WELCOME
to the
NEW WORLD

A Graphic Novel by
Jake Halpern and Michael Sloan

Metropolitan Books
Henry Holt and Company
New York

Metropolitan Books
Henry Holt and Company
Publishers since 1866
120 Broadway
New York, New York 10271

Mohammed Kadalah of Santa Clara University did all of the translations for
this book. His knowledge of Arabic and Syrian culture proved indispensable.

Bruce Headlam was the original editor of our twenty-part series in the
New York Times. His vision for that series helped shape this book.

Library of Congress Cataloging-in-Publication Data

Names: Halpern, Jake, author. | Sloan, Michael, 1963– illustrator.
Title: Welcome to the new world : a graphic novel / Jake Halpern and
  Michael Sloan.
Description: First edition. | New York : Metropolitan Books, 2020. |
  Originally published as a twenty-two part series in the New York Times.
Identifiers: LCCN 2020013950 (print) | LCCN 2020013951 (ebook) | ISBN
  9781250305596 (trade paperback) | ISBN 9781250305602 (ebook)
Subjects: LCSH: Graphic novels.
Classification: LCC PN6727.H2577 Wel 2020 (print) | LCC PN6727.H2577
  (ebook) | DDC 741.5/973—dc23
LC record available at https://lccn.loc.gov/2020013950
LC ebook record available at https://lccn.loc.gov/2020013951

Our books may be purchased in bulk for promotional, educational, or business use. Please contact
your local bookseller or the Macmillan Corporate and Premium Sales Department at (800) 221-7945,
extension 5442, or by e-mail at MacmillanSpecialMarkets@macmillan.com.

First Edition 2020

Designed by Tysha Long

Printed in the United States of America

1 3 5 7 9 10 8 6 4 2

To Peter Kujawinski,
for your many years of friendship.

For Leslie, Dylan, Mia, and Wyatt.
Our love makes everything possible.

Contents

Chapter 1

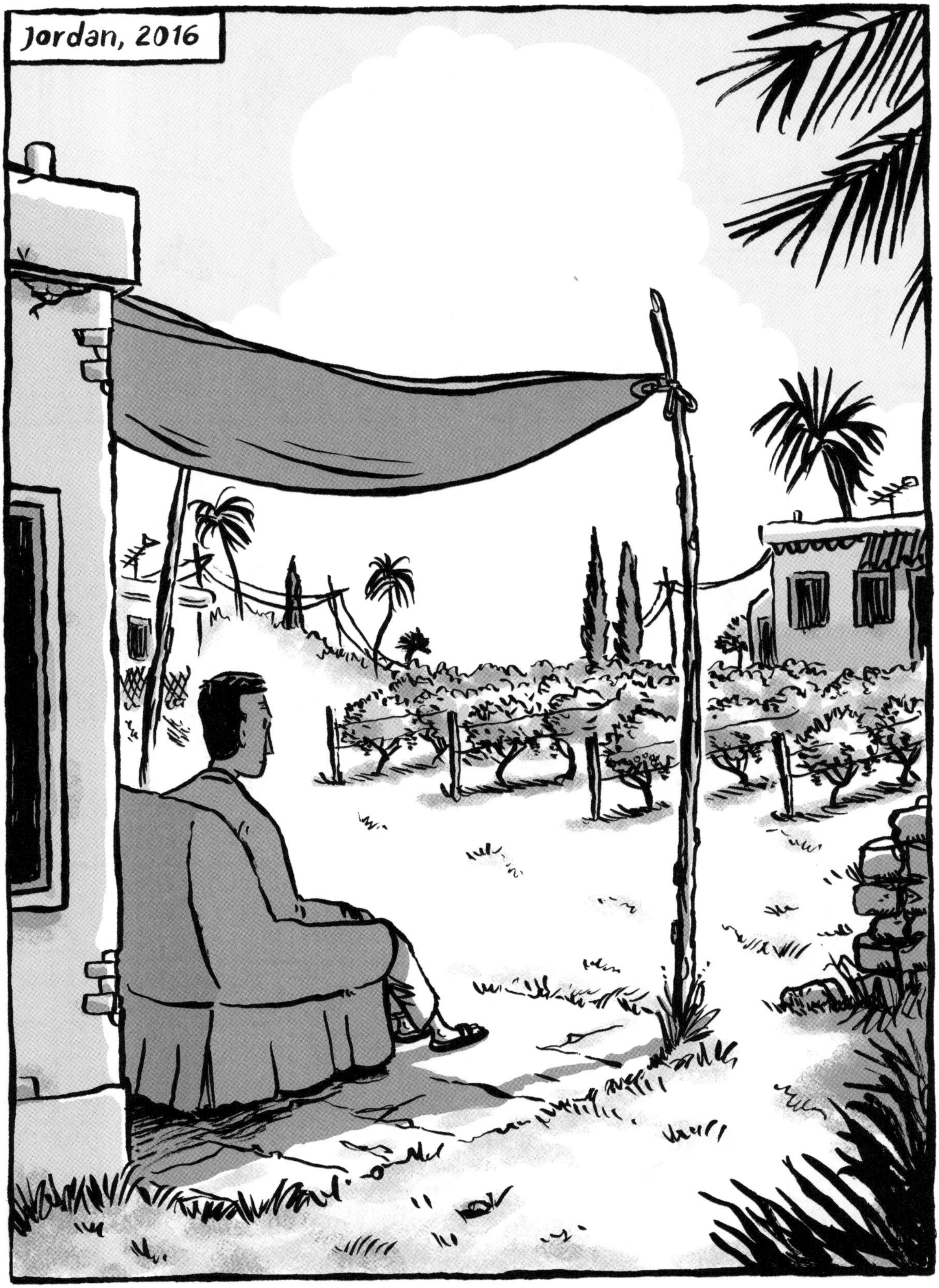
Jordan, 2016

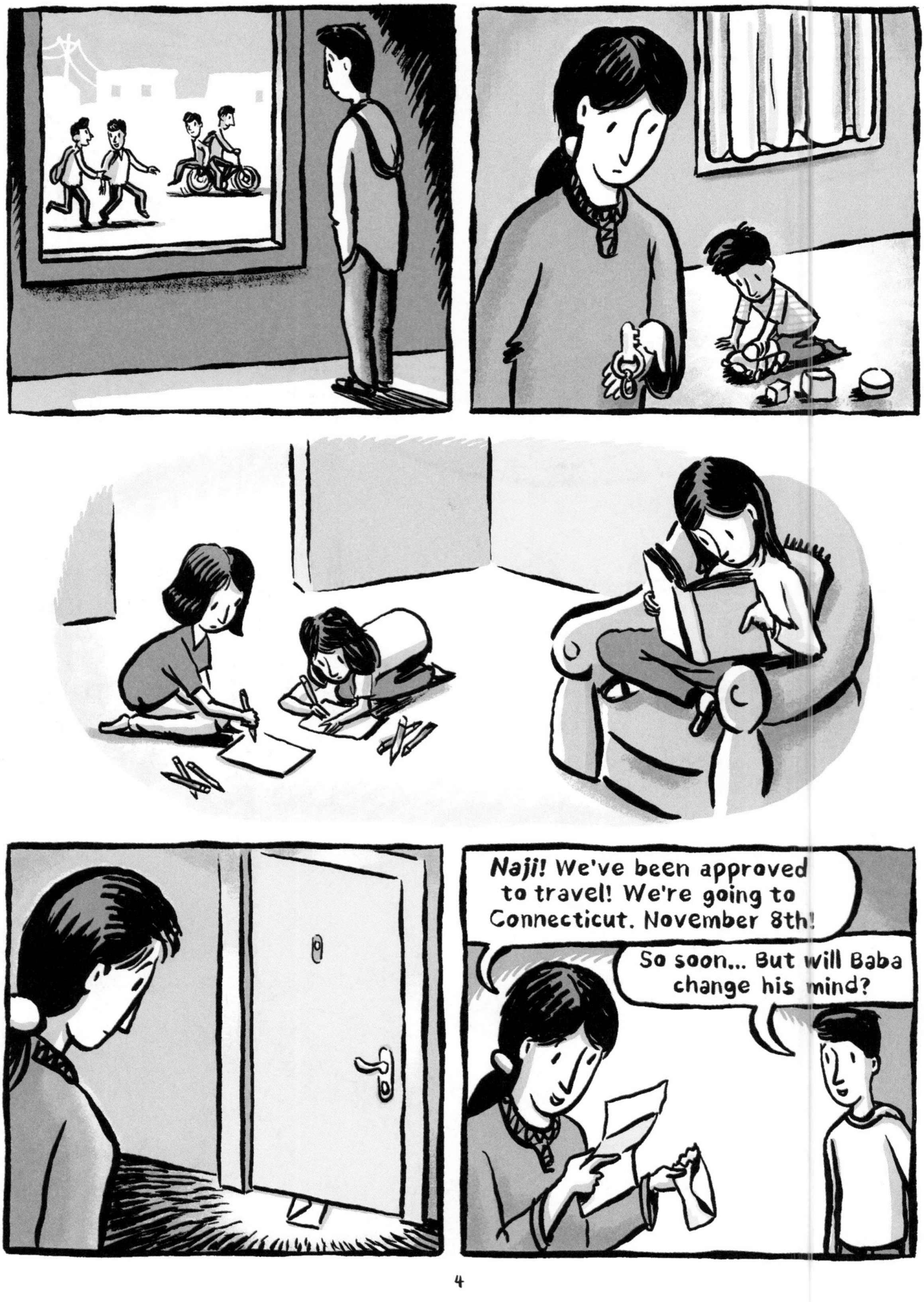
Naji! We've been approved to travel! We're going to Connecticut. November 8th!
So soon... But will Baba change his mind?

Naji, I know you're dying to go...

Shh... Mama. **Please!** You gotta talk quietly. The neighbors might hear.

It's alright...

No! I'm serious. I haven't told **anybody**.

Naji, I think you're taking this whole code of secrecy thing a bit too seriously.

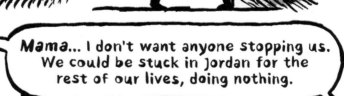

Mama... I don't want anyone stopping us. We could be stuck in Jordan for the rest of our lives, doing nothing.

There's stuff you **can** do. How about English? Have you practiced your words today?

Nope.

Go on, then.

5

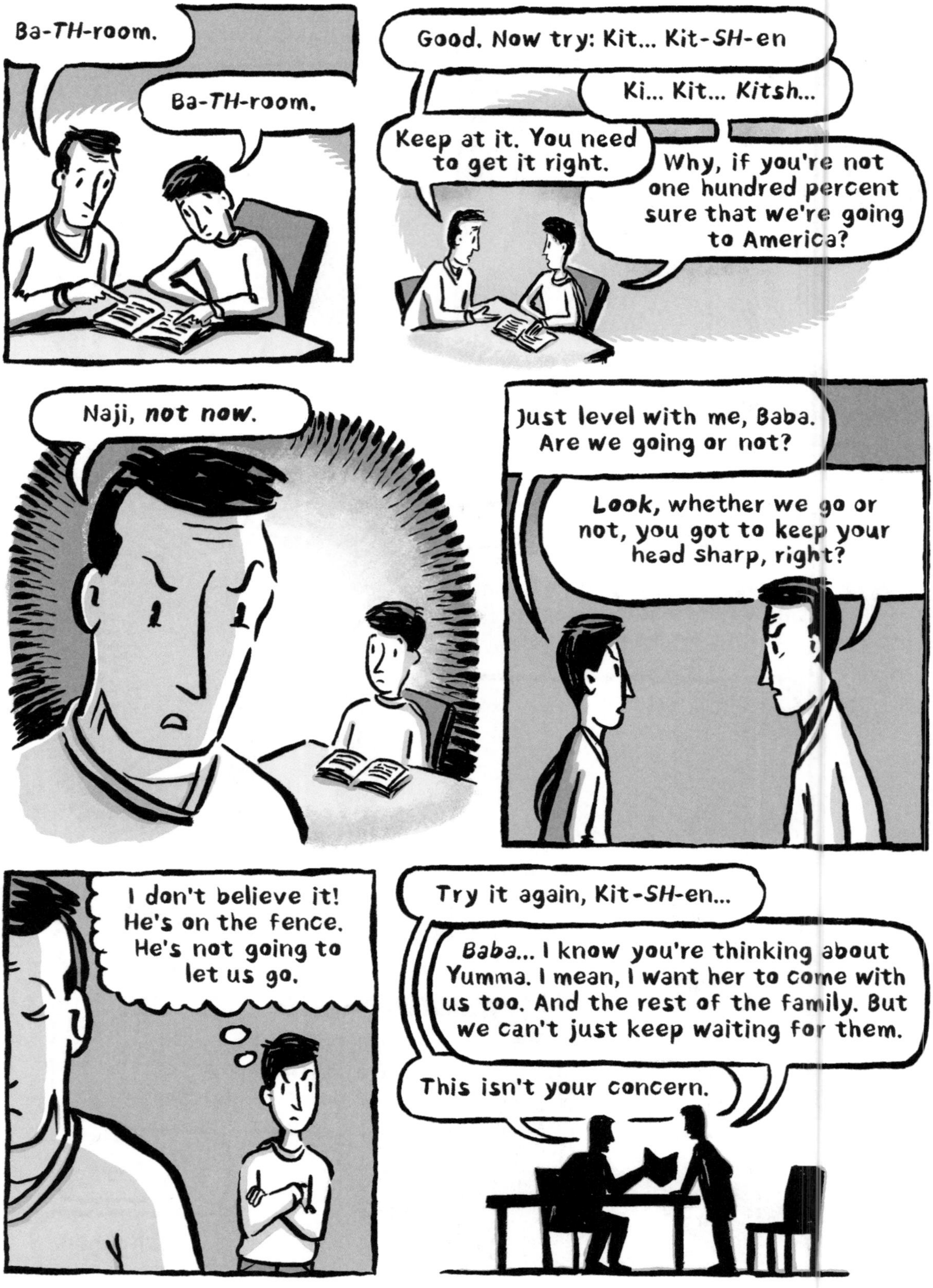
Ba-*TH*-room.
Ba-*TH*-room.
Good. Now try: Kit... Kit-*SH*-en
Ki... Kit... *Kitsh*...
Keep at it. You need to get it right.
Why, if you're not one hundred percent sure that we're going to America?
Naji, ***not now***.
Just level with me, Baba. Are we going or not?
Look, whether we go or not, you got to keep your head sharp, right?
I don't believe it! He's on the fence. He's not going to let us go.
Try it again, Kit-*SH*-en...
Baba... I know you're thinking about Yumma. I mean, I want her to come with us too. And the rest of the family. But we can't just keep waiting for them.
This isn't your concern.

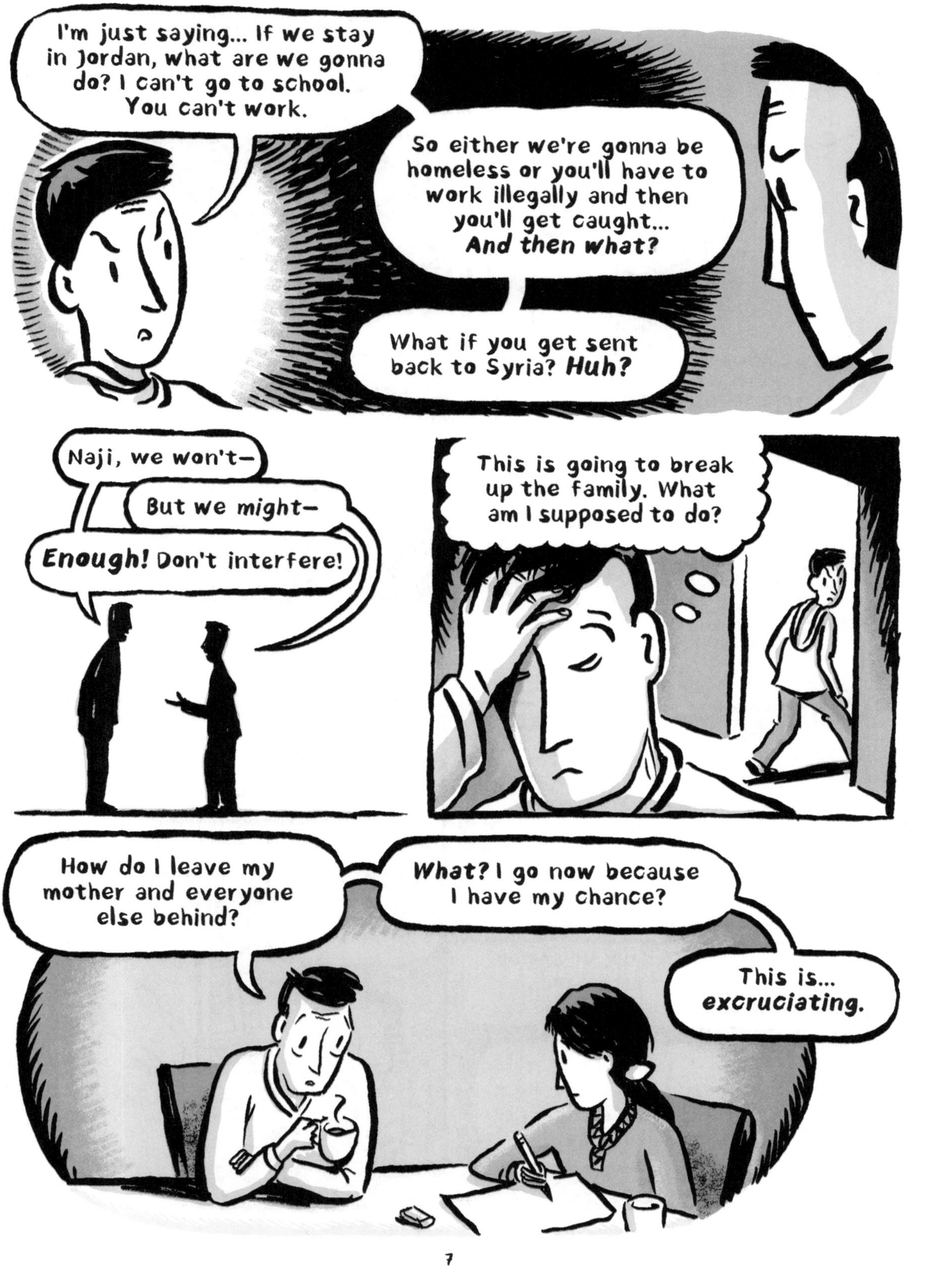
I'm just saying... If we stay in Jordan, what are we gonna do? I can't go to school. You can't work.
So either we're gonna be homeless or you'll have to work illegally and then you'll get caught... *And then what?*
What if you get sent back to Syria? ***Huh?***
Naji, we won't—
But we *might*—
Enough! Don't interfere!
This is going to break up the family. What am I supposed to do?
How do I leave my mother and everyone else behind?
What? I go now because I have my chance?
This is... *excruciating.*

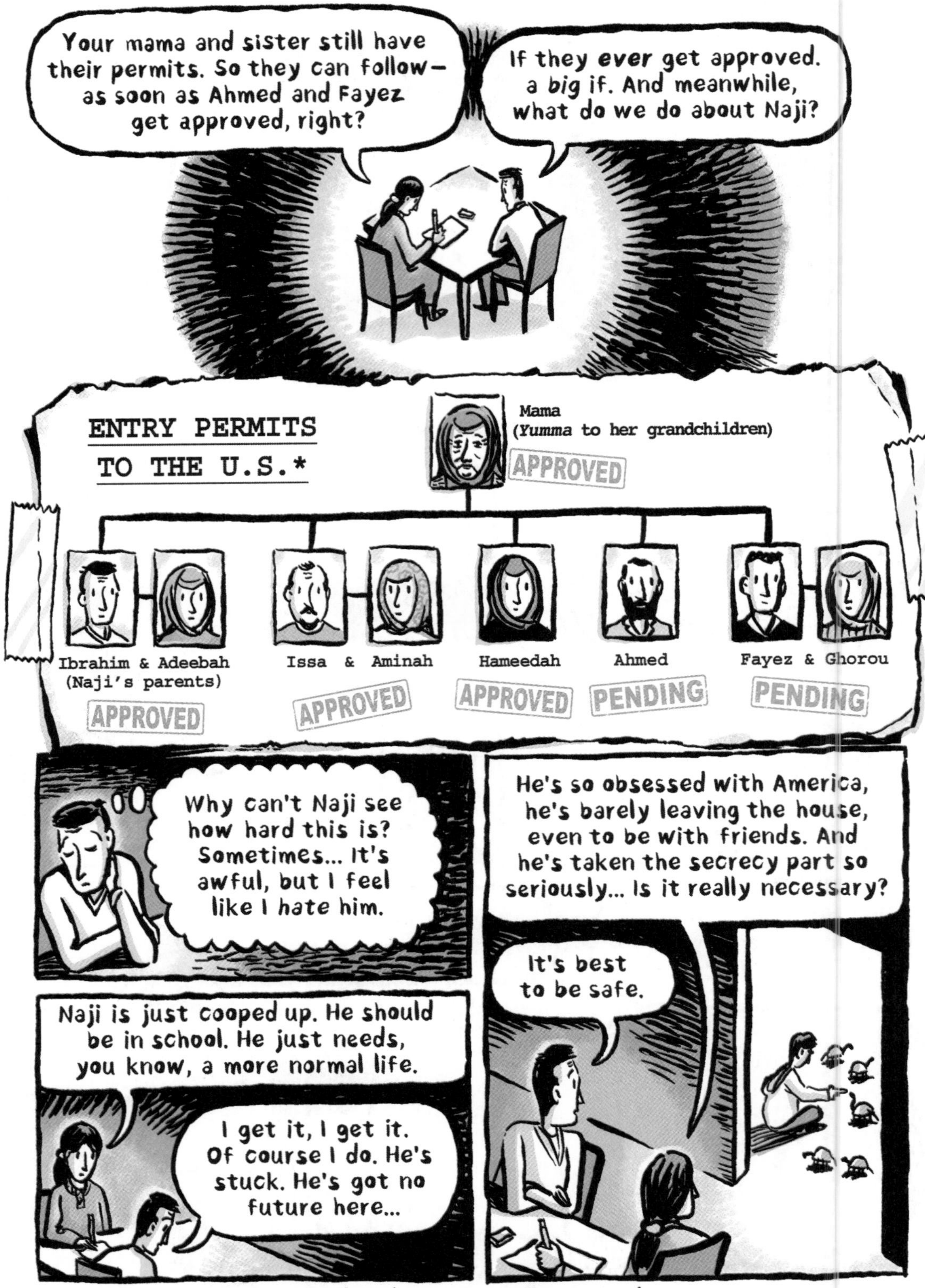
Your mama and sister still have their permits. So they can follow—as soon as Ahmed and Fayez get approved, right?
If they *ever* get approved. a *big* if. And meanwhile, what do we do about Naji?
ENTRY PERMITS TO THE U.S.*
Mama (*Yumma* to her grandchildren)
APPROVED
Ibrahim & Adeebah (Naji's parents)
APPROVED
Issa & Aminah
APPROVED
Hameedah
APPROVED
Ahmed
PENDING
Fayez & Ghorou
PENDING
Why can't Naji see how hard this is? Sometimes... It's awful, but I feel like I *hate* him.
He's so obsessed with America, he's barely leaving the house, even to be with friends. And he's taken the secrecy part so seriously... Is it really necessary?
Naji is just cooped up. He should be in school. He just needs, you know, a more normal life.
I get it, I get it. Of course I do. He's stuck. He's got no future here...
It's best to be safe.

* The fifth brother, Mohammed, had already left for England.

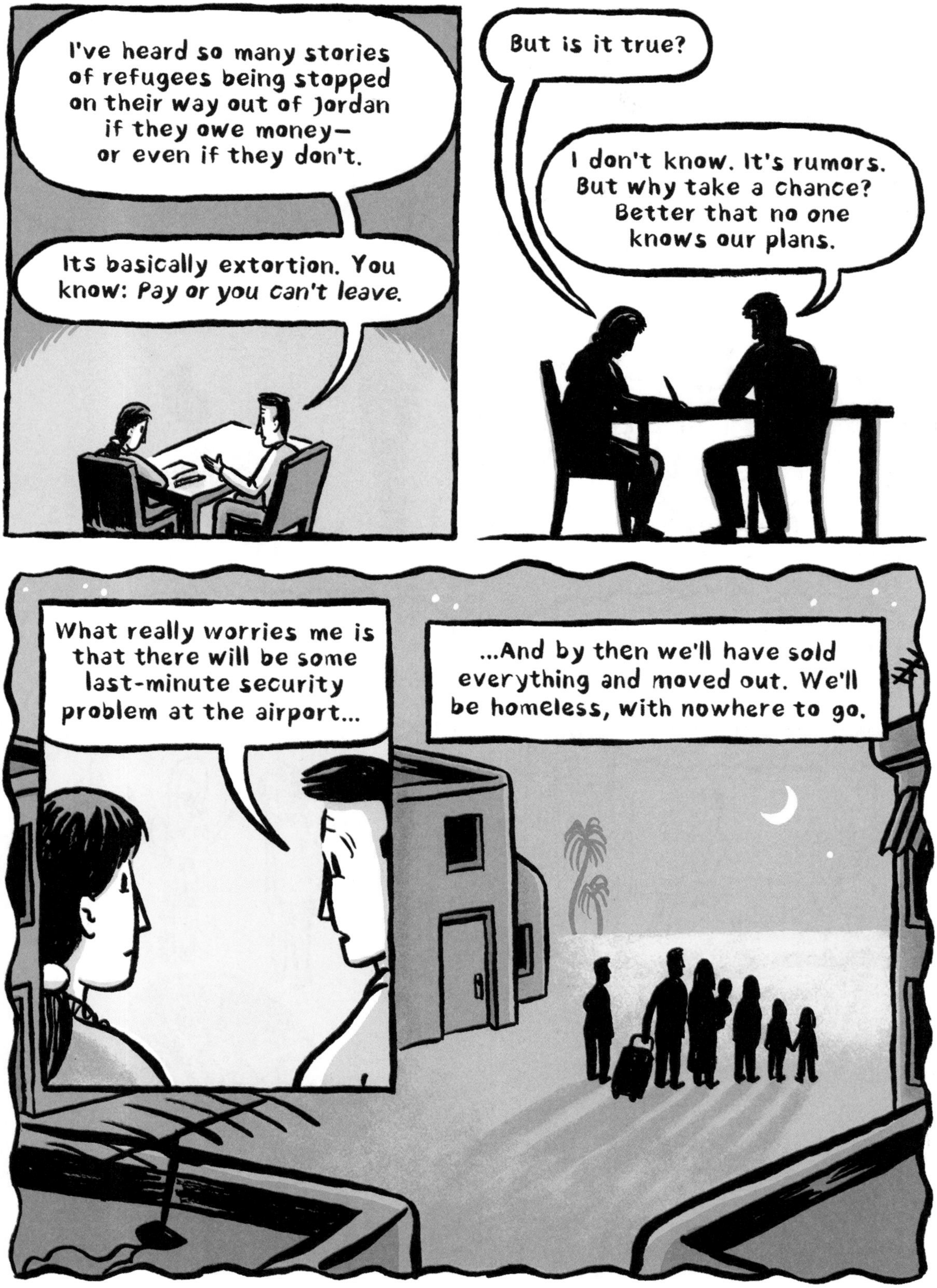
I've heard so many stories of refugees being stopped on their way out of Jordan if they owe money—or even if they don't.
Its basically extortion. You know: *Pay or you can't leave.*
But is it true?
I don't know. It's rumors. But why take a chance? Better that no one knows our plans.
What really worries me is that there will be some last-minute security problem at the airport...
...And by then we'll have sold everything and moved out. We'll be homeless, with nowhere to go.

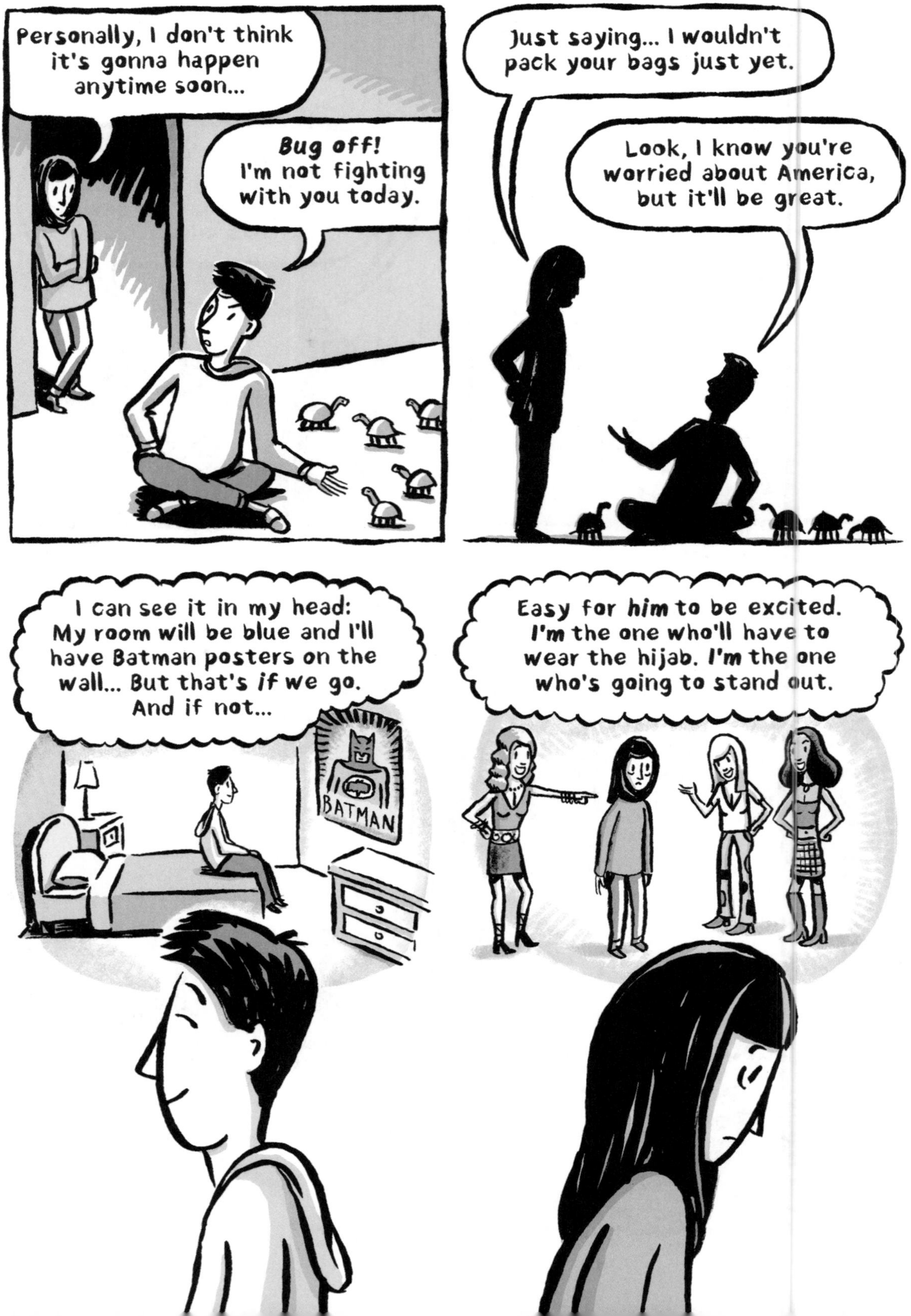
Personally, I don't think it's gonna happen anytime soon...
Bug off! I'm not fighting with you today.
Just saying... I wouldn't pack your bags just yet.
Look, I know you're worried about America, but it'll be great.
I can see it in my head: My room will be blue and I'll have Batman posters on the wall... But that's *if* we go. And if not...
BATMAN
Easy for *him* to be excited. *I'm* the one who'll have to wear the hijab. *I'm* the one who's going to stand out.

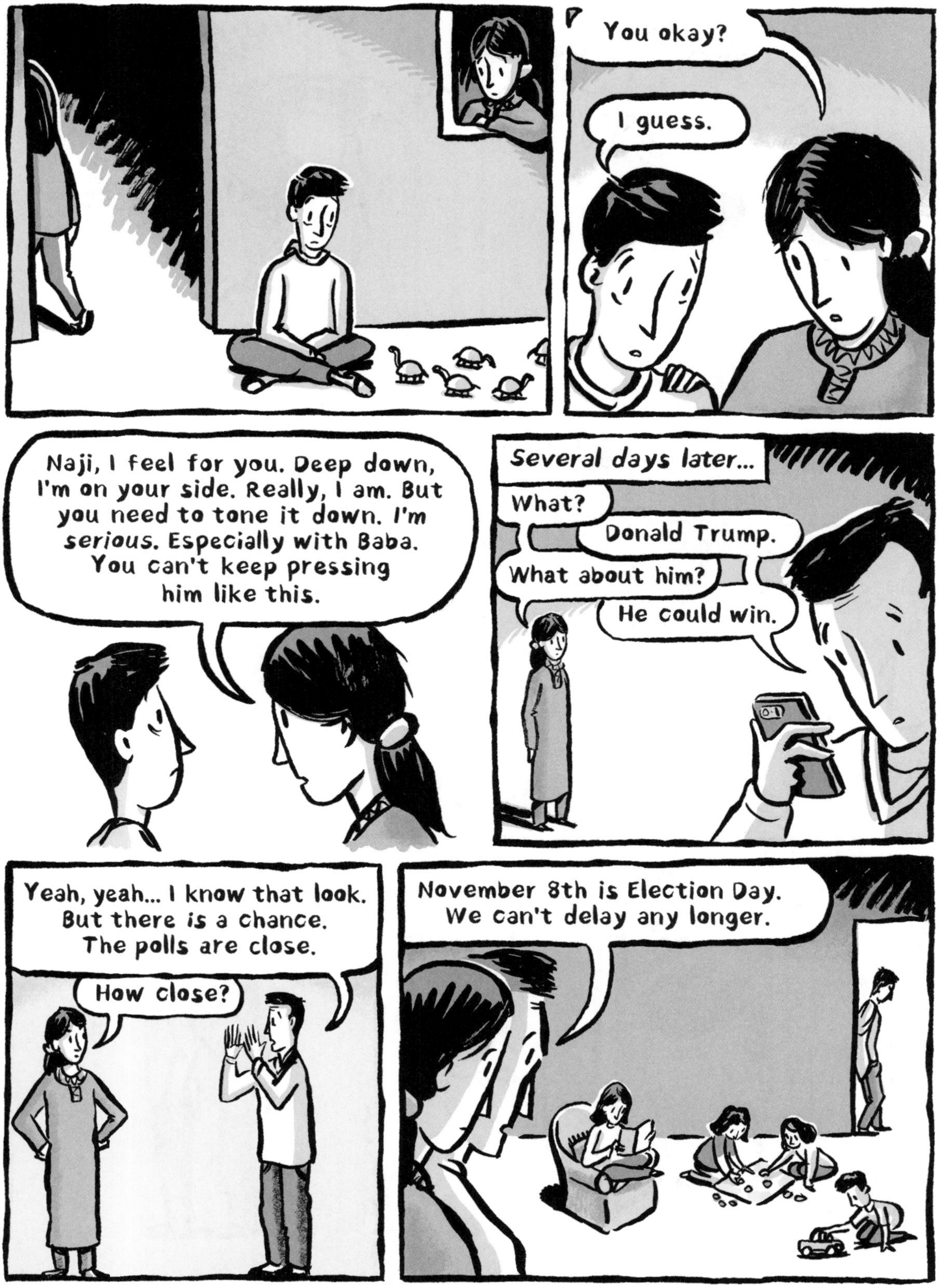

You okay?
I guess.
Naji, I feel for you. Deep down, I'm on your side. Really, I am. But you need to tone it down. I'm *serious*. Especially with Baba. You can't keep pressing him like this.
Several days later...
What?
Donald Trump.
What about him?
He could win.
Yeah, yeah... I know that look. But there is a chance. The polls are close.
How close?
November 8th is Election Day. We can't delay any longer.

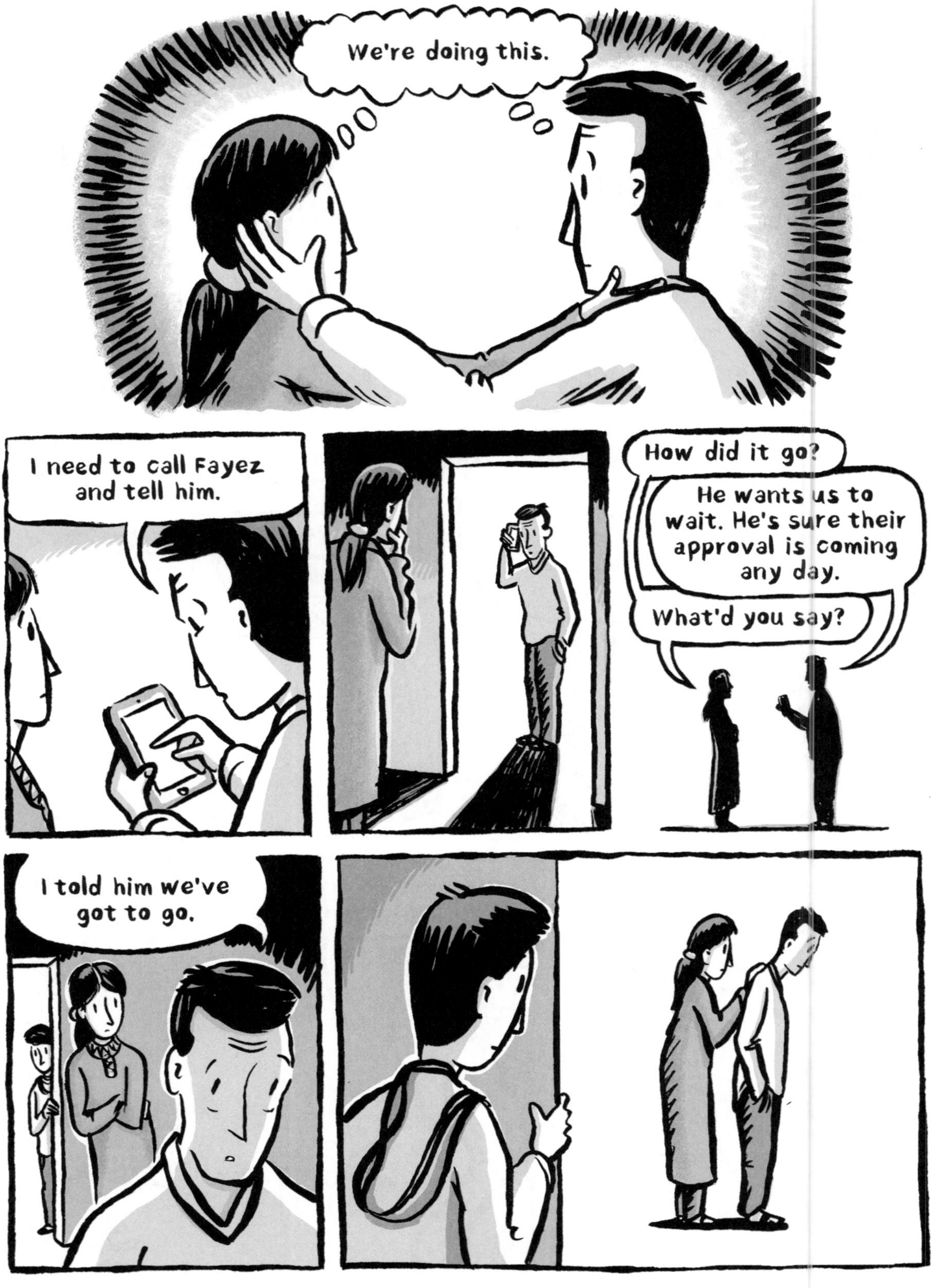
We're doing this.
I need to call Fayez and tell him.
How did it go?
He wants us to wait. He's sure their approval is coming any day.
What'd you say?
I told him we've got to go.

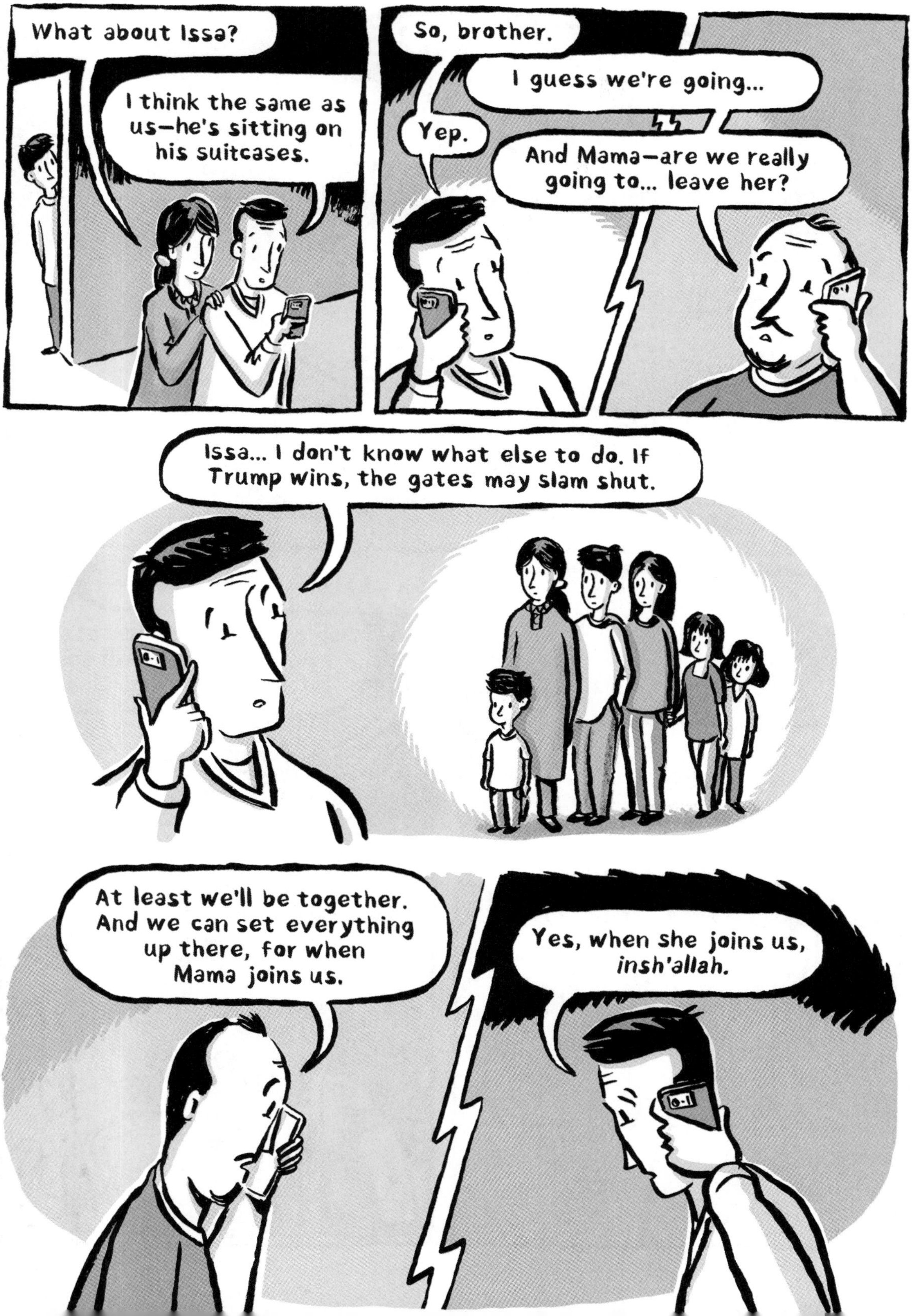
What about Issa?
I think the same as us—he's sitting on his suitcases.
So, brother.
Yep.
I guess we're going...
And Mama—are we really going to... leave her?
Issa... I don't know what else to do. If Trump wins, the gates may slam shut.
At least we'll be together. And we can set everything up there, for when Mama joins us.
Yes, when she joins us, *insh'allah.*

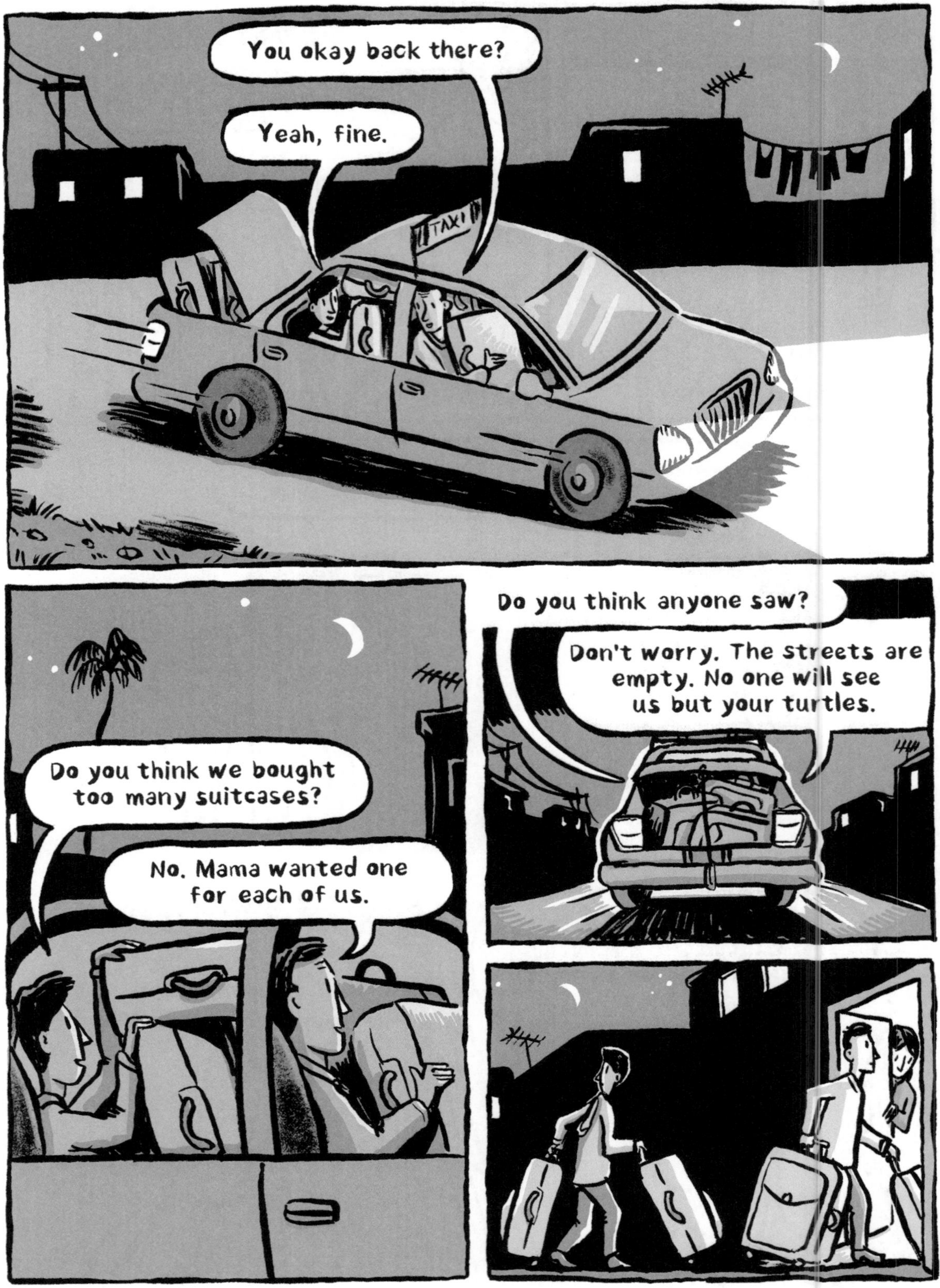
You okay back there?
Yeah, fine.
TAXI
Do you think we bought too many suitcases?
No. Mama wanted one for each of us.
Do you think anyone saw?
Don't worry. The streets are empty. No one will see us but your turtles.

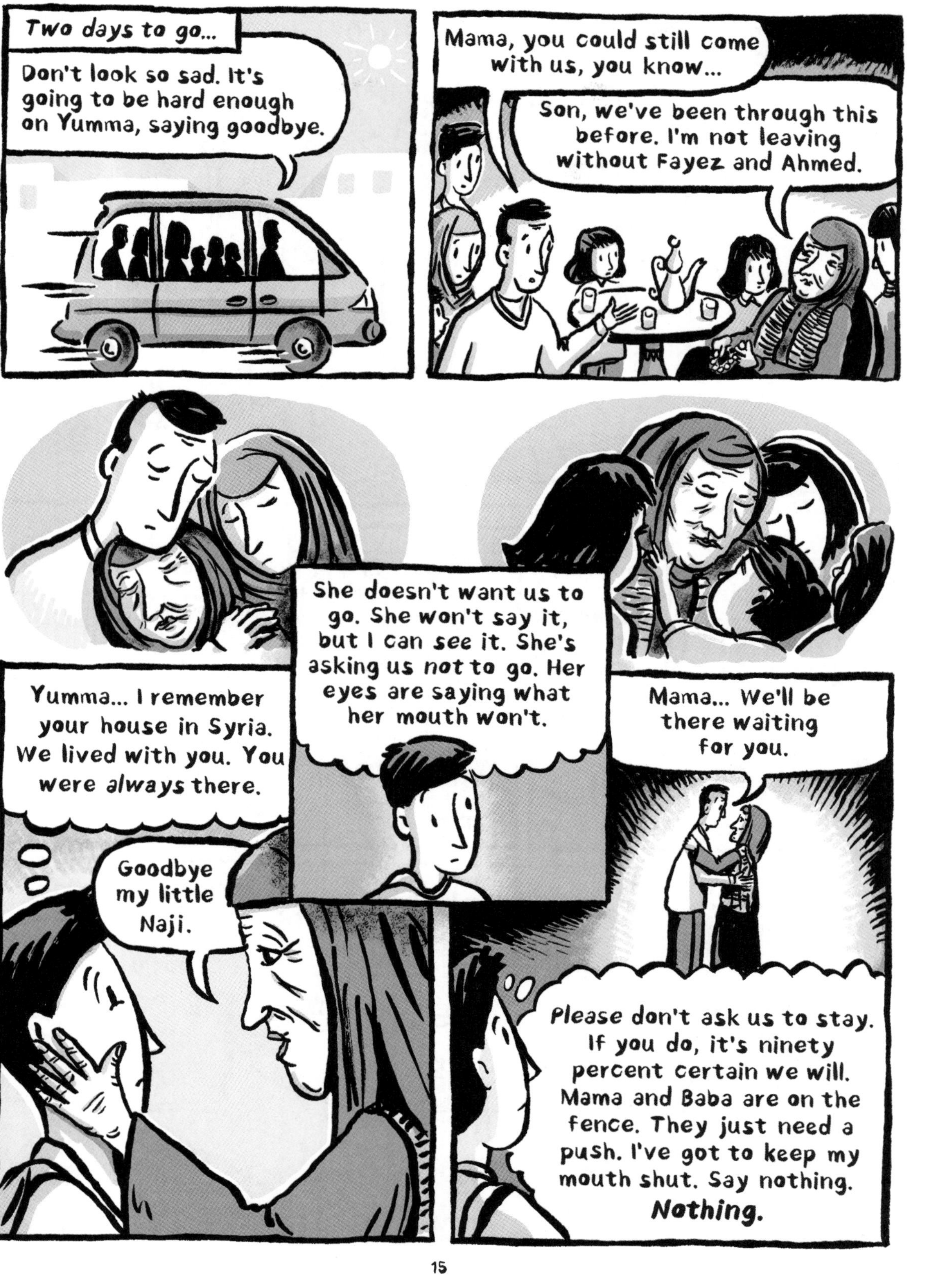
Two days to go...
Don't look so sad. It's going to be hard enough on Yumma, saying goodbye.
Mama, you could still come with us, you know...
Son, we've been through this before. I'm not leaving without Fayez and Ahmed.
She doesn't want us to go. She won't say it, but I can see it. She's asking us not to go. Her eyes are saying what her mouth won't.
Yumma... I remember your house in Syria. We lived with you. You were always there.
Goodbye my little Naji.
Mama... We'll be there waiting for you.
Please don't ask us to stay. If you do, it's ninety percent certain we will. Mama and Baba are on the fence. They just need a push. I've got to keep my mouth shut. Say nothing.
Nothing.

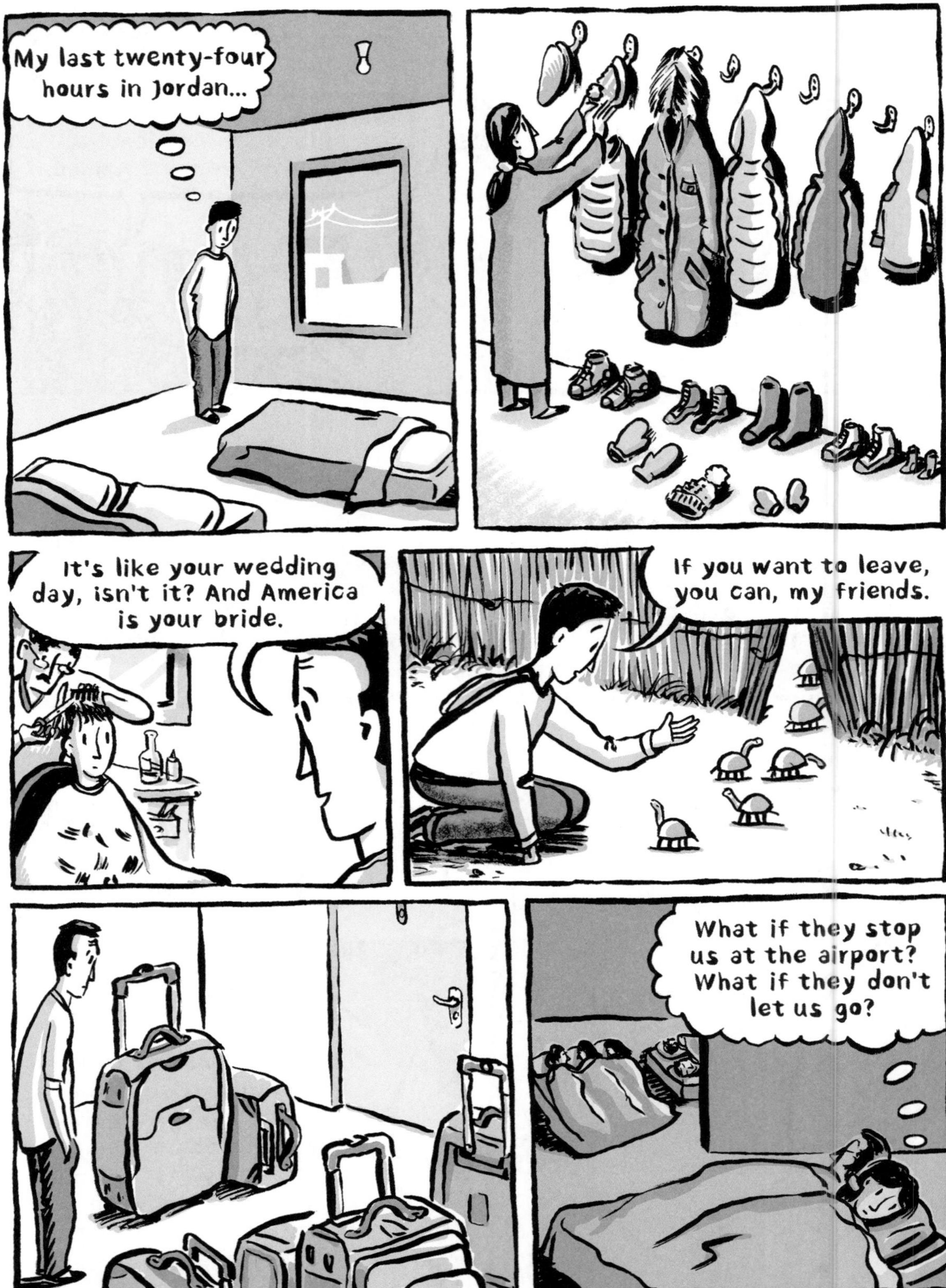
My last twenty-four hours in Jordan...
It's like your wedding day, isn't it? And America is your bride.
If you want to leave, you can, my friends.
What if they stop us at the airport? What if they don't let us go?

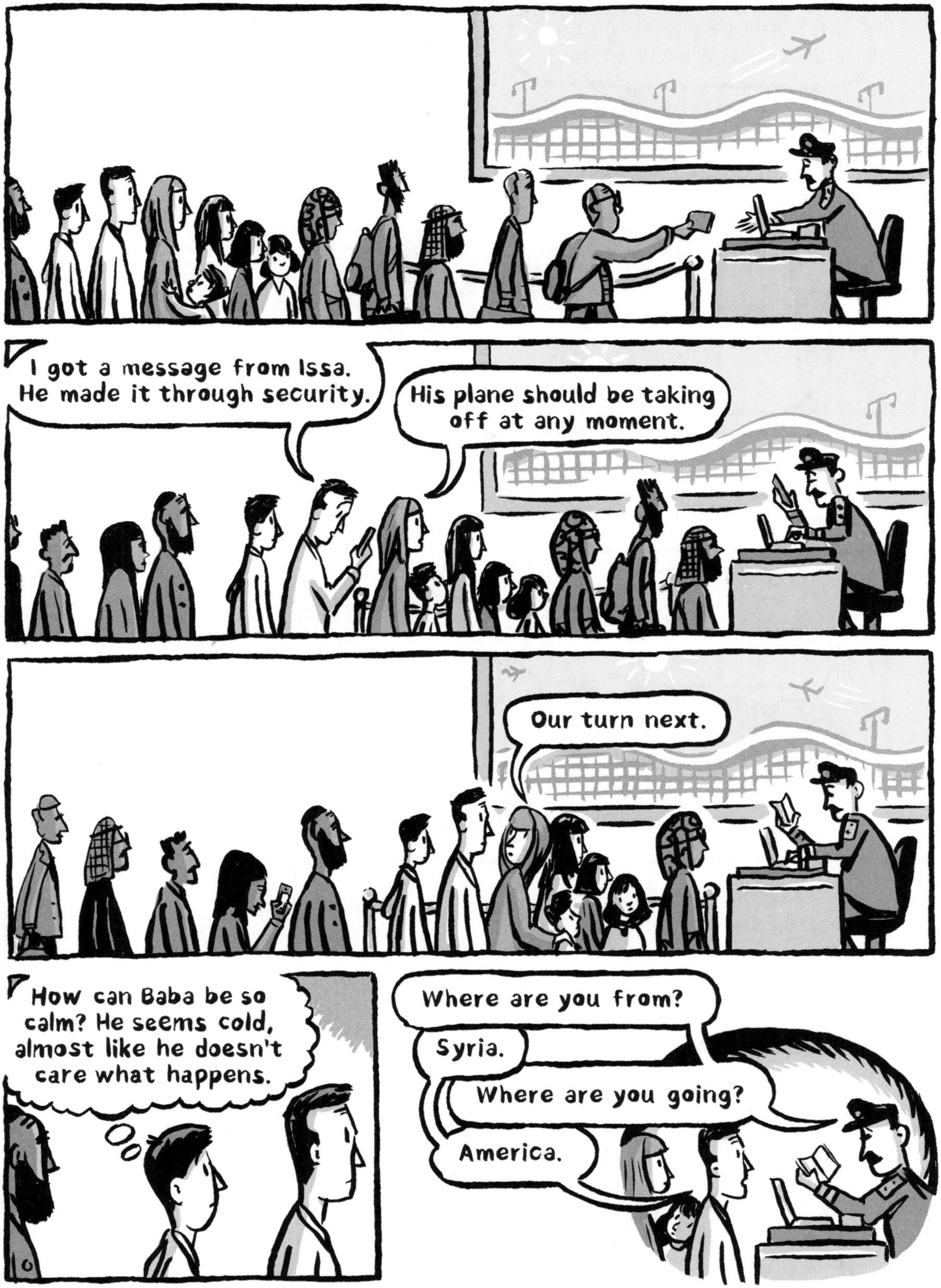
I got a message from Issa. He made it through security.
His plane should be taking off at any moment.
Our turn next.
How can Baba be so calm? He seems cold, almost like he doesn't care what happens.
Where are you from?
Syria.
Where are you going?
America.

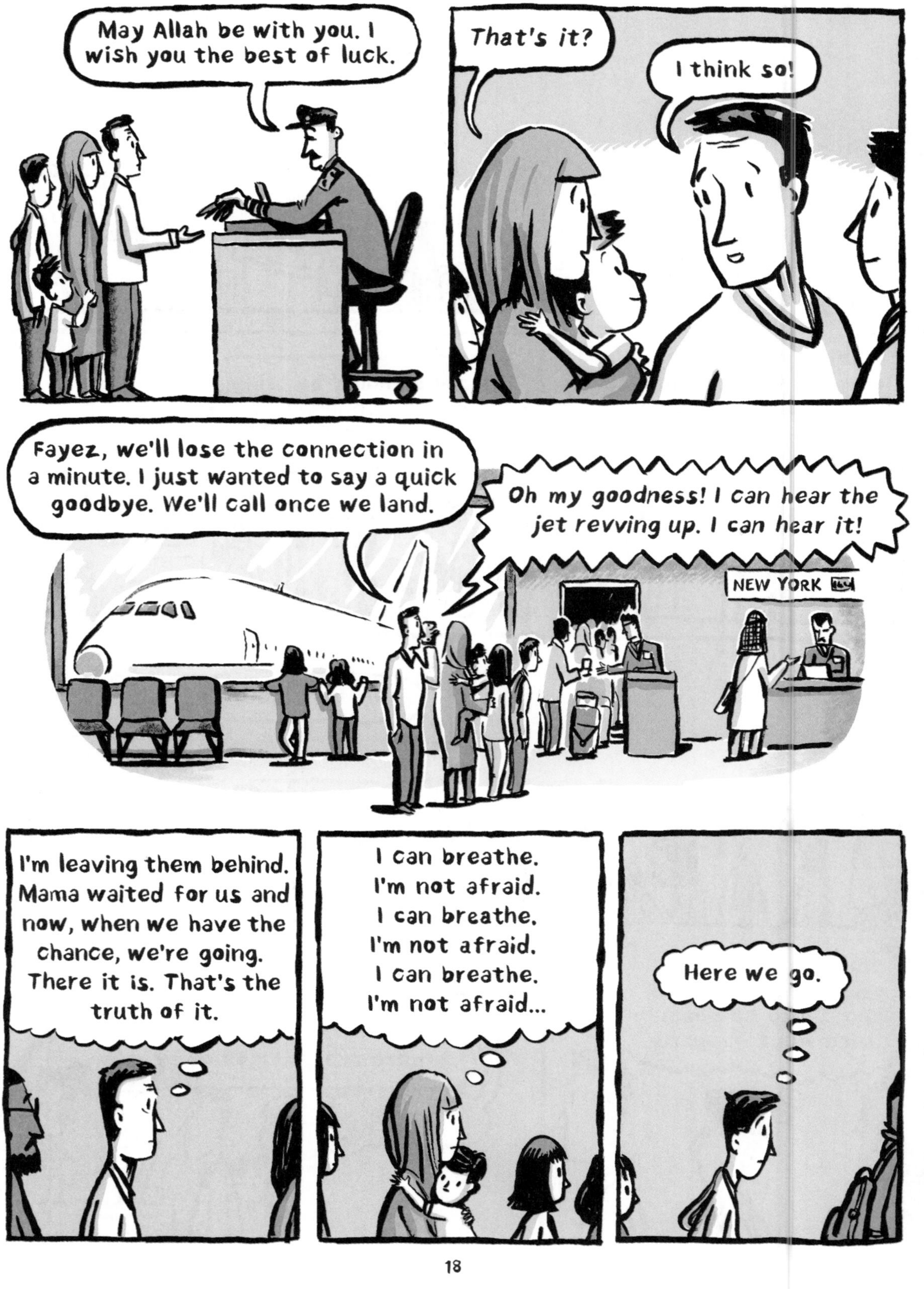
May Allah be with you. I wish you the best of luck.
That's it?
I think so!
Fayez, we'll lose the connection in a minute. I just wanted to say a quick goodbye. We'll call once we land.
Oh my goodness! I can hear the jet revving up. I can hear it!
NEW YORK
I'm leaving them behind. Mama waited for us and now, when we have the chance, we're going. There it is. That's the truth of it.
I can breathe. I'm not afraid. I can breathe. I'm not afraid. I can breathe. I'm not afraid...
Here we go.

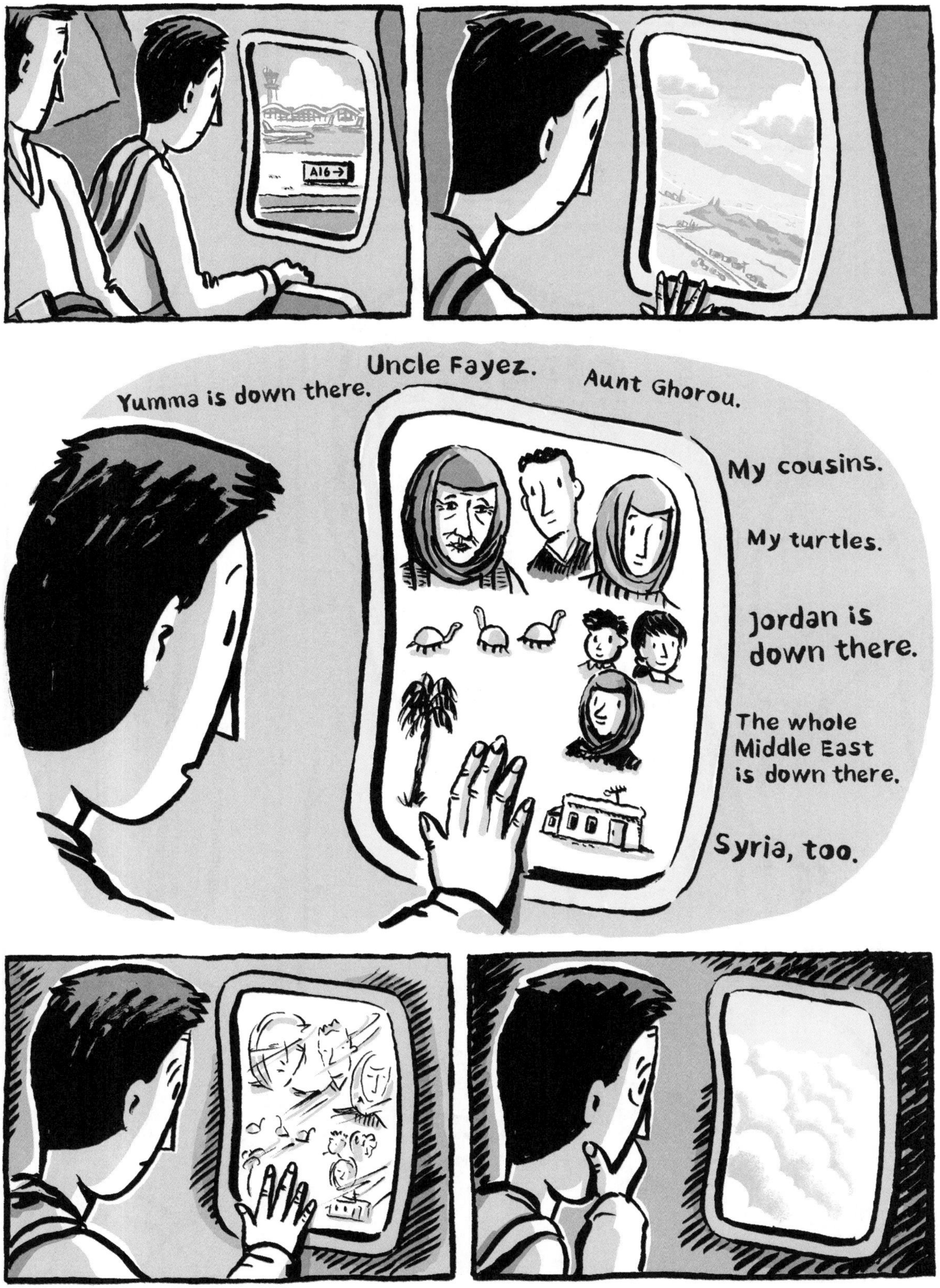
A16 →
Yumma is down there.
Uncle Fayez.
Aunt Ghorou.
My cousins.
My turtles.
Jordan is down there.
The whole Middle East is down there.
Syria, too.

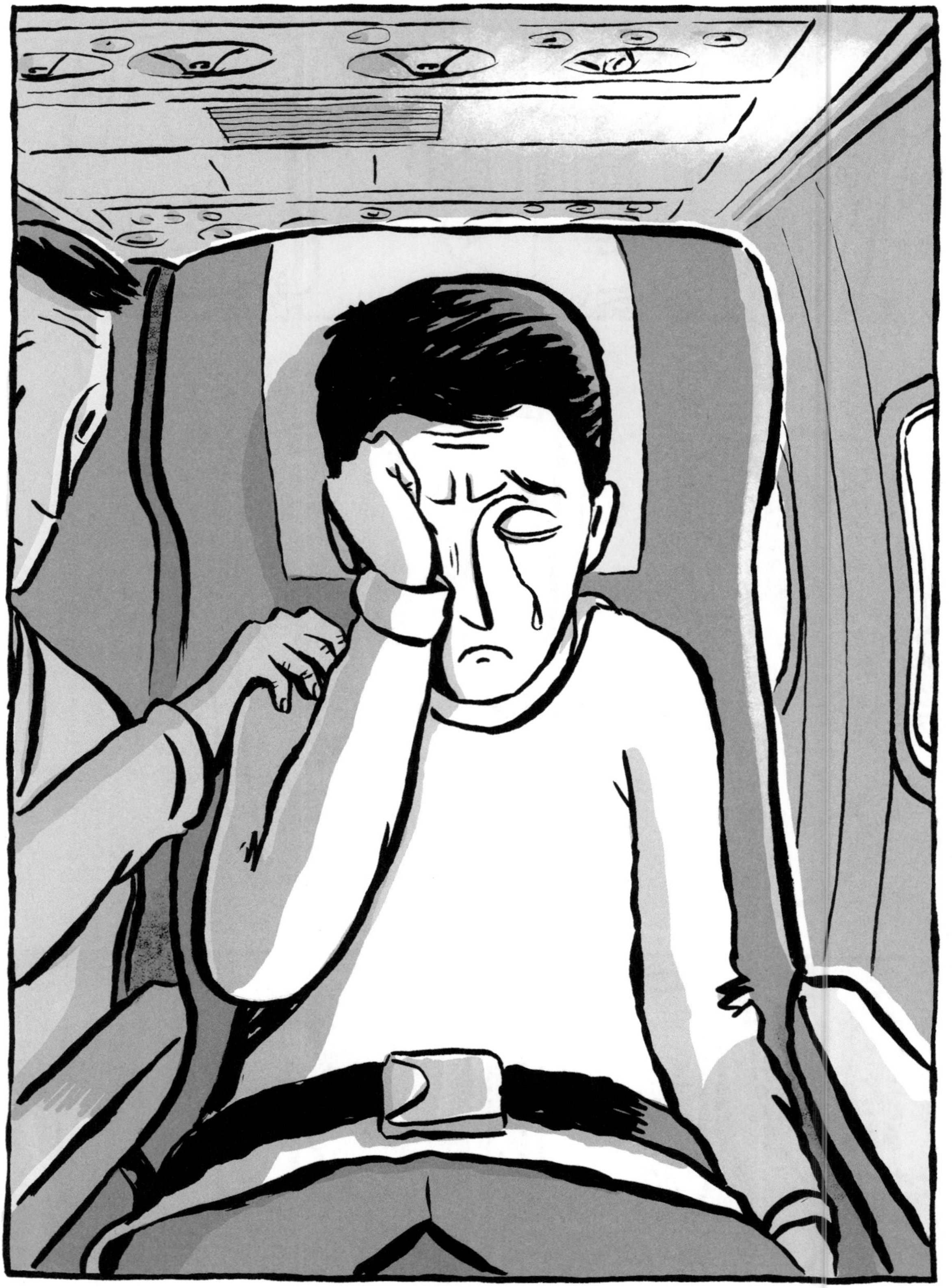

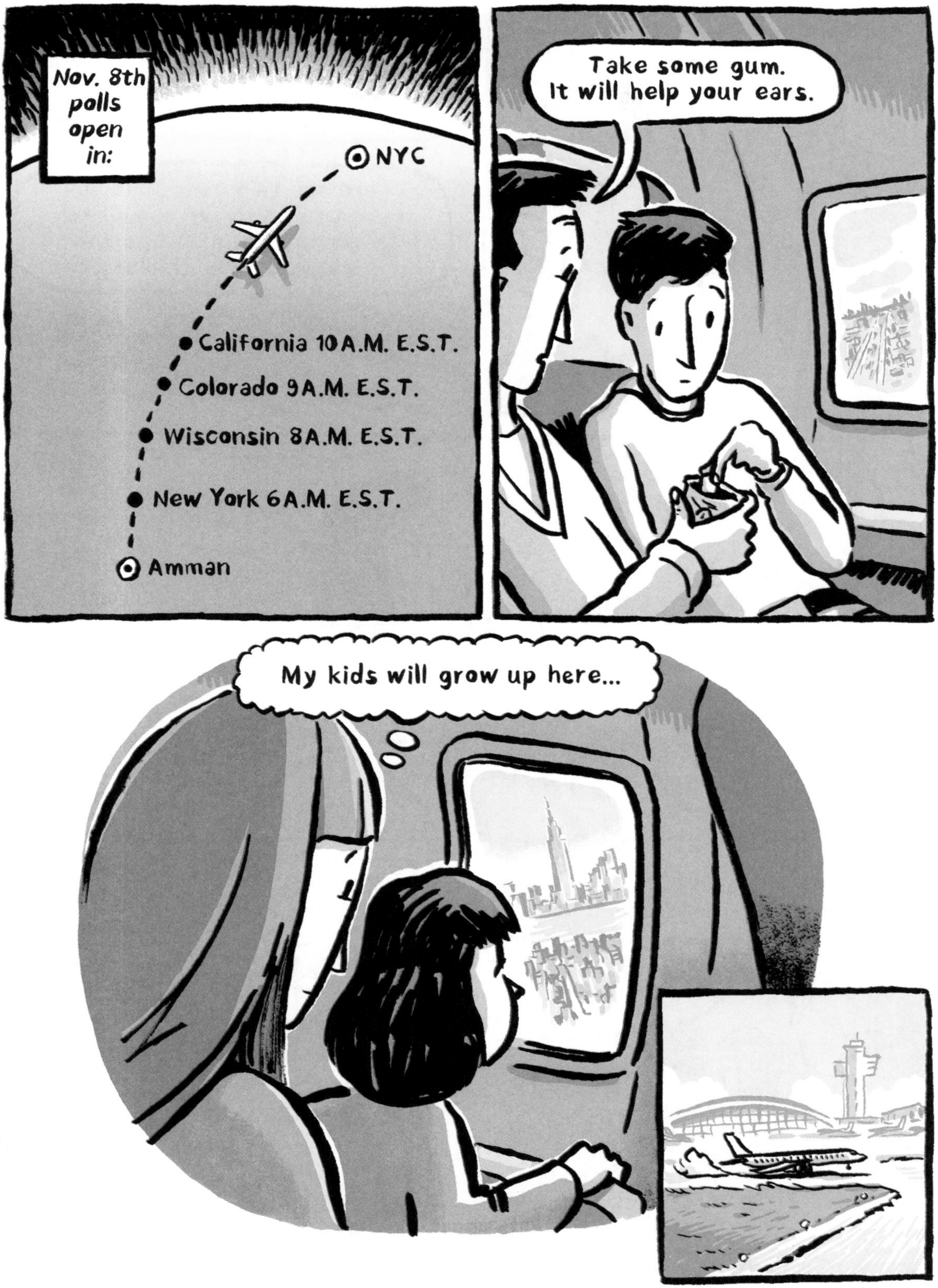
Nov. 8th polls open in:
NYC
California 10 A.M. E.S.T.
Colorado 9 A.M. E.S.T.
Wisconsin 8 A.M. E.S.T.
New York 6 A.M. E.S.T.
Amman
Take some gum. It will help your ears.
My kids will grow up here...

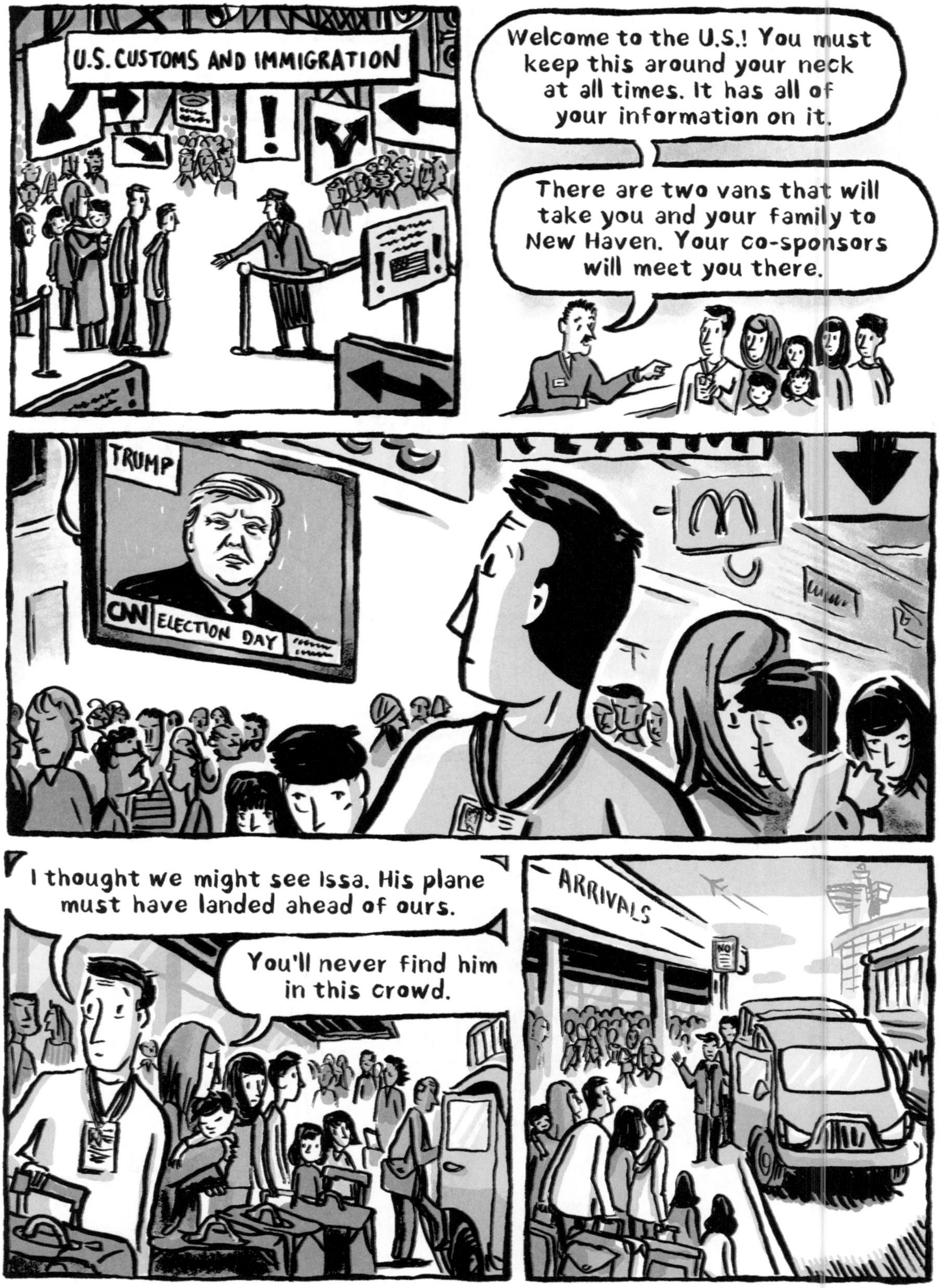
U.S. CUSTOMS AND IMMIGRATION
Welcome to the U.S.! You must keep this around your neck at all times. It has all of your information on it.
There are two vans that will take you and your family to New Haven. Your co-sponsors will meet you there.
TRUMP
CNN ELECTION DAY
I thought we might see Issa. His plane must have landed ahead of ours.
You'll never find him in this crowd.
ARRIVALS

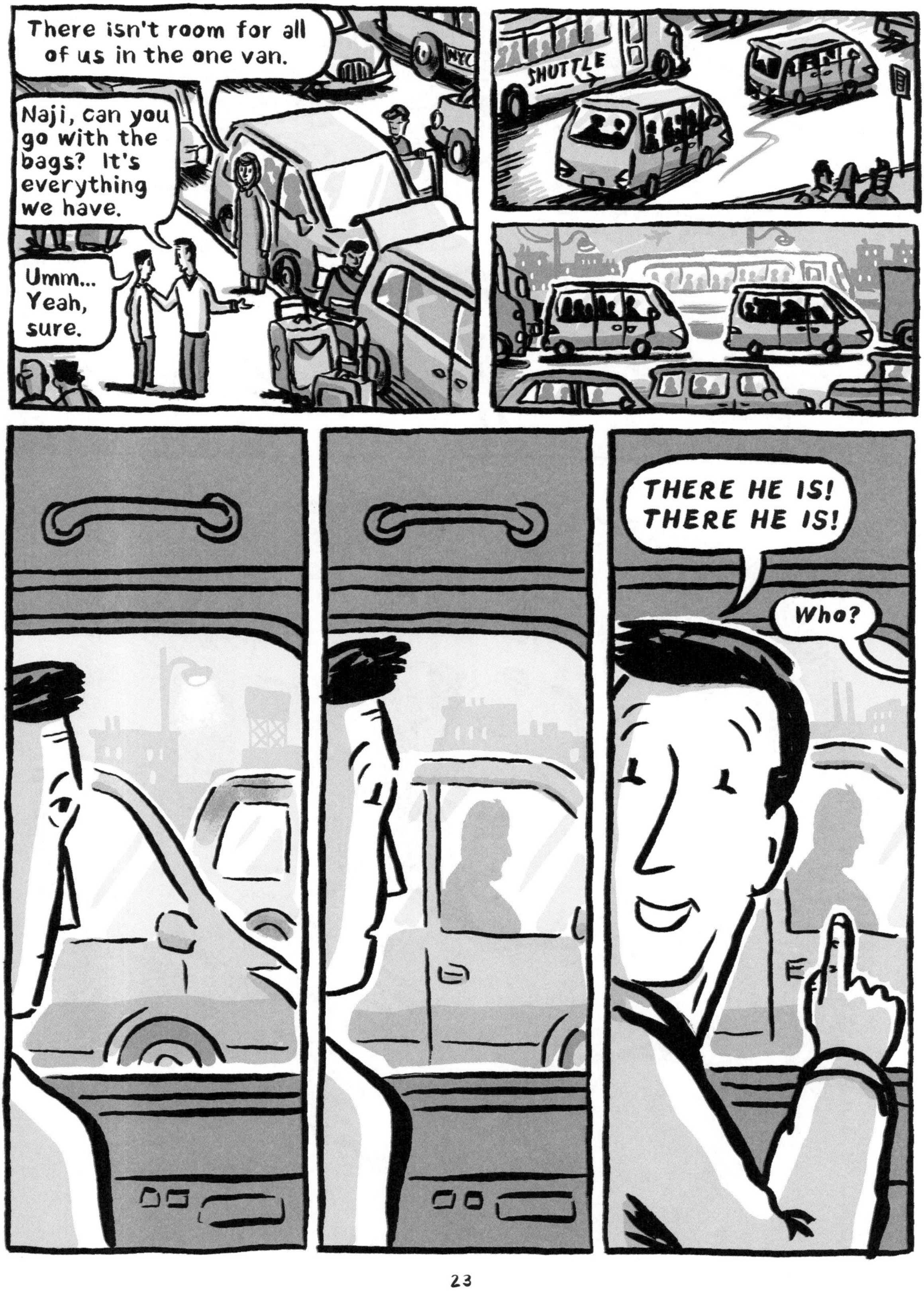
There isn't room for all of us in the one van.
Naji, can you go with the bags? It's everything we have.
Umm... Yeah, sure.
SHUTTLE
THERE HE IS! THERE HE IS!
Who?

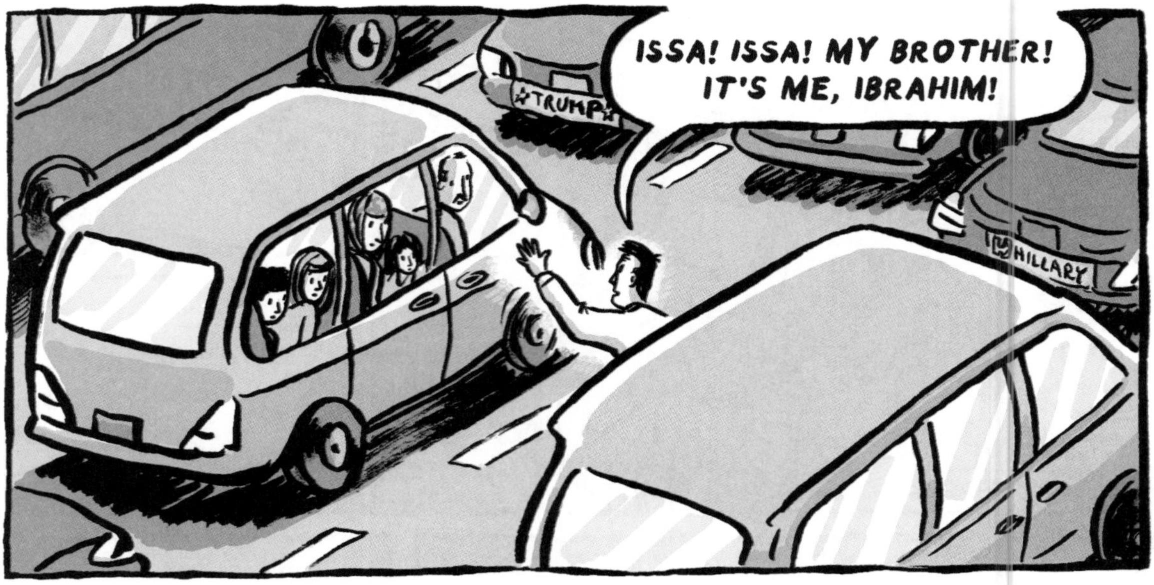
ISSA! ISSA! MY BROTHER! IT'S ME, IBRAHIM!
TRUMP
HILLARY

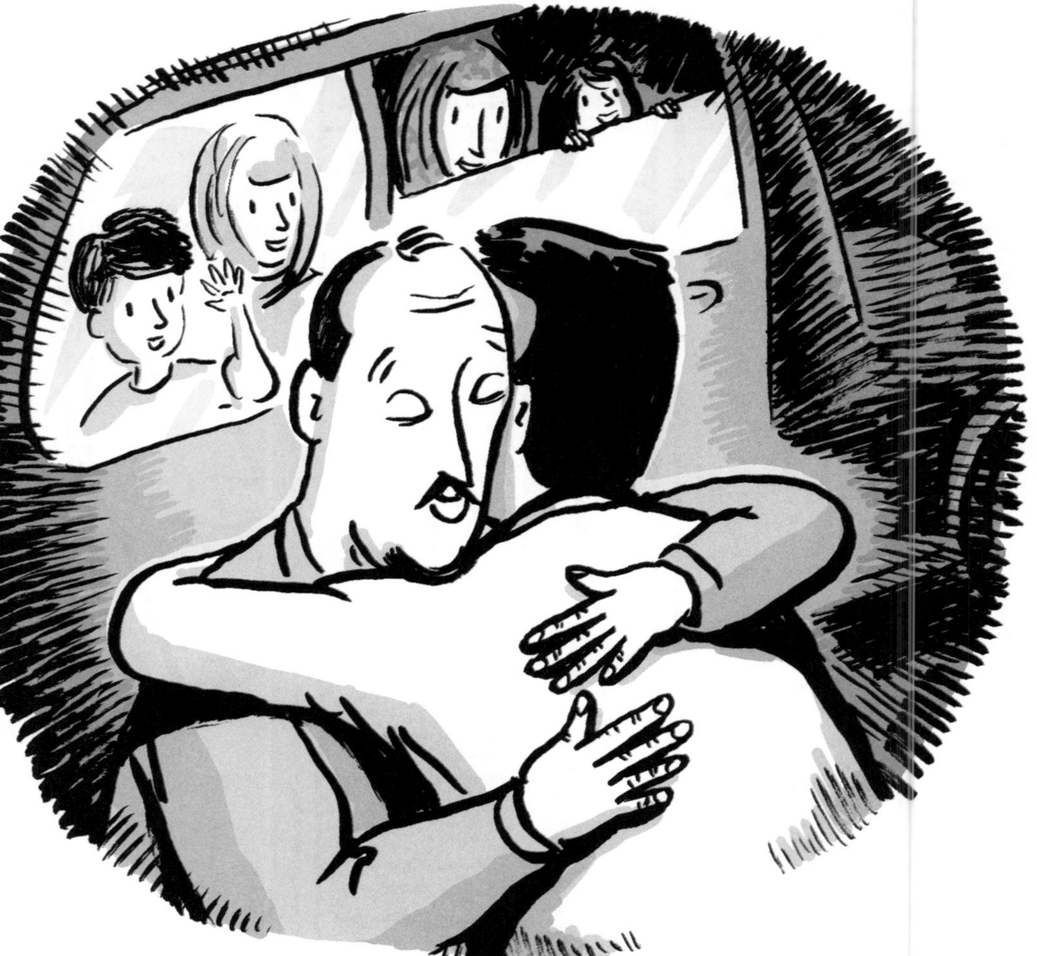

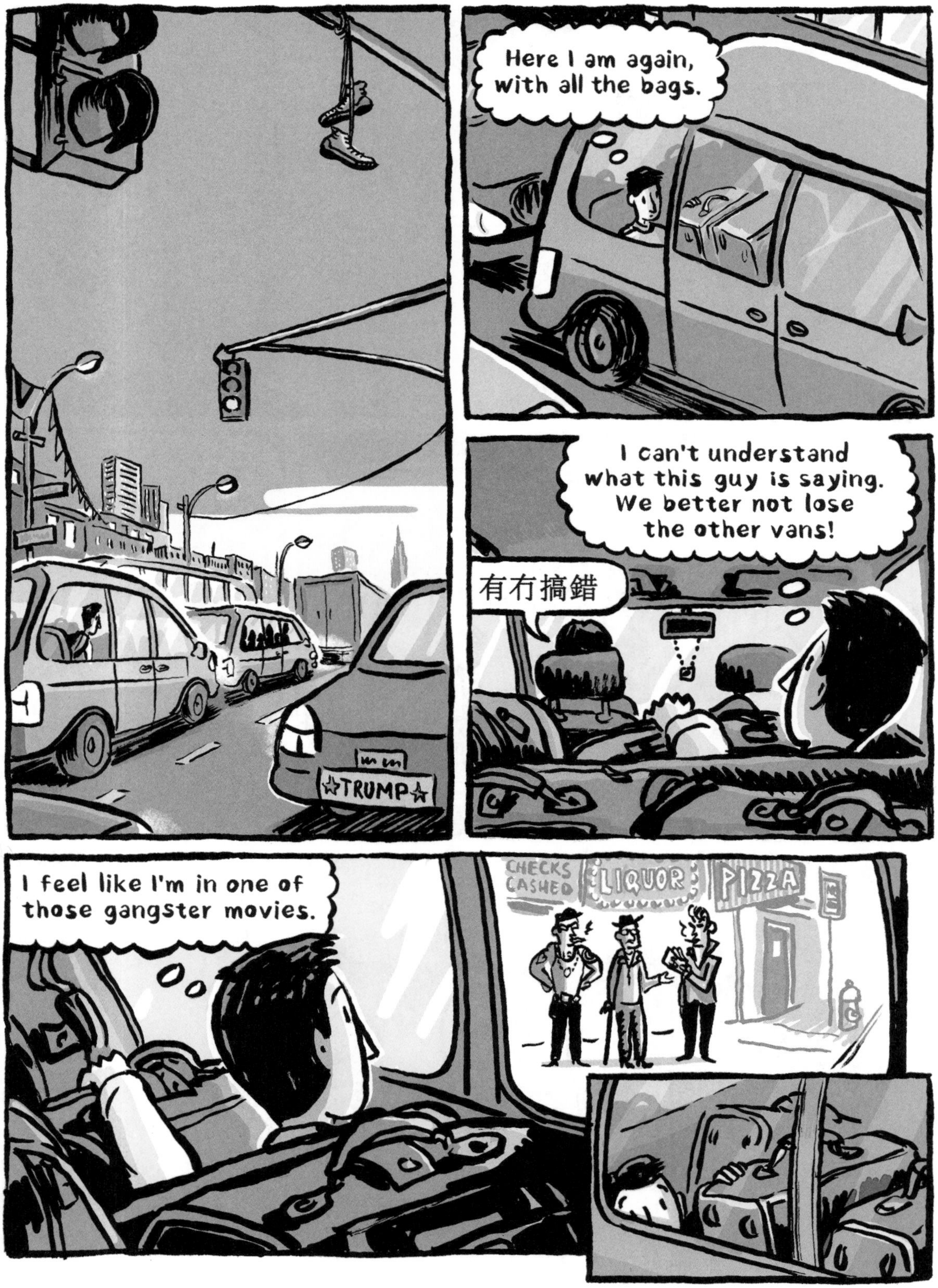
Here I am again, with all the bags.
I can't understand what this guy is saying. We better not lose the other vans!
有冇搞錯
TRUMP
I feel like I'm in one of those gangster movies.
CHECKS CASHED
LIQUOR
PIZZA

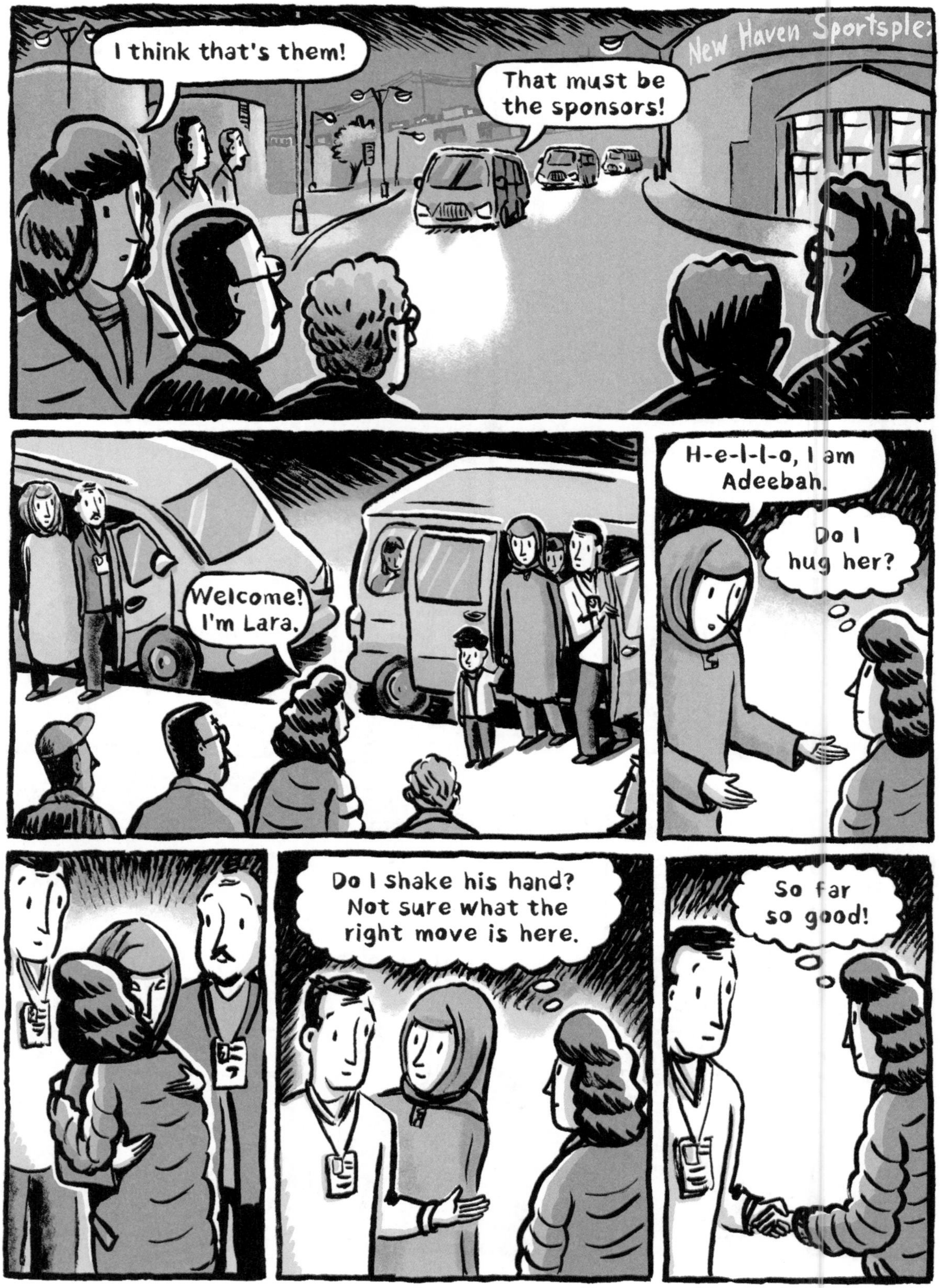
New Haven Sportsplex
I think that's them!
That must be the sponsors!
Welcome! I'm Lara.
H-e-l-l-o, I am Adeebah.
Do I hug her?
Do I shake his hand? Not sure what the right move is here.
So far so good!

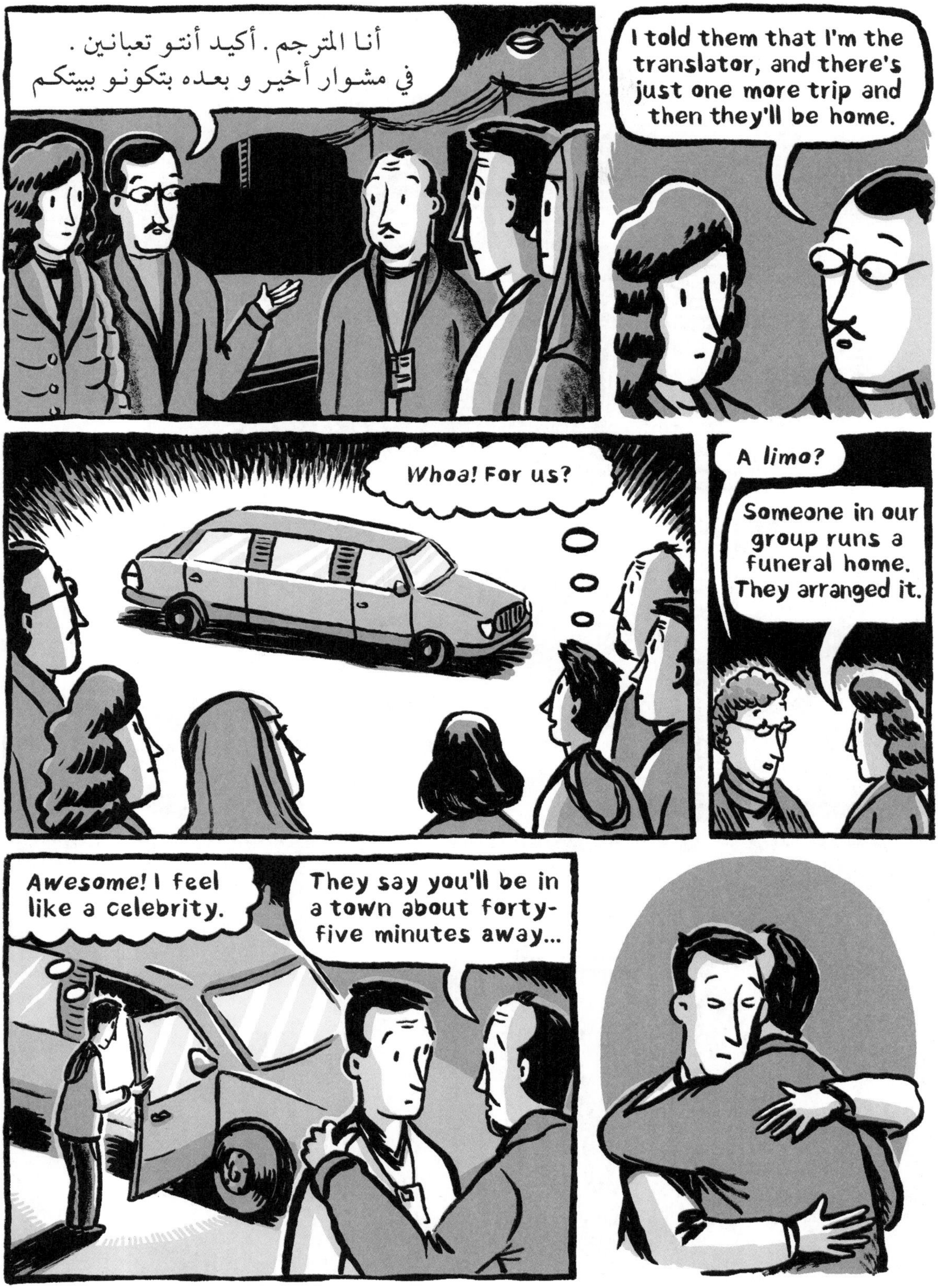
أنا المترجم. أكيد أنتو تعبانين.
في مشوار أخير و بعده بتكونو ببيتكم
I told them that I'm the translator, and there's just one more trip and then they'll be home.
Whoa! For us?
A limo?
Someone in our group runs a funeral home. They arranged it.
Awesome! I feel like a celebrity.
They say you'll be in a town about forty-five minutes away...

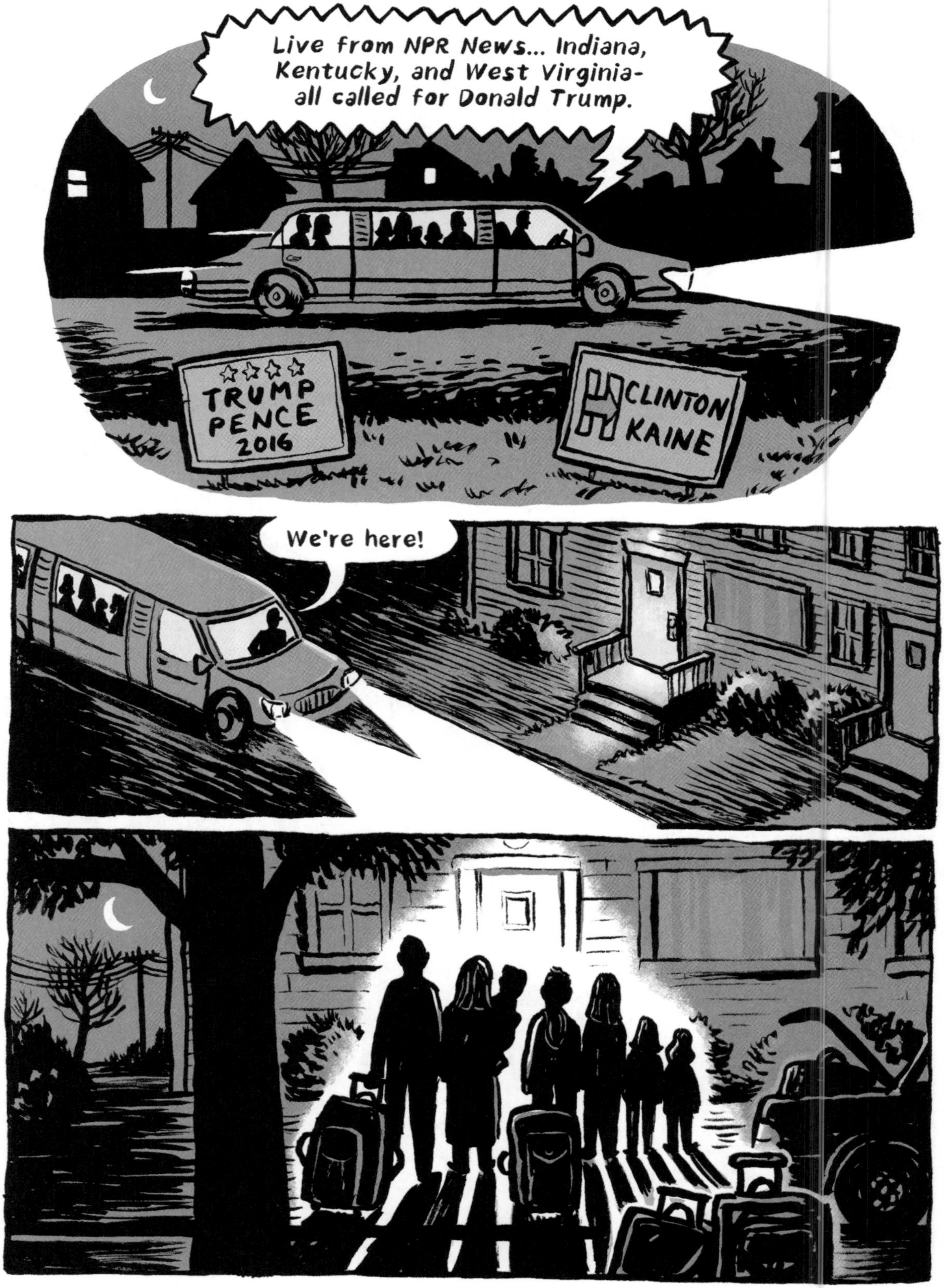
Live from NPR News... Indiana, Kentucky, and West Virginia- all called for Donald Trump.
TRUMP PENCE 2016
CLINTON KAINE
We're here!

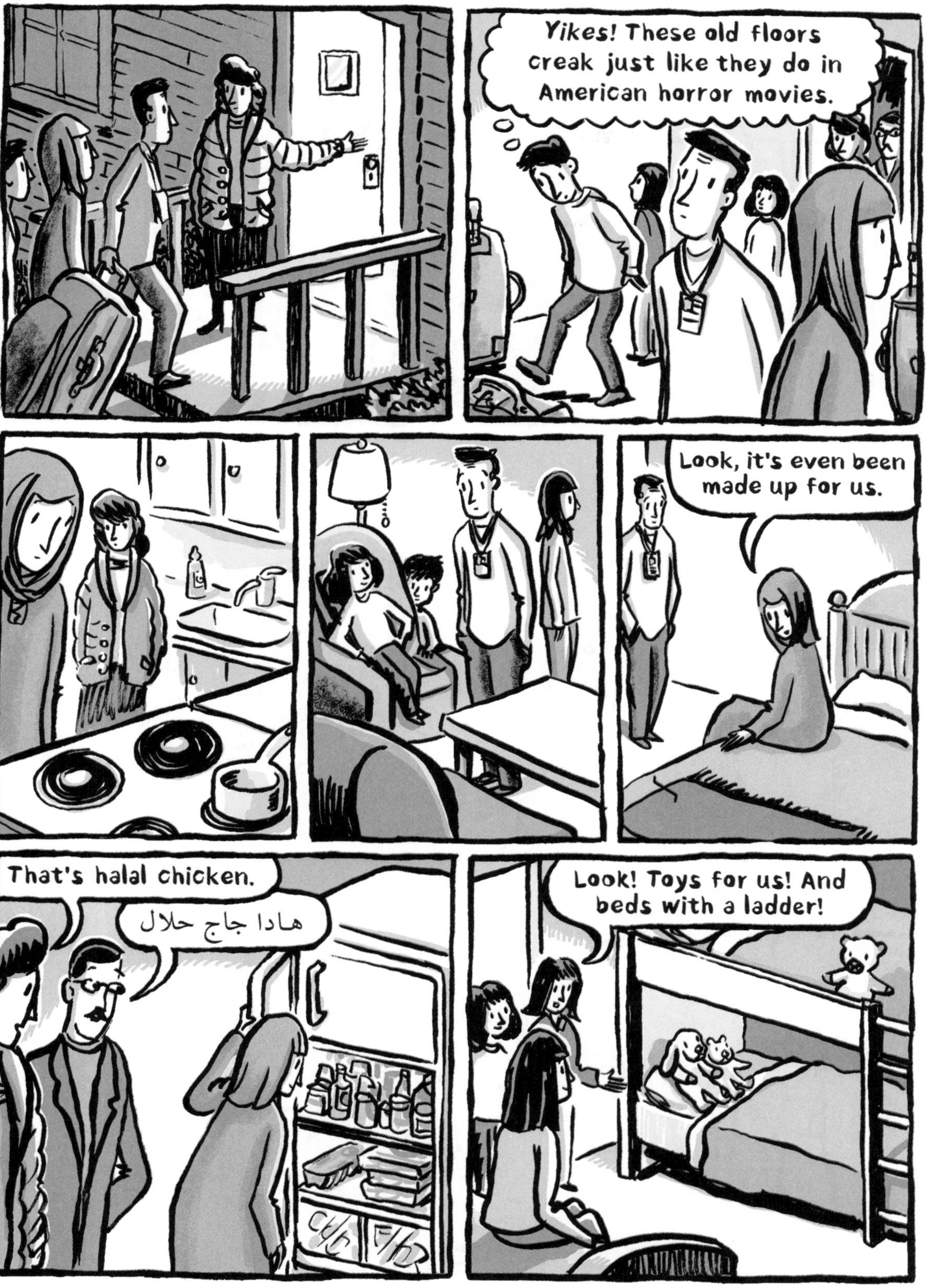
Yikes! These old floors creak just like they do in American horror movies.
Look, it's even been made up for us.
That's halal chicken.
هادا جاج حلال
Look! Toys for us! And beds with a ladder!

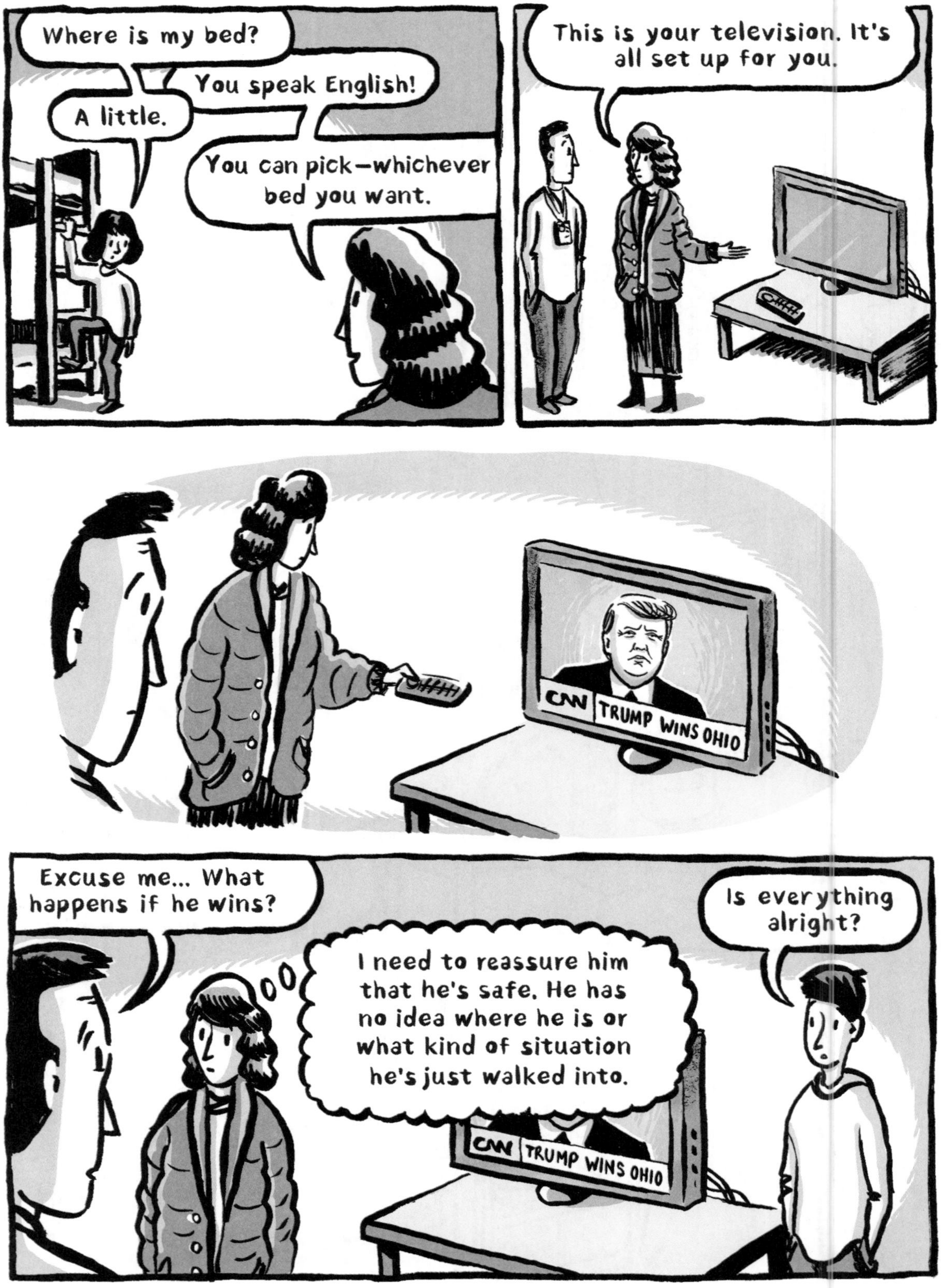
Where is my bed?
You speak English!
A little.
You can pick—whichever bed you want.
This is your television. It's all set up for you.
CNN
TRUMP WINS OHIO
Excuse me... What happens if he wins?
I need to reassure him that he's safe. He has no idea where he is or what kind of situation he's just walked into.
Is everything alright?
CNN
TRUMP WINS OHIO

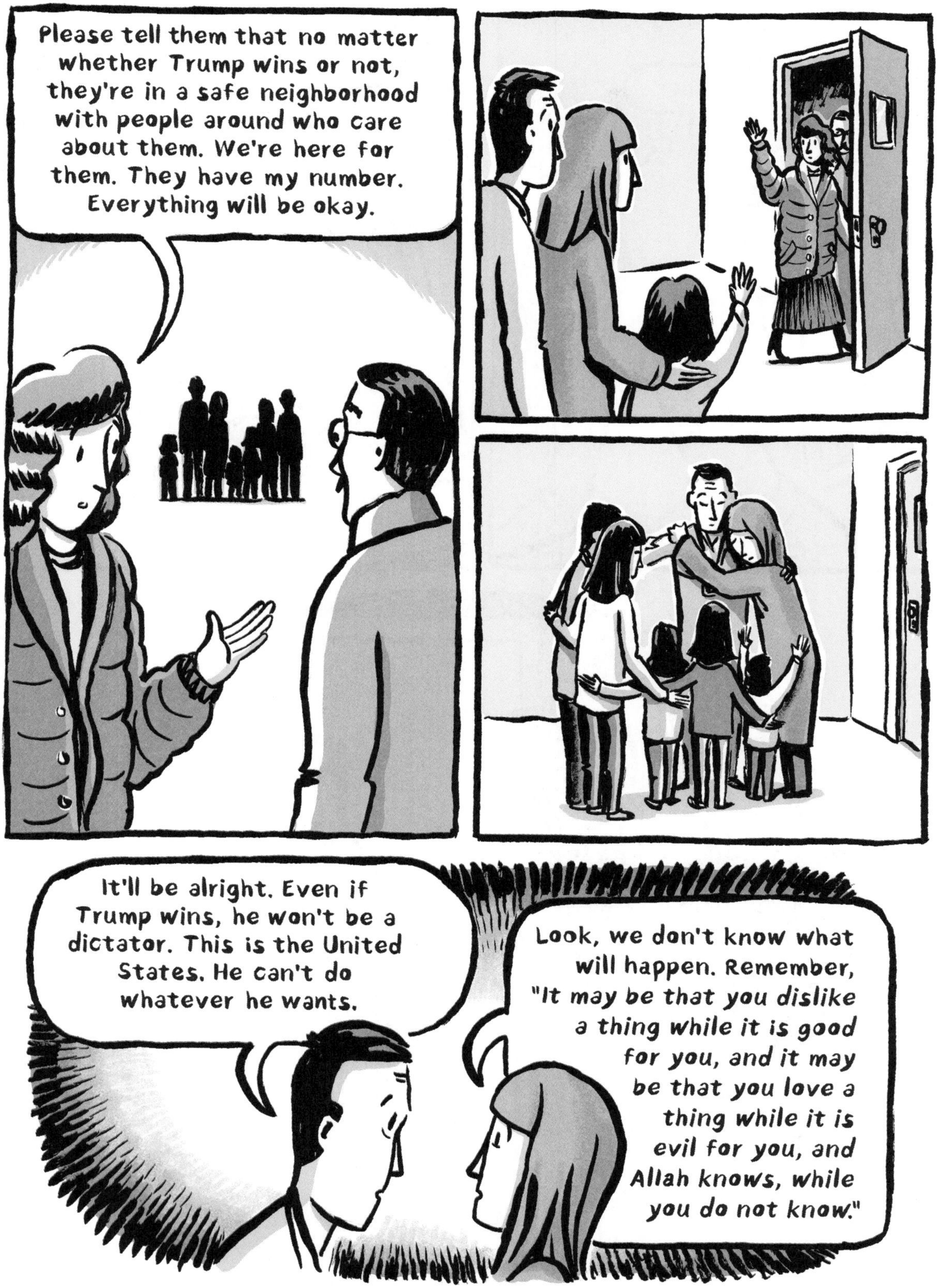
Please tell them that no matter whether Trump wins or not, they're in a safe neighborhood with people around who care about them. We're here for them. They have my number. Everything will be okay.
It'll be alright. Even if Trump wins, he won't be a dictator. This is the United States. He can't do whatever he wants.
Look, we don't know what will happen. Remember, "It may be that you dislike a thing while it is good for you, and it may be that you love a thing while it is evil for you, and Allah knows, while you do not know."

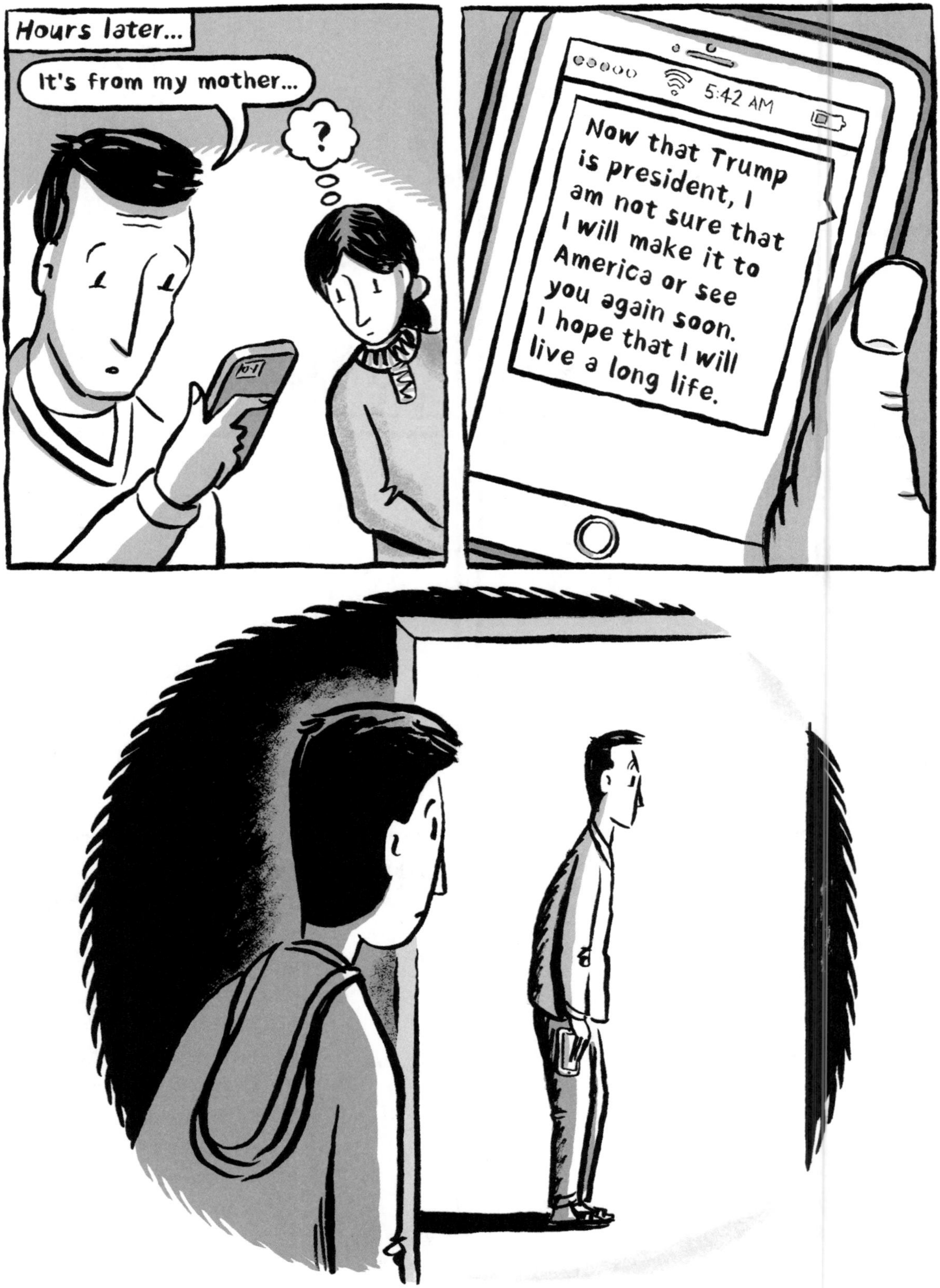
Hours later...
It's from my mother...
?
5:42 AM
Now that Trump is president, I am not sure that I will make it to America or see you again soon. I hope that I will live a long life.

Chapter 2

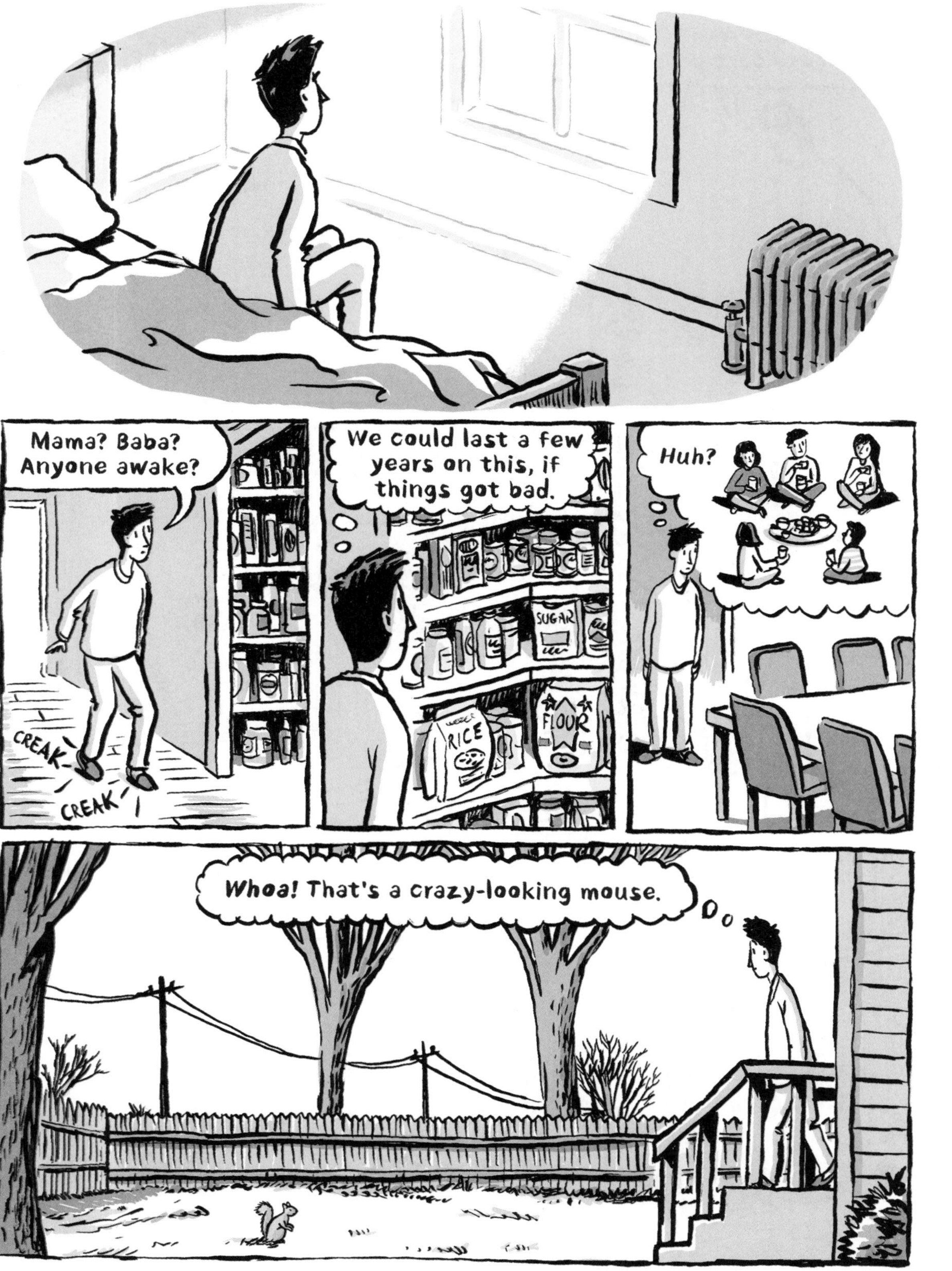

Mama? Baba? Anyone awake?
CREAK
CREAK
We could last a few years on this, if things got bad.
SUGAR
RICE
FLOUR
Huh?
Whoa! That's a crazy-looking mouse.

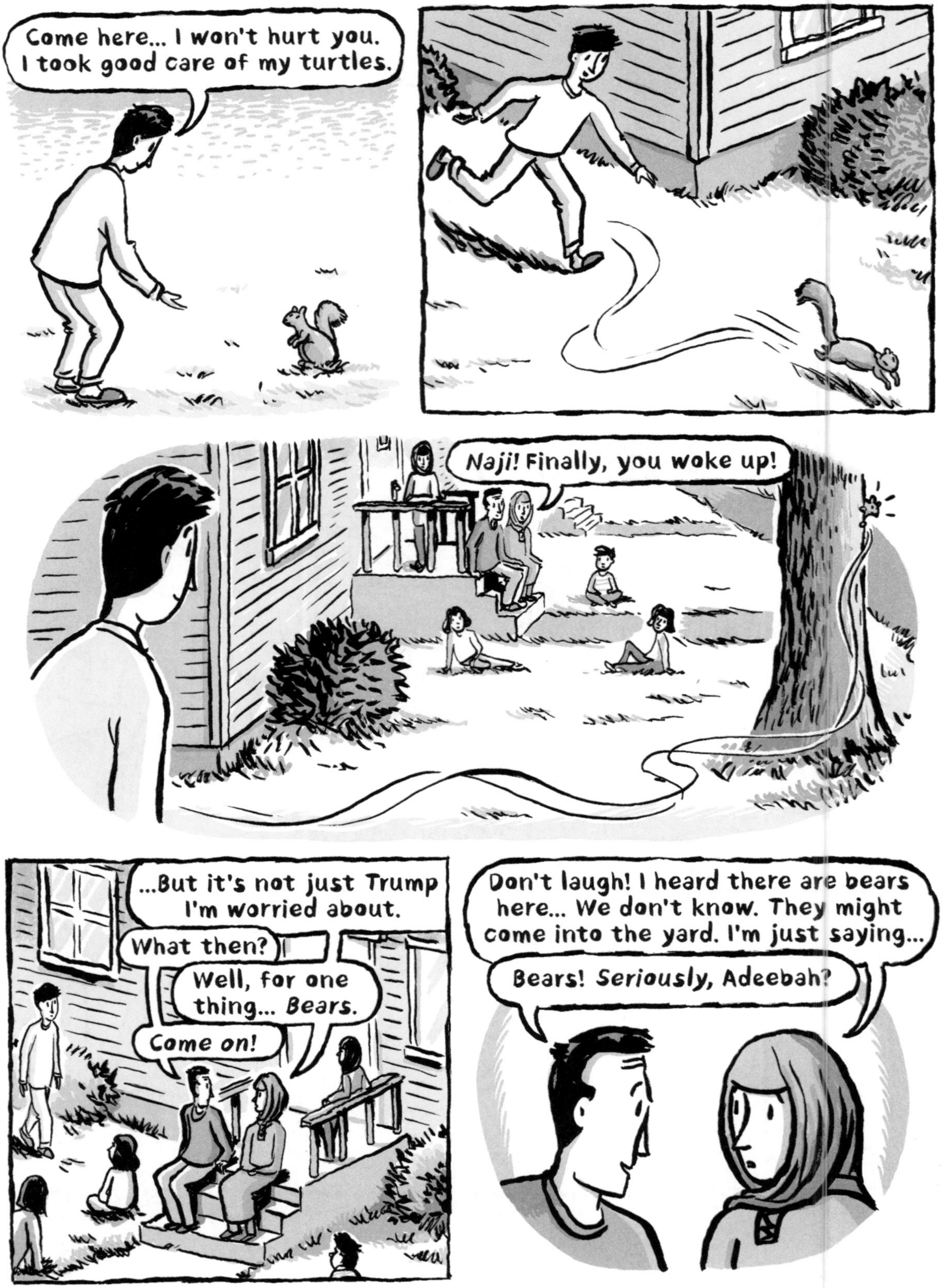
Come here... I won't hurt you. I took good care of my turtles.
Naji! Finally, you woke up!
...But it's not just Trump I'm worried about.
What then?
Well, for one thing... *Bears*.
Come on!
Don't laugh! I heard there are bears here... We don't know. They might come into the yard. I'm just saying...
Bears! *Seriously*, Adeebah?

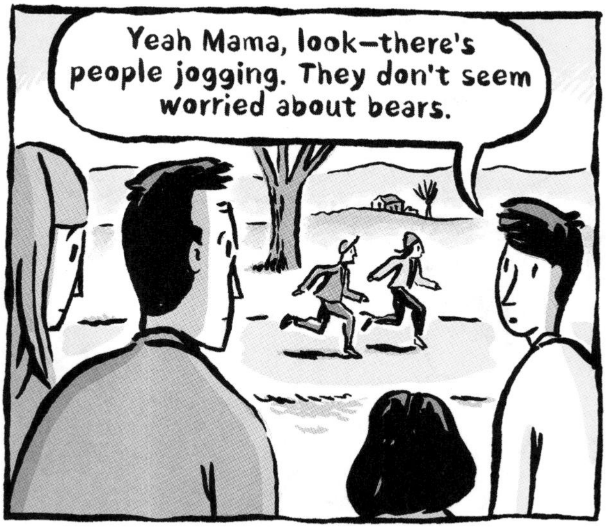

Yeah Mama, look—there's people jogging. They don't seem worried about bears.

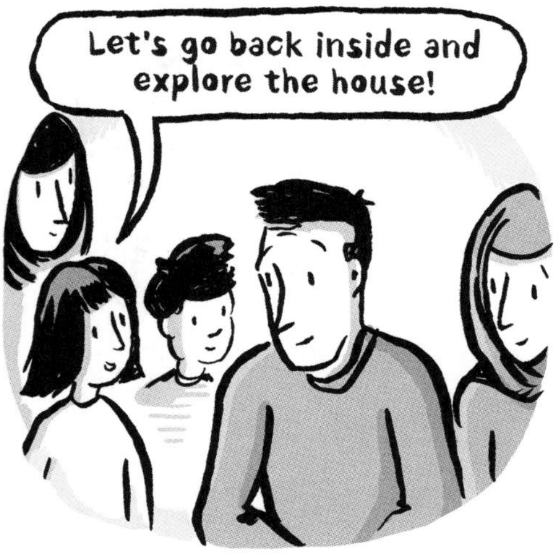

Let's go back inside and explore the house!

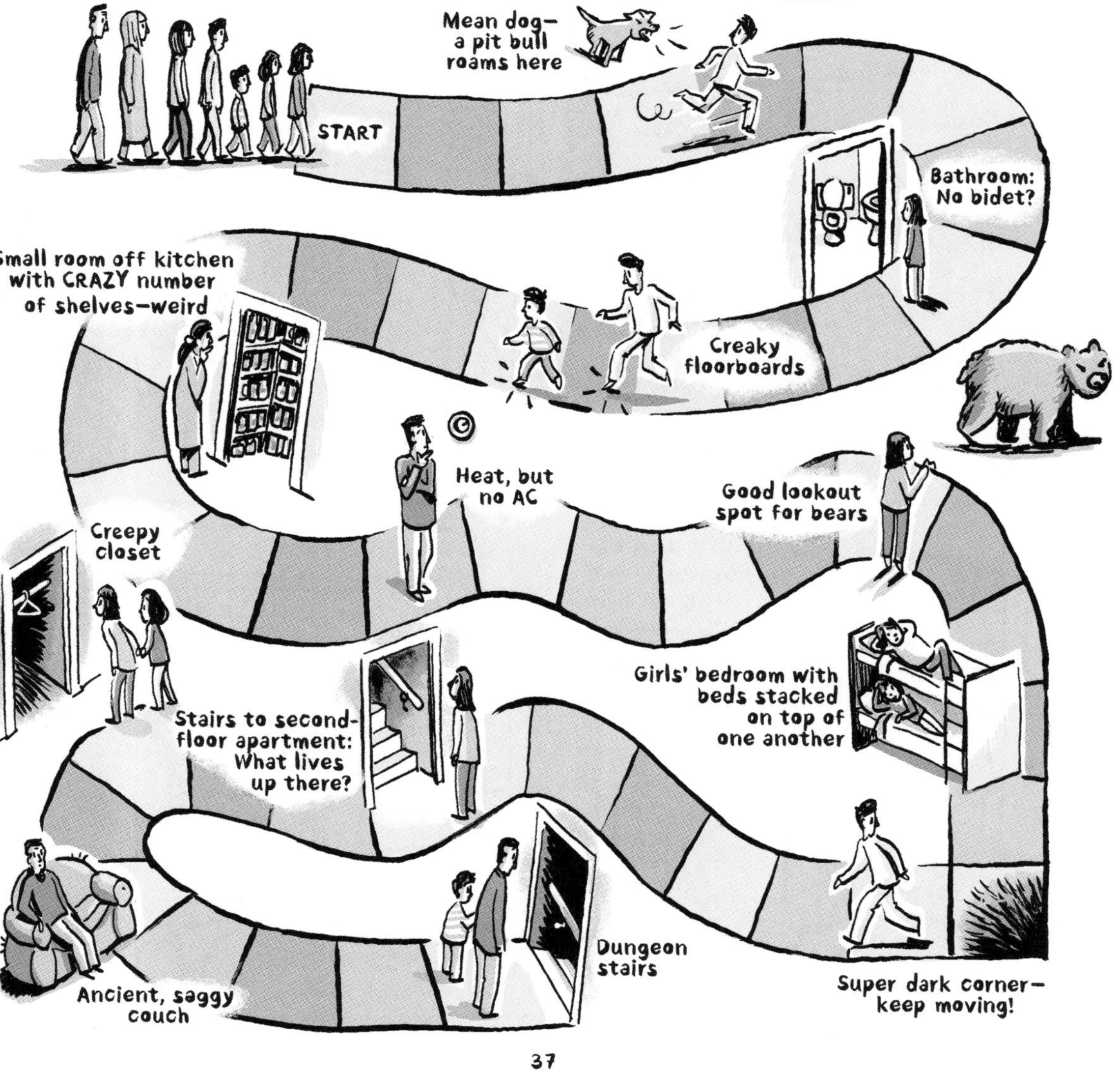

START
Mean dog—a pit bull roams here
Bathroom: No bidet?
Creaky floorboards
Small room off kitchen with CRAZY number of shelves—weird
Heat, but no AC
Good lookout spot for bears
Girls' bedroom with beds stacked on top of one another
Super dark corner—keep moving!
Dungeon stairs
Stairs to second-floor apartment: What lives up there?
Ancient, saggy couch
Creepy closet

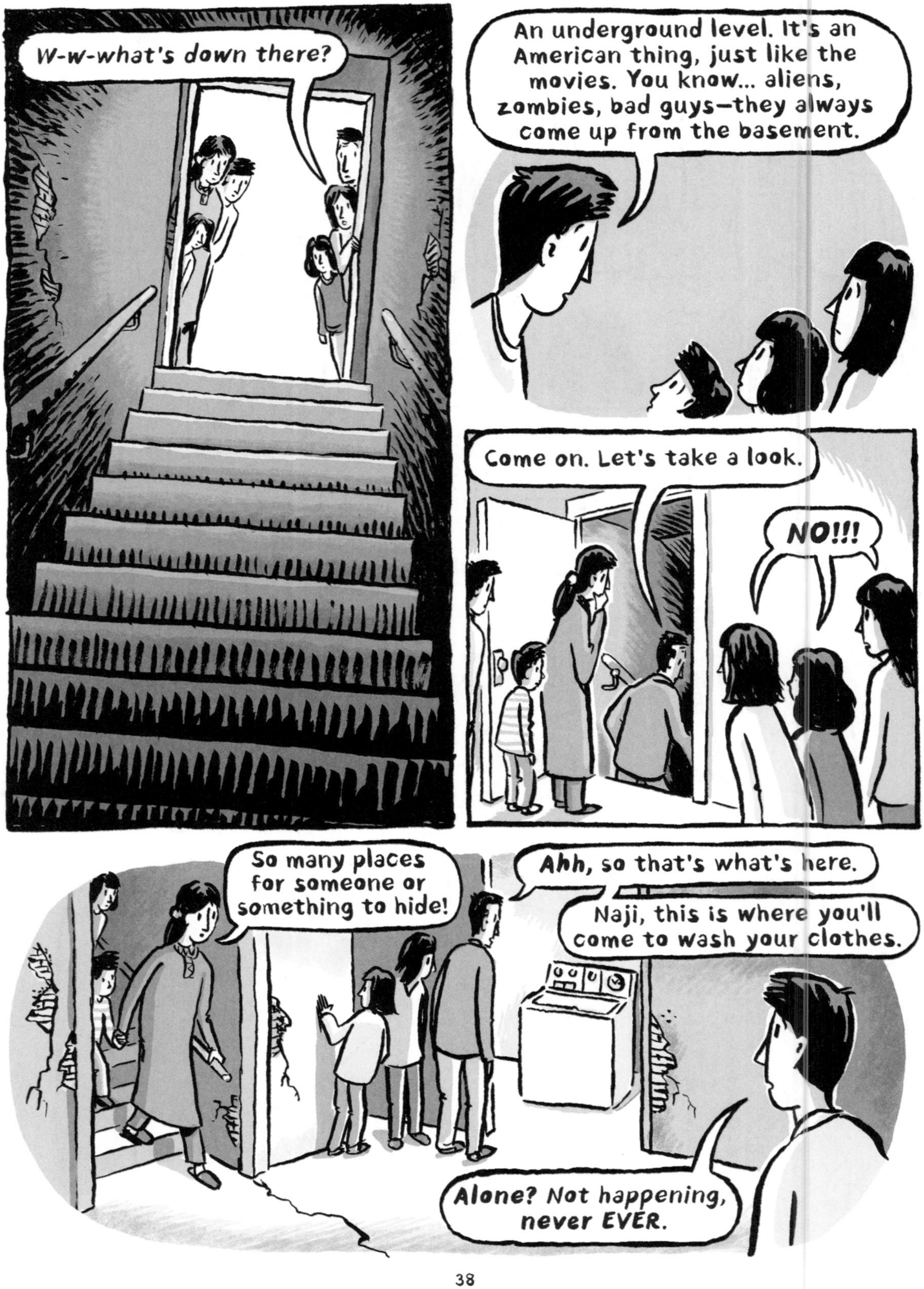
W-w-what's down there?
An underground level. It's an American thing, just like the movies. You know... aliens, zombies, bad guys—they always come up from the basement.
Come on. Let's take a look.
NO!!!
So many places for someone or something to hide!
Ahh, so that's what's here.
Naji, this is where you'll come to wash your clothes.
Alone? Not happening, never EVER.

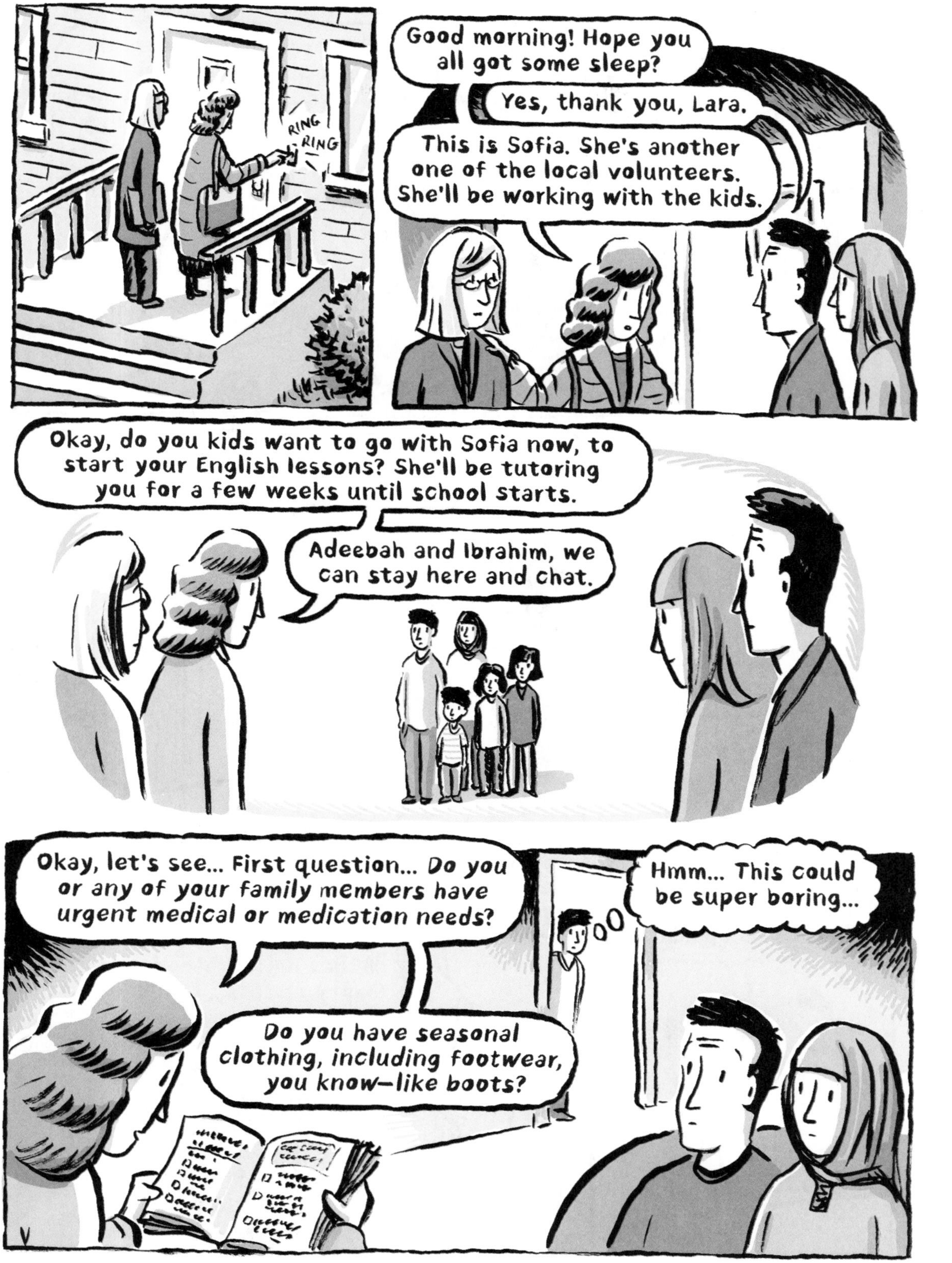
RING
RING
Good morning! Hope you all got some sleep?
Yes, thank you, Lara.
This is Sofia. She's another one of the local volunteers. She'll be working with the kids.
Okay, do you kids want to go with Sofia now, to start your English lessons? She'll be tutoring you for a few weeks until school starts.
Adeebah and Ibrahim, we can stay here and chat.
Okay, let's see... First question... *Do you or any of your family members have urgent medical or medication needs?*
Hmm... This could be super boring...
Do you have seasonal clothing, including footwear, you know—like boots?

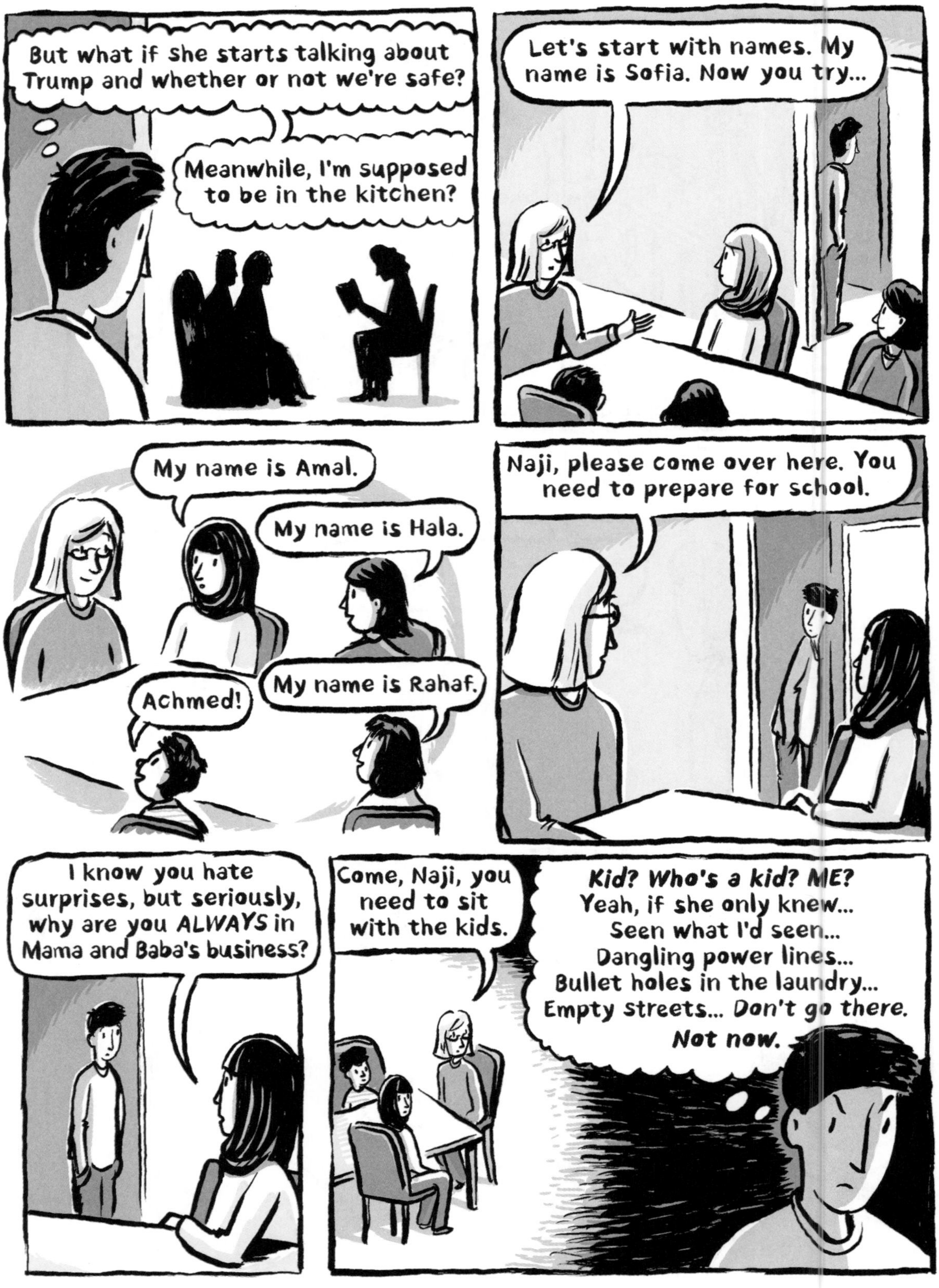

But what if she starts talking about Trump and whether or not we're safe?
Meanwhile, I'm supposed to be in the kitchen?
Let's start with names. My name is Sofia. Now you try...
My name is Amal.
My name is Hala.
Achmed!
My name is Rahaf.
Naji, please come over here. You need to prepare for school.
I know you hate surprises, but seriously, why are you ALWAYS in Mama and Baba's business?
Come, Naji, you need to sit with the kids.
Kid? Who's a kid? ME? Yeah, if she only knew... Seen what I'd seen... Dangling power lines... Bullet holes in the laundry... Empty streets... Don't go there. Not now.

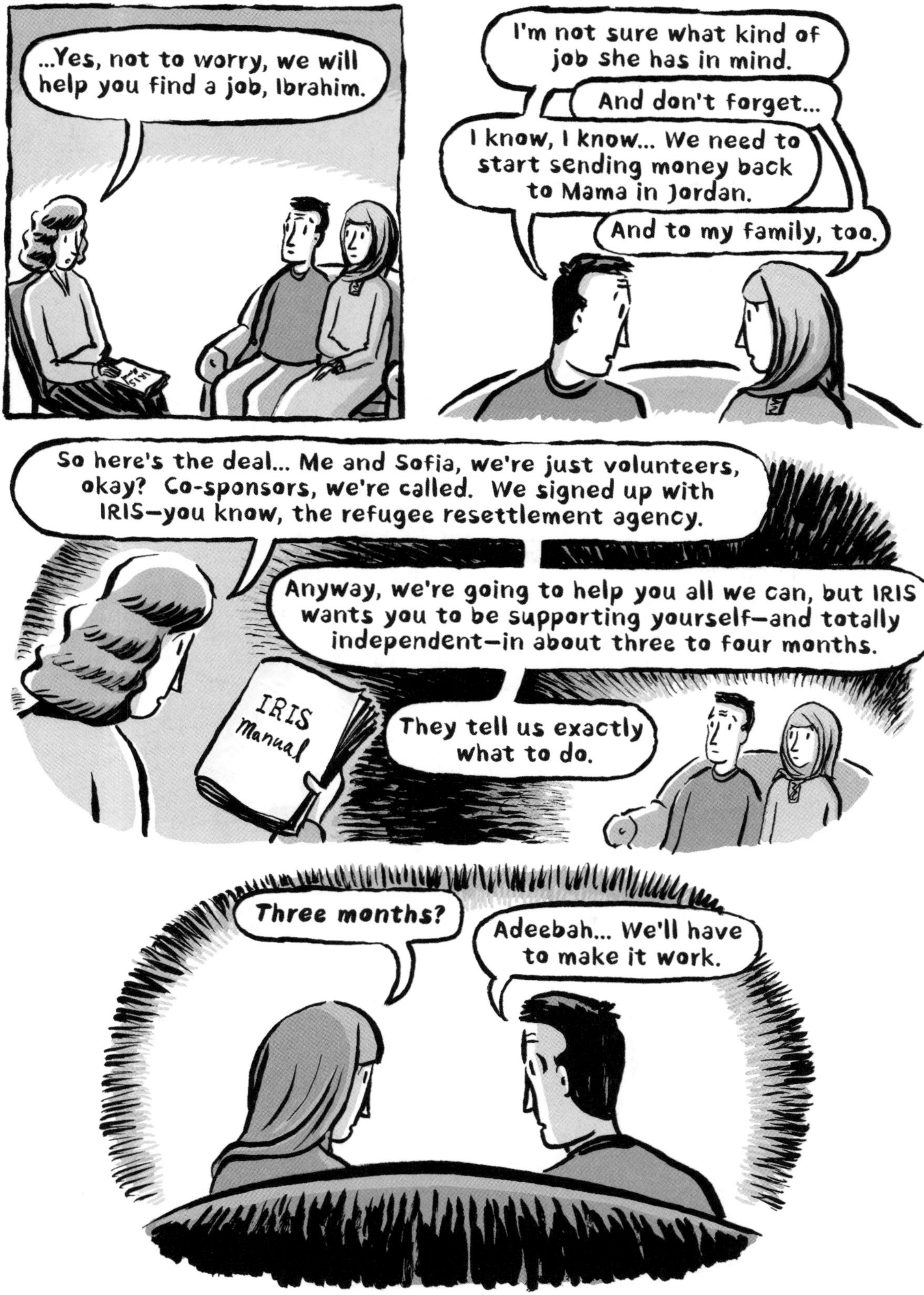
...Yes, not to worry, we will help you find a job, Ibrahim.
I'm not sure what kind of job she has in mind.
And don't forget...
I know, I know... We need to start sending money back to Mama in Jordan.
And to my family, too.
So here's the deal... Me and Sofia, we're just volunteers, okay? Co-sponsors, we're called. We signed up with IRIS—you know, the refugee resettlement agency.
Anyway, we're going to help you all we can, but IRIS wants you to be supporting yourself—and totally independent—in about three to four months.
IRIS Manual
They tell us exactly what to do.
Three months?
Adeebah... We'll have to make it work.

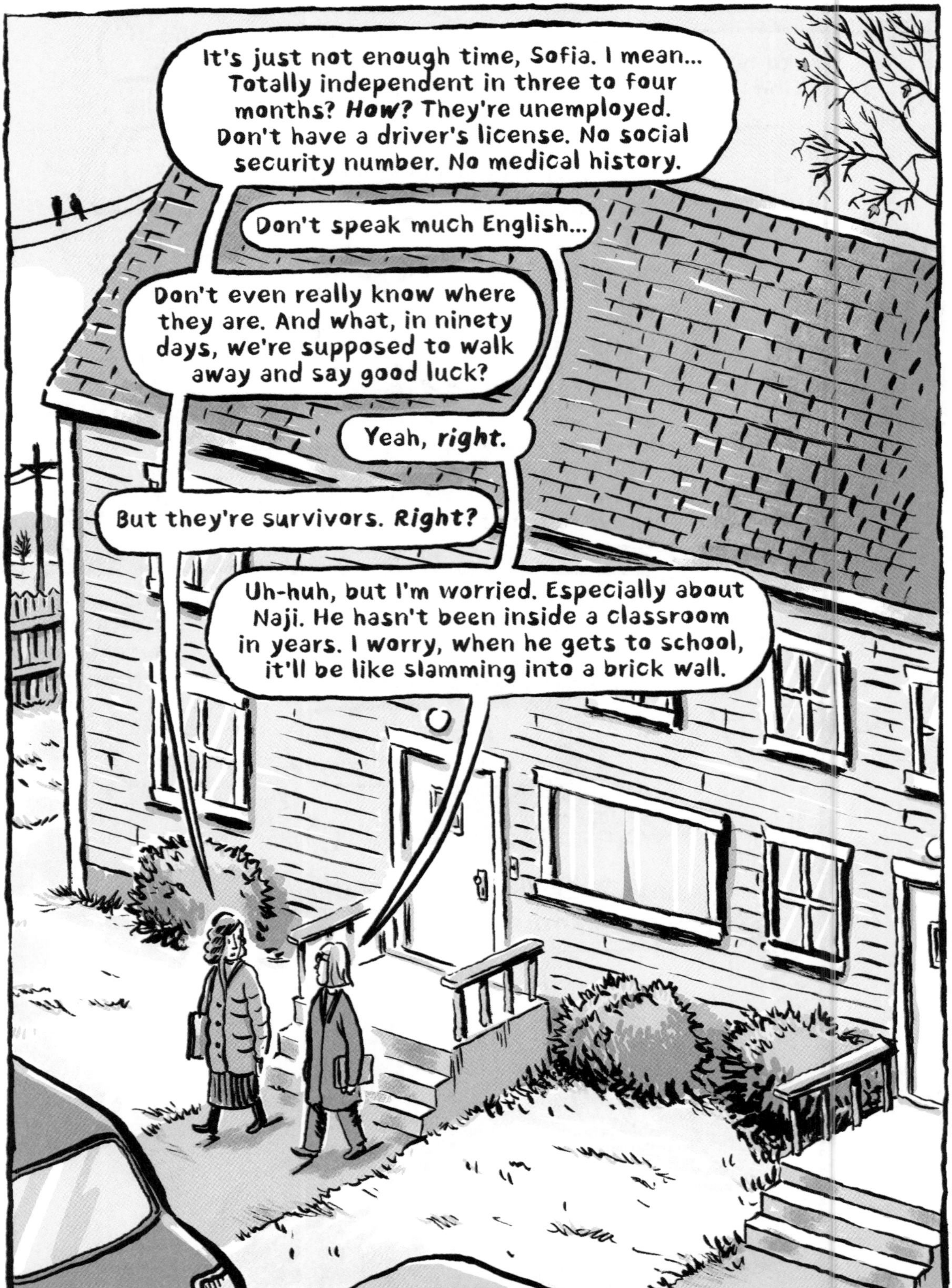
It's just not enough time, Sofia. I mean... Totally independent in three to four months? *How?* They're unemployed. Don't have a driver's license. No social security number. No medical history.
Don't speak much English...
Don't even really know where they are. And what, in ninety days, we're supposed to walk away and say good luck?
Yeah, *right*.
But they're survivors. *Right?*
Uh-huh, but I'm worried. Especially about Naji. He hasn't been inside a classroom in years. I worry, when he gets to school, it'll be like slamming into a brick wall.

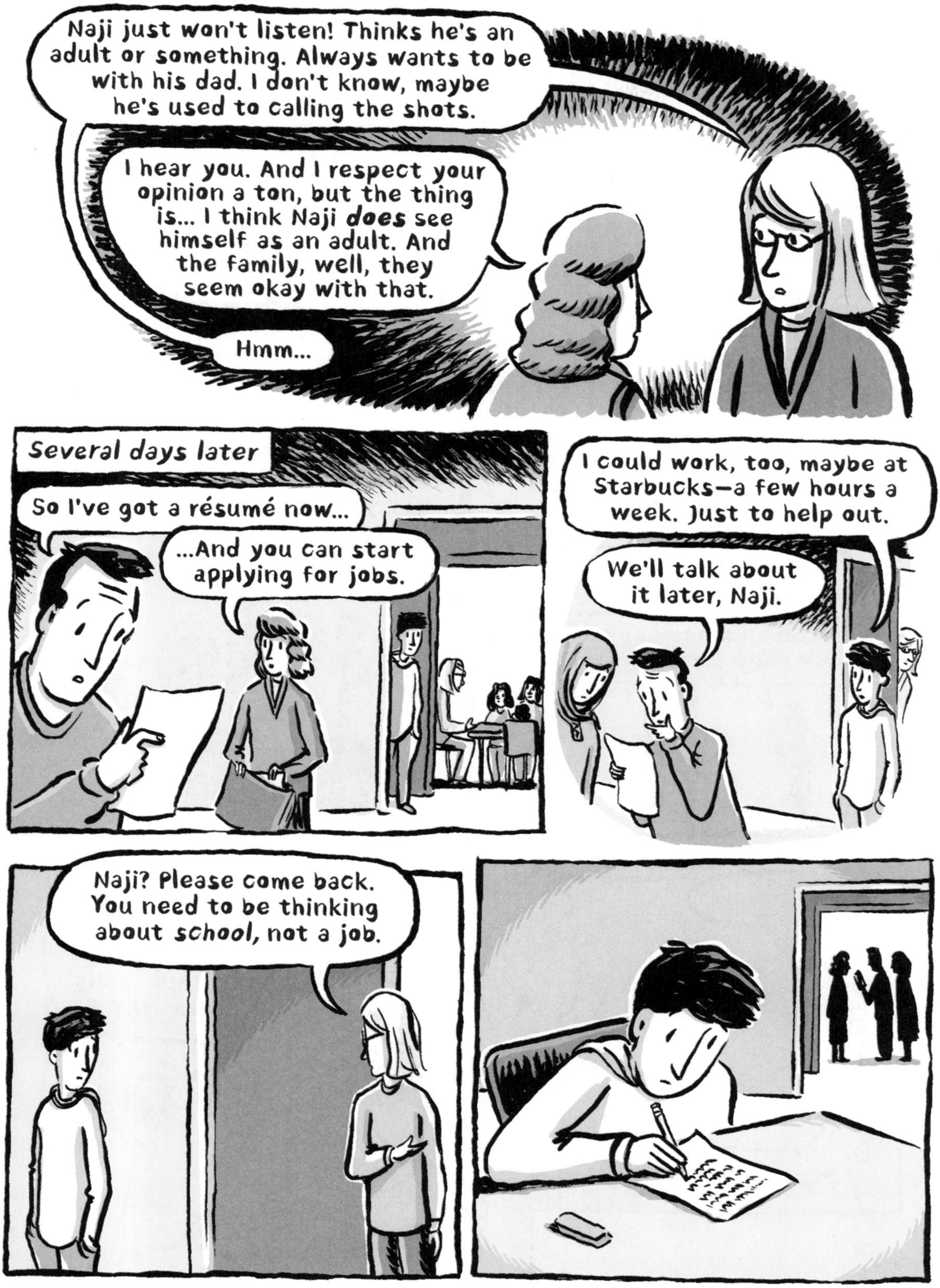
Naji just won't listen! Thinks he's an adult or something. Always wants to be with his dad. I don't know, maybe he's used to calling the shots.
I hear you. And I respect your opinion a ton, but the thing is... I think Naji *does* see himself as an adult. And the family, well, they seem okay with that.
Hmm...
Several days later
So I've got a résumé now...
...And you can start applying for jobs.
I could work, too, maybe at Starbucks—a few hours a week. Just to help out.
We'll talk about it later, Naji.
Naji? Please come back. You need to be thinking about *school*, not a job.

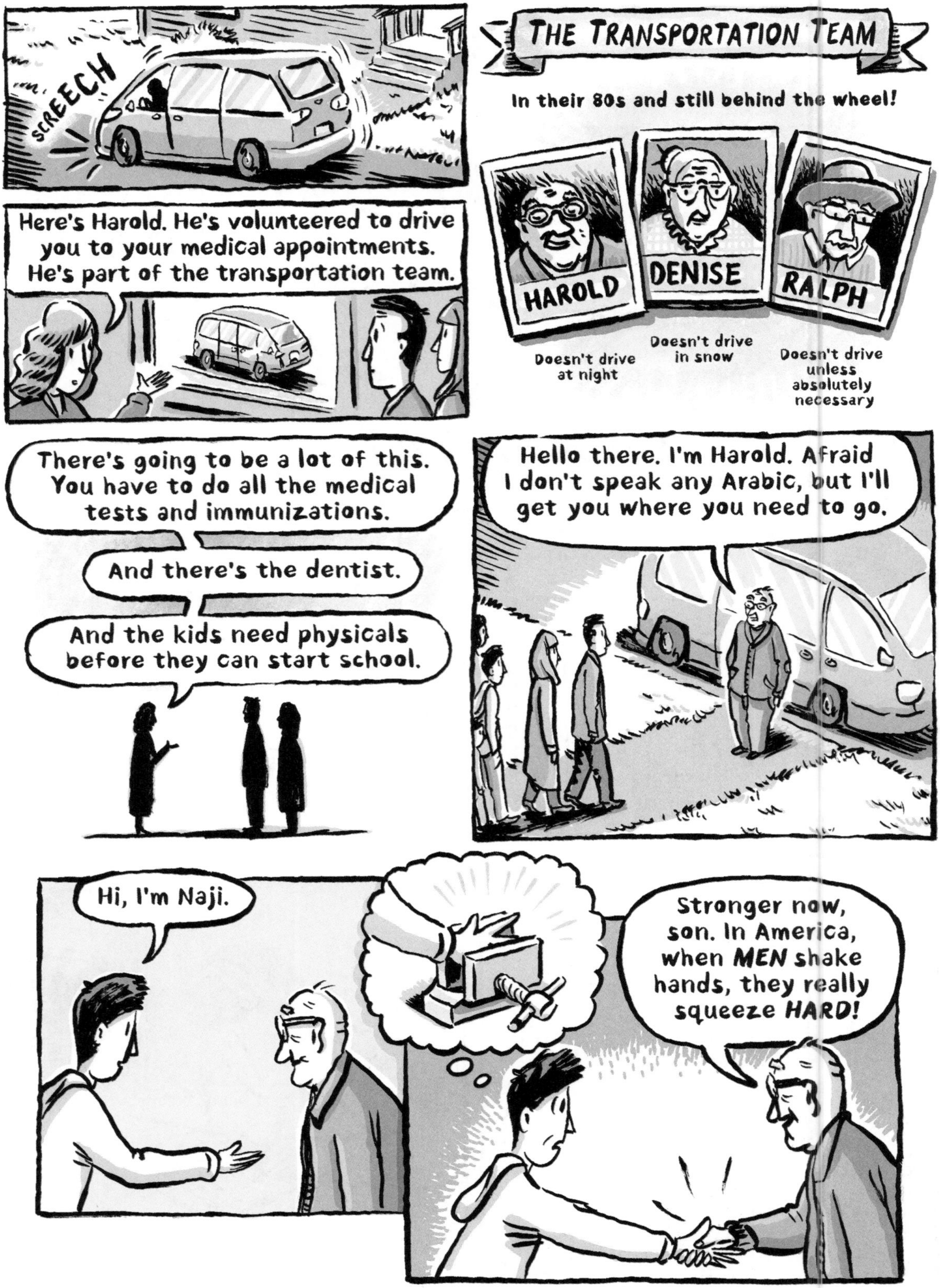
SCREECH
THE TRANSPORTATION TEAM
In their 80s and still behind the wheel!
HAROLD
DENISE
RALPH
Doesn't drive at night
Doesn't drive in snow
Doesn't drive unless absolutely necessary
Here's Harold. He's volunteered to drive you to your medical appointments. He's part of the transportation team.
There's going to be a lot of this. You have to do all the medical tests and immunizations.
And there's the dentist.
And the kids need physicals before they can start school.
Hello there. I'm Harold. Afraid I don't speak any Arabic, but I'll get you where you need to go.
Hi, I'm Naji.
Stronger now, son. In America, when MEN shake hands, they really squeeze HARD!

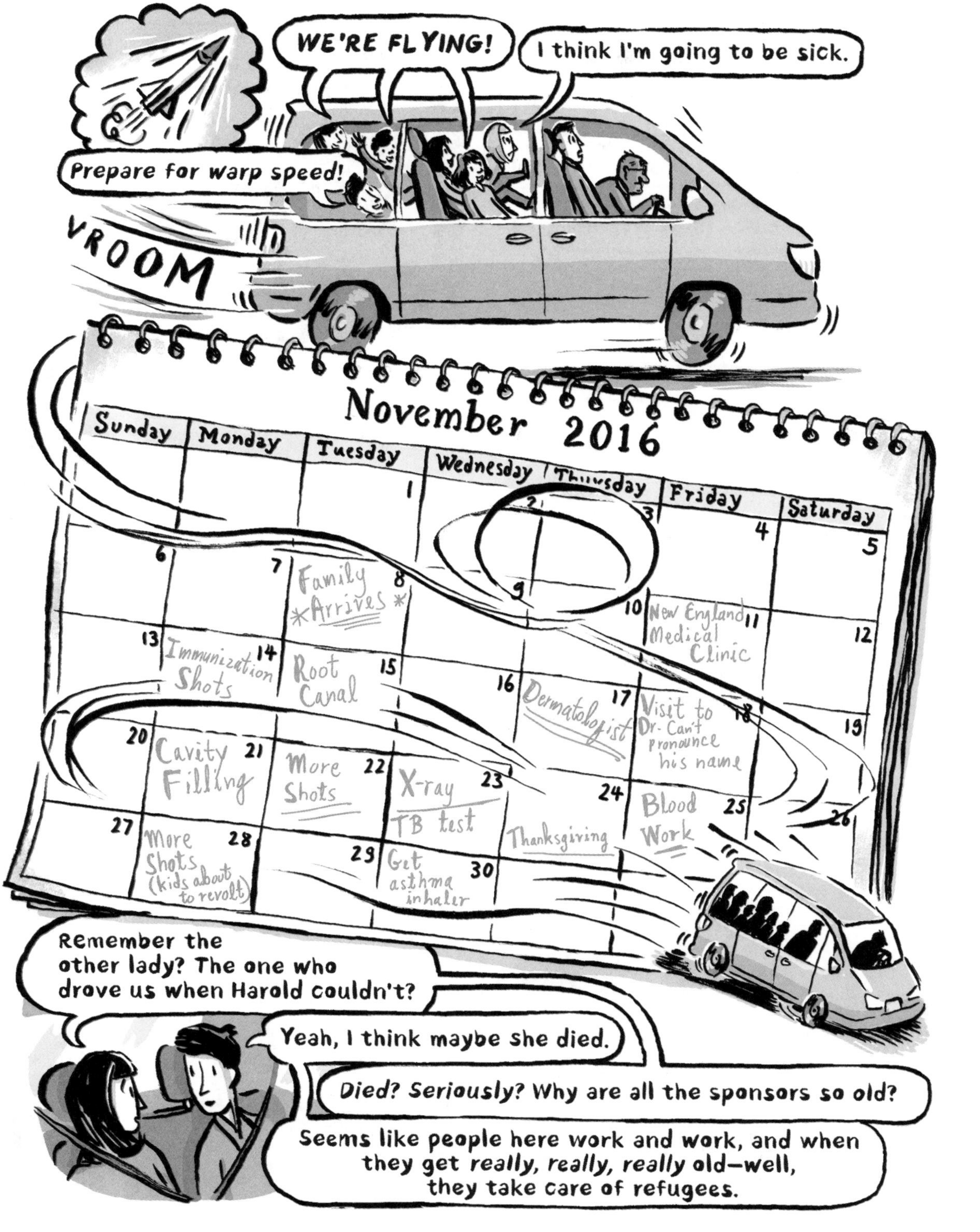
WE'RE FLYING!
I think I'm going to be sick.
Prepare for warp speed!
VROOM
November 2016
Sunday
Monday
Tuesday
Wednesday
Thursday
Friday
Saturday
Family *Arrives*
New England Medical Clinic
Immunization Shots
Root Canal
Dermatologist
Visit to Dr. Can't pronounce his name
Cavity Filling
More Shots
X-ray
TB test
Thanksgiving
Blood Work
More Shots (kids about to revolt)
Get asthma inhaler
Remember the other lady? The one who drove us when Harold couldn't?
Yeah, I think maybe she died.
Died? Seriously? Why are all the sponsors so old?
Seems like people here work and work, and when they get *really, really, really* old—well, they take care of refugees.

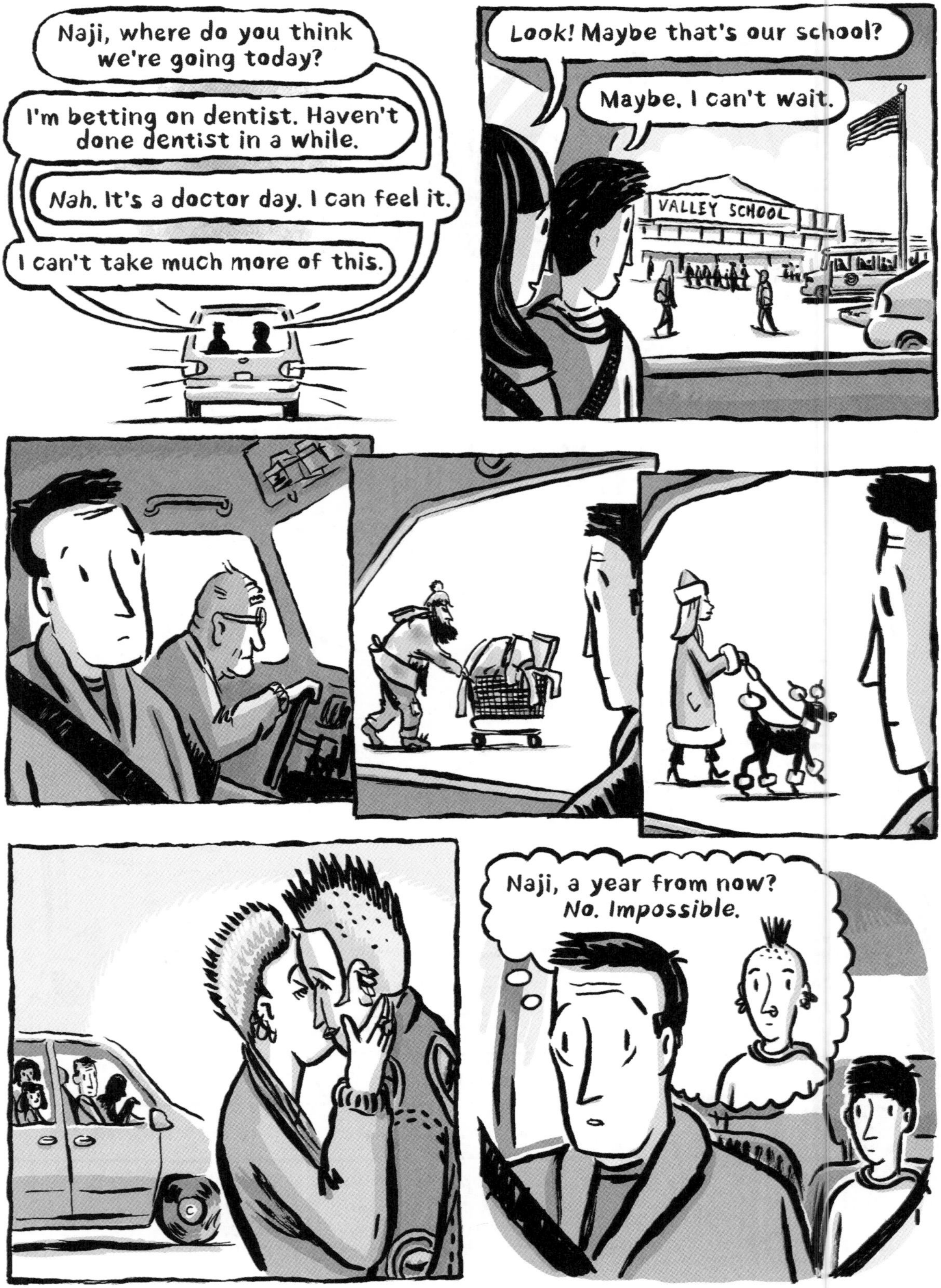
Naji, where do you think we're going today?
I'm betting on dentist. Haven't done dentist in a while.
Nah. It's a doctor day. I can feel it.
I can't take much more of this.
Look! Maybe that's our school?
Maybe. I can't wait.
VALLEY SCHOOL
Naji, a year from now? No. Impossible.

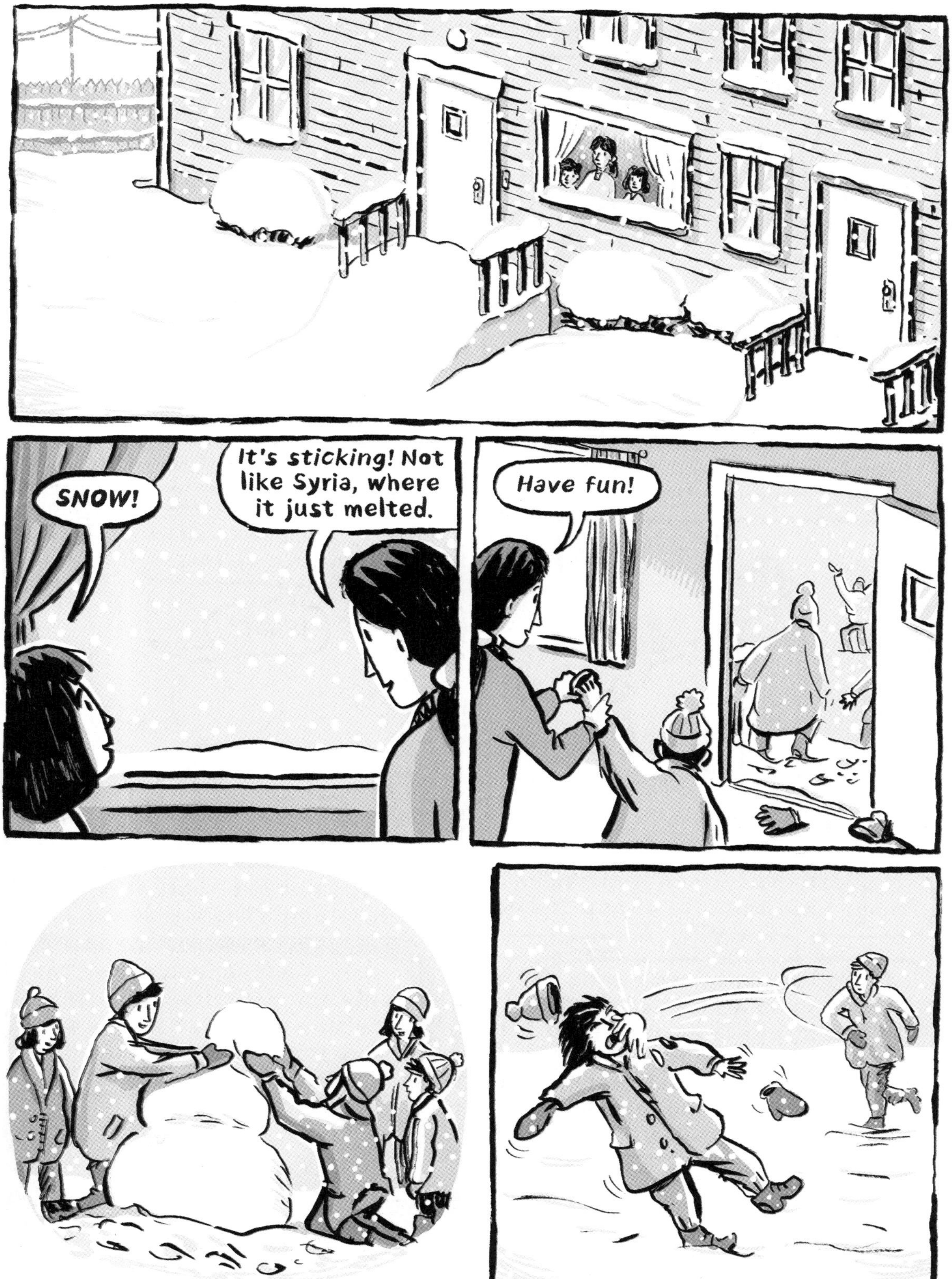
SNOW!
It's sticking! Not like Syria, where it just melted.
Have fun!

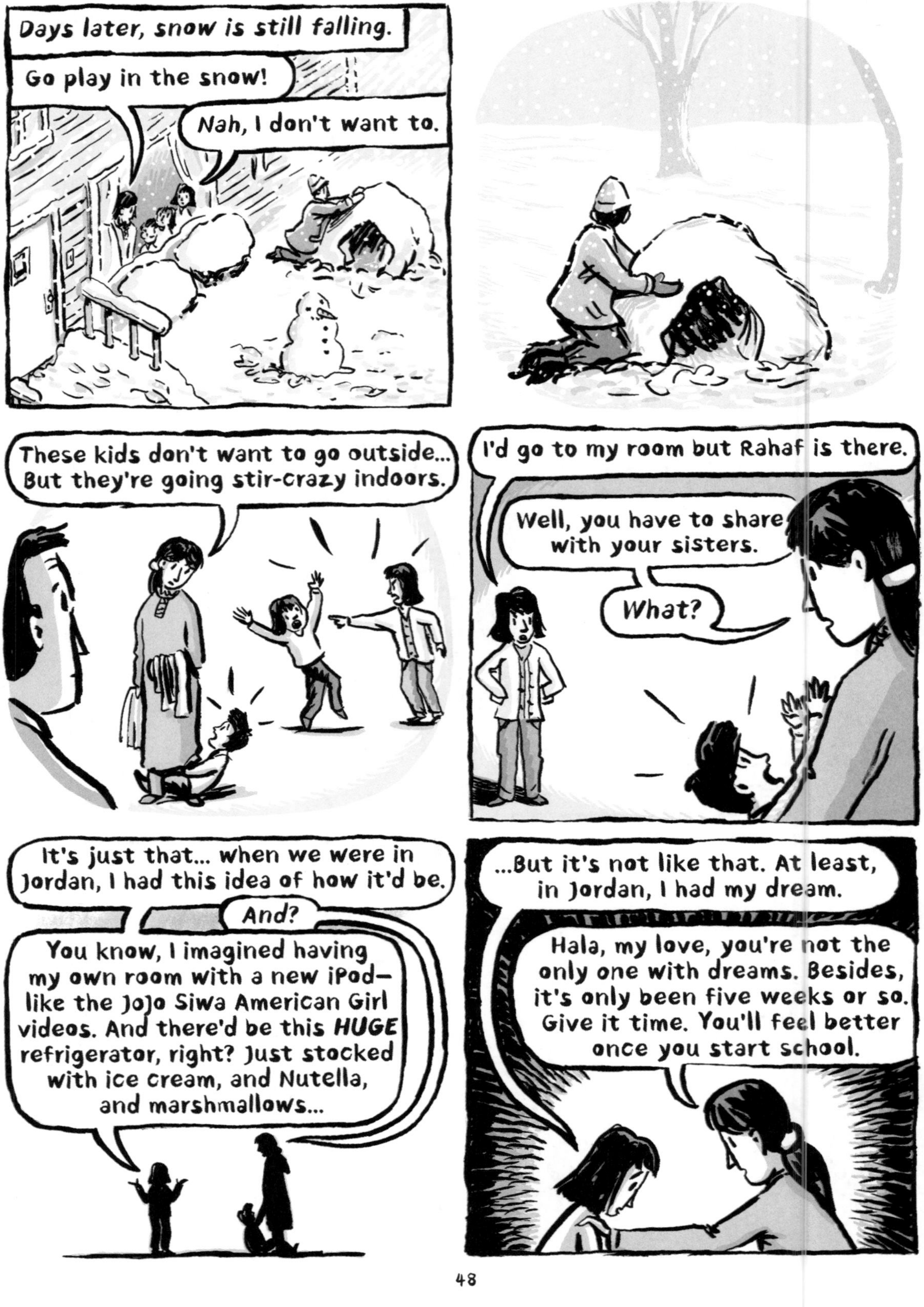

Days later, snow is still falling.
Go play in the snow!
Nah, I don't want to.
These kids don't want to go outside... But they're going stir-crazy indoors.
I'd go to my room but Rahaf is there.
Well, you have to share with your sisters.
What?
It's just that... when we were in Jordan, I had this idea of how it'd be.
And?
You know, I imagined having my own room with a new iPod— like the JoJo Siwa American Girl videos. And there'd be this *HUGE* refrigerator, right? Just stocked with ice cream, and Nutella, and marshmallows...
...But it's not like that. At least, in Jordan, I had my dream.
Hala, my love, you're not the only one with dreams. Besides, it's only been five weeks or so. Give it time. You'll feel better once you start school.

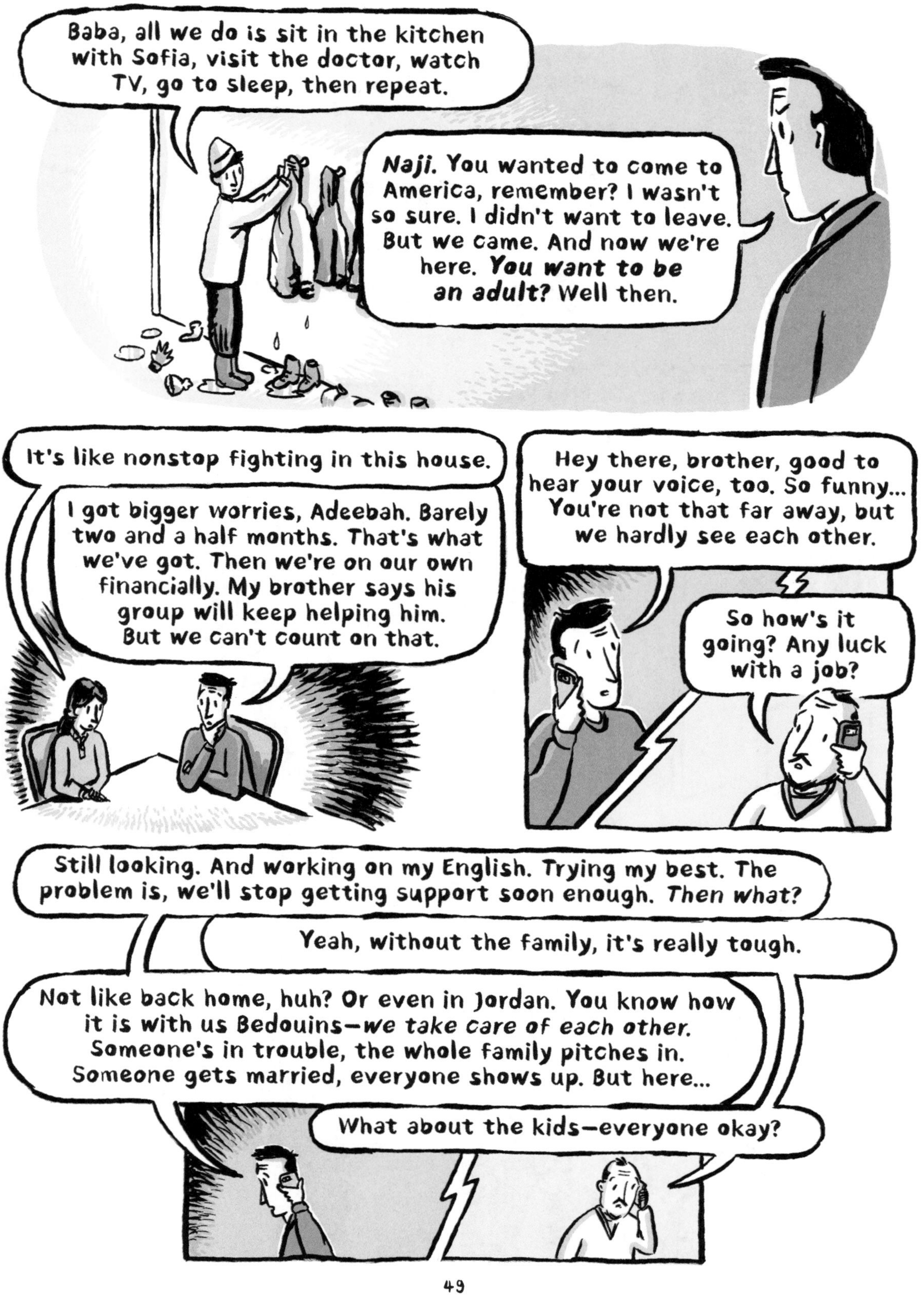
Baba, all we do is sit in the kitchen with Sofia, visit the doctor, watch TV, go to sleep, then repeat.
Naji. You wanted to come to America, remember? I wasn't so sure. I didn't want to leave. But we came. And now we're here. ***You want to be an adult?*** Well then.
It's like nonstop fighting in this house.
I got bigger worries, Adeebah. Barely two and a half months. That's what we've got. Then we're on our own financially. My brother says his group will keep helping him. But we can't count on that.
Hey there, brother, good to hear your voice, too. So funny... You're not that far away, but we hardly see each other.
So how's it going? Any luck with a job?
Still looking. And working on my English. Trying my best. The problem is, we'll stop getting support soon enough. *Then what?*
Yeah, without the family, it's really tough.
Not like back home, huh? Or even in Jordan. You know how it is with us Bedouins—*we take care of each other.* Someone's in trouble, the whole family pitches in. Someone gets married, everyone shows up. But here...
What about the kids—everyone okay?

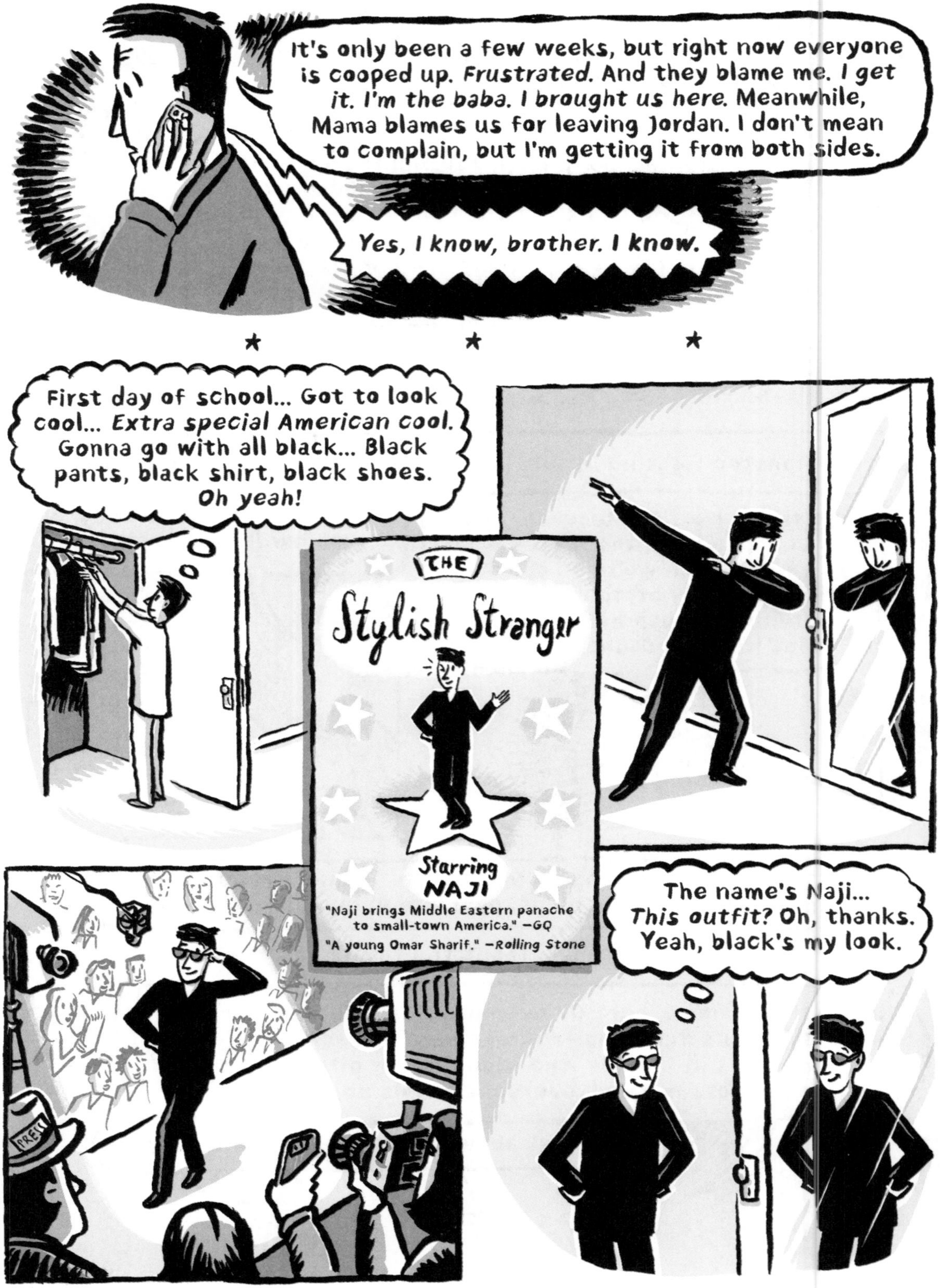
It's only been a few weeks, but right now everyone is cooped up. *Frustrated.* And they blame me. *I get it. I'm the baba. I brought us here.* Meanwhile, Mama blames us for leaving Jordan. I don't mean to complain, but I'm getting it from both sides.
Yes, I know, brother. I know.
First day of school... Got to look cool... *Extra special American cool.* Gonna go with all black... Black pants, black shirt, black shoes. *Oh yeah!*
THE
Stylish Stranger
Starring
NAJI
"Naji brings Middle Eastern panache to small-town America." —GQ
"A young Omar Sharif." —Rolling Stone
PRESS
The name's Naji... *This outfit?* Oh, thanks. Yeah, black's my look.

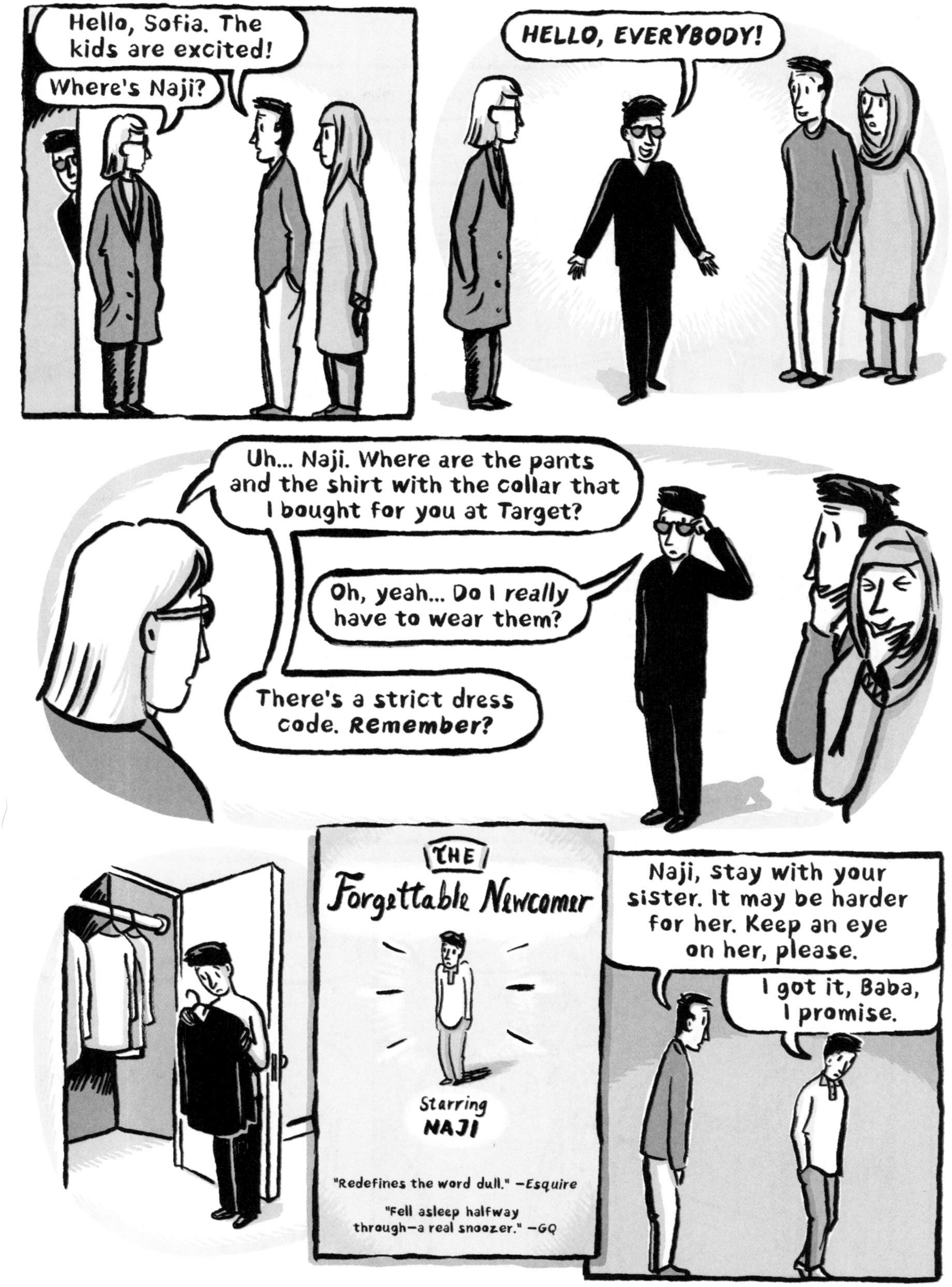

Hello, Sofia. The kids are excited!
Where's Naji?
HELLO, EVERYBODY!
Uh... Naji. Where are the pants and the shirt with the collar that I bought for you at Target?
Oh, yeah... Do I really have to wear them?
There's a strict dress code. Remember?
THE
Forgettable Newcomer
Starring
NAJI
"Redefines the word dull." –Esquire
"Fell asleep halfway through—a real snoozer." –GQ
Naji, stay with your sister. It may be harder for her. Keep an eye on her, please.
I got it, Baba, I promise.

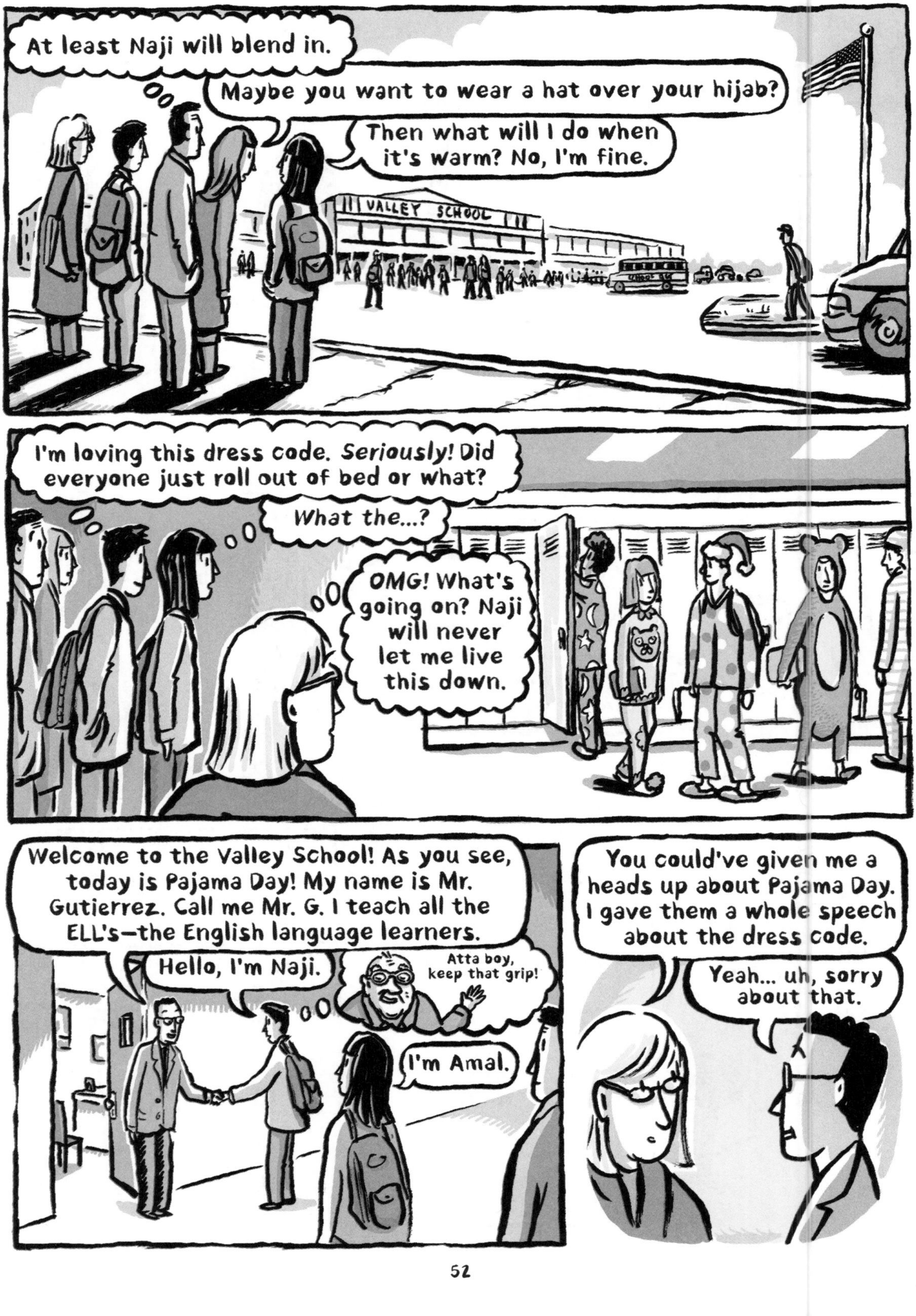
At least Naji will blend in.
Maybe you want to wear a hat over your hijab?
Then what will I do when it's warm? No, I'm fine.
VALLEY SCHOOL
I'm loving this dress code. *Seriously!* Did everyone just roll out of bed or what?
What the...?
OMG! What's going on? Naji will never let me live this down.
Welcome to the Valley School! As you see, today is Pajama Day! My name is Mr. Gutierrez. Call me Mr. G. I teach all the ELL's—the English language learners.
Hello, I'm Naji.
Atta boy, keep that grip!
I'm Amal.
You could've given me a heads up about Pajama Day. I gave them a whole speech about the dress code.
Yeah... uh, sorry about that.

...As you can see, Amal plans to keep her hijab.

That's just fine.

Thank you... but I don't want the kids to stick out too much. To be honest, Mr. G, I'm concerned about their safety—especially them wandering home on their own.

Don't worry. We'll see them onto the school bus.

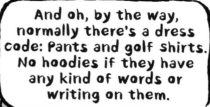

And oh, by the way, normally there's a dress code: Pants and golf shirts. No hoodies if they have any kind of words or writing on them.

These are our new ELL students. They're from Syria. Can you introduce yourselves?

Hey, I'm Yasmine, from Algeria.

Hi, I'm Cristina, from Peru.

Today I want everyone to draw his or her dream house. This is your ideal, perfect home. Then I want you to present it to the class—in English.

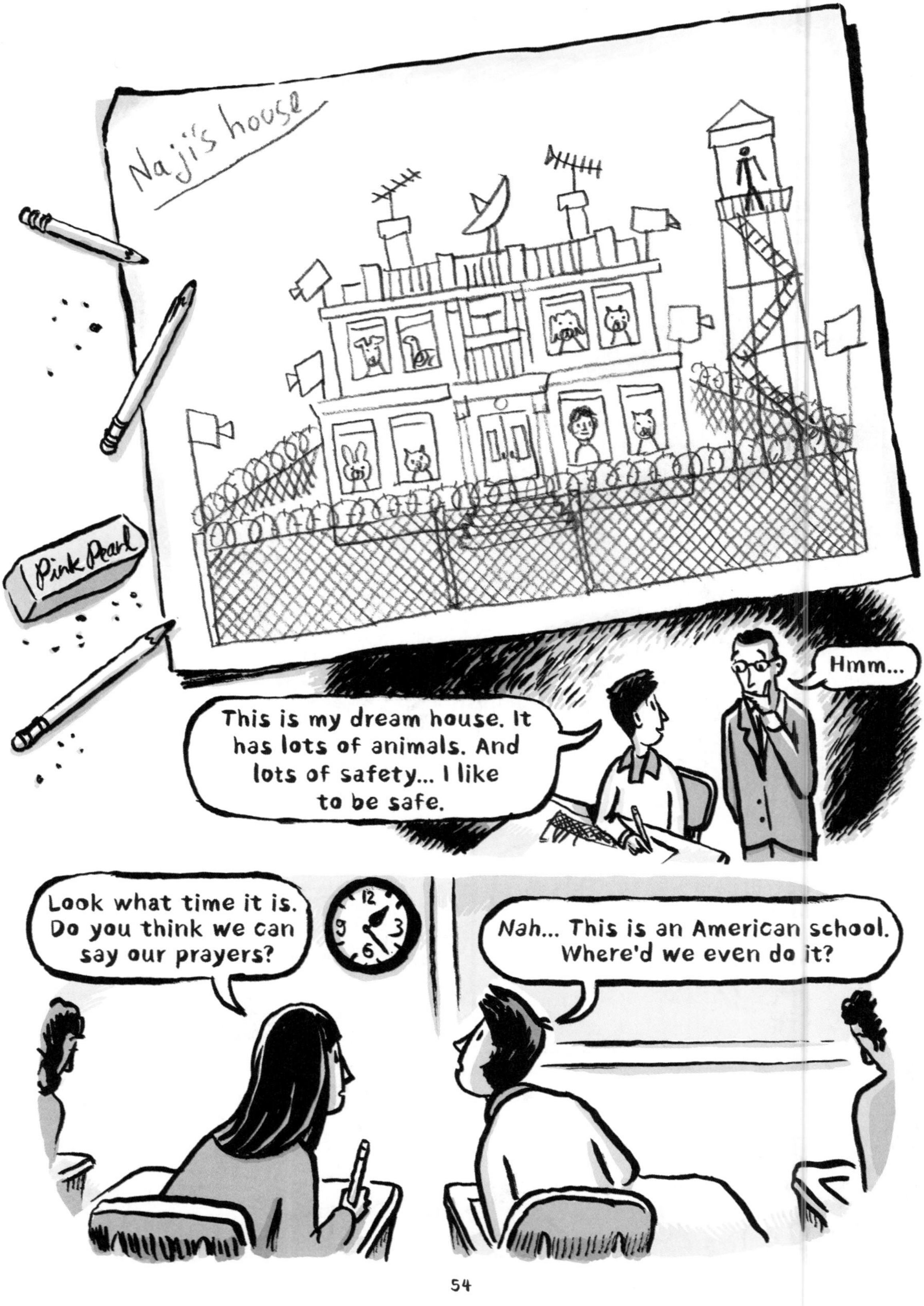
Naji's house
Pink Pearl
This is my dream house. It has lots of animals. And lots of safety... I like to be safe.
Hmm...
Look what time it is. Do you think we can say our prayers?
Nah... This is an American school. Where'd we even do it?

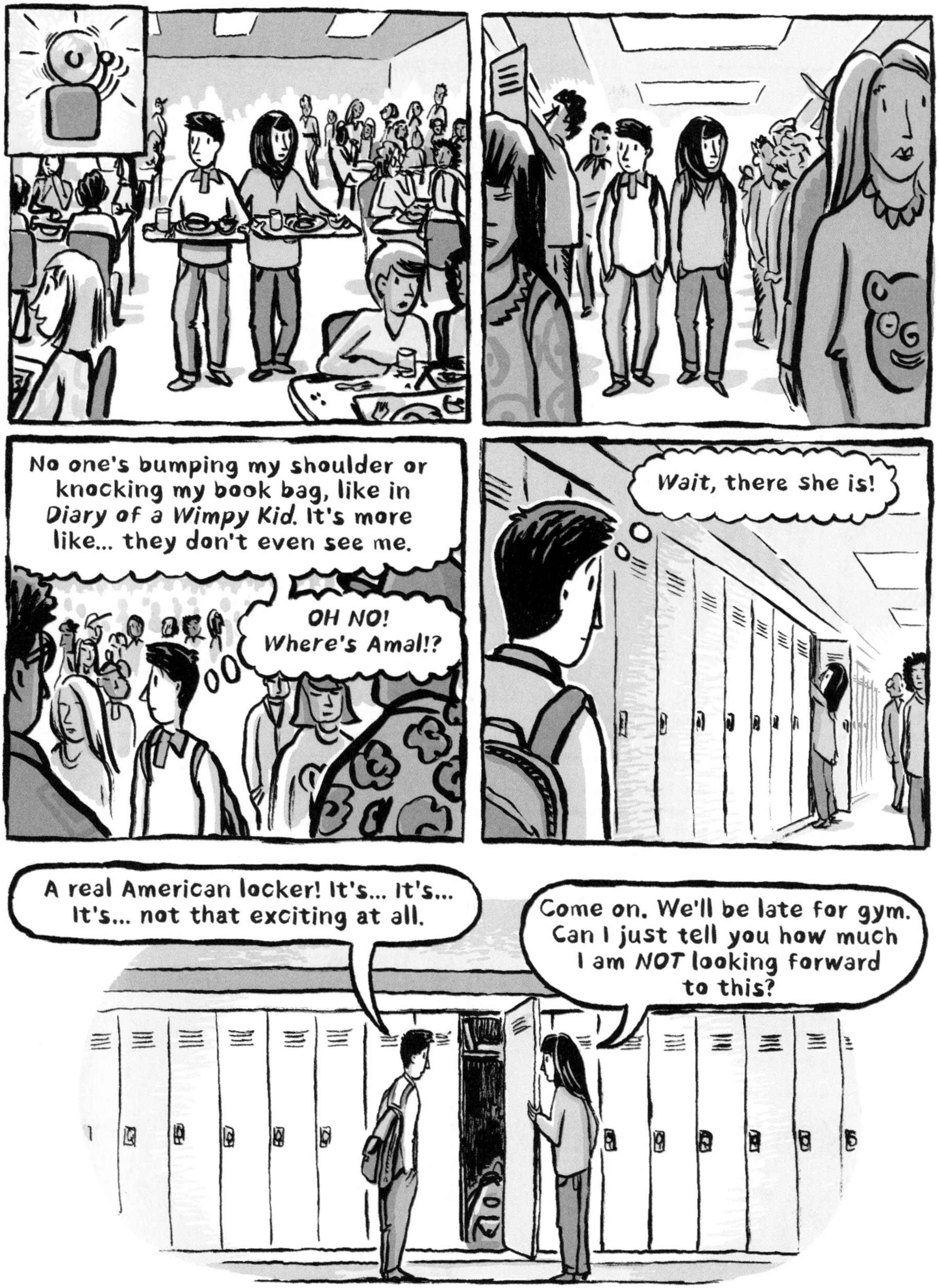
No one's bumping my shoulder or knocking my book bag, like in *Diary of a Wimpy Kid*. It's more like... they don't even see me.
OH NO! Where's Amal!?
Wait, there she is!
A real American locker! It's... It's... It's... not that exciting at all.
Come on. We'll be late for gym. Can I just tell you how much I am *NOT* looking forward to this?

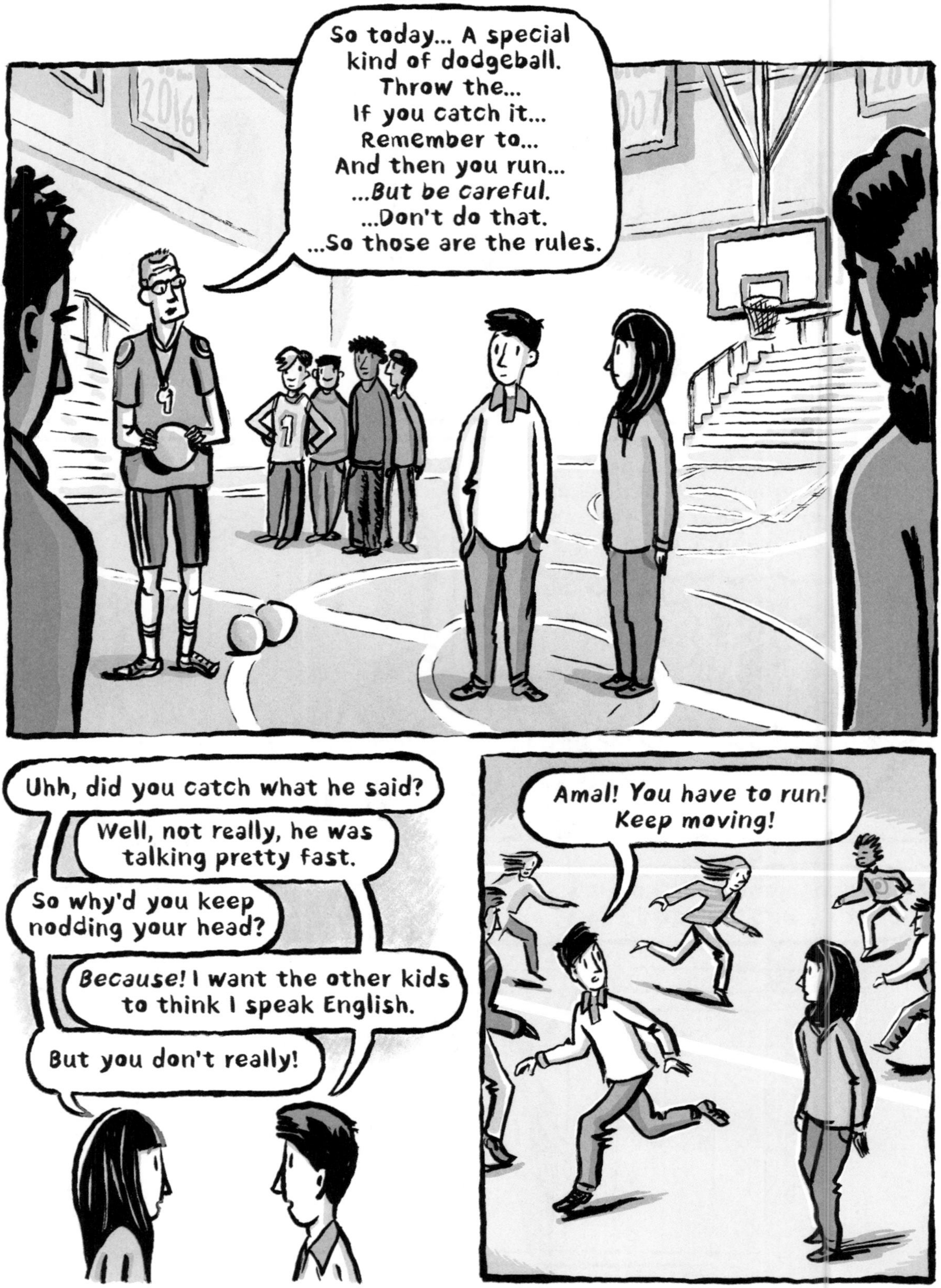
So today... A special kind of dodgeball. Throw the... If you catch it... Remember to... And then you run... ...But be careful. ...Don't do that. ...So those are the rules.
Uhh, did you catch what he said?
Well, not really, he was talking pretty fast.
So why'd you keep nodding your head?
Because! I want the other kids to think I speak English.
But you don't really!
Amal! You have to run! Keep moving!

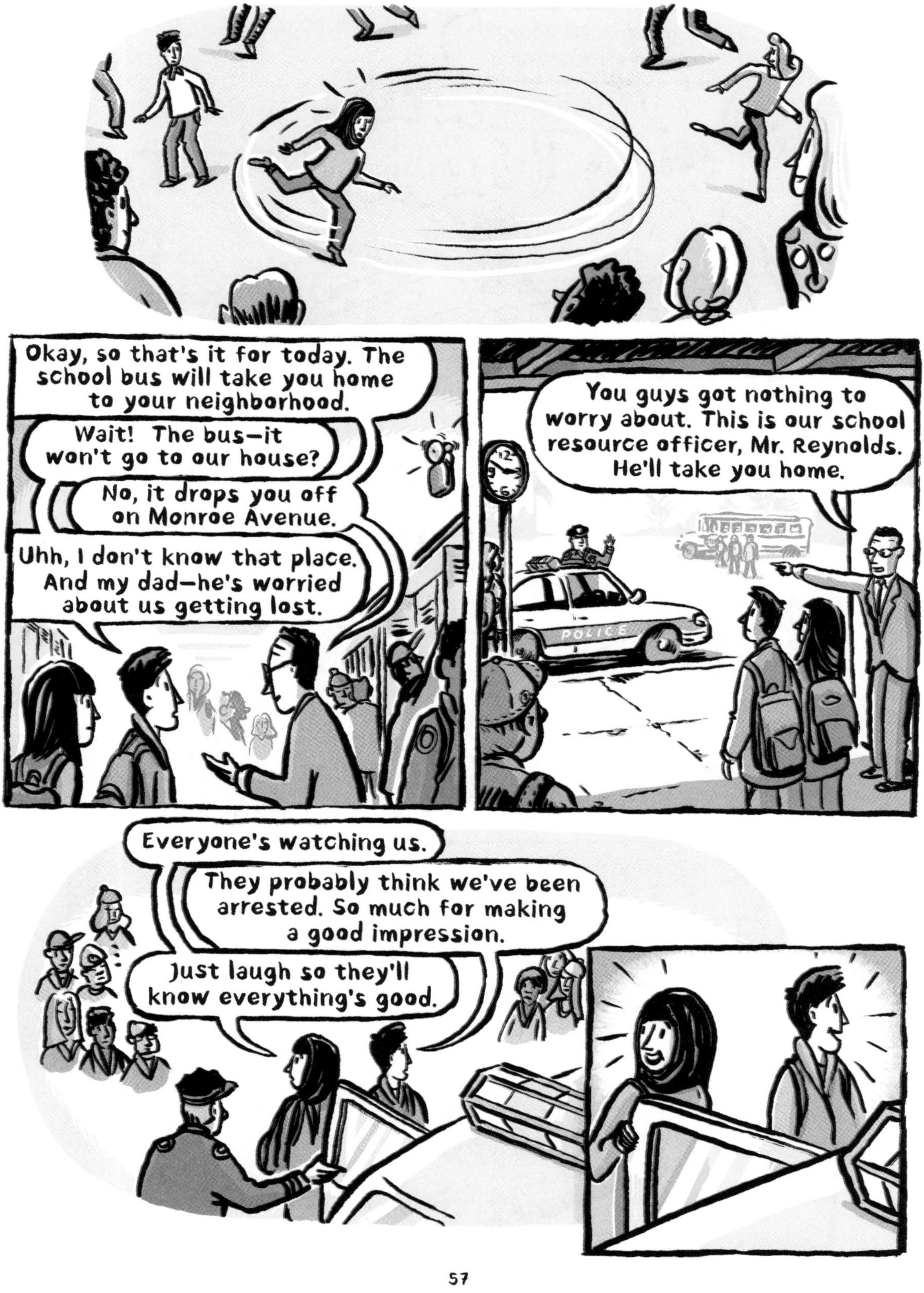

Okay, so that's it for today. The school bus will take you home to your neighborhood.
Wait! The bus—it won't go to our house?
No, it drops you off on Monroe Avenue.
Uhh, I don't know that place. And my dad—he's worried about us getting lost.
You guys got nothing to worry about. This is our school resource officer, Mr. Reynolds. He'll take you home.
POLICE
Everyone's watching us.
They probably think we've been arrested. So much for making a good impression.
Just laugh so they'll know everything's good.

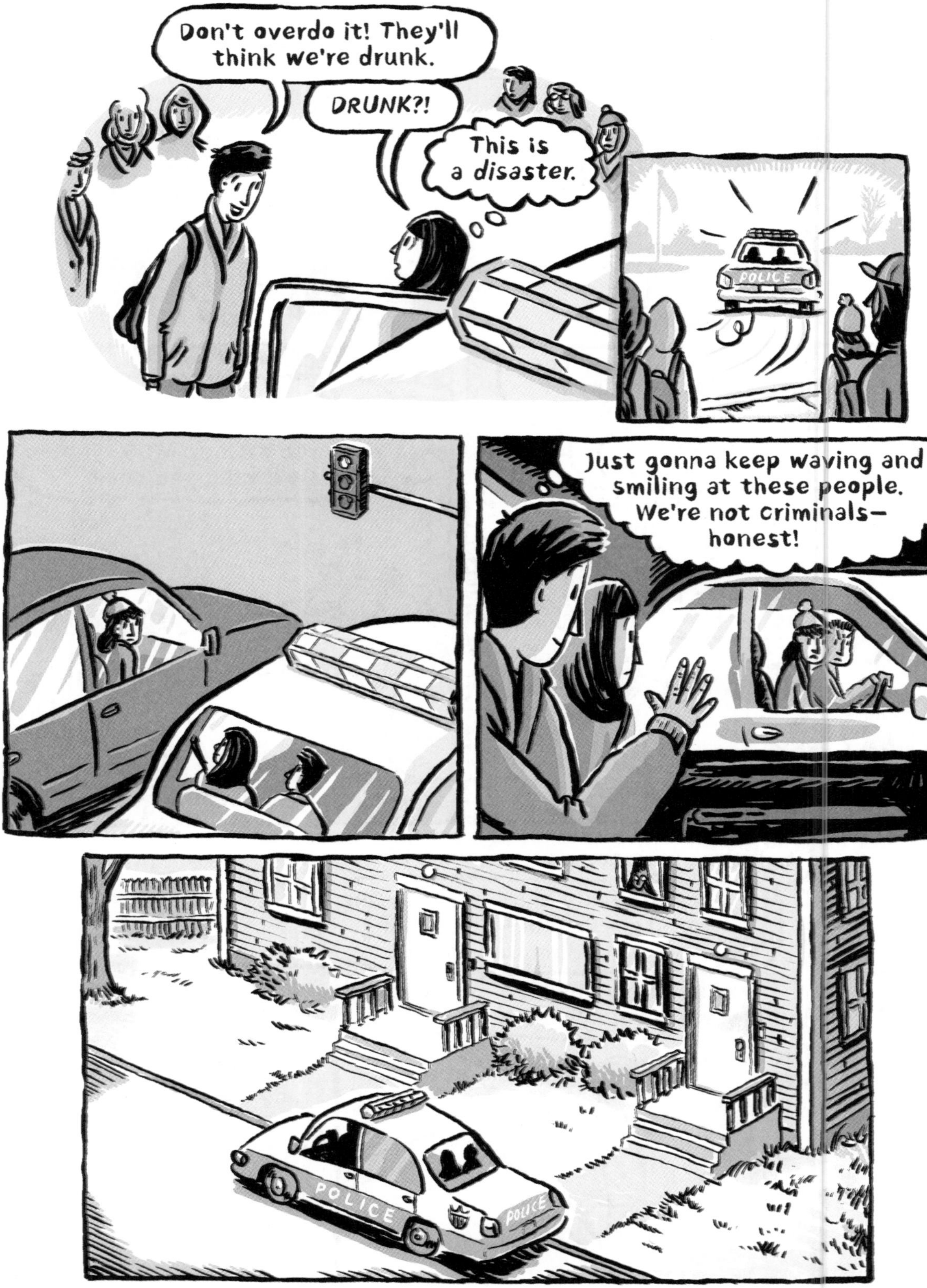
Don't overdo it! They'll think we're drunk.
DRUNK?!
This is a disaster.
POLICE
Just gonna keep waving and smiling at these people. We're not criminals— honest!
POLICE
POLICE

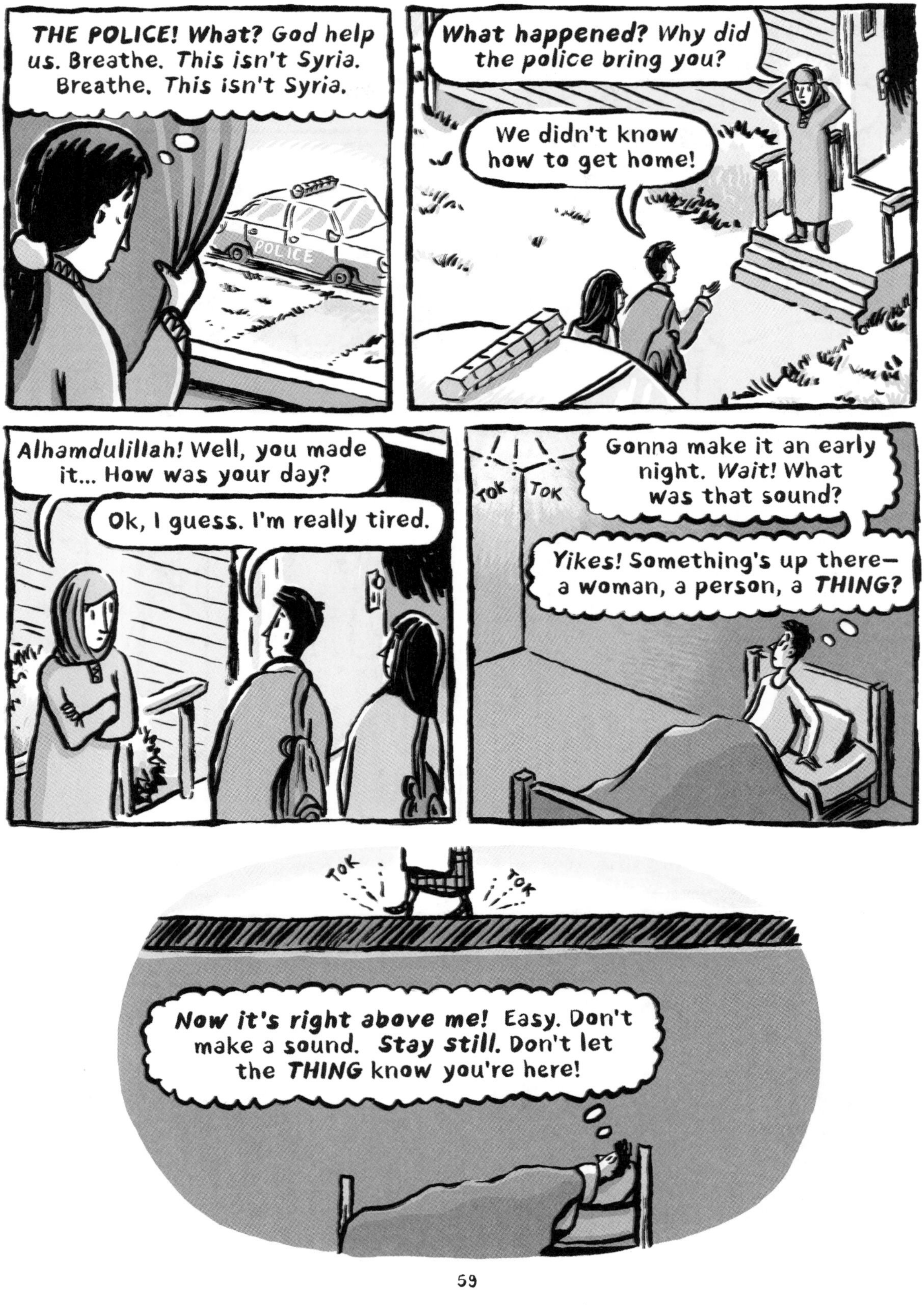
THE POLICE! What? God help us. Breathe. This isn't Syria. Breathe. This isn't Syria.
What happened? Why did the police bring you?
We didn't know how to get home!
Alhamdulillah! Well, you made it... How was your day?
Ok, I guess. I'm really tired.
TOK
TOK
Gonna make it an early night. Wait! What was that sound?
Yikes! Something's up there—a woman, a person, a THING?
TOK
TOK
Now it's right above me! Easy. Don't make a sound. Stay still. Don't let the THING know you're here!

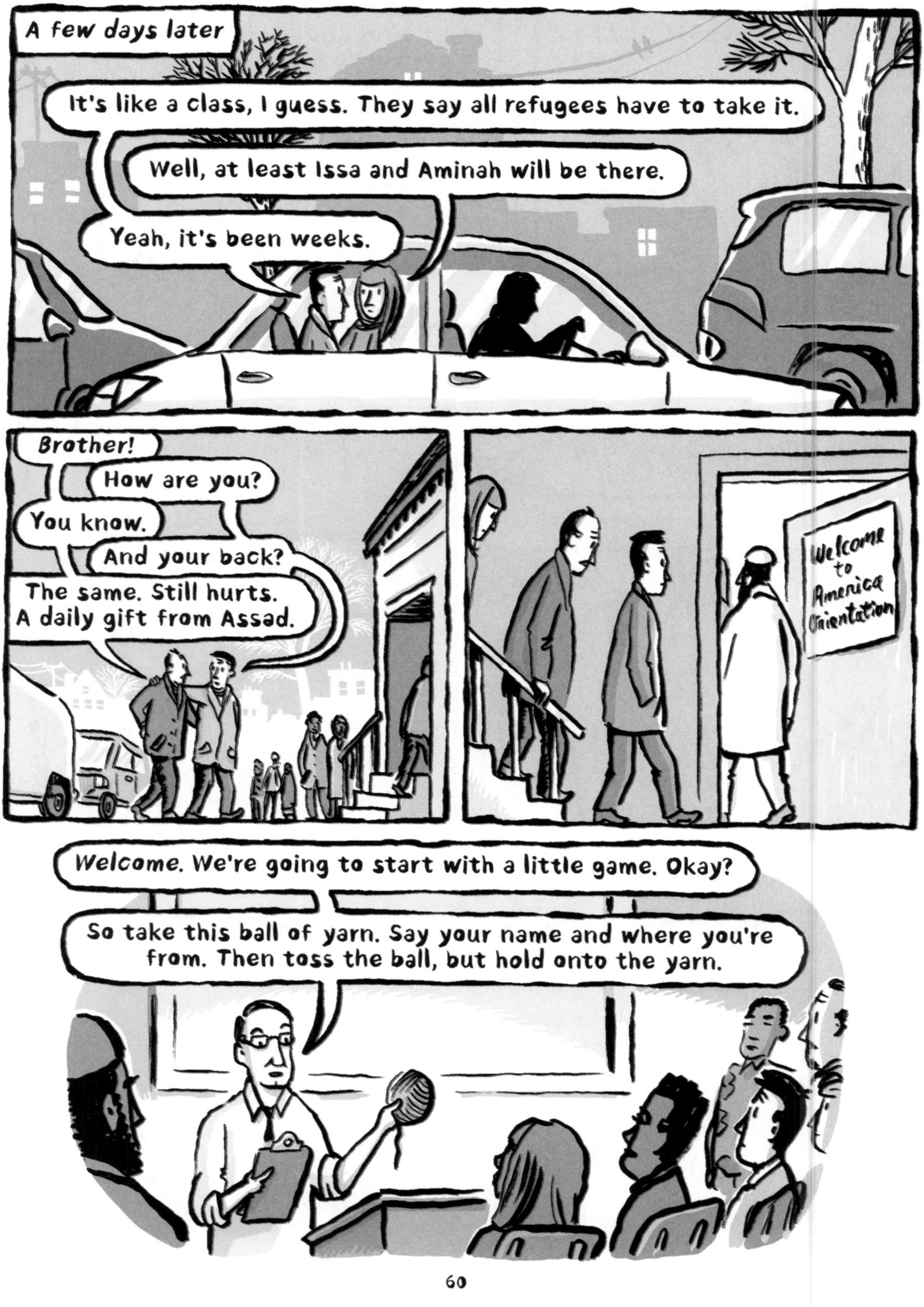
A few days later
It's like a class, I guess. They say all refugees have to take it.
Well, at least Issa and Aminah will be there.
Yeah, it's been weeks.
Brother!
How are you?
You know.
And your back?
The same. Still hurts.
A daily gift from Assad.
Welcome to America Orientation
Welcome. We're going to start with a little game. Okay?
So take this ball of yarn. Say your name and where you're from. Then toss the ball, but hold onto the yarn.

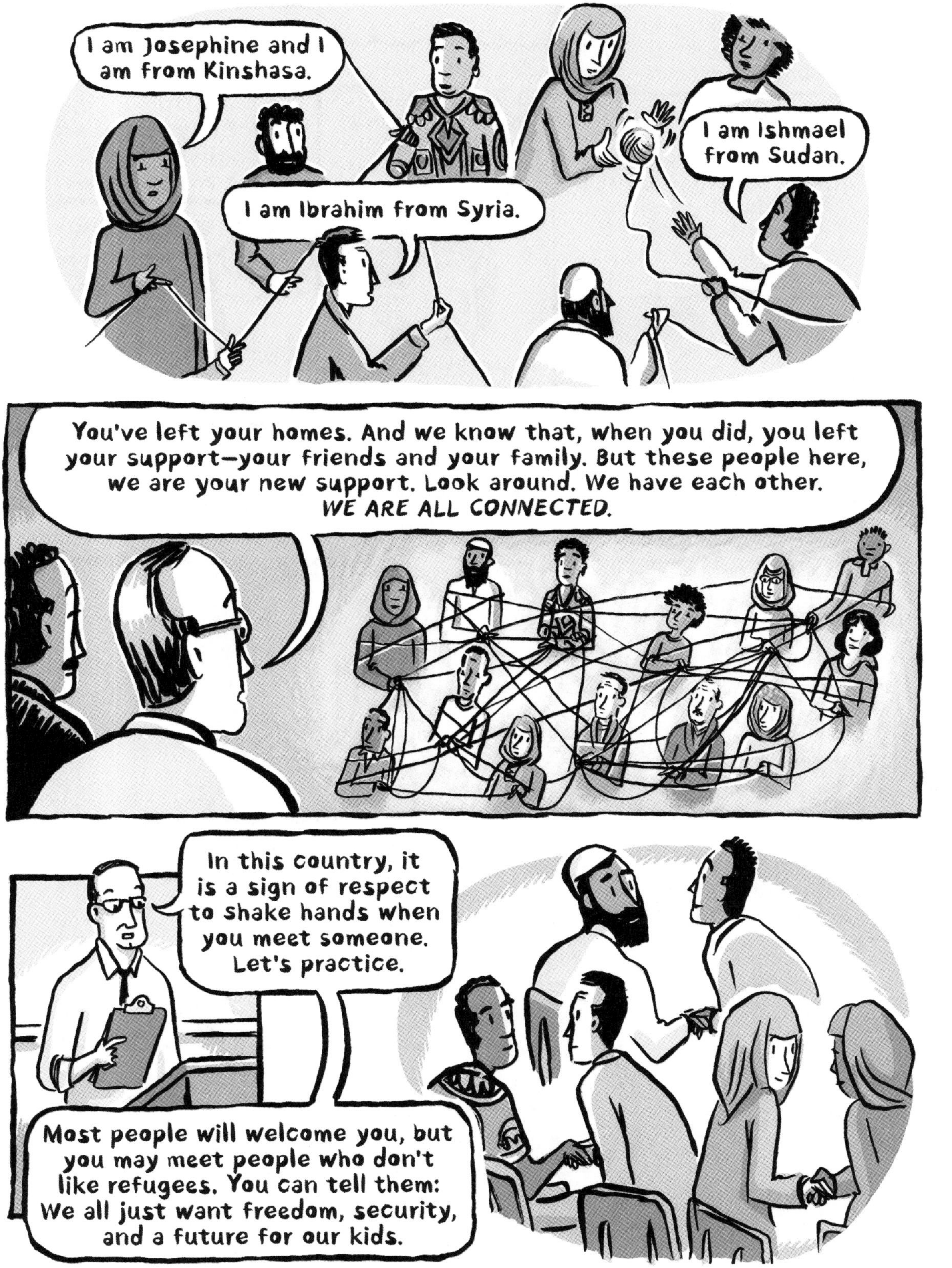
I am Josephine and I am from Kinshasa.
I am Ibrahim from Syria.
I am Ishmael from Sudan.
You've left your homes. And we know that, when you did, you left your support—your friends and your family. But these people here, we are your new support. Look around. We have each other. WE ARE ALL CONNECTED.
In this country, it is a sign of respect to shake hands when you meet someone. Let's practice.
Most people will welcome you, but you may meet people who don't like refugees. You can tell them: We all just want freedom, security, and a future for our kids.

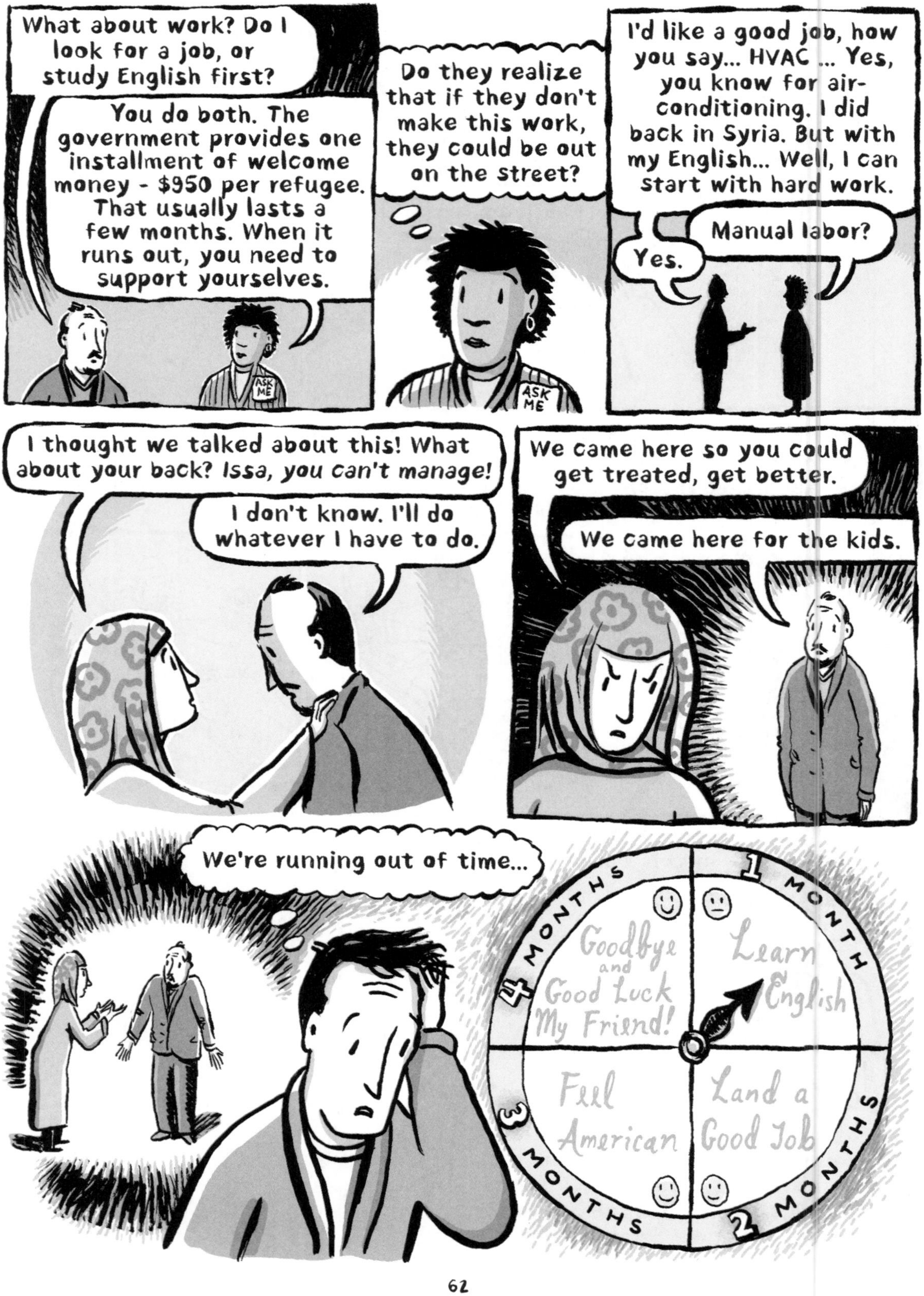
What about work? Do I look for a job, or study English first?
You do both. The government provides one installment of welcome money - $950 per refugee. That usually lasts a few months. When it runs out, you need to support yourselves.
ASK ME
Do they realize that if they don't make this work, they could be out on the street?
ASK ME
I'd like a good job, how you say... HVAC ... Yes, you know for air-conditioning. I did back in Syria. But with my English... Well, I can start with hard work.
Manual labor?
Yes.
I thought we talked about this! What about your back? Issa, you can't manage!
I don't know. I'll do whatever I have to do.
We came here so you could get treated, get better.
We came here for the kids.
We're running out of time...
1 MONTH
Learn English
2 MONTHS
Land a Good Job
3 MONTHS
Feel American
4 MONTHS
Goodbye and Good Luck My Friend!

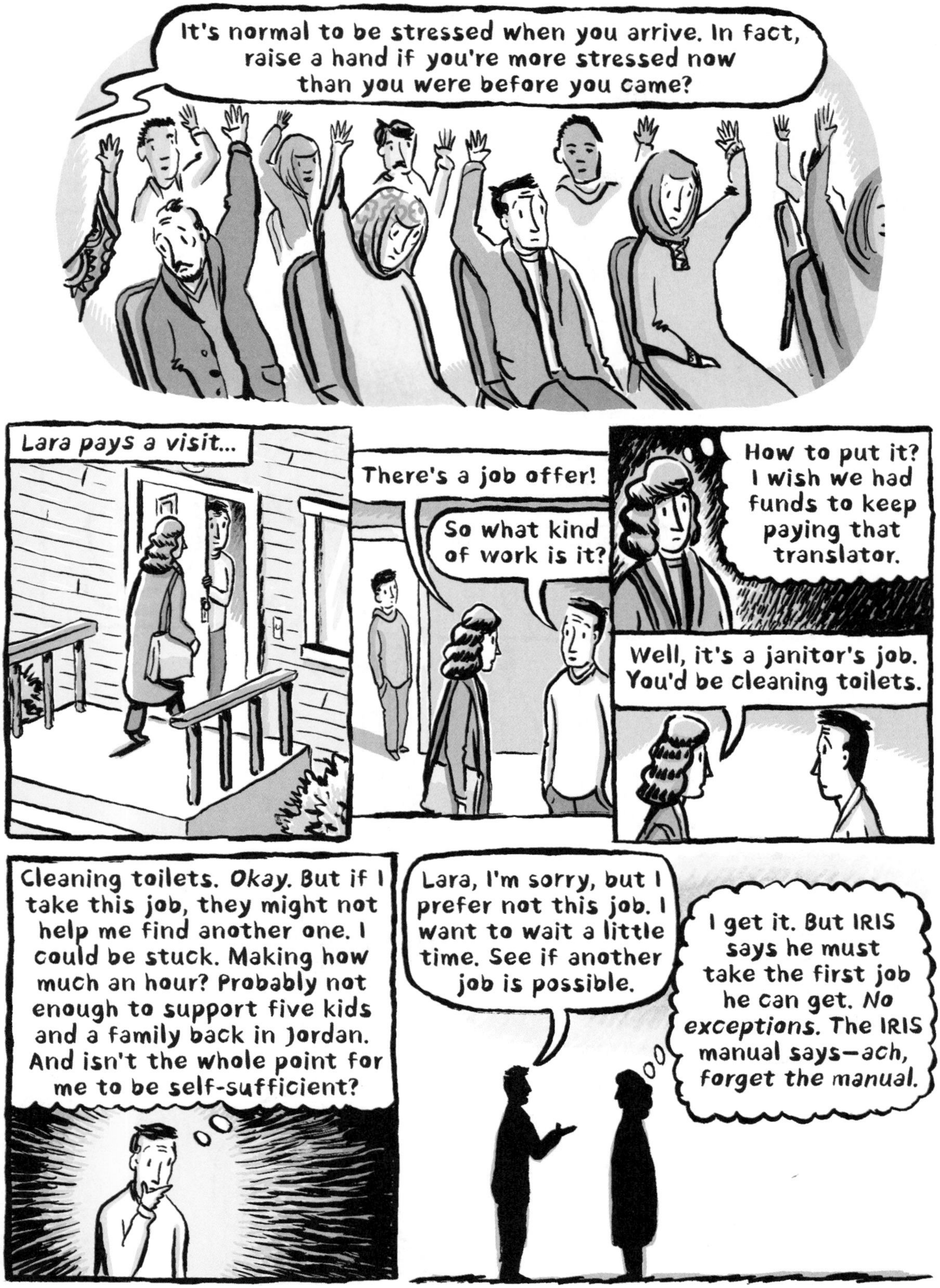

It's normal to be stressed when you arrive. In fact, raise a hand if you're more stressed now than you were before you came?
Lara pays a visit...
There's a job offer!
So what kind of work is it?
How to put it? I wish we had funds to keep paying that translator.
Well, it's a janitor's job. You'd be cleaning toilets.
Cleaning toilets. *Okay.* But if I take this job, they might not help me find another one. I could be stuck. Making how much an hour? Probably not enough to support five kids and a family back in Jordan. And isn't the whole point for me to be self-sufficient?
Lara, I'm sorry, but I prefer not this job. I want to wait a little time. See if another job is possible.
I get it. But IRIS says he must take the first job he can get. *No exceptions.* The IRIS manual says—*ach, forget the manual.*

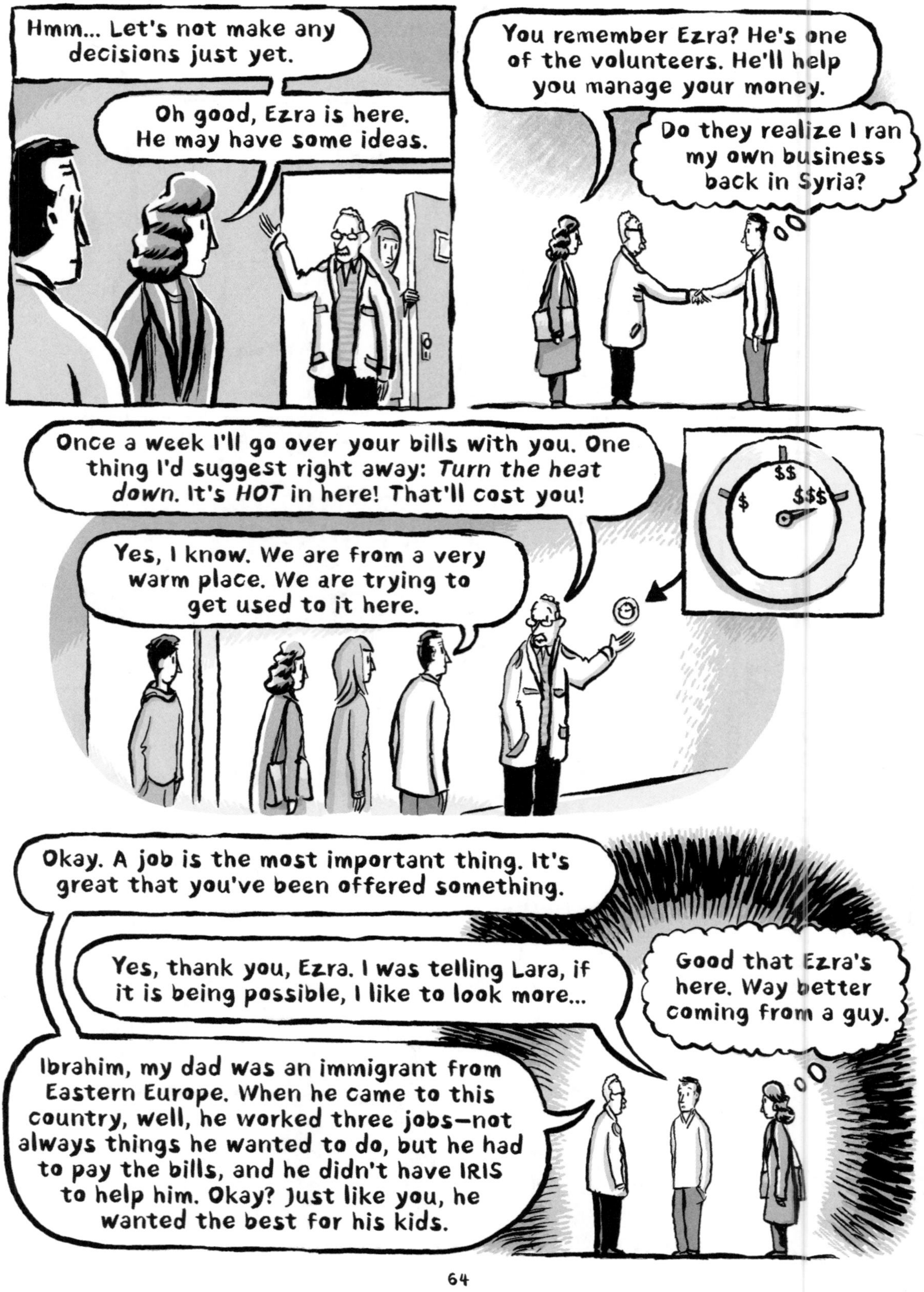

Hmm... Let's not make any decisions just yet.
Oh good, Ezra is here. He may have some ideas.
You remember Ezra? He's one of the volunteers. He'll help you manage your money.
Do they realize I ran my own business back in Syria?
Once a week I'll go over your bills with you. One thing I'd suggest right away: *Turn the heat down.* It's *HOT* in here! That'll cost you!
$$
$
$$$
Yes, I know. We are from a very warm place. We are trying to get used to it here.
Okay. A job is the most important thing. It's great that you've been offered something.
Yes, thank you, Ezra. I was telling Lara, if it is being possible, I like to look more...
Good that Ezra's here. Way better coming from a guy.
Ibrahim, my dad was an immigrant from Eastern Europe. When he came to this country, well, he worked three jobs—not always things he wanted to do, but he had to pay the bills, and he didn't have IRIS to help him. Okay? Just like you, he wanted the best for his kids.

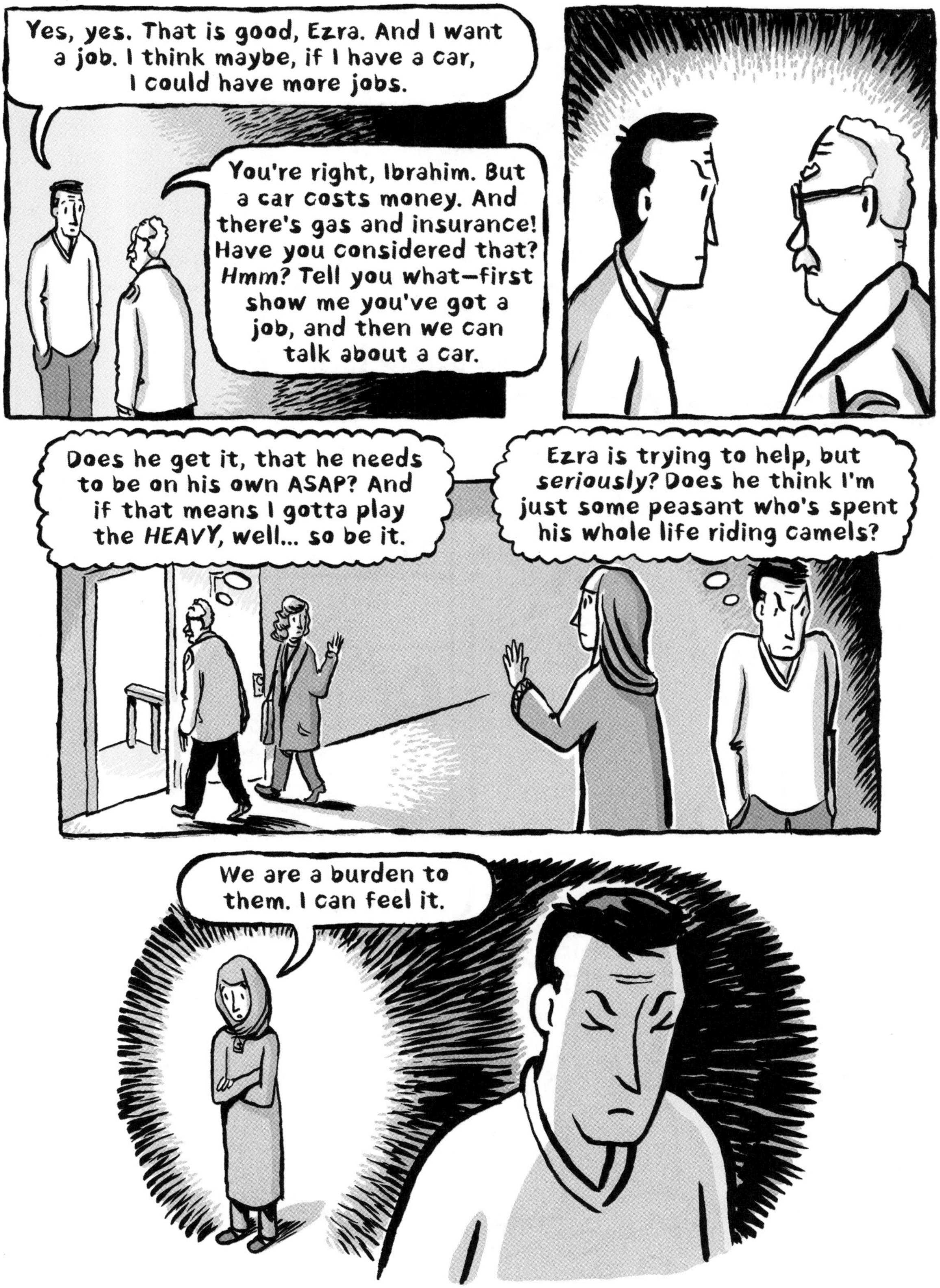
Yes, yes. That is good, Ezra. And I want a job. I think maybe, if I have a car, I could have more jobs.
You're right, Ibrahim. But a car costs money. And there's gas and insurance! Have you considered that? *Hmm?* Tell you what—first show me you've got a job, and then we can talk about a car.
Does he get it, that he needs to be on his own ASAP? And if that means I gotta play the *HEAVY*, well... so be it.
Ezra is trying to help, but *seriously*? Does he think I'm just some peasant who's spent his whole life riding camels?
We are a burden to them. I can feel it.

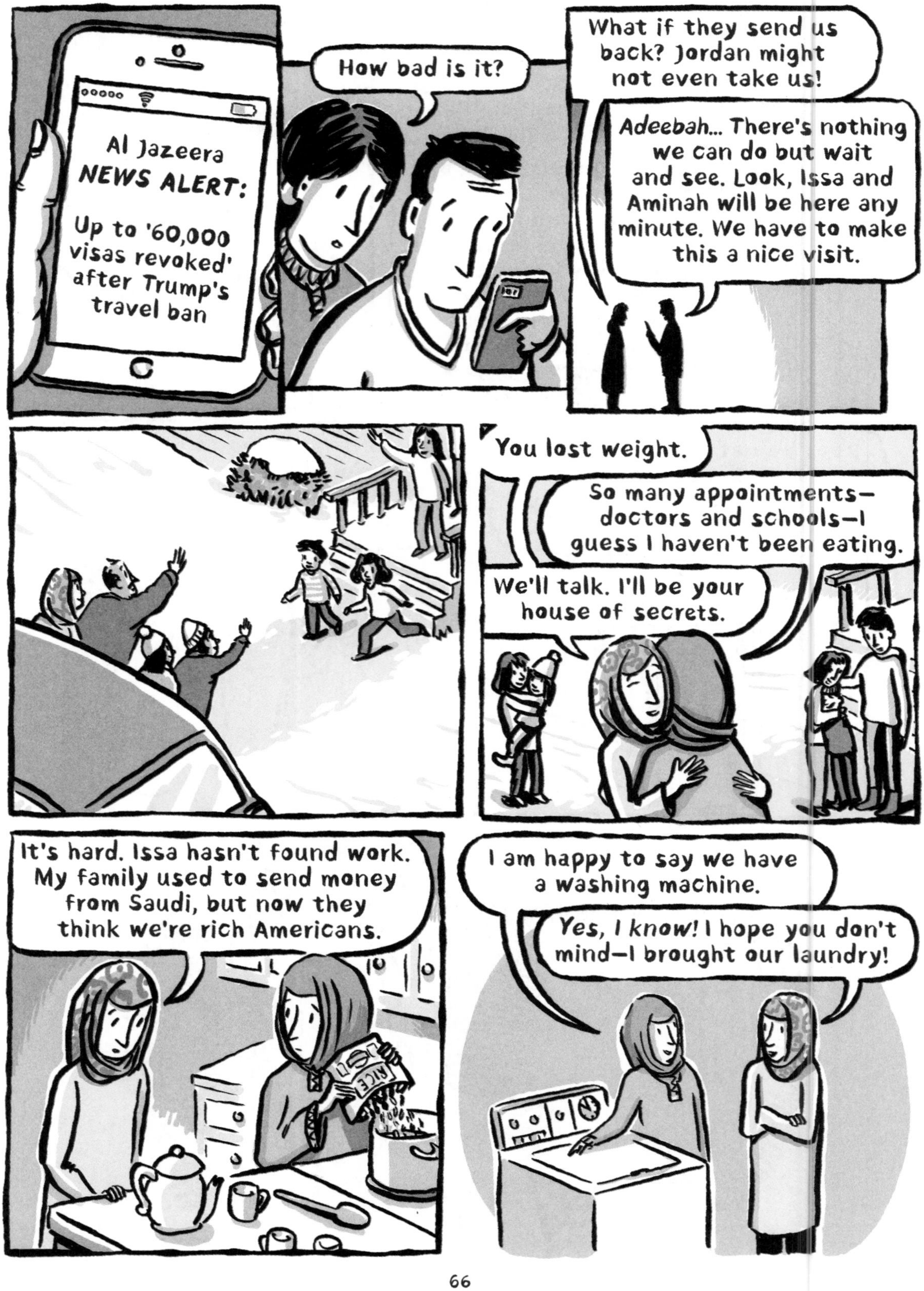

Al Jazeera
NEWS ALERT:
Up to '60,000 visas revoked' after Trump's travel ban
How bad is it?
What if they send us back? Jordan might not even take us!
Adeebah... There's nothing we can do but wait and see. Look, Issa and Aminah will be here any minute. We have to make this a nice visit.
You lost weight.
So many appointments—doctors and schools—I guess I haven't been eating.
We'll talk. I'll be your house of secrets.
It's hard. Issa hasn't found work. My family used to send money from Saudi, but now they think we're rich Americans.
RICE
I am happy to say we have a washing machine.
Yes, I know! I hope you don't mind—I brought our laundry!

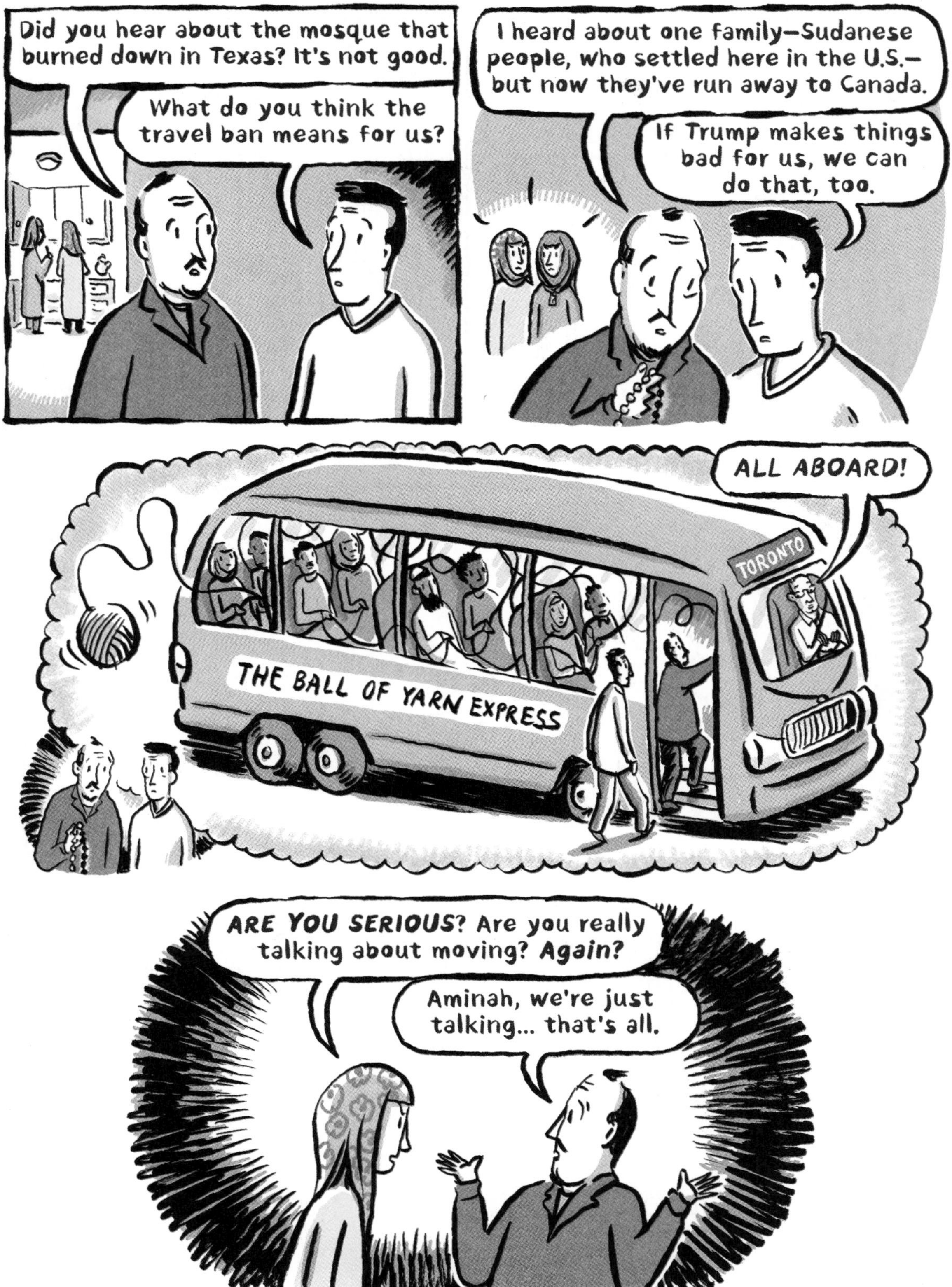
Did you hear about the mosque that burned down in Texas? It's not good.
What do you think the travel ban means for us?
I heard about one family—Sudanese people, who settled here in the U.S.—but now they've run away to Canada.
If Trump makes things bad for us, we can do that, too.
ALL ABOARD!
TORONTO
THE BALL OF YARN EXPRESS
ARE YOU SERIOUS? Are you really talking about moving? Again?
Aminah, we're just talking... that's all.

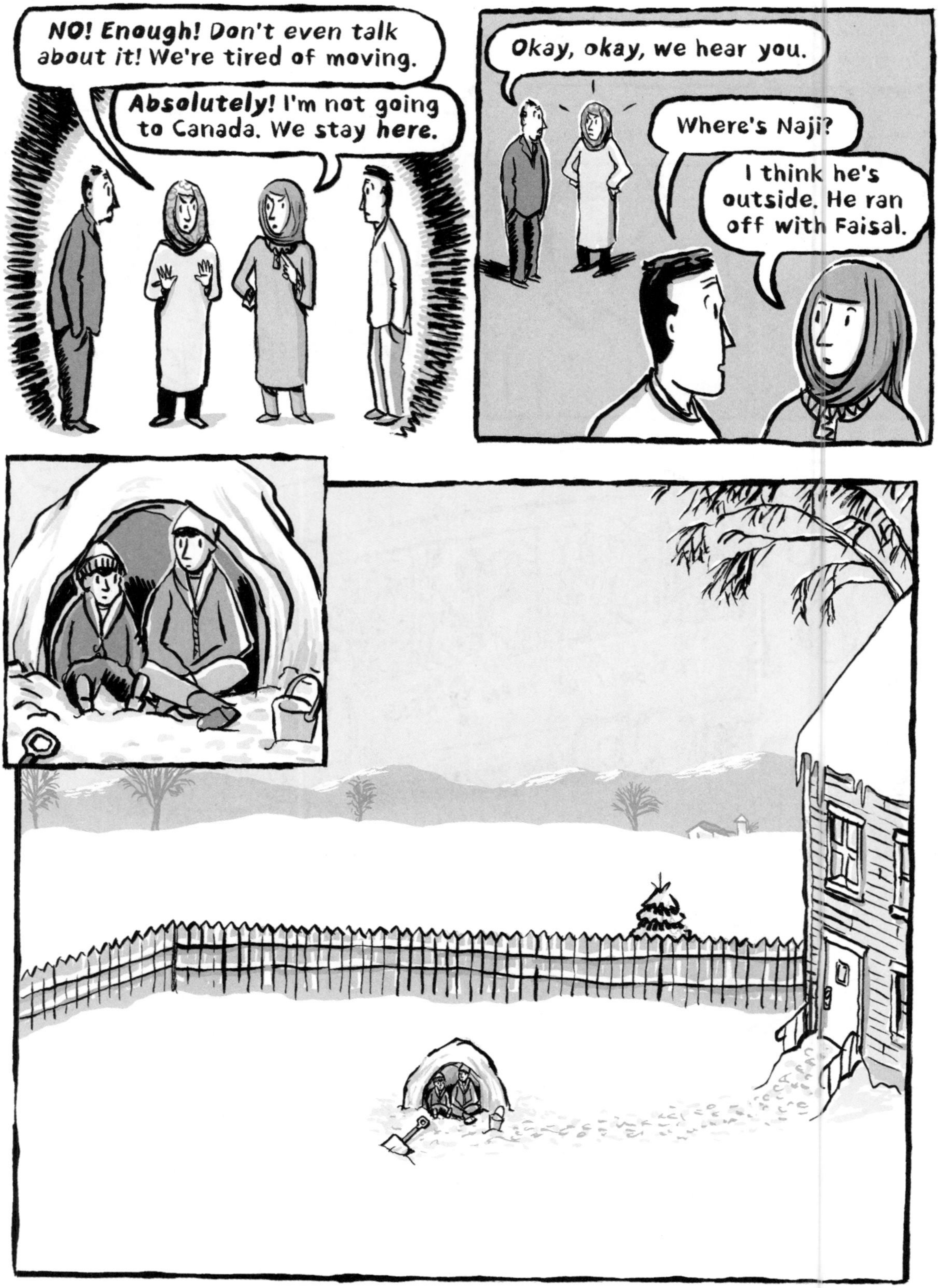
NO! Enough! Don't even talk about it! We're tired of moving.
Absolutely! I'm not going to Canada. We stay here.
Okay, okay, we hear you.
Where's Naji?
I think he's outside. He ran off with Faisal.

Chapter 3

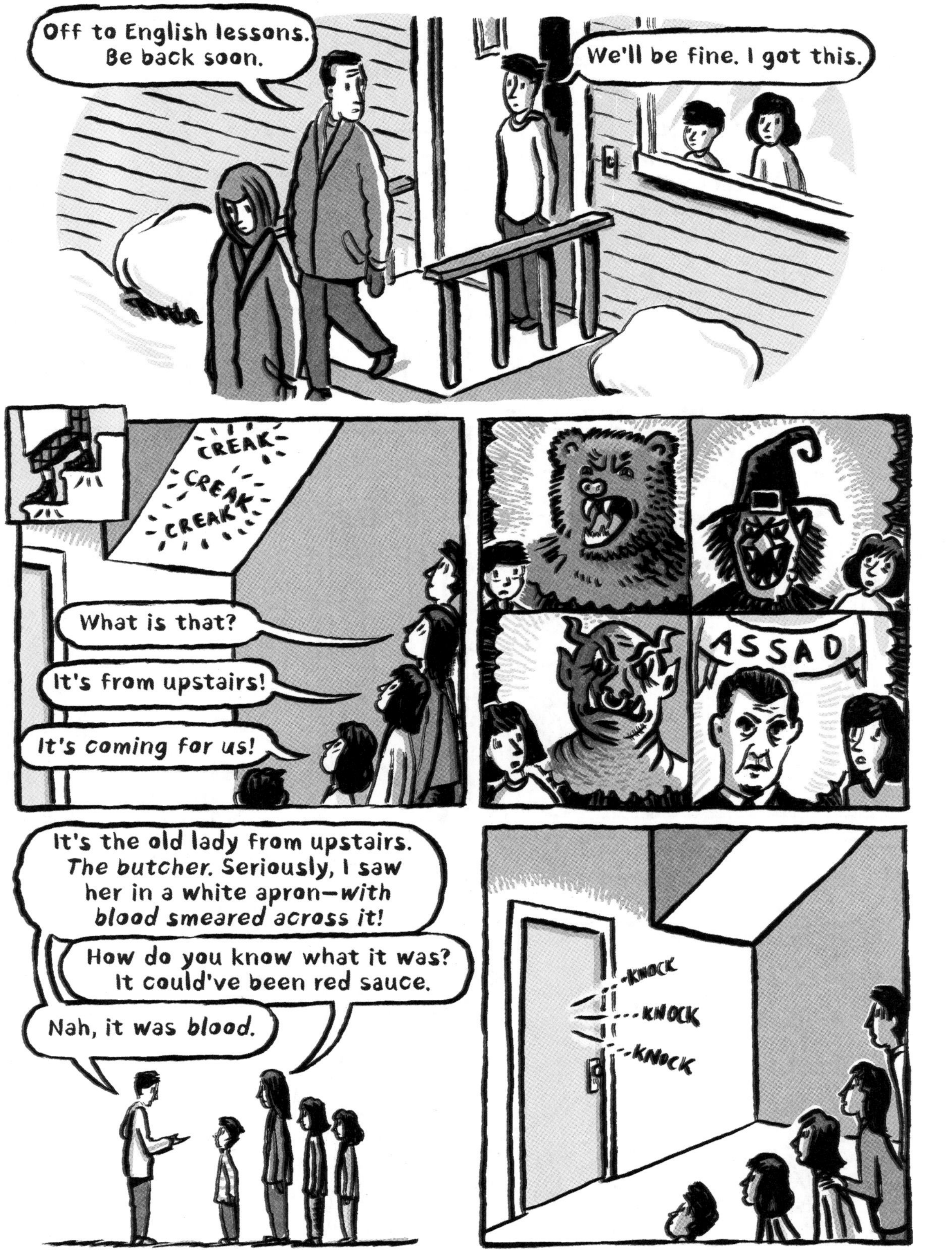
Off to English lessons. Be back soon.
We'll be fine. I got this.
CREAK
CREAK
CREAK
What is that?
It's from upstairs!
It's coming for us!
ASSAD
It's the old lady from upstairs. *The butcher.* Seriously, I saw her in a white apron—*with blood smeared across it!*
How do you know what it was? It could've been red sauce.
Nah, it was *blood.*
KNOCK
KNOCK
KNOCK

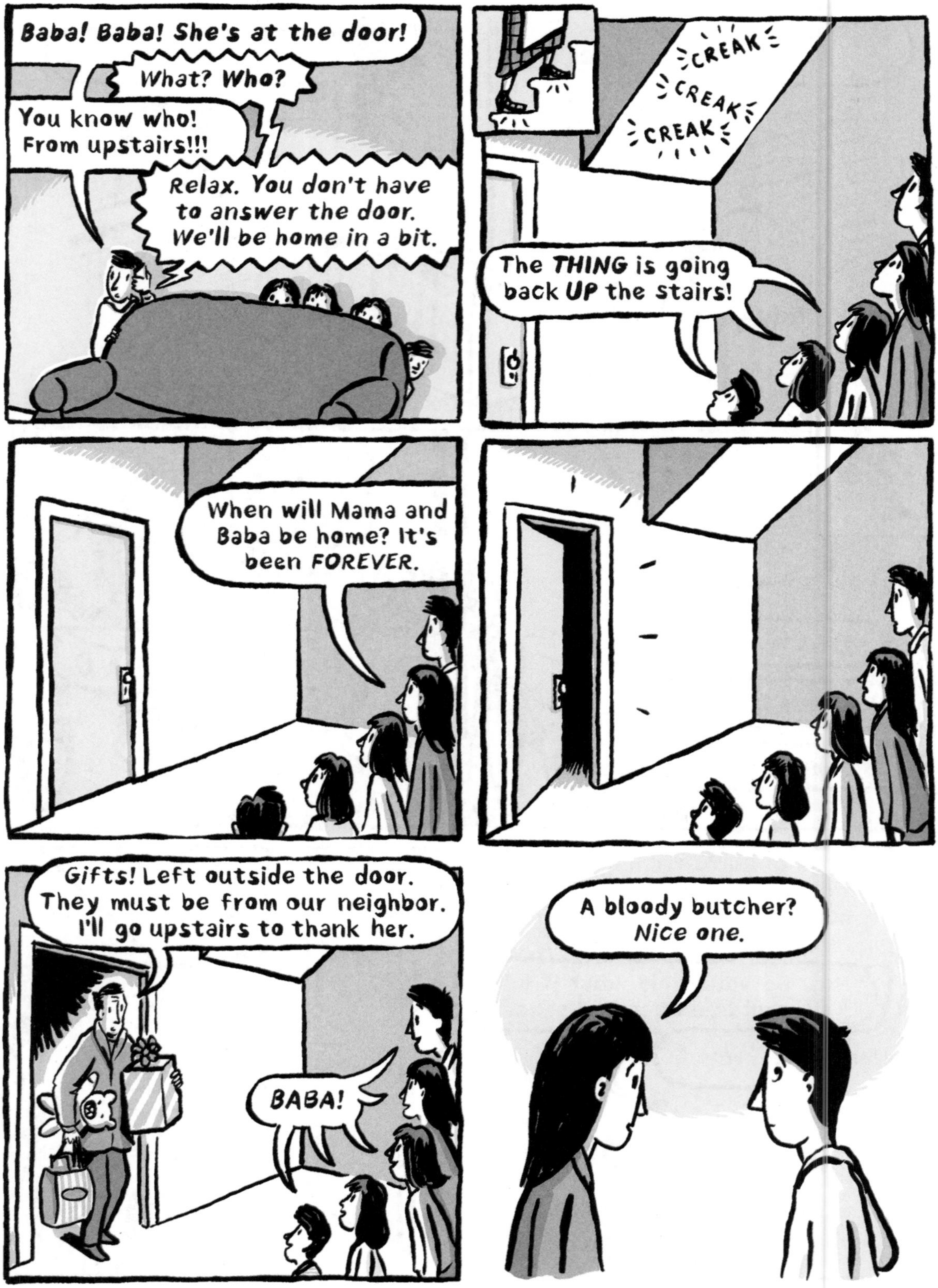
Baba! Baba! She's at the door!
What? Who?
You know who! From upstairs!!!
Relax. You don't have to answer the door. We'll be home in a bit.
CREAK
CREAK
CREAK
The THING is going back UP the stairs!
When will Mama and Baba be home? It's been FOREVER.
Gifts! Left outside the door. They must be from our neighbor. I'll go upstairs to thank her.
BABA!
A bloody butcher? Nice one.

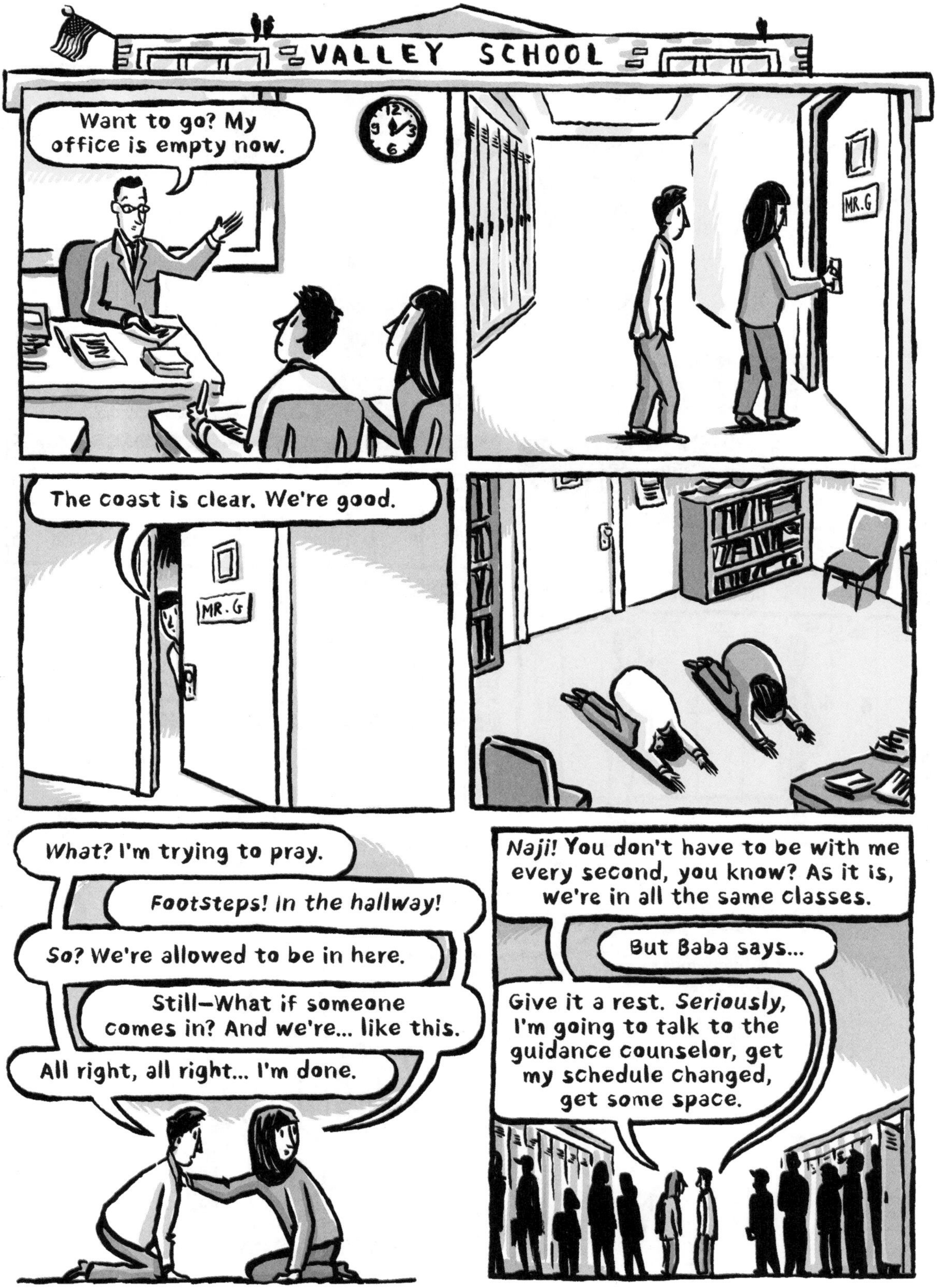
VALLEY SCHOOL
Want to go? My office is empty now.
MR. G
The coast is clear. We're good.
MR. G
What? I'm trying to pray.
Footsteps! In the hallway!
So? We're allowed to be in here.
Still—What if someone comes in? And we're... like this.
All right, all right... I'm done.
Naji! You don't have to be with me every second, you know? As it is, we're in all the same classes.
But Baba says...
Give it a rest. Seriously, I'm going to talk to the guidance counselor, get my schedule changed, get some space.

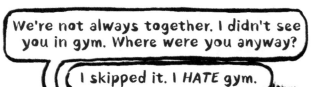
We're not always together. I didn't see you in gym. Where were you anyway?

I skipped it. I *HATE* gym.

You better hope you don't get busted. And different schedules? That's a good one. Good luck with that. Baba'll never go for it.

Naji. A little space? *Please...*

Easier to blend in without her anyway. Right?

Hey.

What's up?

How come you don't wear one of them head thingies, like your sister?

Head thingies? Is he messing with me?

Uh, yeah, where we come from, only girls wear them.

Hmm.

I like those hoodies. They're tough looking. That's gonna be my new look.

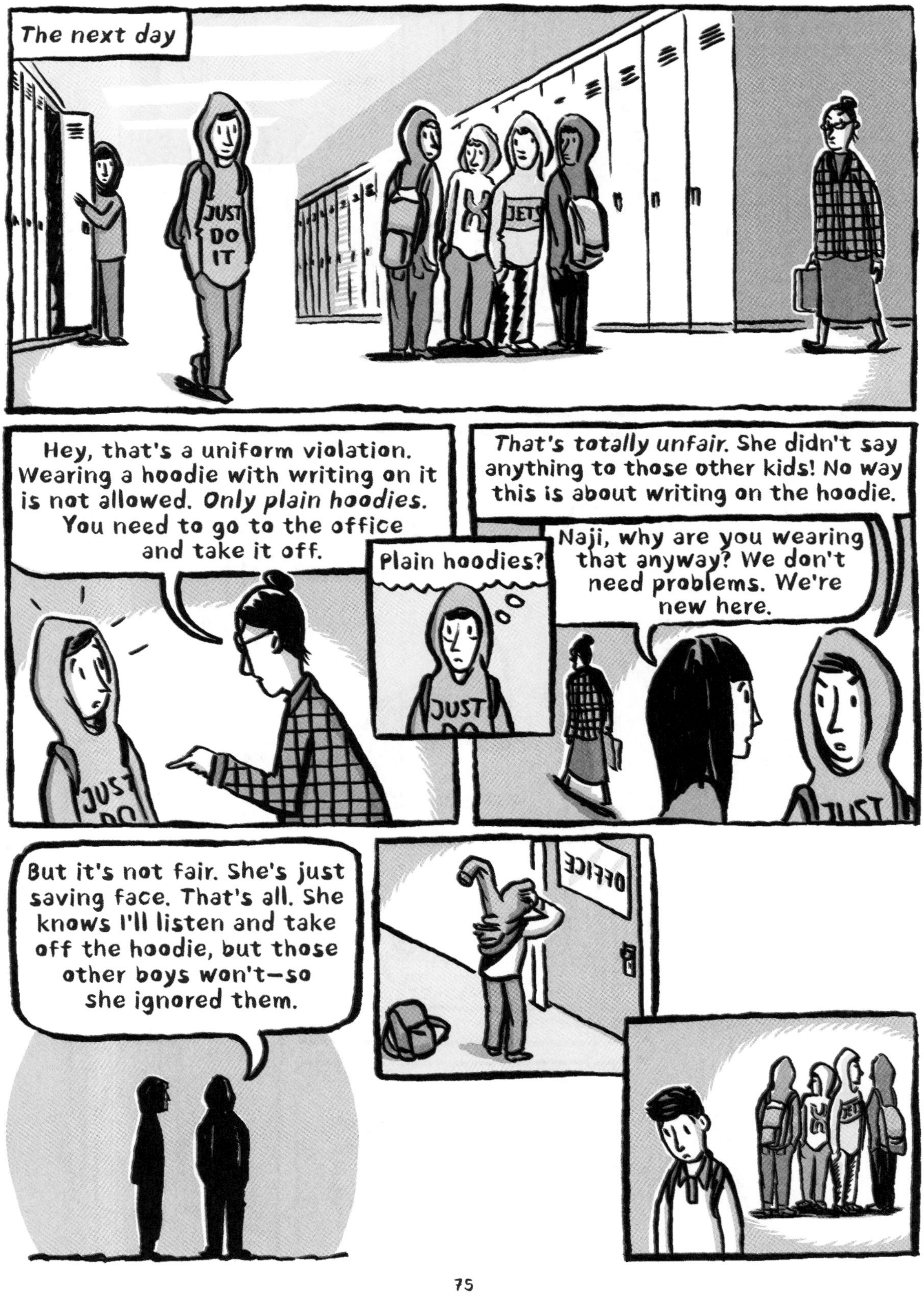
The next day
JUST DO IT
JETS
Hey, that's a uniform violation. Wearing a hoodie with writing on it is not allowed. Only plain hoodies. You need to go to the office and take it off.
Plain hoodies?
That's totally unfair. She didn't say anything to those other kids! No way this is about writing on the hoodie.
Naji, why are you wearing that anyway? We don't need problems. We're new here.
But it's not fair. She's just saving face. That's all. She knows I'll listen and take off the hoodie, but those other boys won't—so she ignored them.
OFFICE
JETS

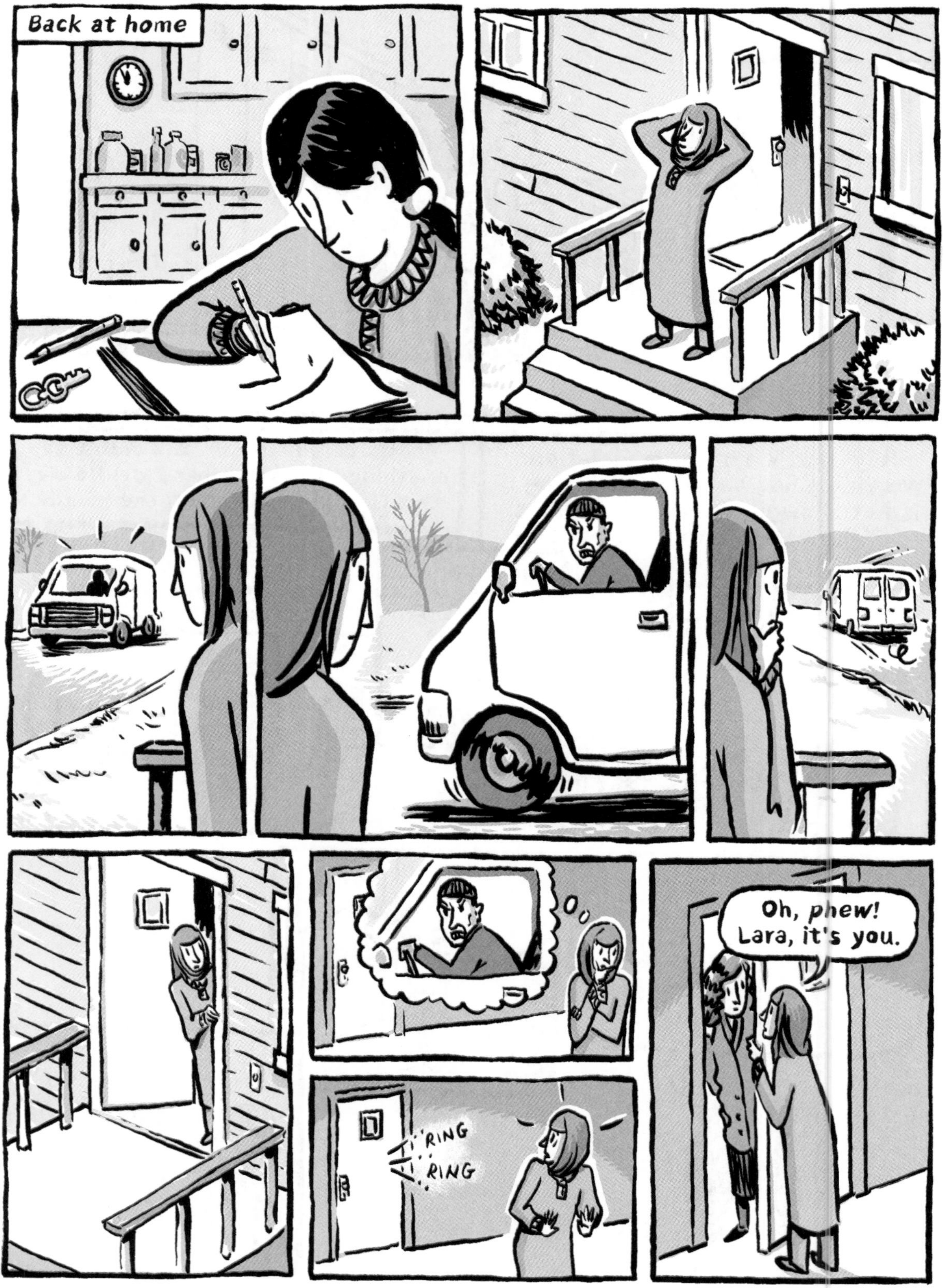
Back at home
RING
RING
Oh, phew!
Lara, it's you.

What are you working on at the moment?

Yes, trying... I was doing like this in Jordan.

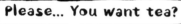
Please... You want tea?

Yes, thanks.

We really need the translator right now.

How are you doing, Adeebah?

Where even to begin? No friends. No money. Nowhere to go. My family stranded in Syria. No words to explain...

Doing okay.

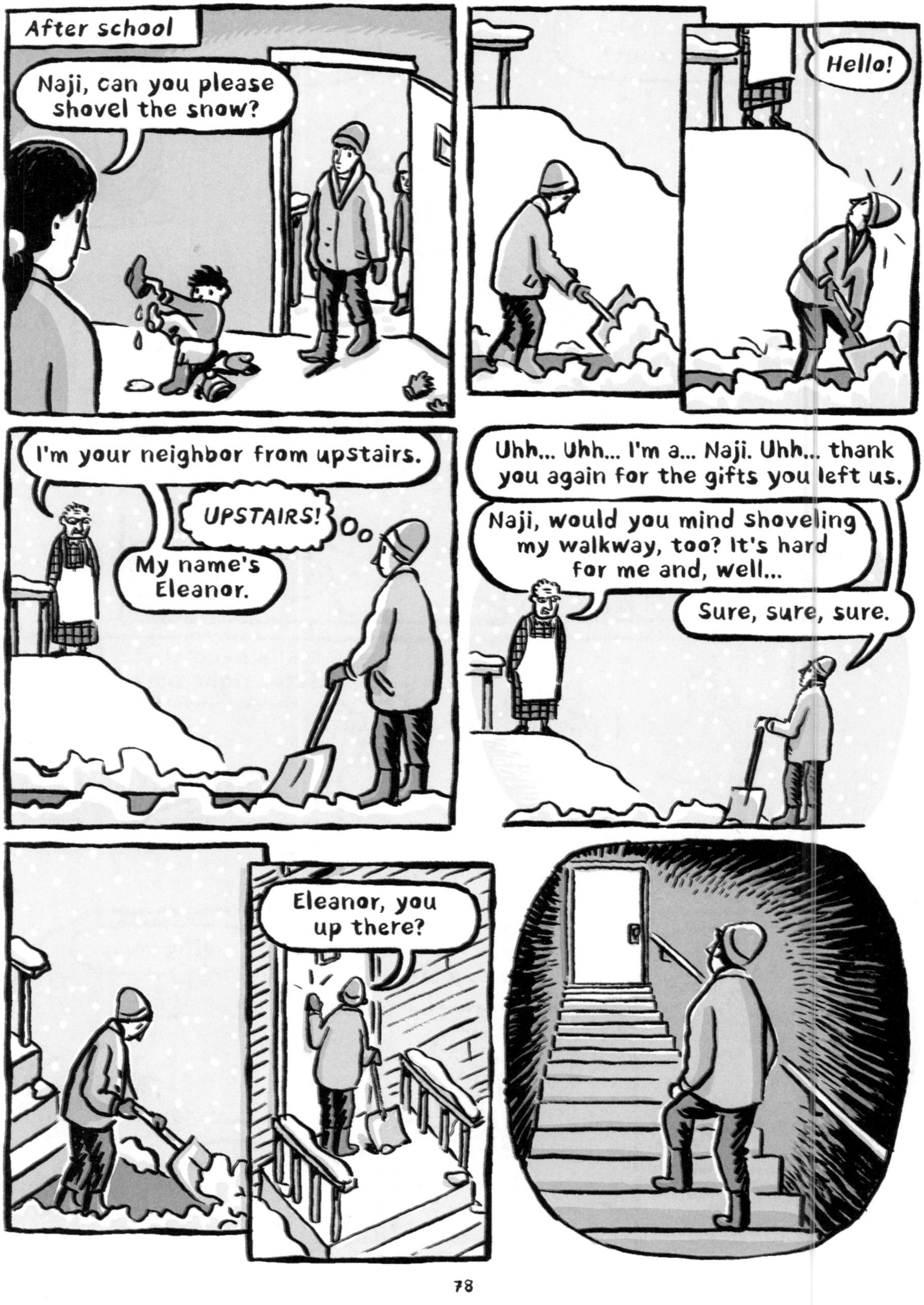
After school
Naji, can you please shovel the snow?
Hello!
I'm your neighbor from upstairs.
UPSTAIRS!
My name's Eleanor.
Uhh... Uhh... I'm a... Naji. Uhh... thank you again for the gifts you left us.
Naji, would you mind shoveling my walkway, too? It's hard for me and, well...
Sure, sure, sure.
Eleanor, you up there?

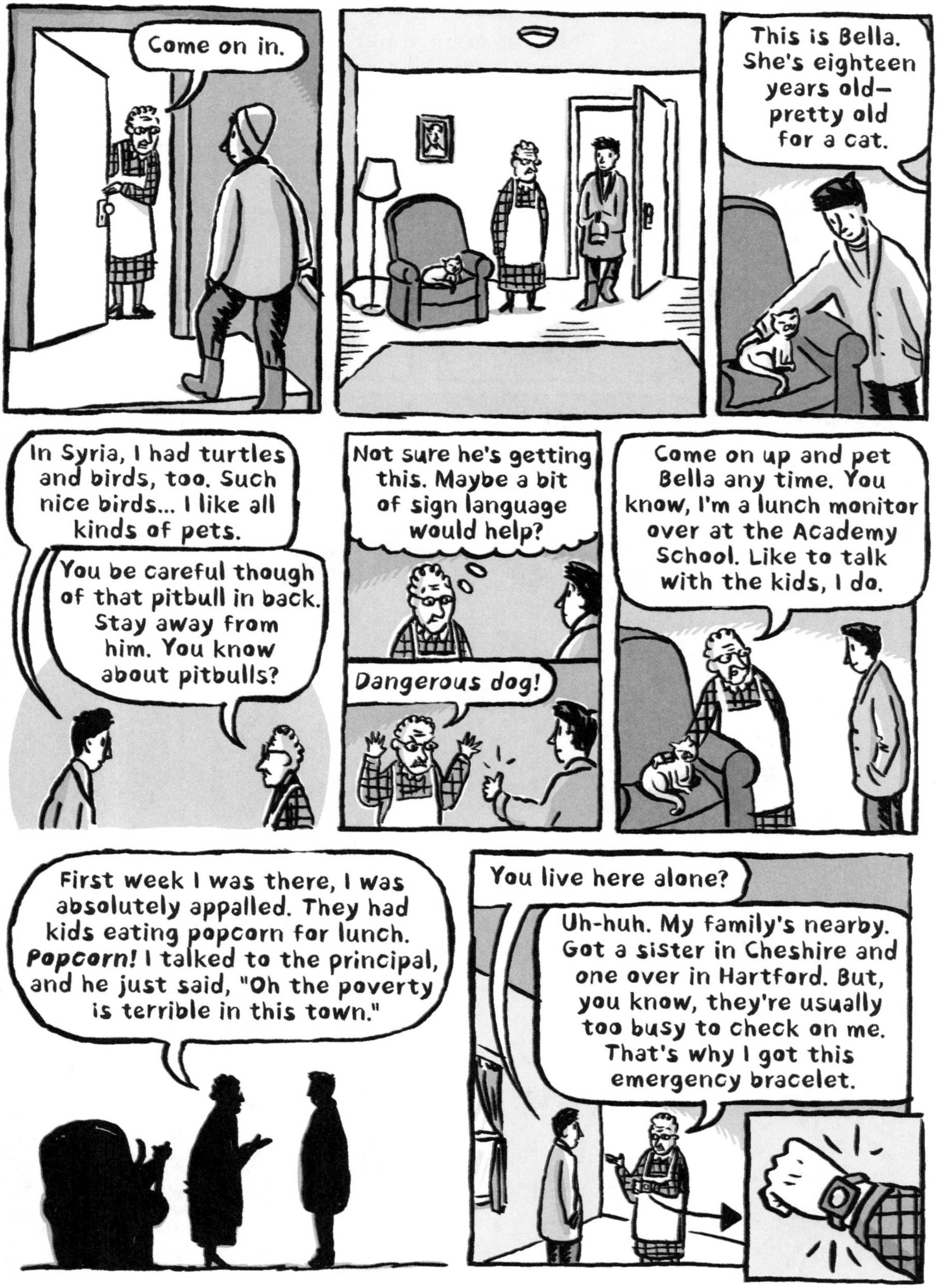

Come on in.
This is Bella. She's eighteen years old— pretty old for a cat.
In Syria, I had turtles and birds, too. Such nice birds... I like all kinds of pets.
You be careful though of that pitbull in back. Stay away from him. You know about pitbulls?
Not sure he's getting this. Maybe a bit of sign language would help?
Dangerous dog!
Come on up and pet Bella any time. You know, I'm a lunch monitor over at the Academy School. Like to talk with the kids, I do.
First week I was there, I was absolutely appalled. They had kids eating popcorn for lunch. *Popcorn!* I talked to the principal, and he just said, "Oh the poverty is terrible in this town."
You live here alone?
Uh-huh. My family's nearby. Got a sister in Cheshire and one over in Hartford. But, you know, they're usually too busy to check on me. That's why I got this emergency bracelet.

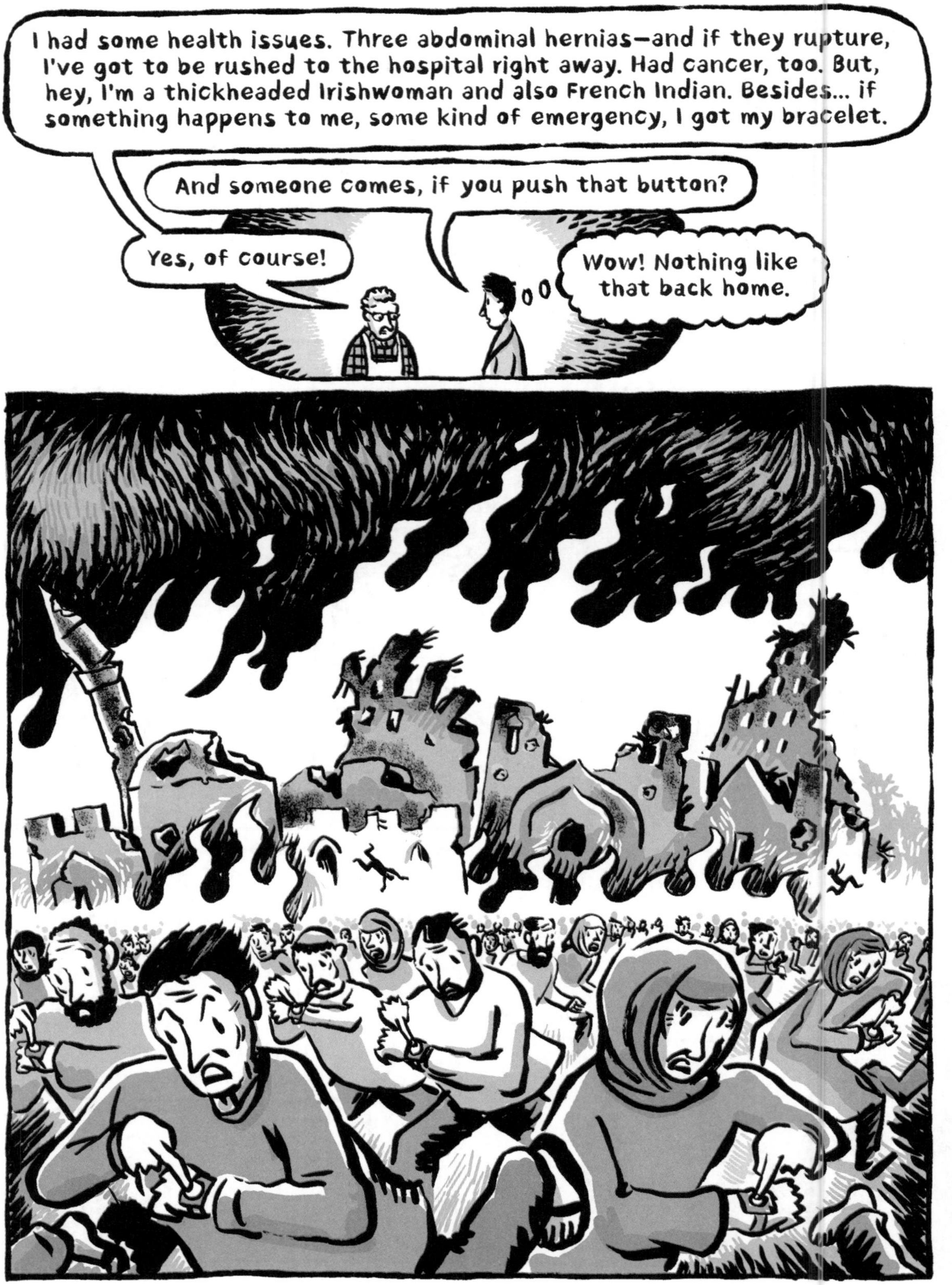
I had some health issues. Three abdominal hernias—and if they rupture, I've got to be rushed to the hospital right away. Had cancer, too. But, hey, I'm a thickheaded Irishwoman and also French Indian. Besides... if something happens to me, some kind of emergency, I got my bracelet.
And someone comes, if you push that button?
Yes, of course!
Wow! Nothing like that back home.

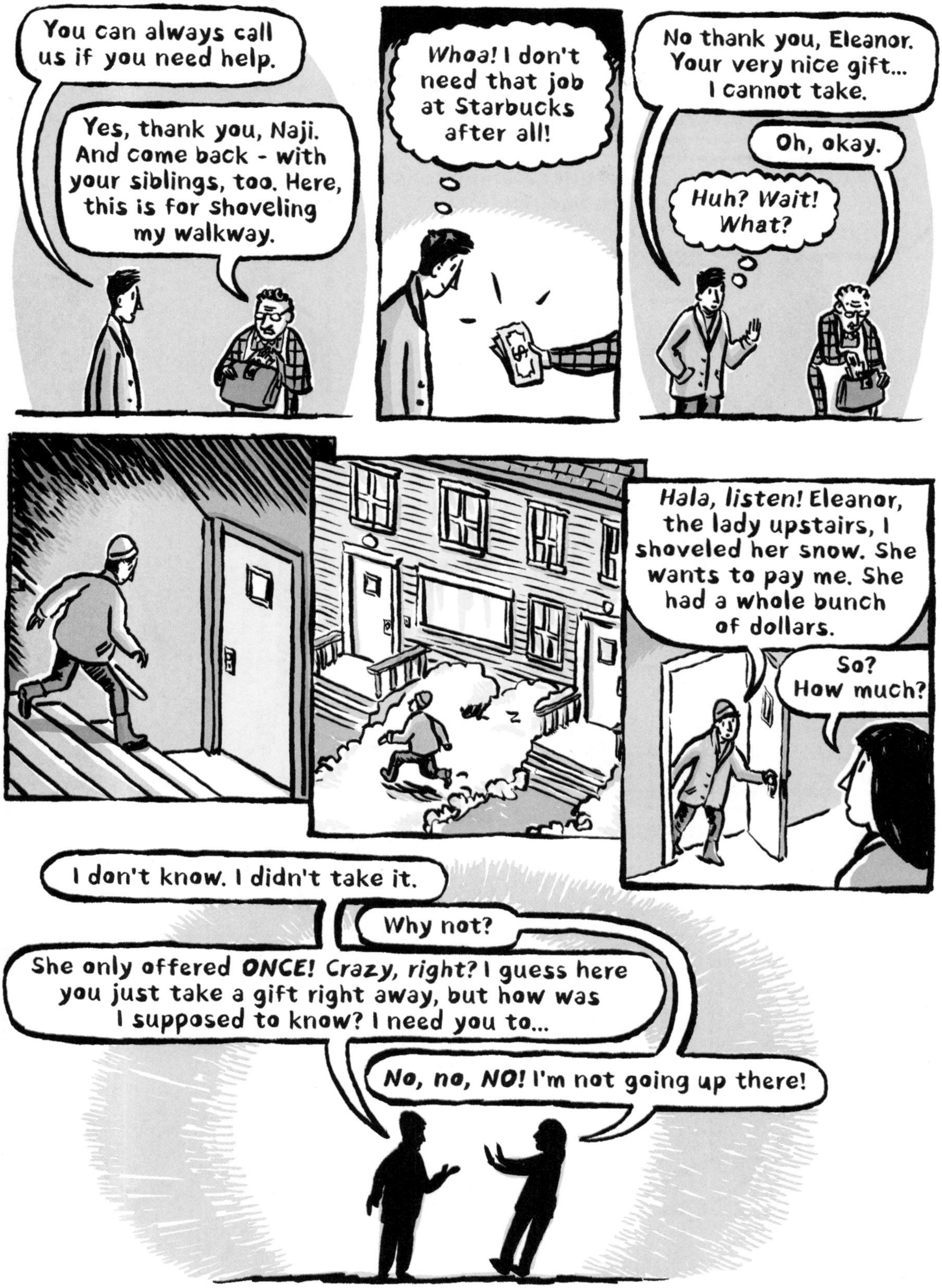

You can always call us if you need help.
Yes, thank you, Naji. And come back - with your siblings, too. Here, this is for shoveling my walkway.
Whoa! I don't need that job at Starbucks after all!
No thank you, Eleanor. Your very nice gift... I cannot take.
Oh, okay.
Huh? Wait! What?
Hala, listen! Eleanor, the lady upstairs, I shoveled her snow. She wants to pay me. She had a whole bunch of dollars.
So? How much?
I don't know. I didn't take it.
Why not?
She only offered ONCE! Crazy, right? I guess here you just take a gift right away, but how was I supposed to know? I need you to...
No, no, NO! I'm not going up there!

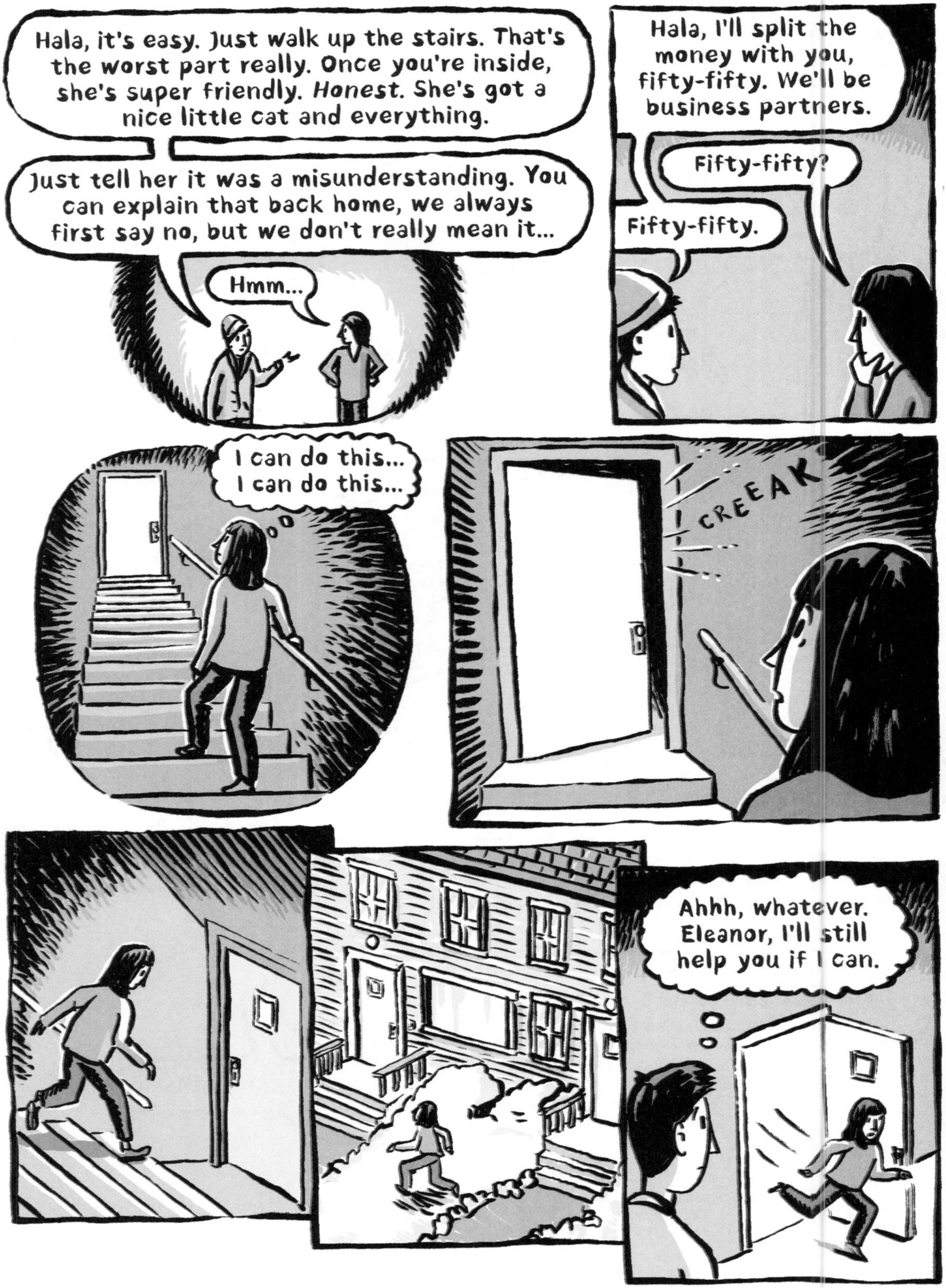
Hala, it's easy. Just walk up the stairs. That's the worst part really. Once you're inside, she's super friendly. *Honest*. She's got a nice little cat and everything.
Just tell her it was a misunderstanding. You can explain that back home, we always first say no, but we don't really mean it...
Hmm...
Hala, I'll split the money with you, fifty-fifty. We'll be business partners.
Fifty-fifty?
Fifty-fifty.
I can do this... I can do this...
CREEAK
Ahhh, whatever. Eleanor, I'll still help you if I can.

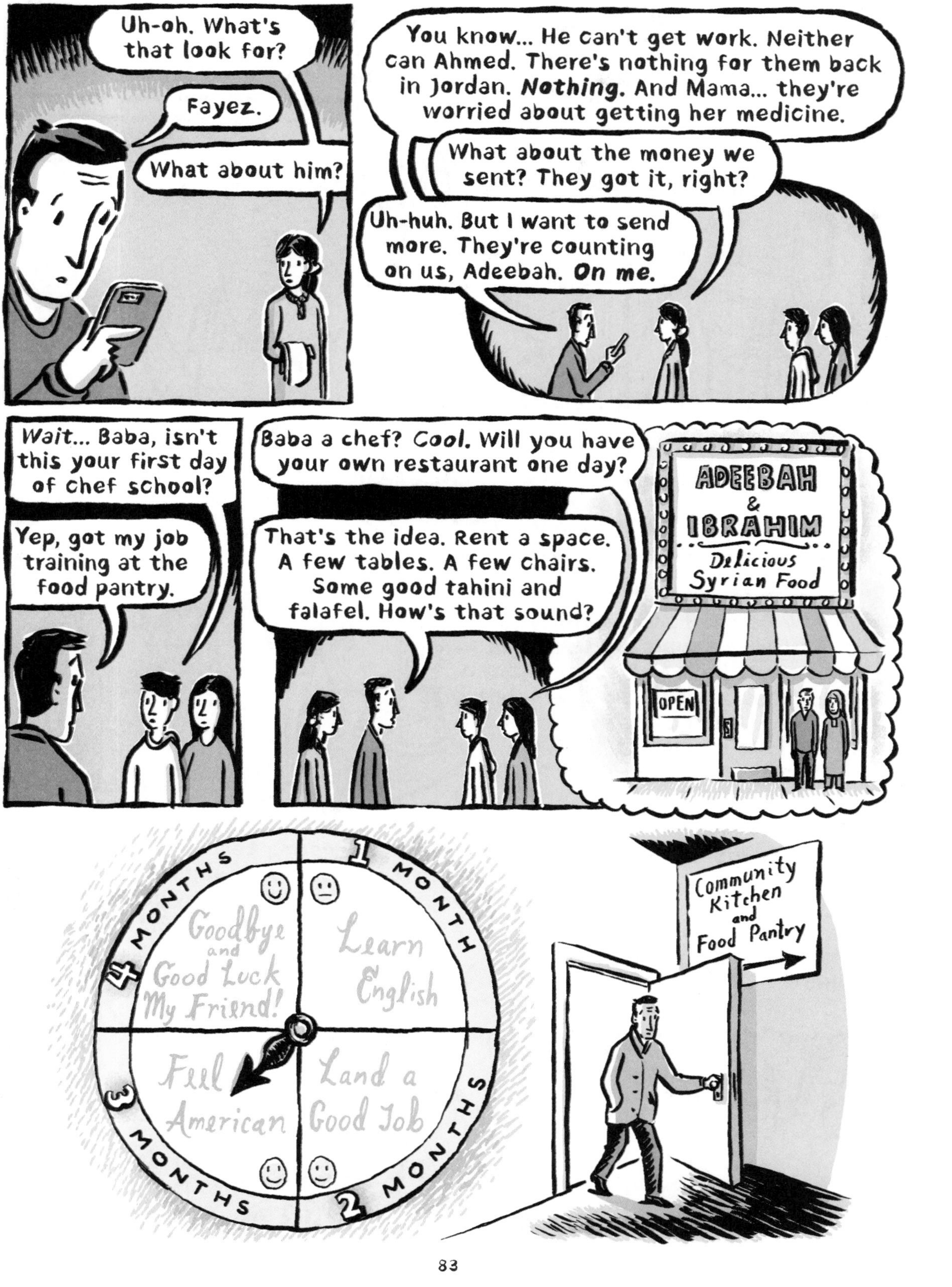
Uh-oh. What's that look for?
Fayez.
What about him?
You know... He can't get work. Neither can Ahmed. There's nothing for them back in Jordan. *Nothing.* And Mama... they're worried about getting her medicine.
What about the money we sent? They got it, right?
Uh-huh. But I want to send more. They're counting on us, Adeebah. *On me.*
Wait... Baba, isn't this your first day of chef school?
Yep, got my job training at the food pantry.
Baba a chef? *Cool.* Will you have your own restaurant one day?
That's the idea. Rent a space. A few tables. A few chairs. Some good tahini and falafel. How's that sound?
ADEEBAH & IBRAHIM
Delicious Syrian Food
OPEN
1 MONTH
Learn English
2 MONTHS
Land a Good Job
3 MONTHS
Feel American
4 MONTHS
Goodbye and Good Luck My Friend!
Community Kitchen and Food Pantry

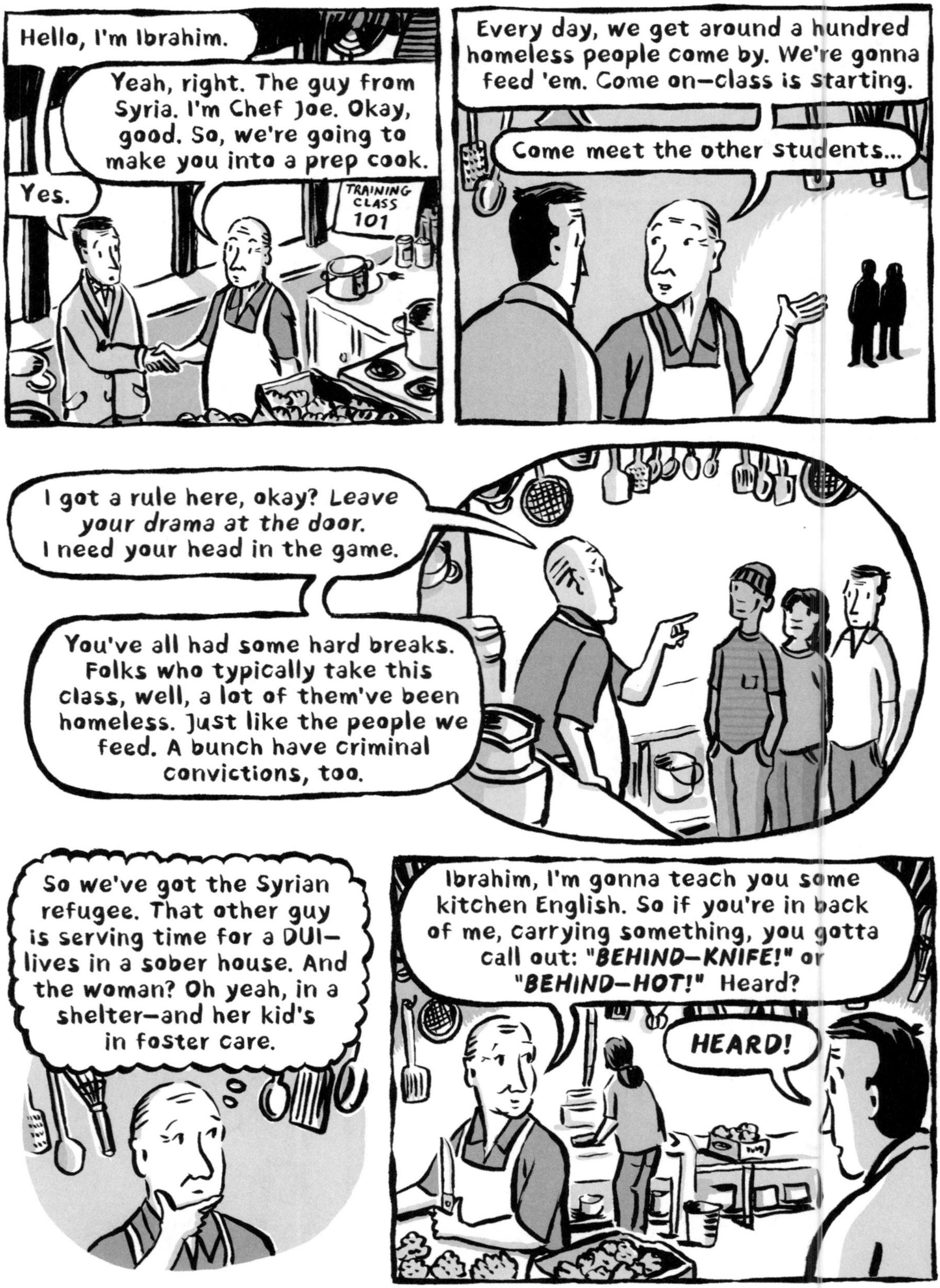
Hello, I'm Ibrahim.
Yeah, right. The guy from Syria. I'm Chef Joe. Okay, good. So, we're going to make you into a prep cook.
Yes.
TRAINING CLASS 101
Every day, we get around a hundred homeless people come by. We're gonna feed 'em. Come on—class is starting.
Come meet the other students...
I got a rule here, okay? *Leave your drama at the door.* I need your head in the game.
You've all had some hard breaks. Folks who typically take this class, well, a lot of them've been homeless. Just like the people we feed. A bunch have criminal convictions, too.
So we've got the Syrian refugee. That other guy is serving time for a DUI—lives in a sober house. And the woman? Oh yeah, in a shelter—and her kid's in foster care.
Ibrahim, I'm gonna teach you some kitchen English. So if you're in back of me, carrying something, you gotta call out: "*BEHIND—KNIFE!*" or "*BEHIND—HOT!*" Heard?
HEARD!

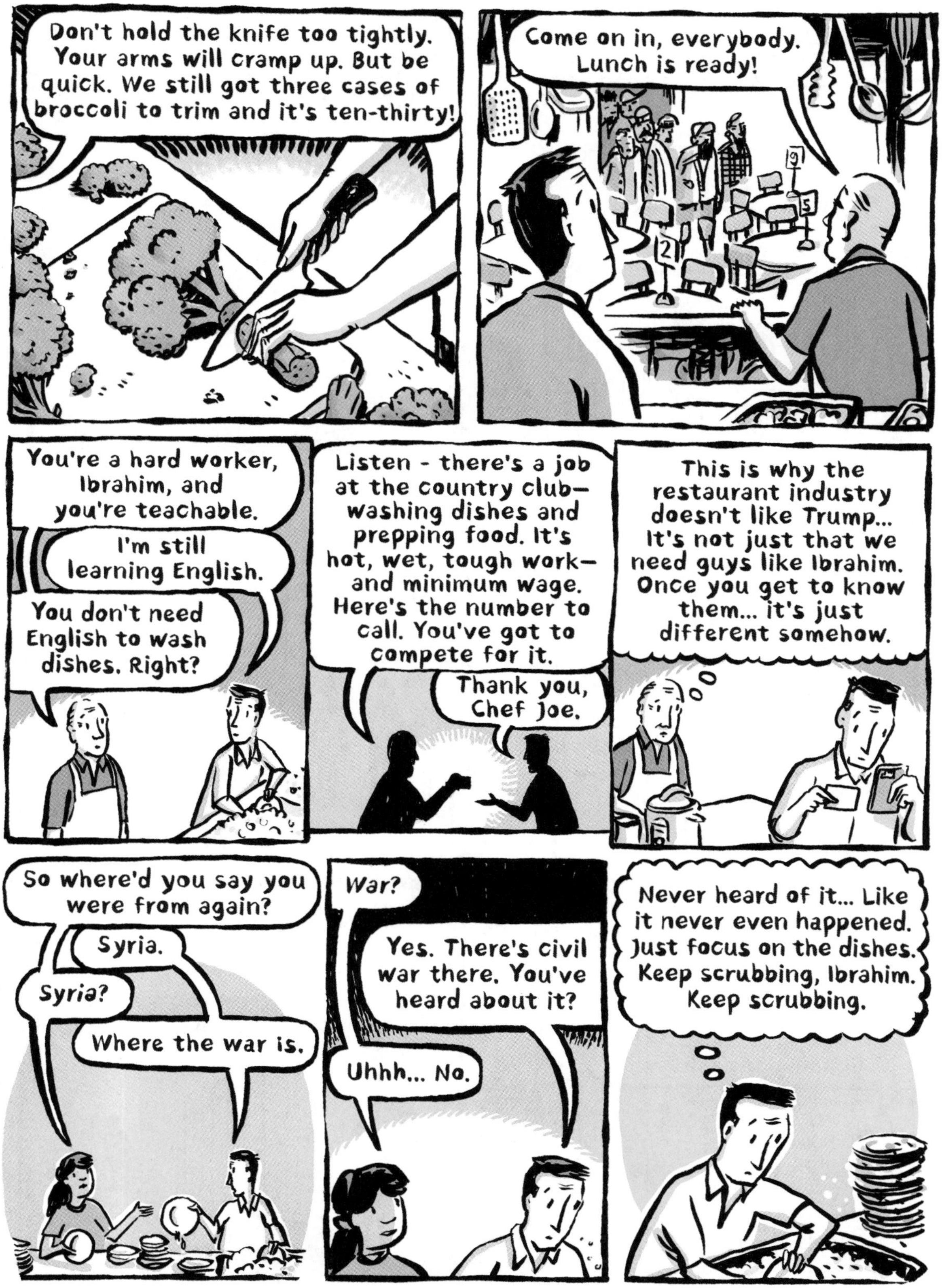
Don't hold the knife too tightly. Your arms will cramp up. But be quick. We still got three cases of broccoli to trim and it's ten-thirty!
Come on in, everybody. Lunch is ready!
You're a hard worker, Ibrahim, and you're teachable.
I'm still learning English.
You don't need English to wash dishes. Right?
Listen - there's a job at the country club— washing dishes and prepping food. It's hot, wet, tough work— and minimum wage. Here's the number to call. You've got to compete for it.
Thank you, Chef Joe.
This is why the restaurant industry doesn't like Trump... It's not just that we need guys like Ibrahim. Once you get to know them... it's just different somehow.
So where'd you say you were from again?
Syria.
Syria?
Where the war is.
War?
Yes. There's civil war there. You've heard about it?
Uhhh... No.
Never heard of it... Like it never even happened. Just focus on the dishes. Keep scrubbing, Ibrahim. Keep scrubbing.

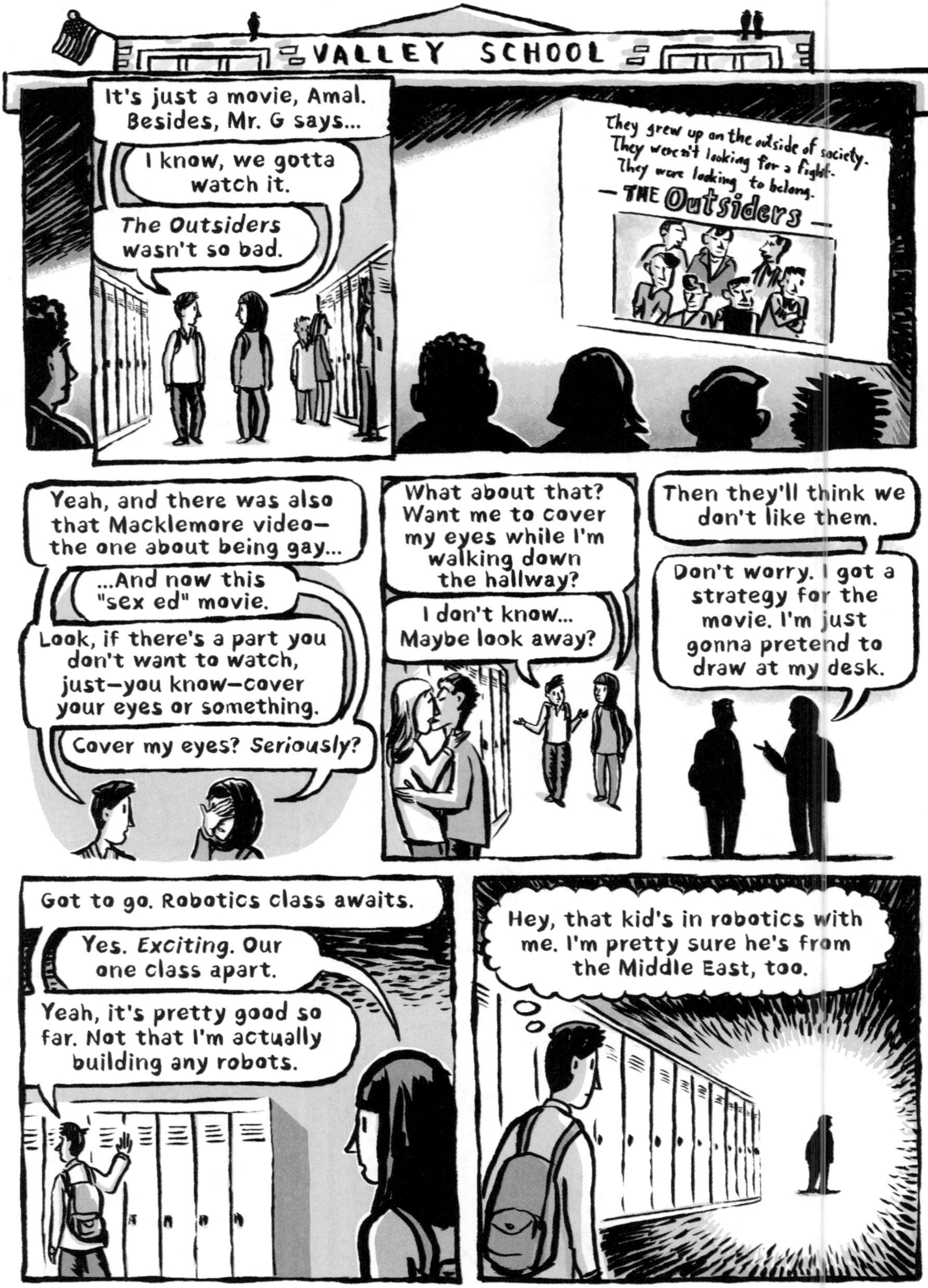
VALLEY SCHOOL
It's just a movie, Amal. Besides, Mr. G says...
I know, we gotta watch it.
The Outsiders wasn't so bad.
They grew up on the outside of society. They weren't looking for a fight. They were looking to belong.
— THE Outsiders —
Yeah, and there was also that Macklemore video—the one about being gay...
...And now this "sex ed" movie.
Look, if there's a part you don't want to watch, just—you know—cover your eyes or something.
Cover my eyes? Seriously?
What about that? Want me to cover my eyes while I'm walking down the hallway?
I don't know... Maybe look away?
Then they'll think we don't like them.
Don't worry. I got a strategy for the movie. I'm just gonna pretend to draw at my desk.
Got to go. Robotics class awaits.
Yes. Exciting. Our one class apart.
Yeah, it's pretty good so far. Not that I'm actually building any robots.
Hey, that kid's in robotics with me. I'm pretty sure he's from the Middle East, too.

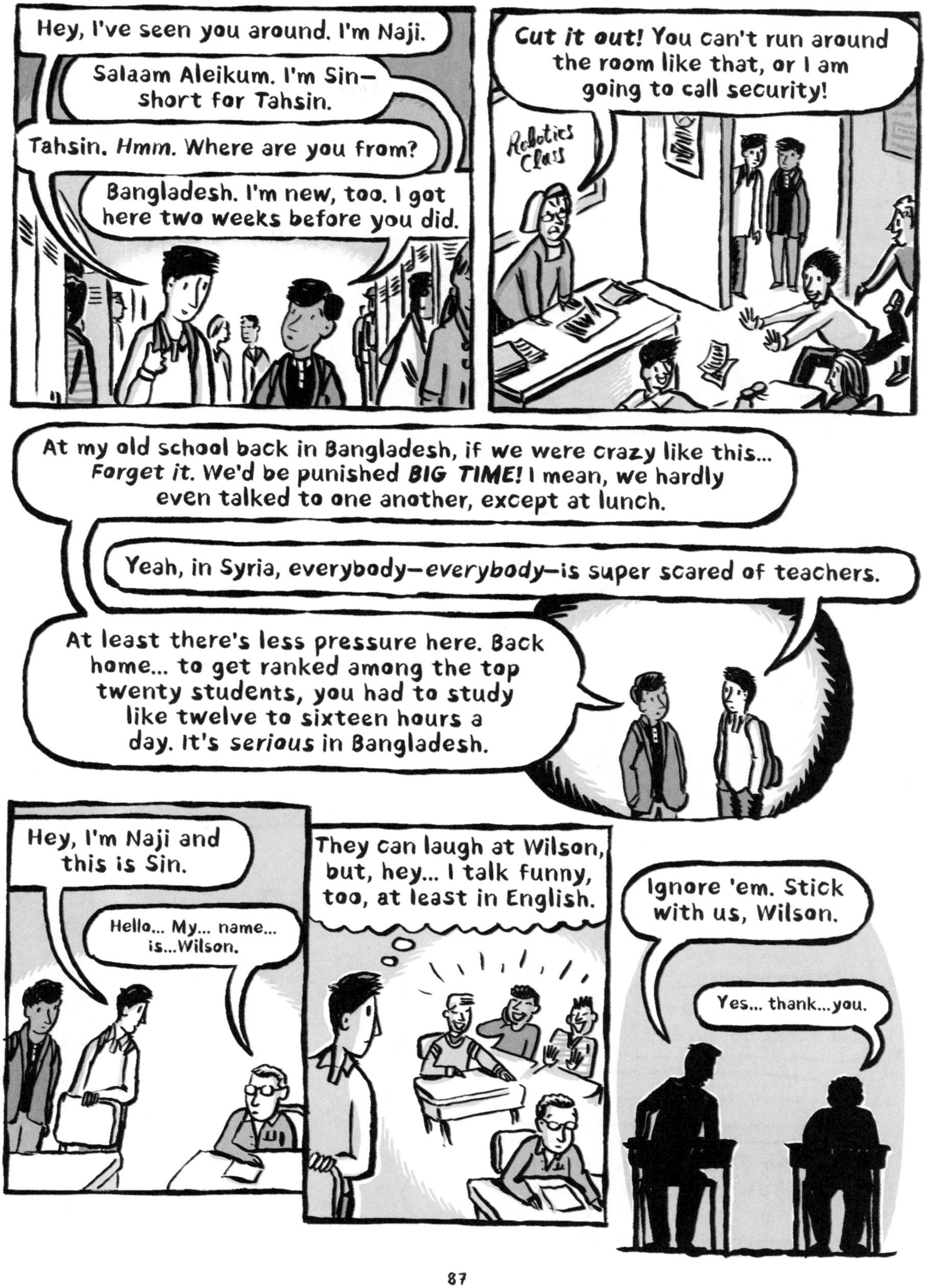
Hey, I've seen you around. I'm Naji.
Salaam Aleikum. I'm Sin—short for Tahsin.
Tahsin. Hmm. Where are you from?
Bangladesh. I'm new, too. I got here two weeks before you did.
Cut it out! You can't run around the room like that, or I am going to call security!
Robotics Class
At my old school back in Bangladesh, if we were crazy like this... Forget it. We'd be punished BIG TIME! I mean, we hardly even talked to one another, except at lunch.
Yeah, in Syria, everybody—everybody—is super scared of teachers.
At least there's less pressure here. Back home... to get ranked among the top twenty students, you had to study like twelve to sixteen hours a day. It's serious in Bangladesh.
Hey, I'm Naji and this is Sin.
Hello... My... name... is...Wilson.
They can laugh at Wilson, but, hey... I talk funny, too, at least in English.
Ignore 'em. Stick with us, Wilson.
Yes... thank...you.

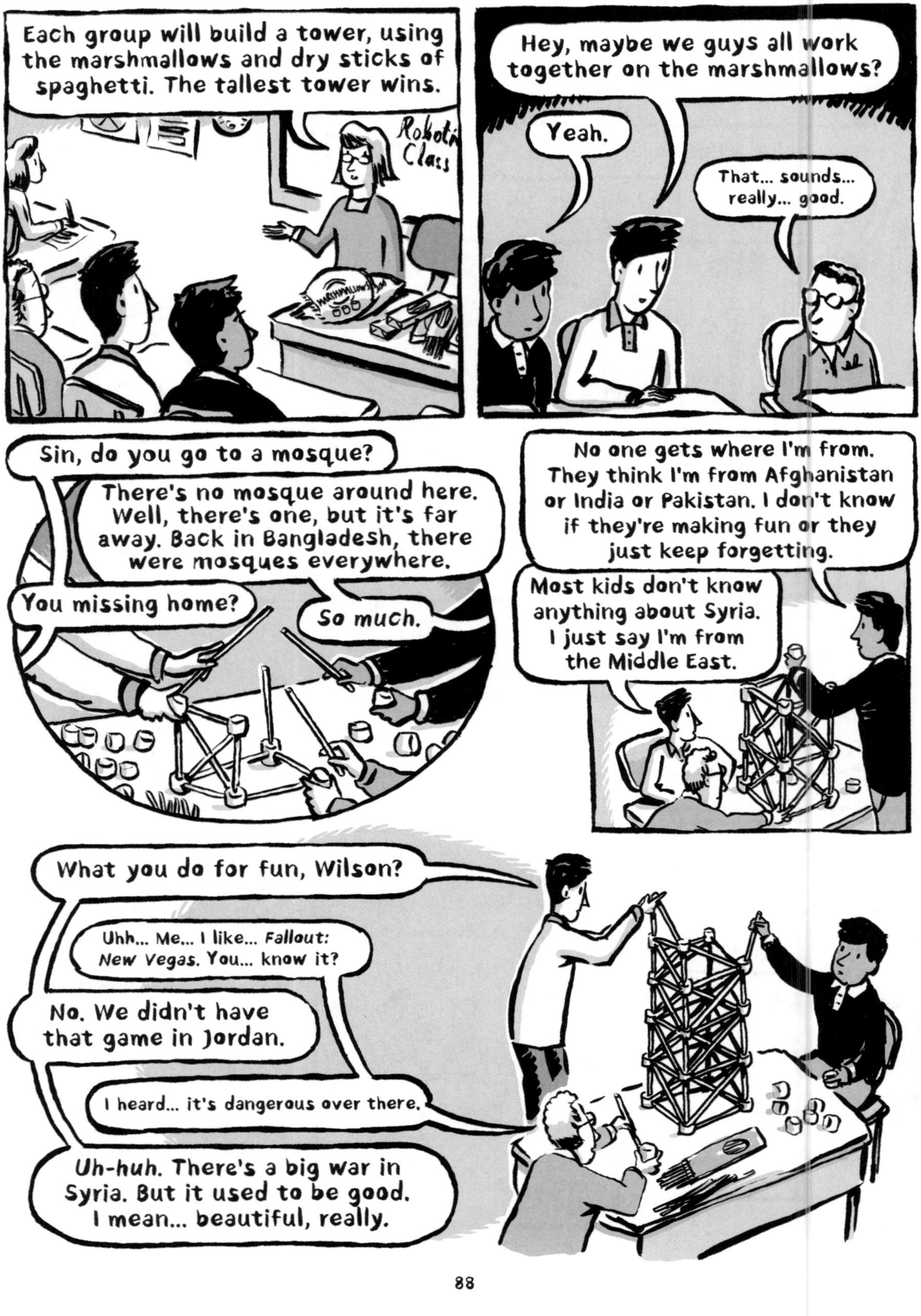
Each group will build a tower, using the marshmallows and dry sticks of spaghetti. The tallest tower wins.
Robotics Class
Hey, maybe we guys all work together on the marshmallows?
Yeah.
That... sounds... really... good.
Sin, do you go to a mosque?
There's no mosque around here. Well, there's one, but it's far away. Back in Bangladesh, there were mosques everywhere.
You missing home?
So much.
No one gets where I'm from. They think I'm from Afghanistan or India or Pakistan. I don't know if they're making fun or they just keep forgetting.
Most kids don't know anything about Syria. I just say I'm from the Middle East.
What you do for fun, Wilson?
Uhh... Me... I like... *Fallout: New Vegas*. You... know it?
No. We didn't have that game in Jordan.
I heard... it's dangerous over there.
Uh-huh. There's a big war in Syria. But it used to be good. I mean... beautiful, really.

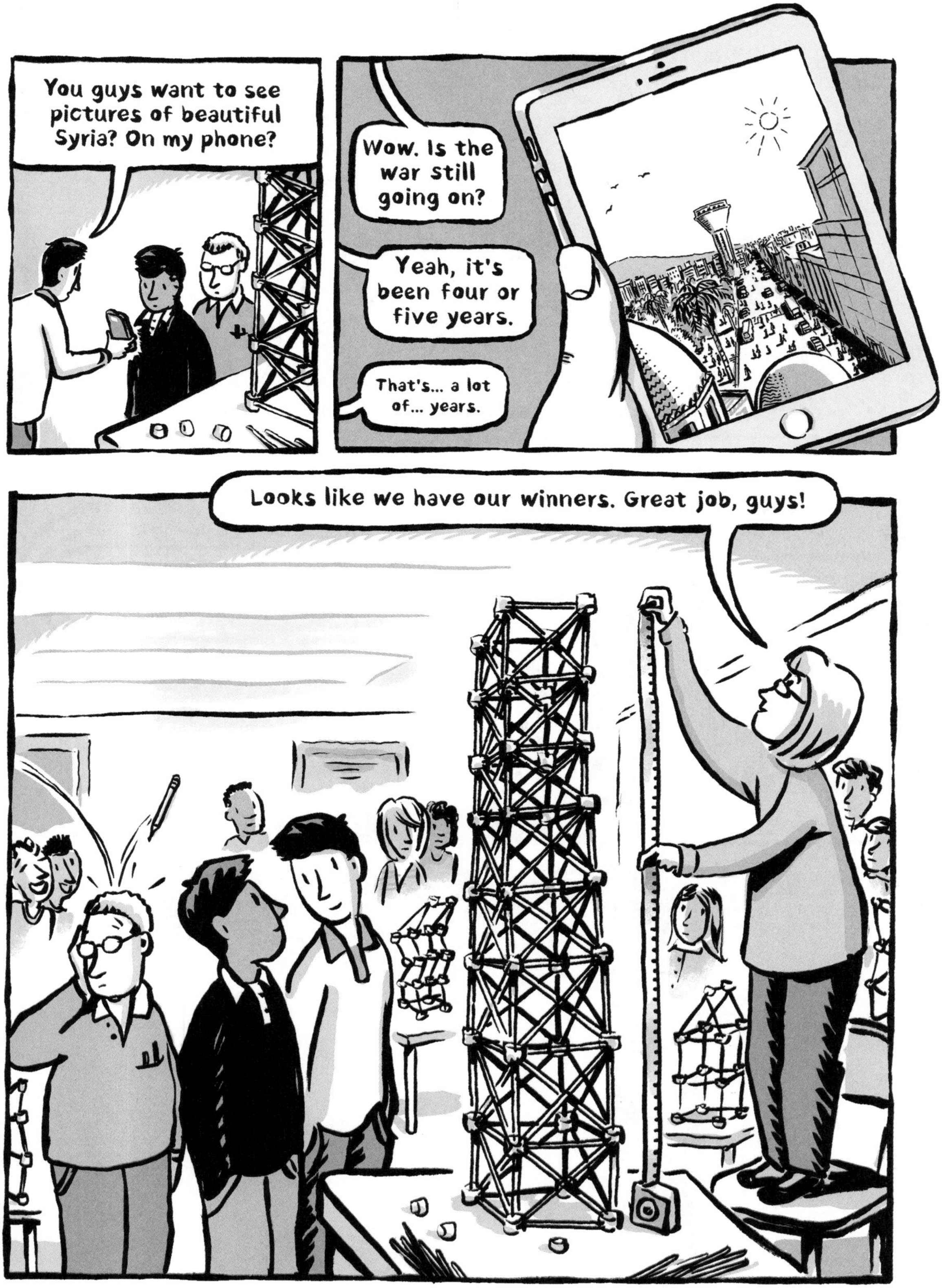
You guys want to see pictures of beautiful Syria? On my phone?
Wow. Is the war still going on?
Yeah, it's been four or five years.
That's... a lot of... years.
Looks like we have our winners. Great job, guys!

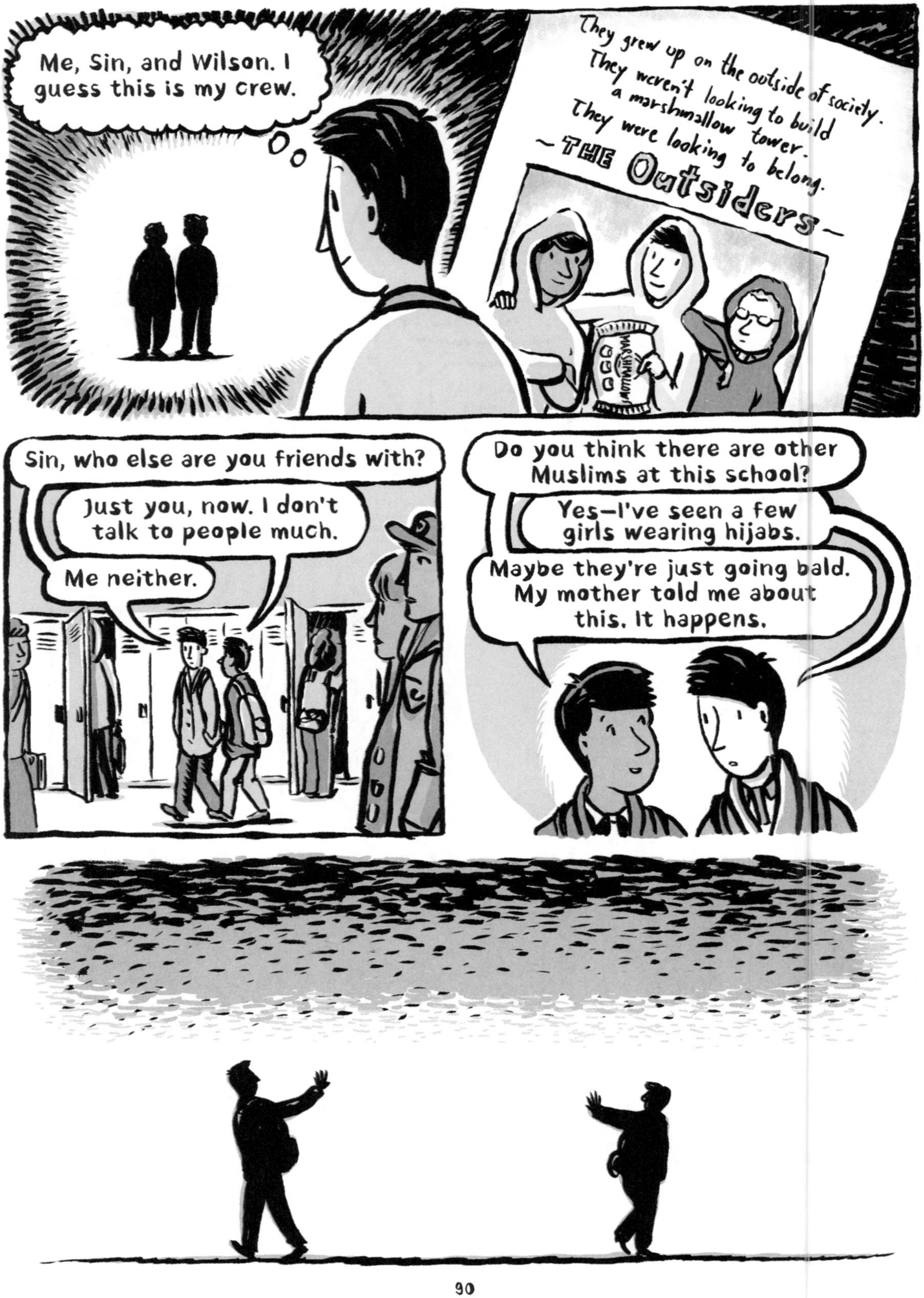
Me, Sin, and Wilson. I guess this is my crew.
They grew up on the outside of society. They weren't looking to build a marshmallow tower. They were looking to belong. ~THE Outsiders~
Sin, who else are you friends with?
Just you, now. I don't talk to people much.
Me neither.
Do you think there are other Muslims at this school?
Yes—I've seen a few girls wearing hijabs.
Maybe they're just going bald. My mother told me about this. It happens.

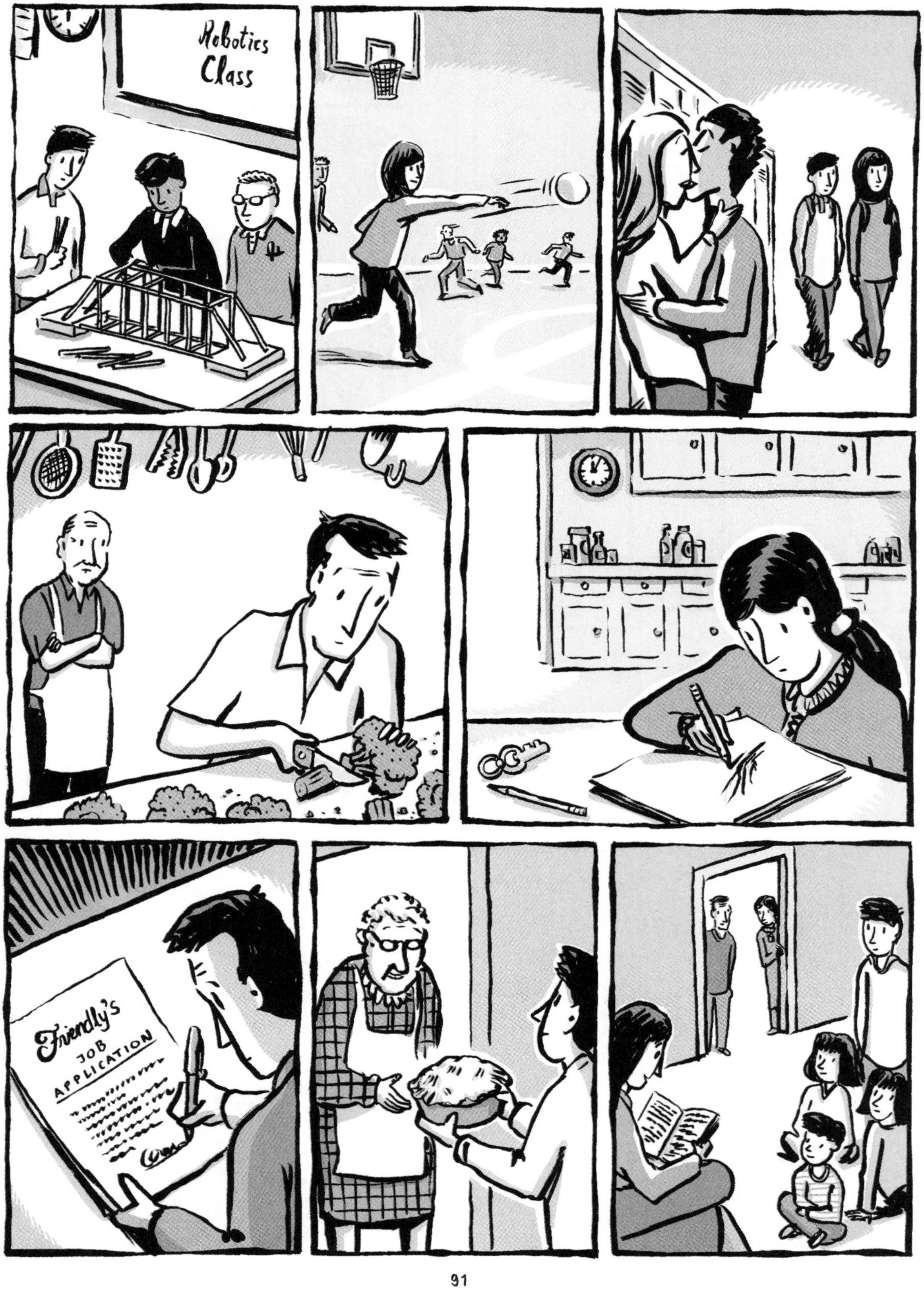
Robotics
Class
Friendly's
JOB
APPLICATION

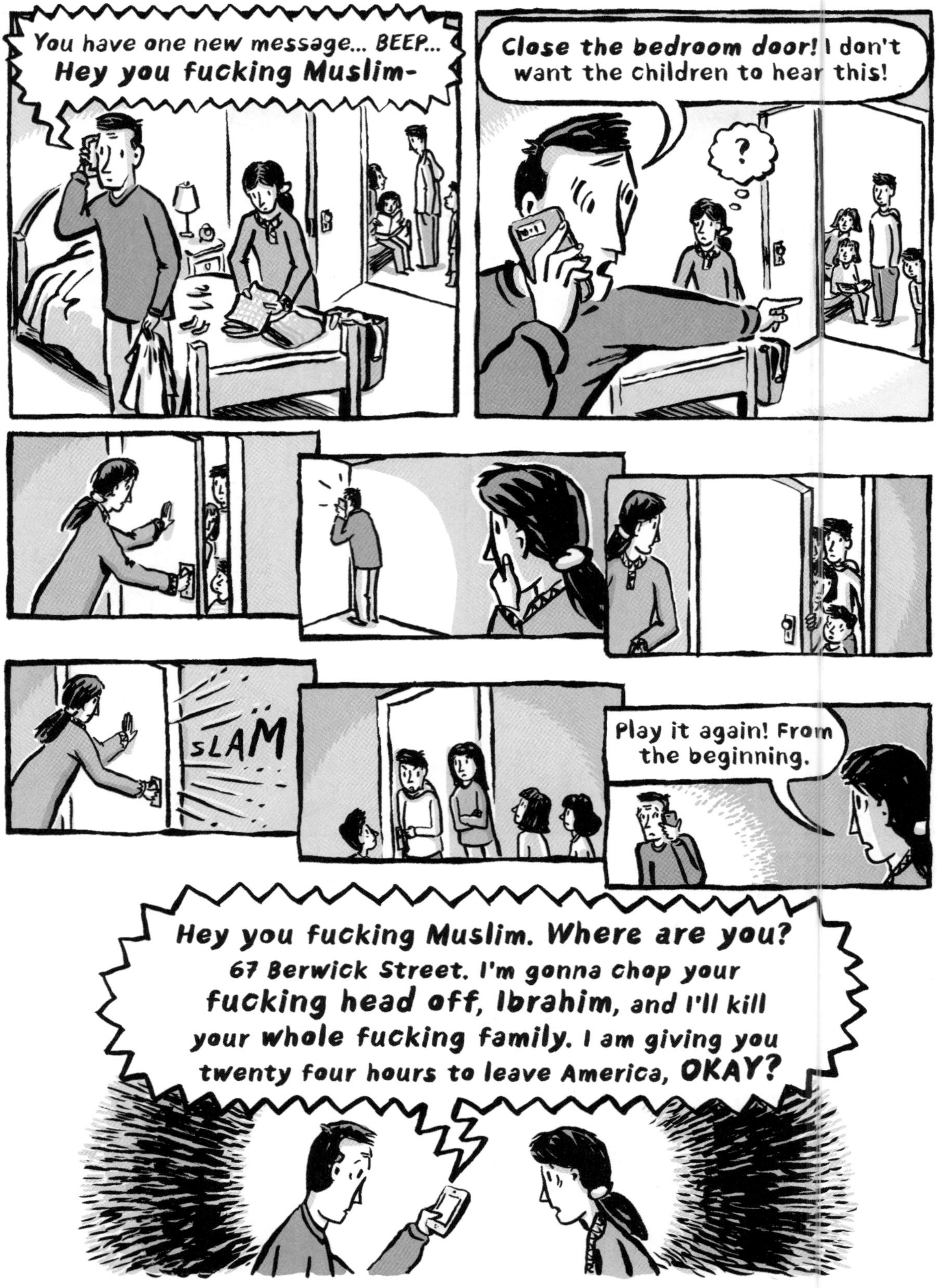

You have one new message... BEEP... Hey you fucking Muslim-
Close the bedroom door! I don't want the children to hear this!
?
SLAM
Play it again! From the beginning.
Hey you fucking Muslim. Where are you? 67 Berwick Street. I'm gonna chop your fucking head off, Ibrahim, and I'll kill your whole fucking family. I am giving you twenty four hours to leave America, OKAY?

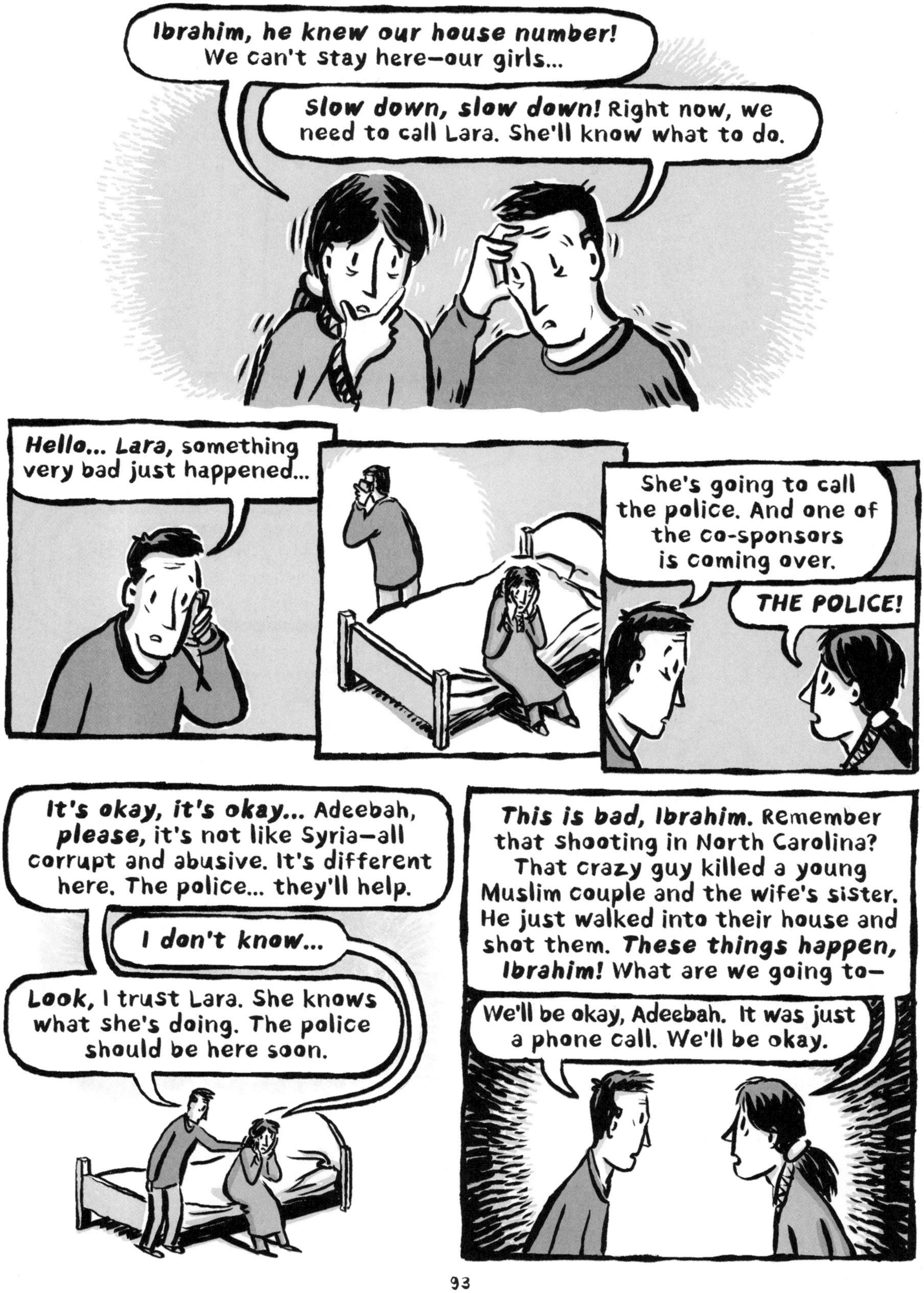

Ibrahim, he knew our house number! We can't stay here—our girls...
Slow down, slow down! Right now, we need to call Lara. She'll know what to do.
Hello... Lara, something very bad just happened...
She's going to call the police. And one of the co-sponsors is coming over.
THE POLICE!
It's okay, it's okay... Adeebah, ***please,*** it's not like Syria—all corrupt and abusive. It's different here. The police... they'll help.
I don't know...
Look, I trust Lara. She knows what she's doing. The police should be here soon.
This is bad, Ibrahim. Remember that shooting in North Carolina? That crazy guy killed a young Muslim couple and the wife's sister. He just walked into their house and shot them. ***These things happen, Ibrahim!*** What are we going to—
We'll be okay, Adeebah. It was just a phone call. We'll be okay.

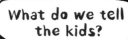

What do we tell the kids?

Nothing for now.

Ibrahim, when the police come, we'll have to say something to the kids.

I know.

We'll probably have to replay that voice mail. One way or another, the kids will find out. Naji has already asked me.

I'll talk to him.

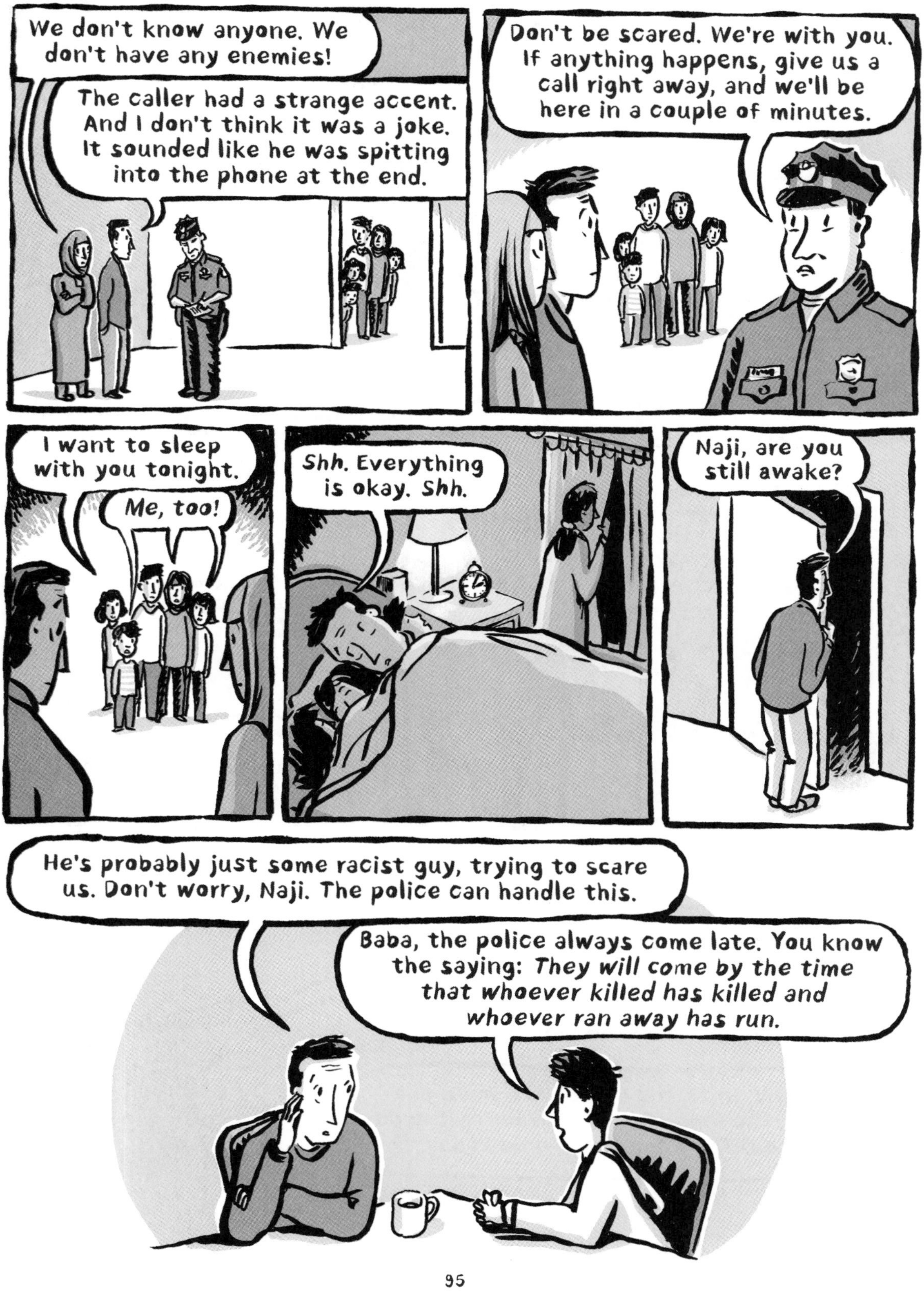

We don't know anyone. We don't have any enemies!
The caller had a strange accent. And I don't think it was a joke. It sounded like he was spitting into the phone at the end.
Don't be scared. We're with you. If anything happens, give us a call right away, and we'll be here in a couple of minutes.
I want to sleep with you tonight.
Me, too!
Shh. Everything is okay. *Shh.*
Naji, are you still awake?
He's probably just some racist guy, trying to scare us. Don't worry, Naji. The police can handle this.
Baba, the police always come late. You know the saying: *They will come by the time that whoever killed has killed and whoever ran away has run.*

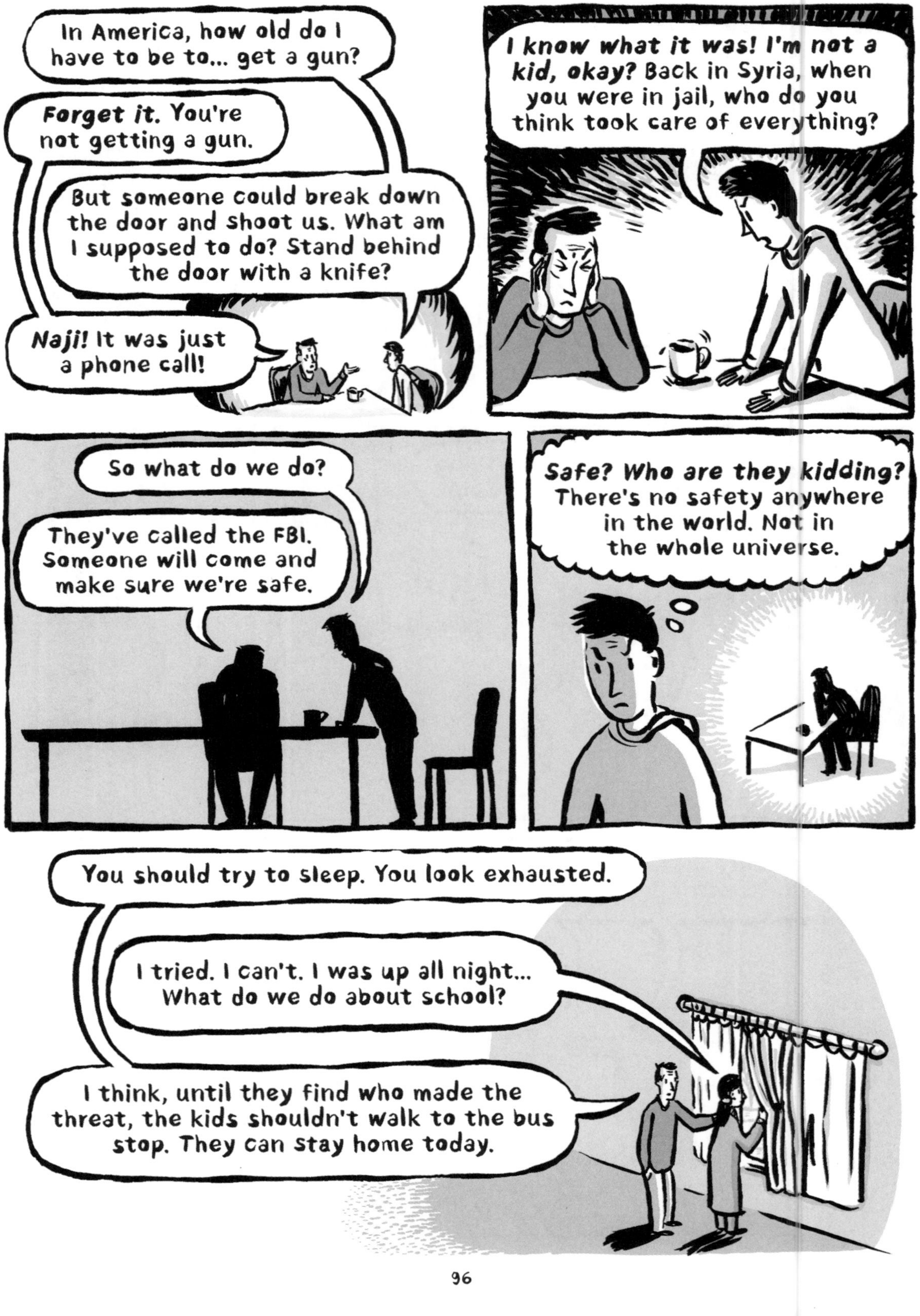
In America, how old do I have to be to... get a gun?
Forget it. You're not getting a gun.
But someone could break down the door and shoot us. What am I supposed to do? Stand behind the door with a knife?
Naji! It was just a phone call!
I know what it was! I'm not a kid, okay? Back in Syria, when you were in jail, who do you think took care of everything?
So what do we do?
They've called the FBI. Someone will come and make sure we're safe.
Safe? Who are they kidding? There's no safety anywhere in the world. Not in the whole universe.
You should try to sleep. You look exhausted.
I tried. I can't. I was up all night... What do we do about school?
I think, until they find who made the threat, the kids shouldn't walk to the bus stop. They can stay home today.

The man who called... I suppose he might just be a crazy person, but that makes me even more scared. It means he's not rational. He could do anything.

I don't want to stay here. In this house.

But the kids! They're just getting used to school. And my training program...

So what do we do, Ibrahim?

Maybe another house, near the center of town. So we're not out here by ourselves

Somewhere very close to a police station.

I guess there's always my brother, but we're too many, with our five. We'd never fit. Maybe a hotel room?

Someone's at the door!

It's probably the FBI agent. They said he'd be here around now.

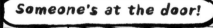

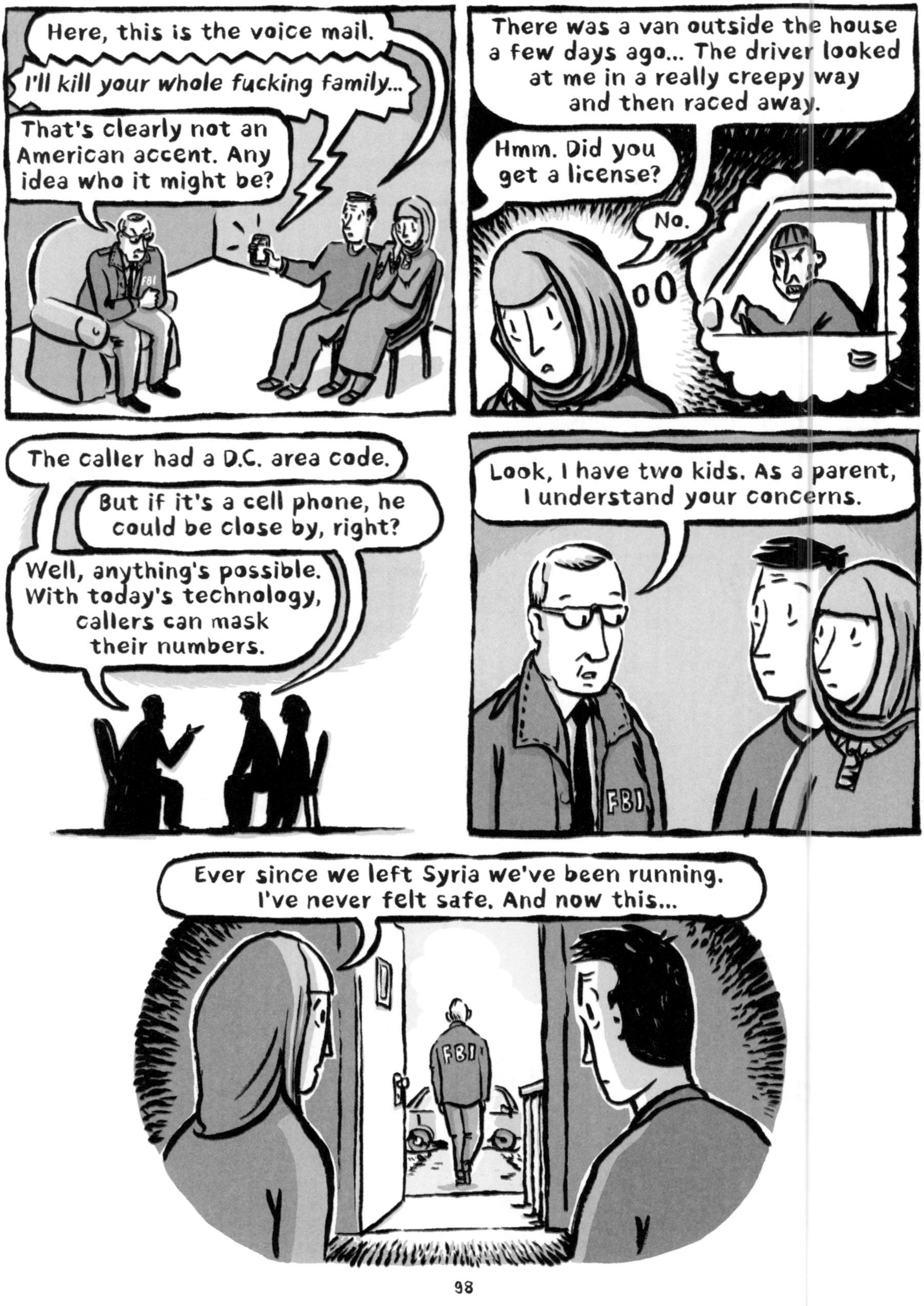

Here, this is the voice mail.
I'll kill your whole fucking family...
That's clearly not an American accent. Any idea who it might be?
FBI
There was a van outside the house a few days ago... The driver looked at me in a really creepy way and then raced away.
Hmm. Did you get a license?
No.
The caller had a D.C. area code.
But if it's a cell phone, he could be close by, right?
Well, anything's possible. With today's technology, callers can mask their numbers.
Look, I have two kids. As a parent, I understand your concerns.
FBI
Ever since we left Syria we've been running. I've never felt safe. And now this...
FBI

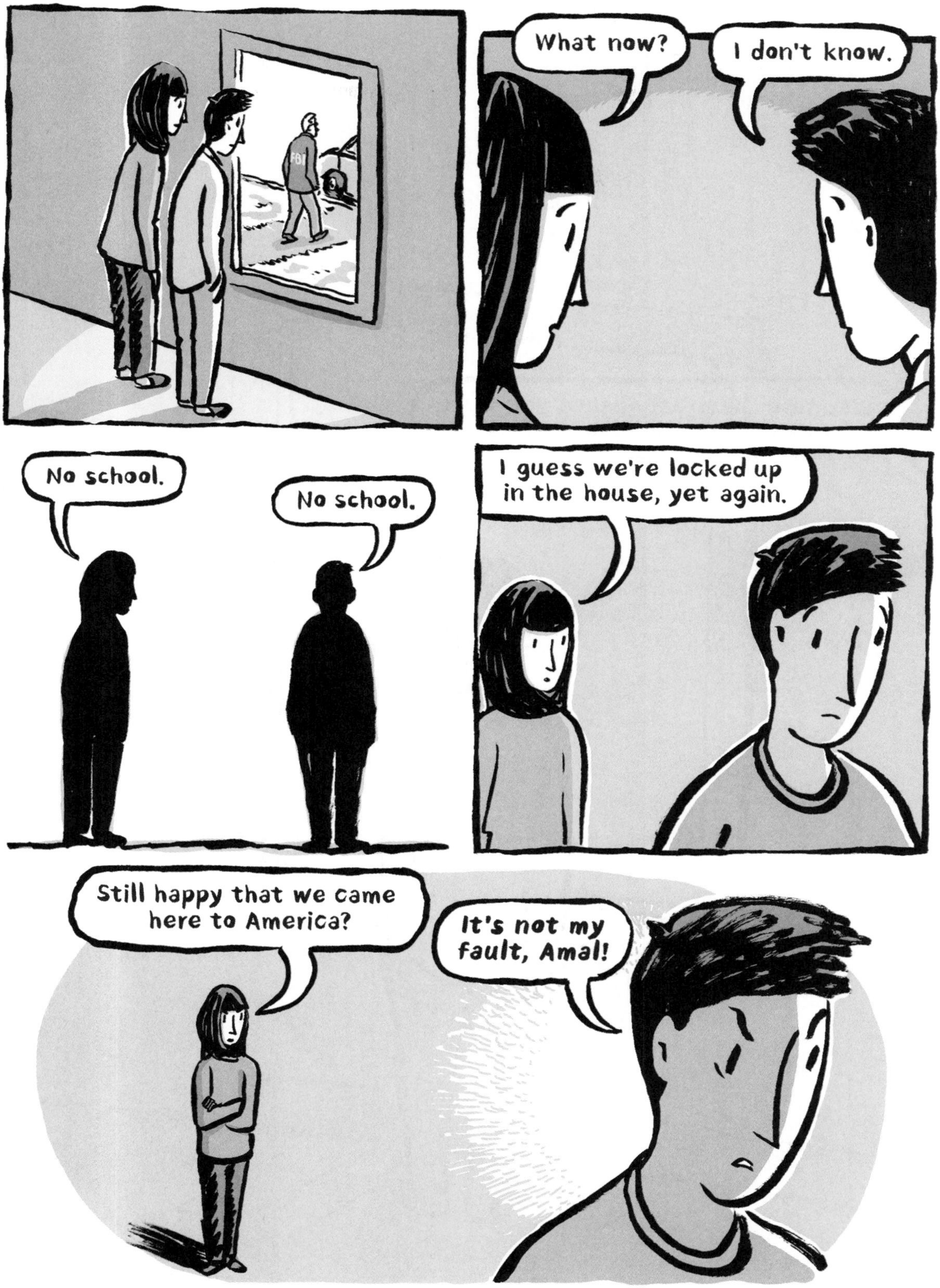
What now?
I don't know.
No school.
No school.
I guess we're locked up in the house, yet again.
Still happy that we came here to America?
It's not my fault, Amal!

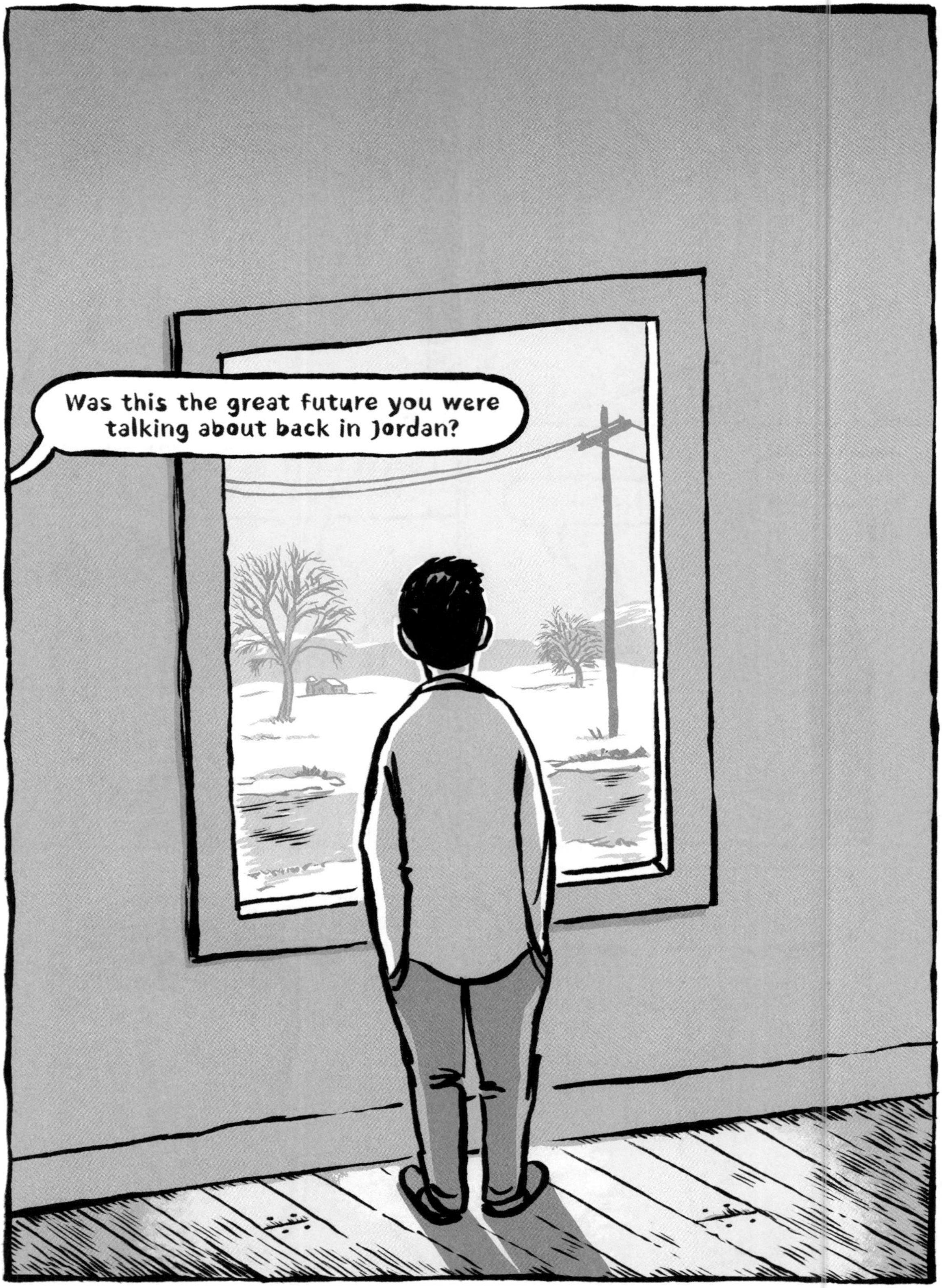
Was this the great future you were talking about back in Jordan?

Chapter 4

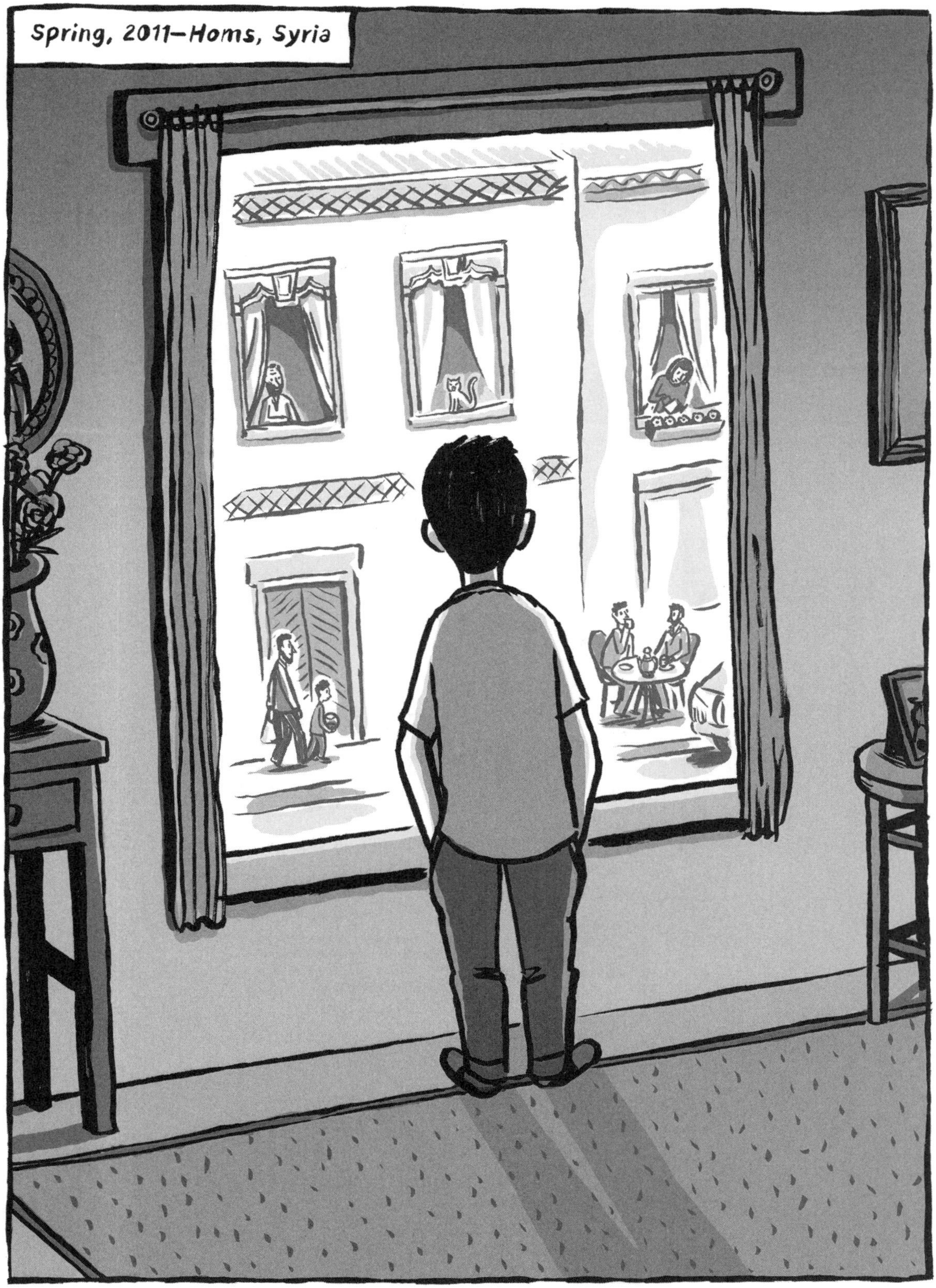
Spring, 2011—Homs, Syria

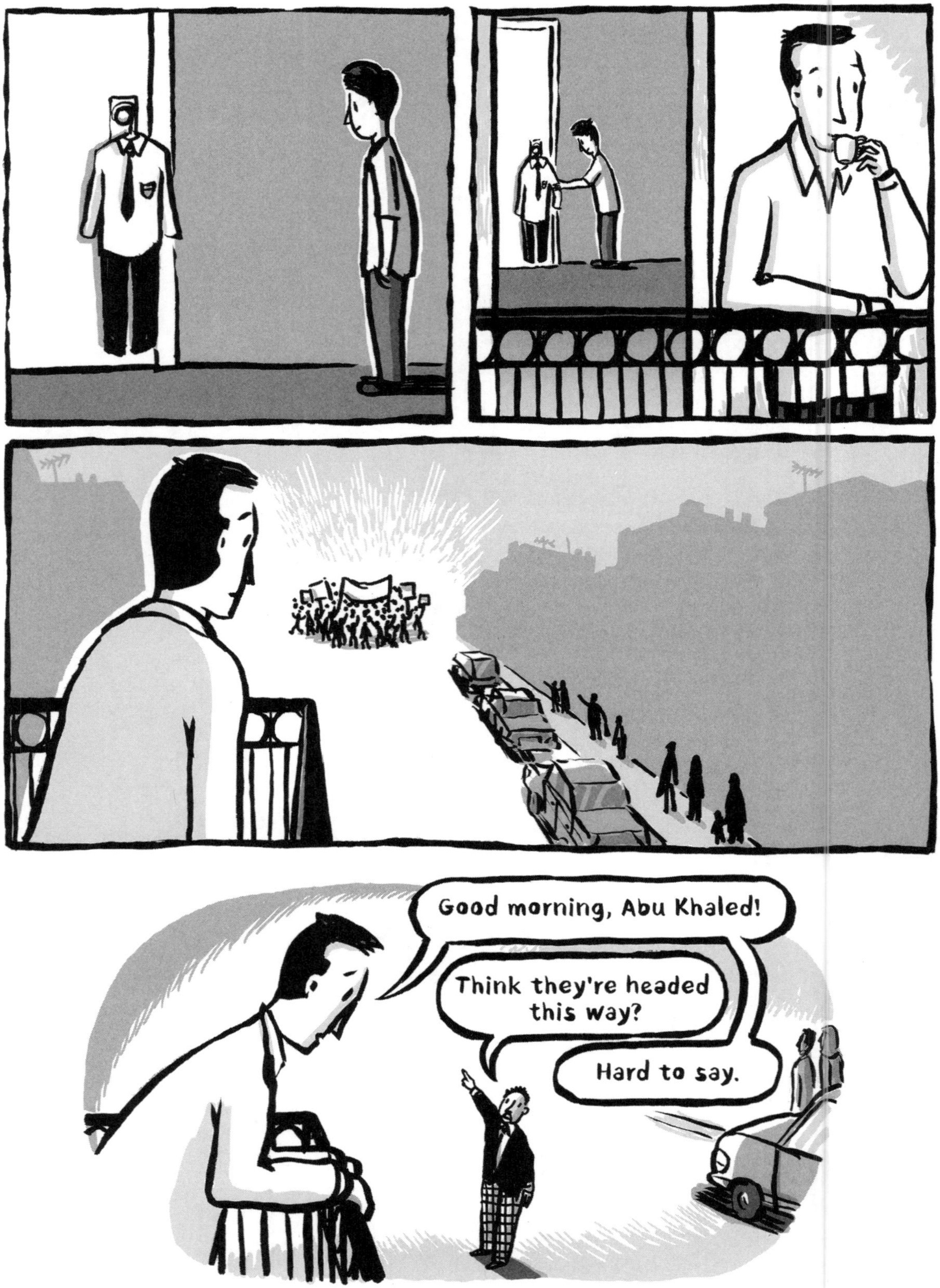
Good morning, Abu Khaled!
Think they're headed this way?
Hard to say.

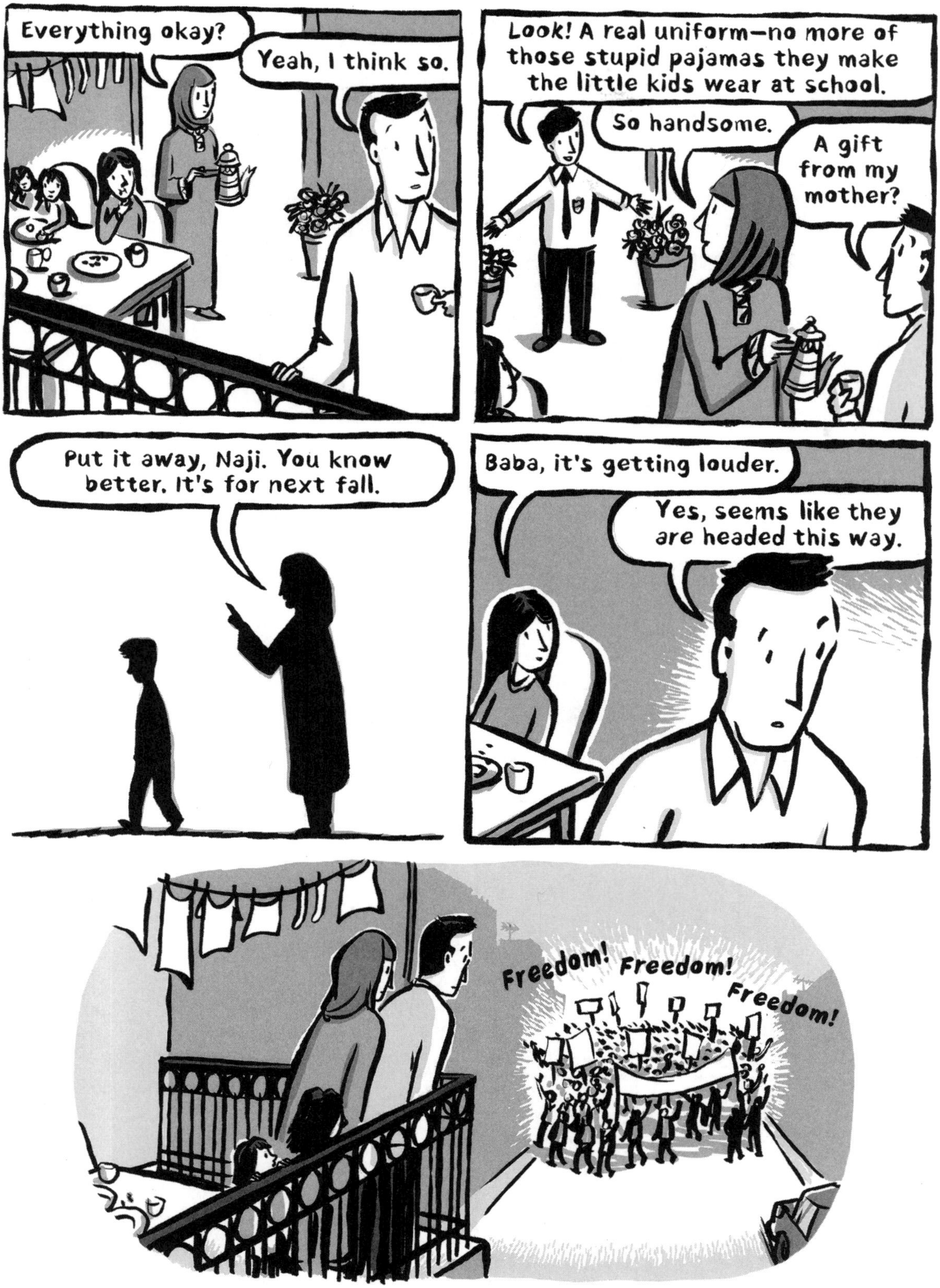
Everything okay?
Yeah, I think so.
Look! A real uniform—no more of those stupid pajamas they make the little kids wear at school.
So handsome.
A gift from my mother?
Put it away, Naji. You know better. It's for next fall.
Baba, it's getting louder.
Yes, seems like they are headed this way.
Freedom!
Freedom!
Freedom!

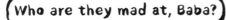

Who are they mad at, Baba?

President Assad. The governor. The police. The corrupt thieves who make us pay bribes until our businesses go broke...

ALDABAAN'S MOBILE PHONES

Out of Business

Almost every Friday now... And it's growing.

My father always said, *Blood will rise up to our knees before the government falls.*

Yeah... like in '82.

Look, they're throwing petals!

Don't you dare, Amal! Those are my roses!

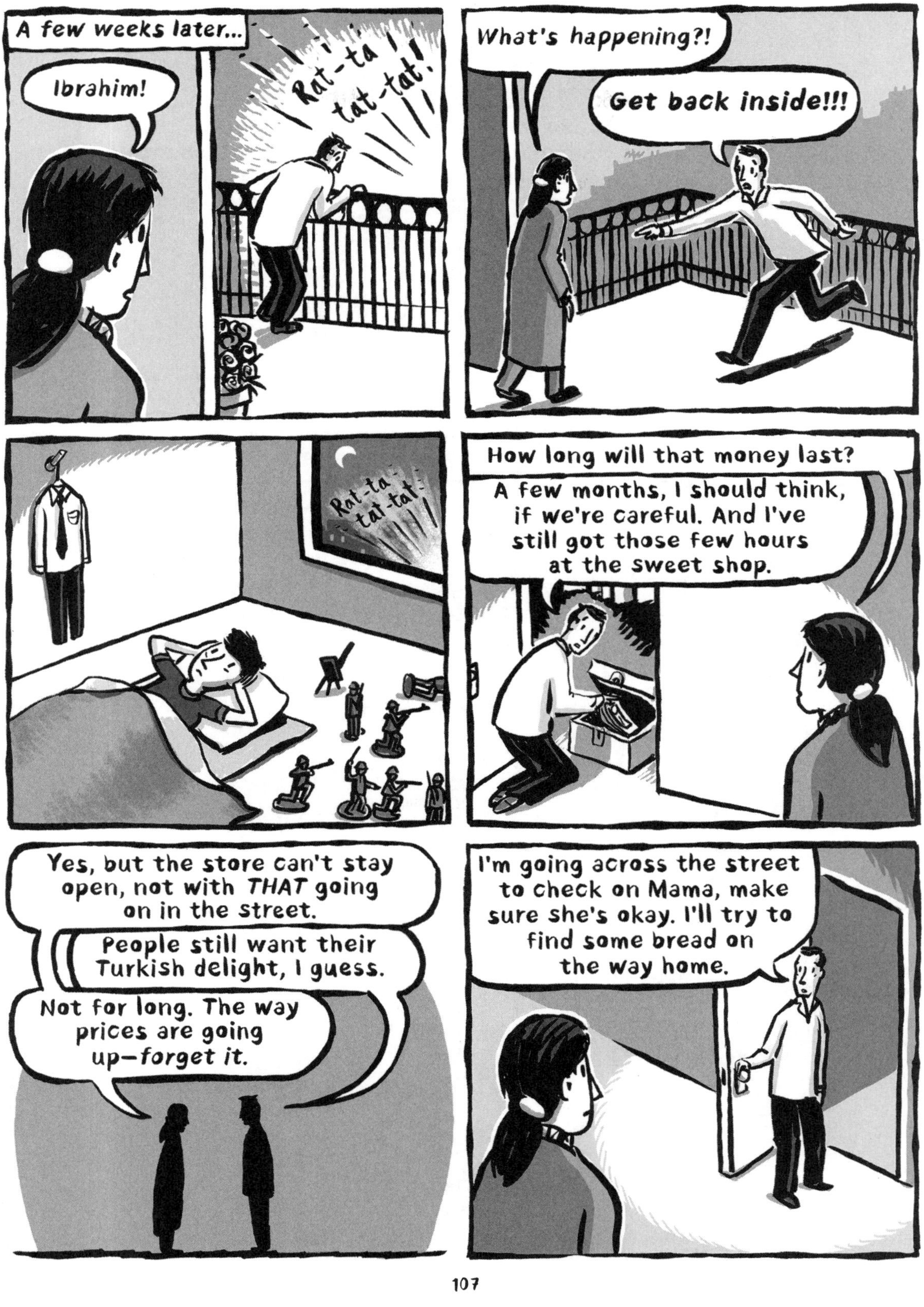
A few weeks later...
Ibrahim!
Rat-ta tat-tat!
What's happening?!
Get back inside!!!
Rat-ta tat-tat
How long will that money last?
A few months, I should think, if we're careful. And I've still got those few hours at the sweet shop.
Yes, but the store can't stay open, not with THAT going on in the street.
People still want their Turkish delight, I guess.
Not for long. The way prices are going up—forget it.
I'm going across the street to check on Mama, make sure she's okay. I'll try to find some bread on the way home.

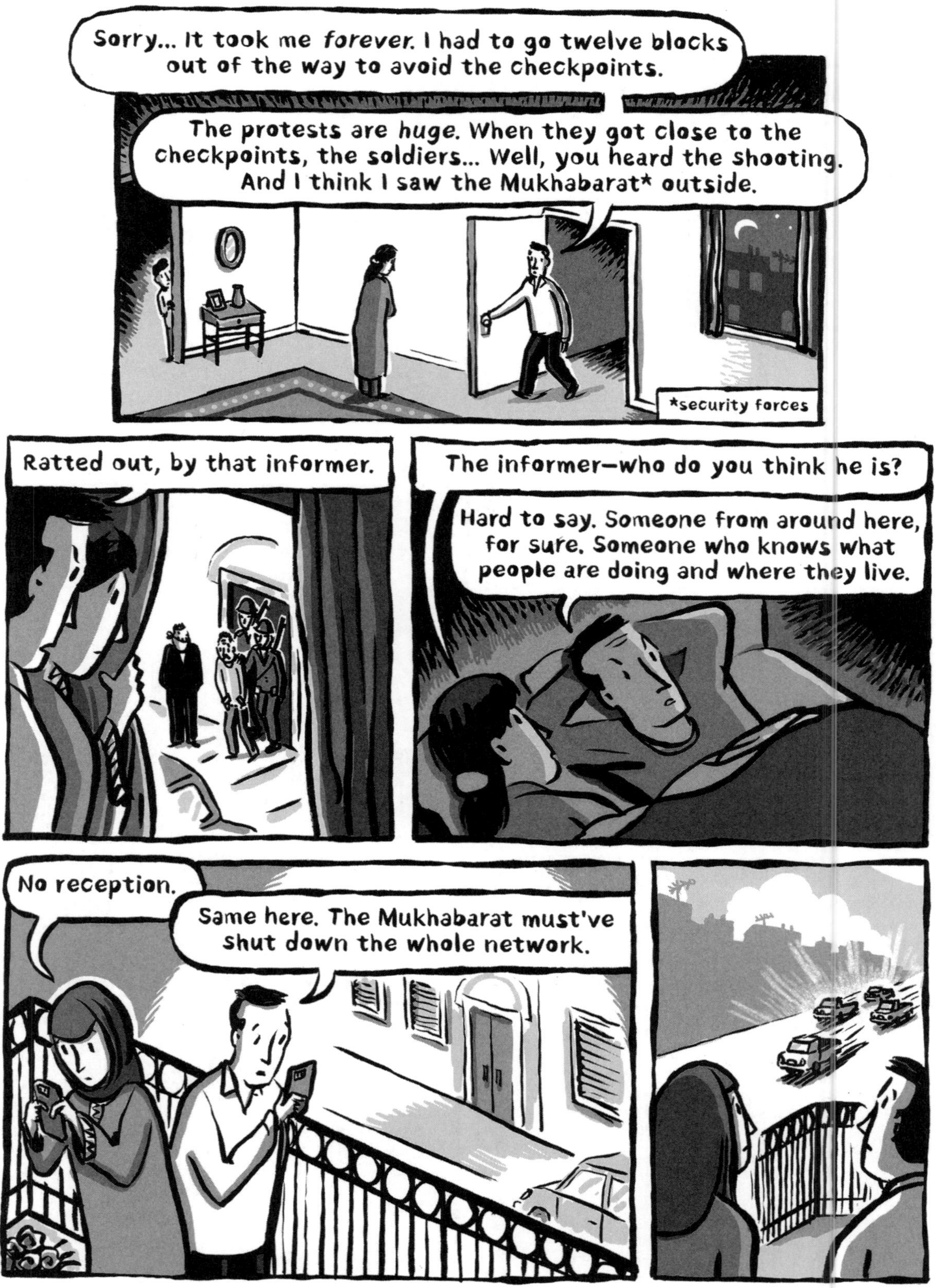
Sorry... It took me *forever.* I had to go twelve blocks out of the way to avoid the checkpoints.
The protests are *huge.* When they got close to the checkpoints, the soldiers... Well, you heard the shooting. And I think I saw the Mukhabarat* outside.
*security forces
Ratted out, by that informer.
The informer—who do you think he is?
Hard to say. Someone from around here, for sure. Someone who knows what people are doing and where they live.
No reception.
Same here. The Mukhabarat must've shut down the whole network.

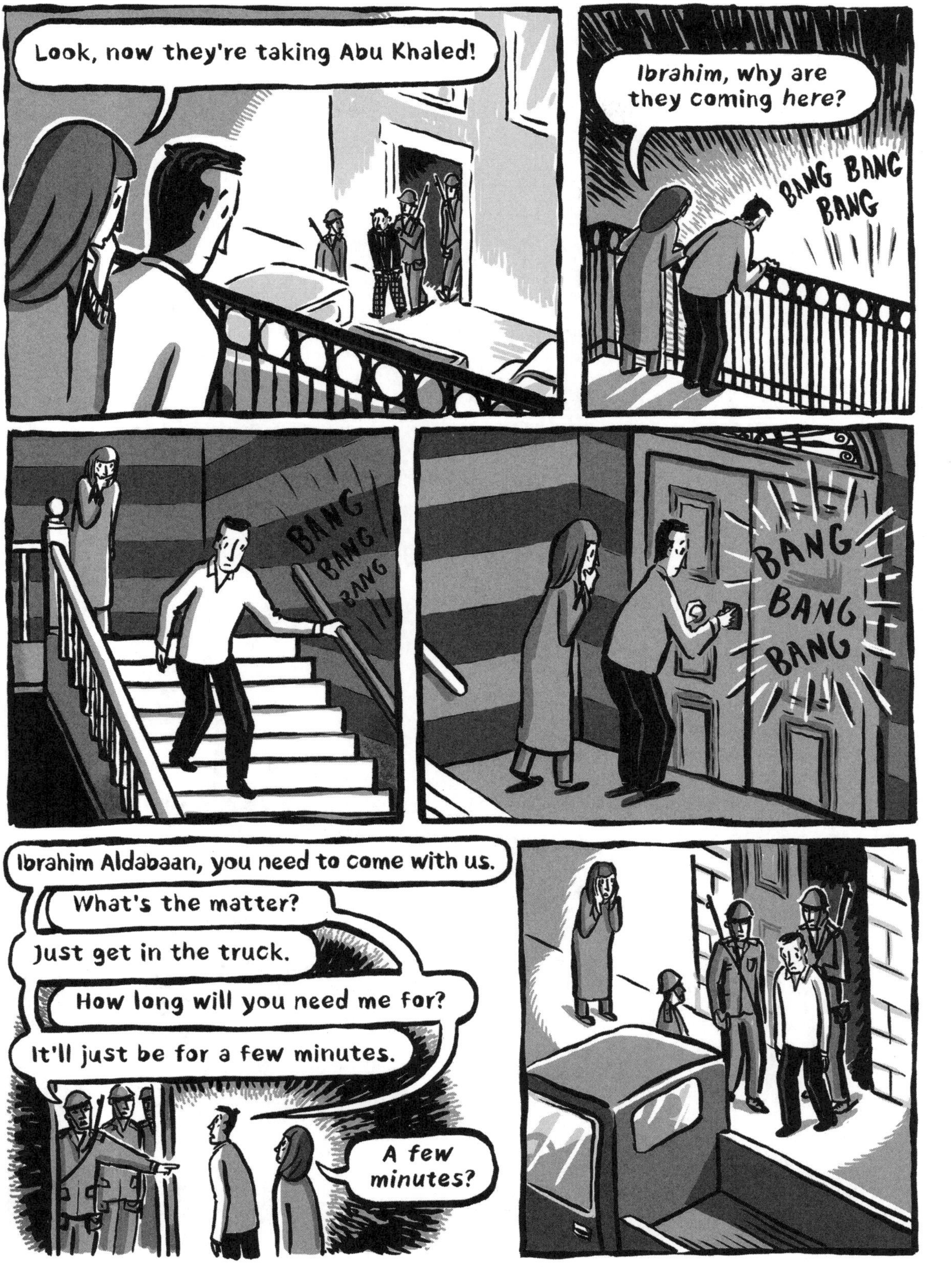
Look, now they're taking Abu Khaled!
Ibrahim, why are they coming here?
BANG BANG BANG
BANG BANG BANG
BANG BANG BANG
Ibrahim Aldabaan, you need to come with us.
What's the matter?
Just get in the truck.
How long will you need me for?
It'll just be for a few minutes.
A few minutes?

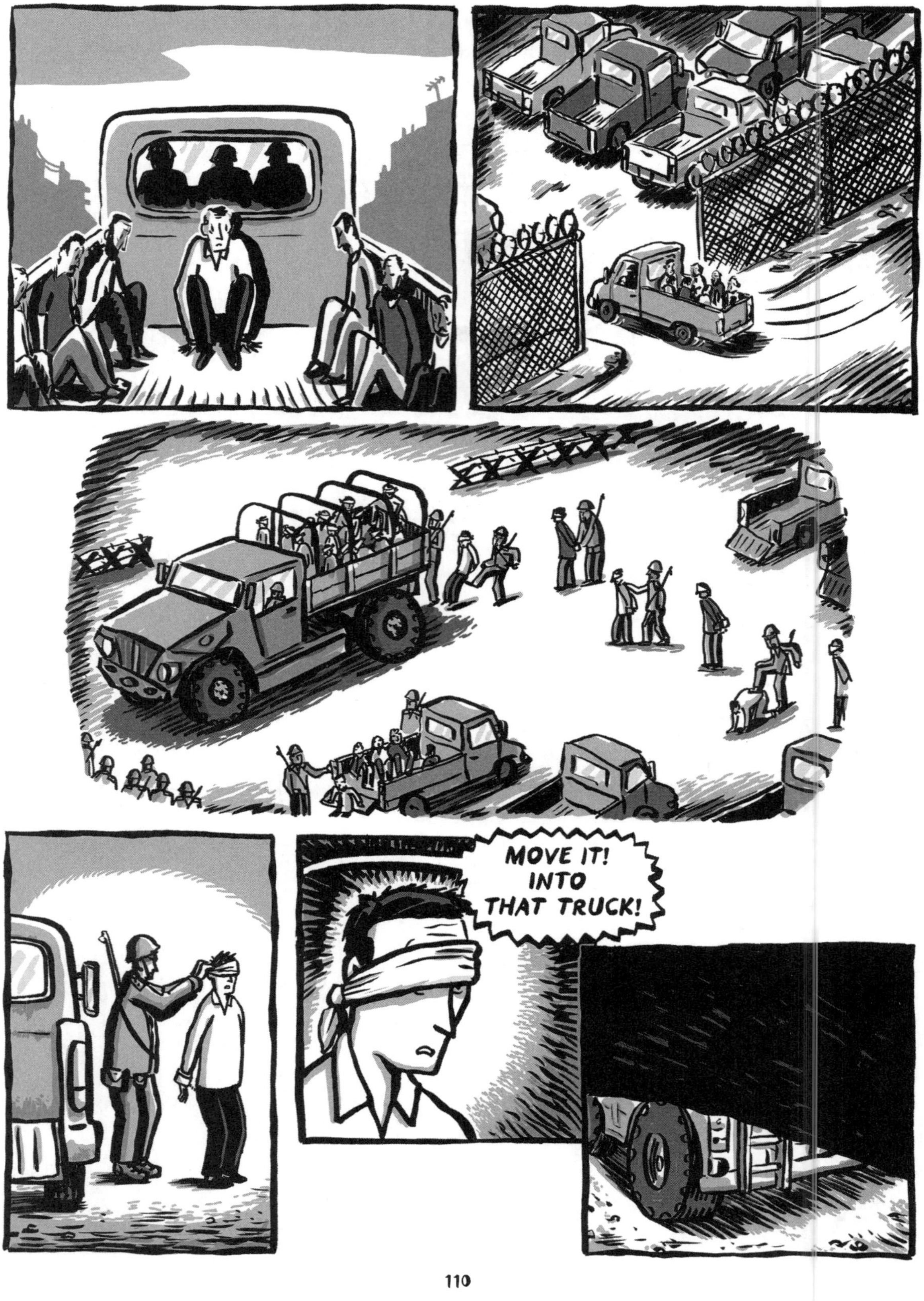
MOVE IT! INTO THAT TRUCK!

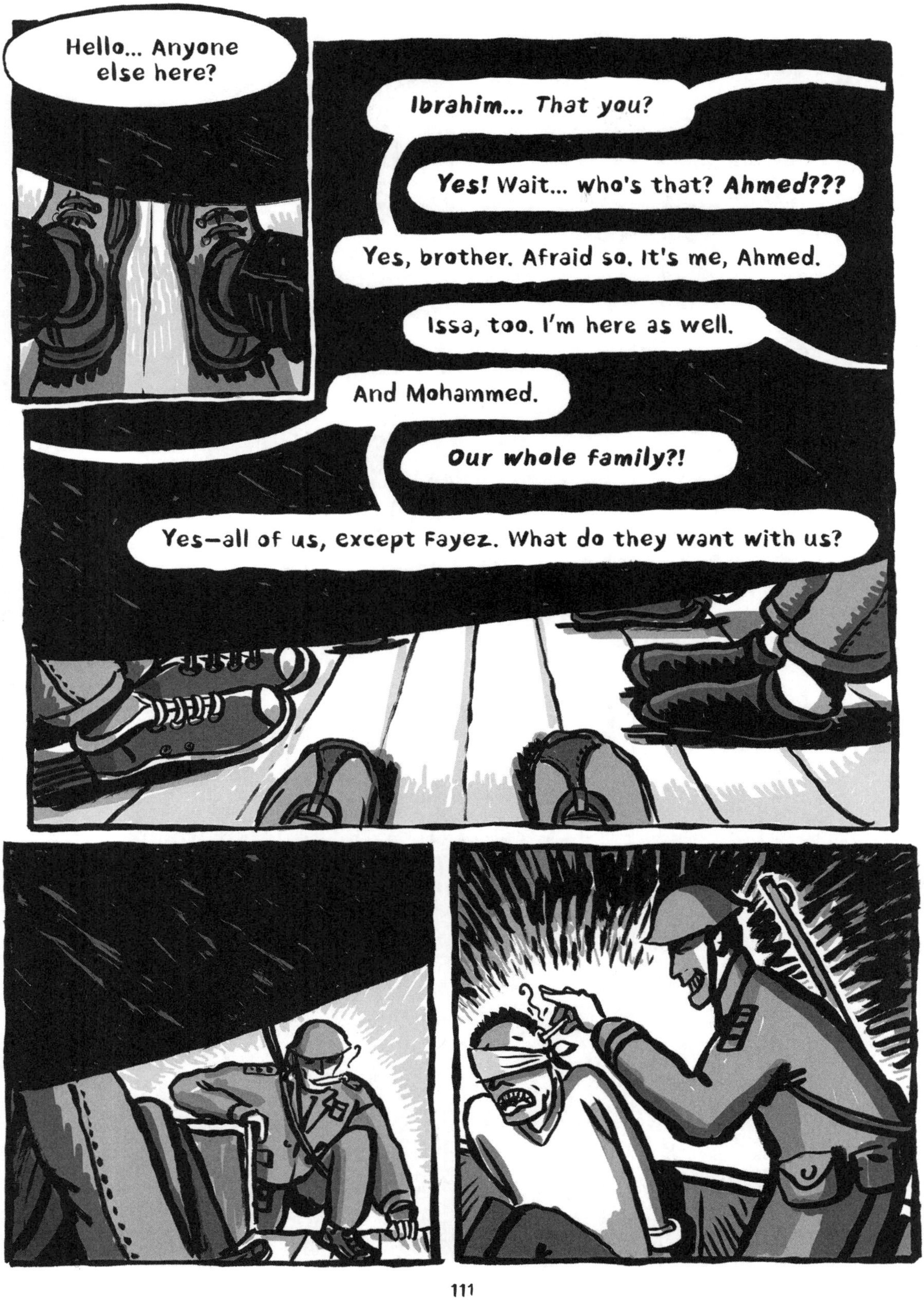
Hello... Anyone else here?
Ibrahim... That you?
Yes! Wait... who's that? Ahmed???
Yes, brother. Afraid so. It's me, Ahmed.
Issa, too. I'm here as well.
And Mohammed.
Our whole family?!
Yes—all of us, except Fayez. What do they want with us?

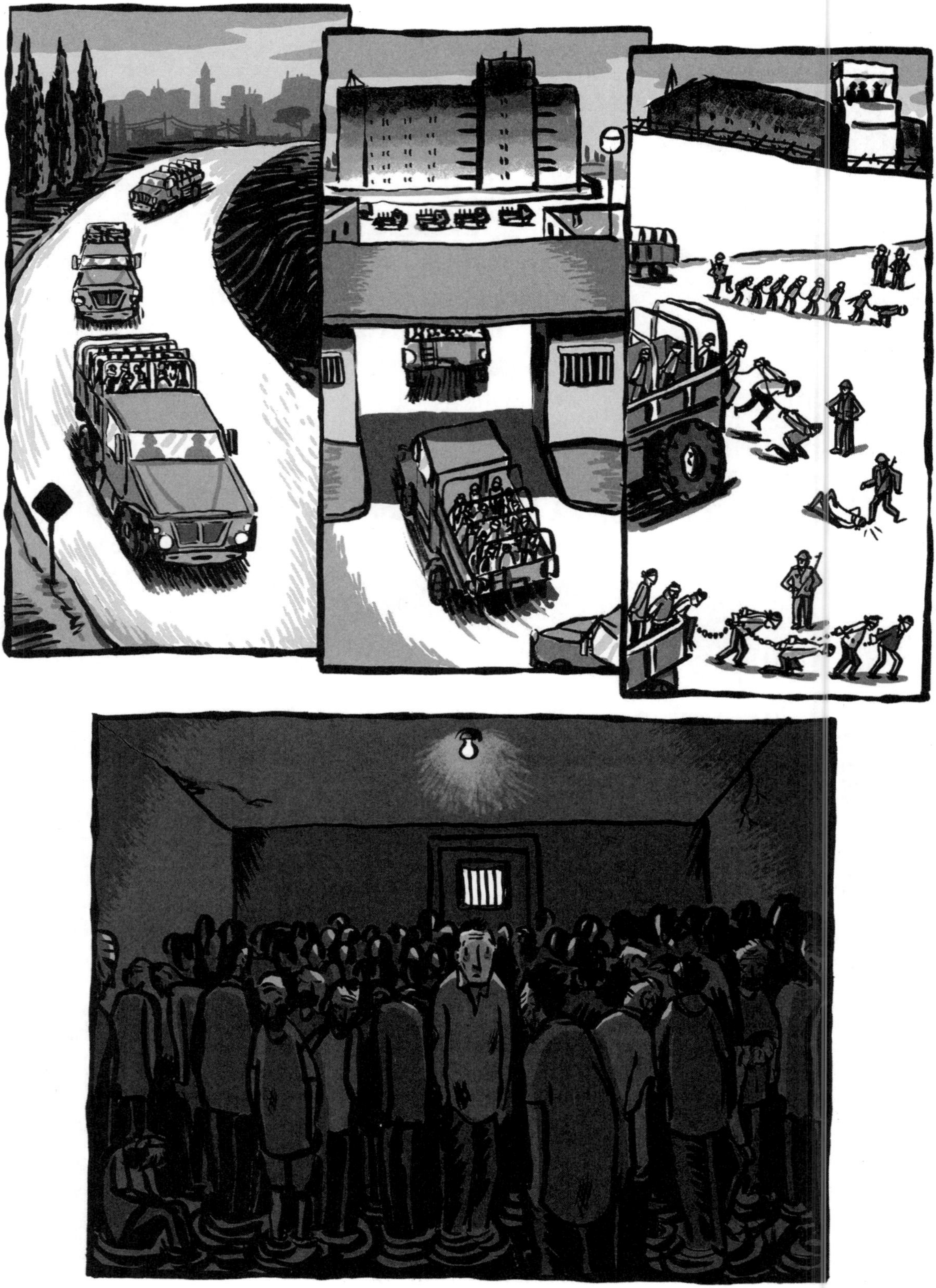

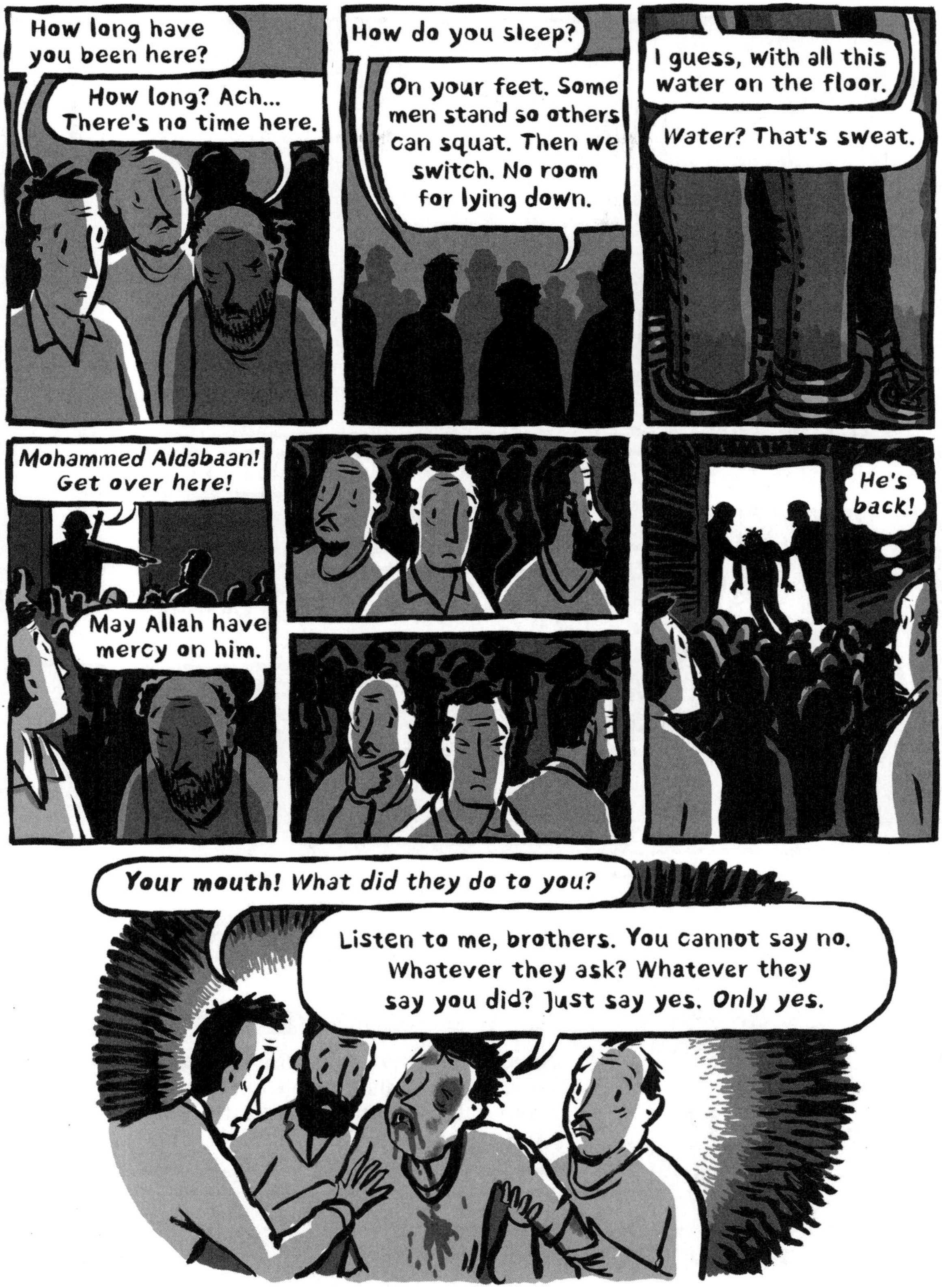
How long have you been here?
How long? Ach... There's no time here.
How do you sleep?
On your feet. Some men stand so others can squat. Then we switch. No room for lying down.
I guess, with all this water on the floor.
Water? That's sweat.
Mohammed Aldabaan! Get over here!
May Allah have mercy on him.
He's back!
Your mouth! What did they do to you?
Listen to me, brothers. You cannot say no. Whatever they ask? Whatever they say you did? Just say yes. Only yes.

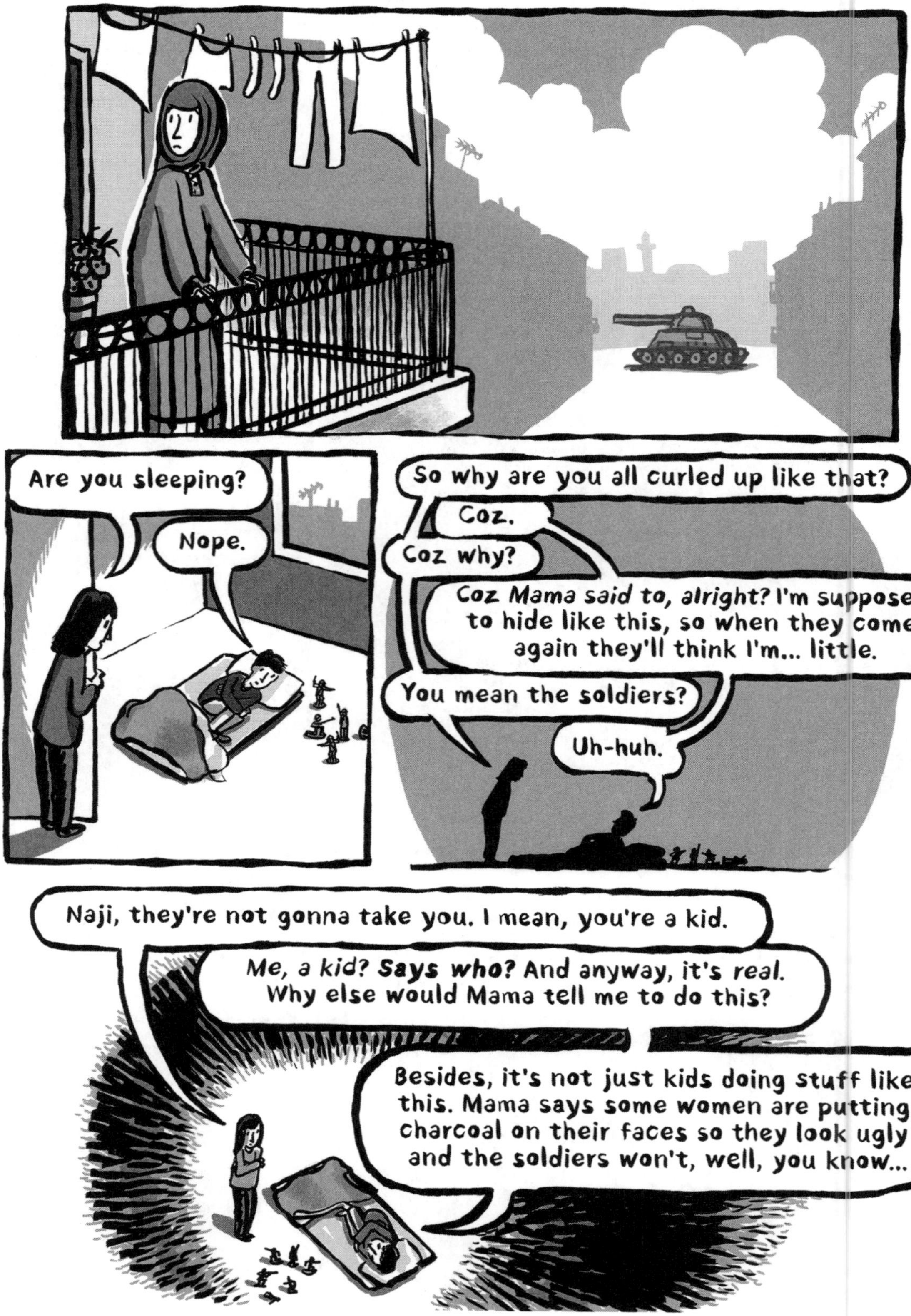

Are you sleeping?
Nope.
So why are you all curled up like that?
Coz.
Coz why?
Coz Mama said to, alright? I'm supposed to hide like this, so when they come again they'll think I'm... little.
You mean the soldiers?
Uh-huh.
Naji, they're not gonna take you. I mean, you're a kid.
Me, a kid? **Says who?** And anyway, it's *real*. Why else would Mama tell me to do this?
Besides, it's not just kids doing stuff like this. Mama says some women are putting charcoal on their faces so they look ugly and the soldiers won't, well, you know...

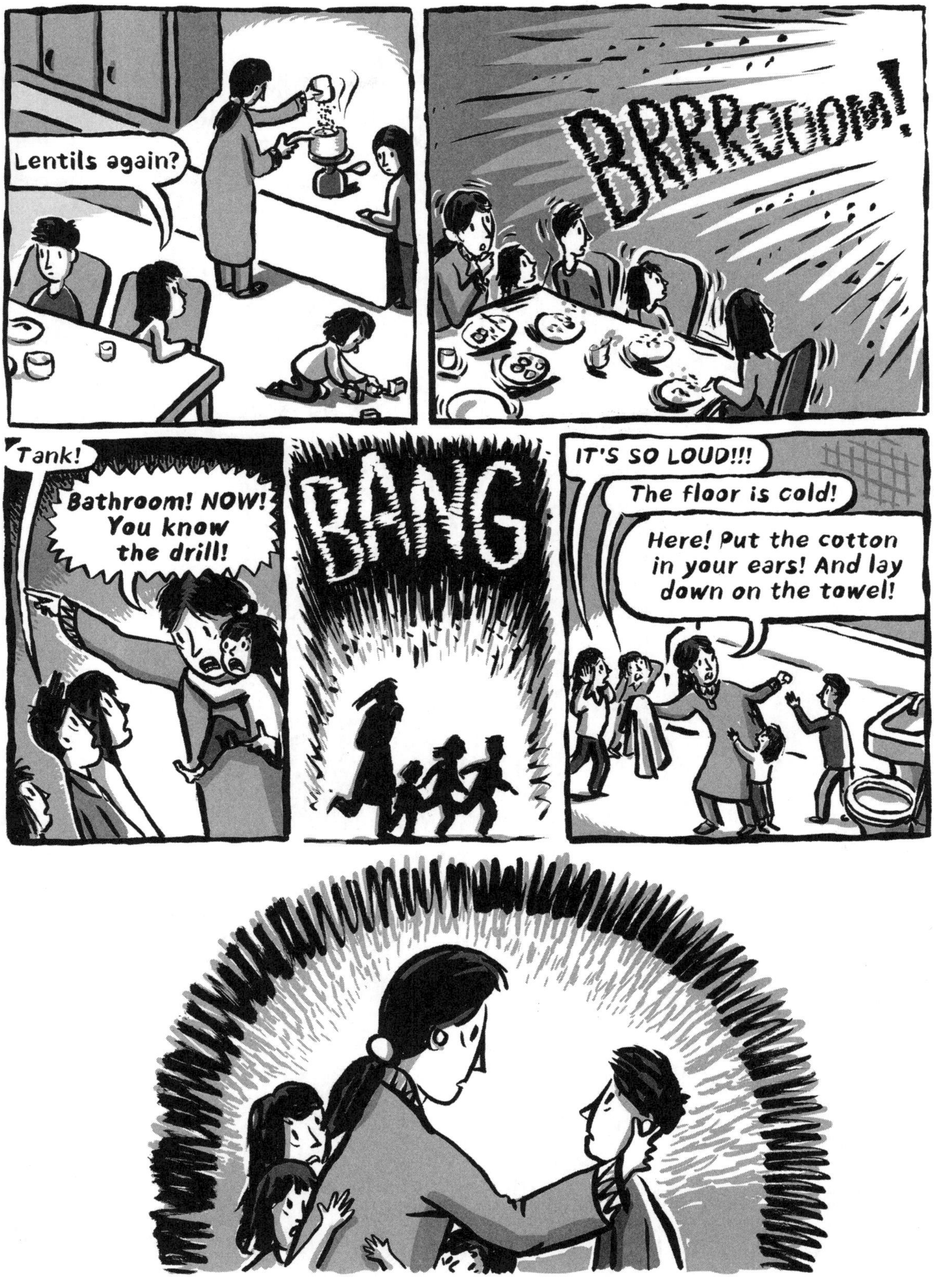
Lentils again?
BRRROOOM!
Tank!
Bathroom! NOW! You know the drill!
BANG
IT'S SO LOUD!!!
The floor is cold!
Here! Put the cotton in your ears! And lay down on the towel!

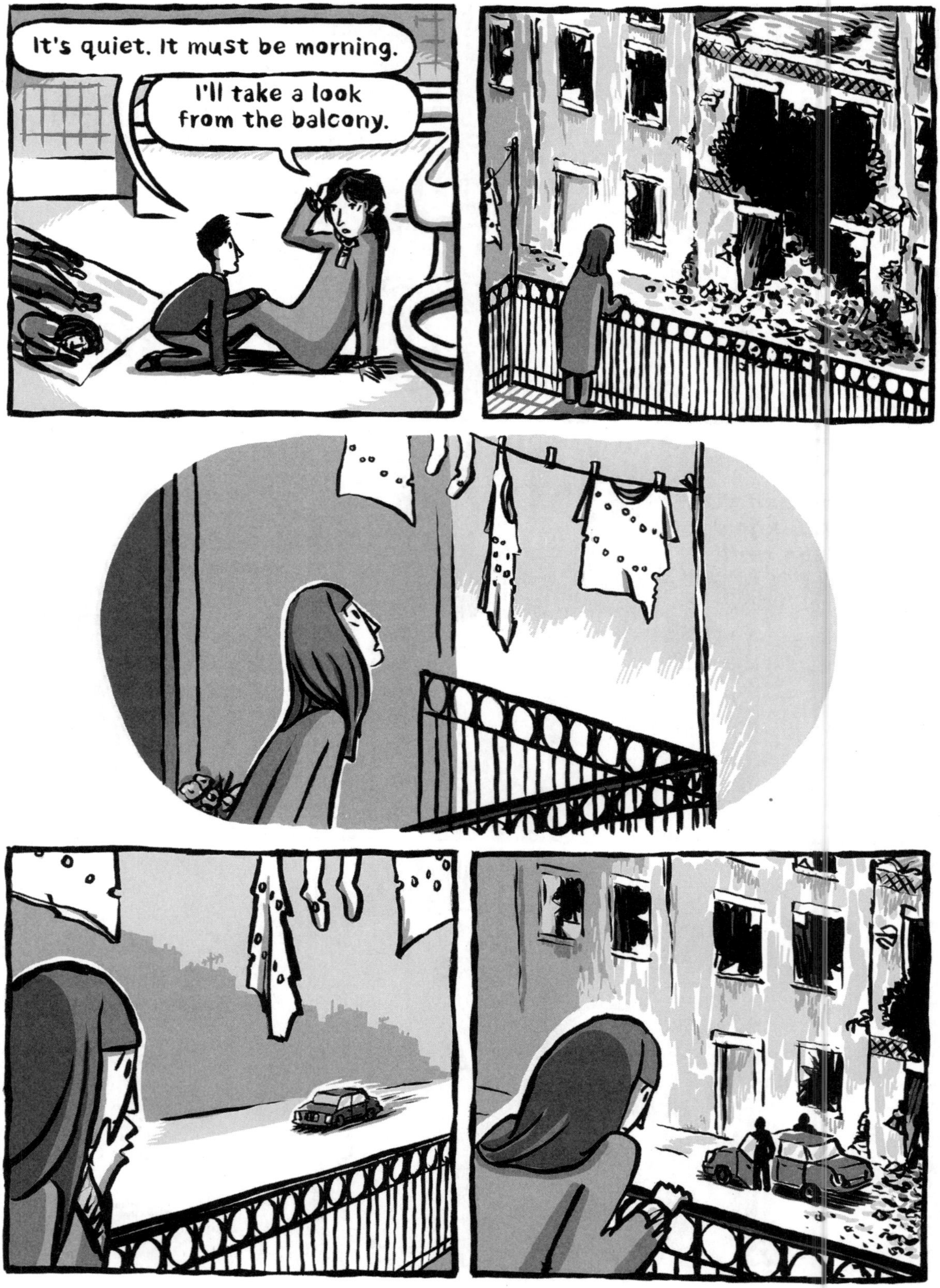
It's quiet. It must be morning.
I'll take a look from the balcony.

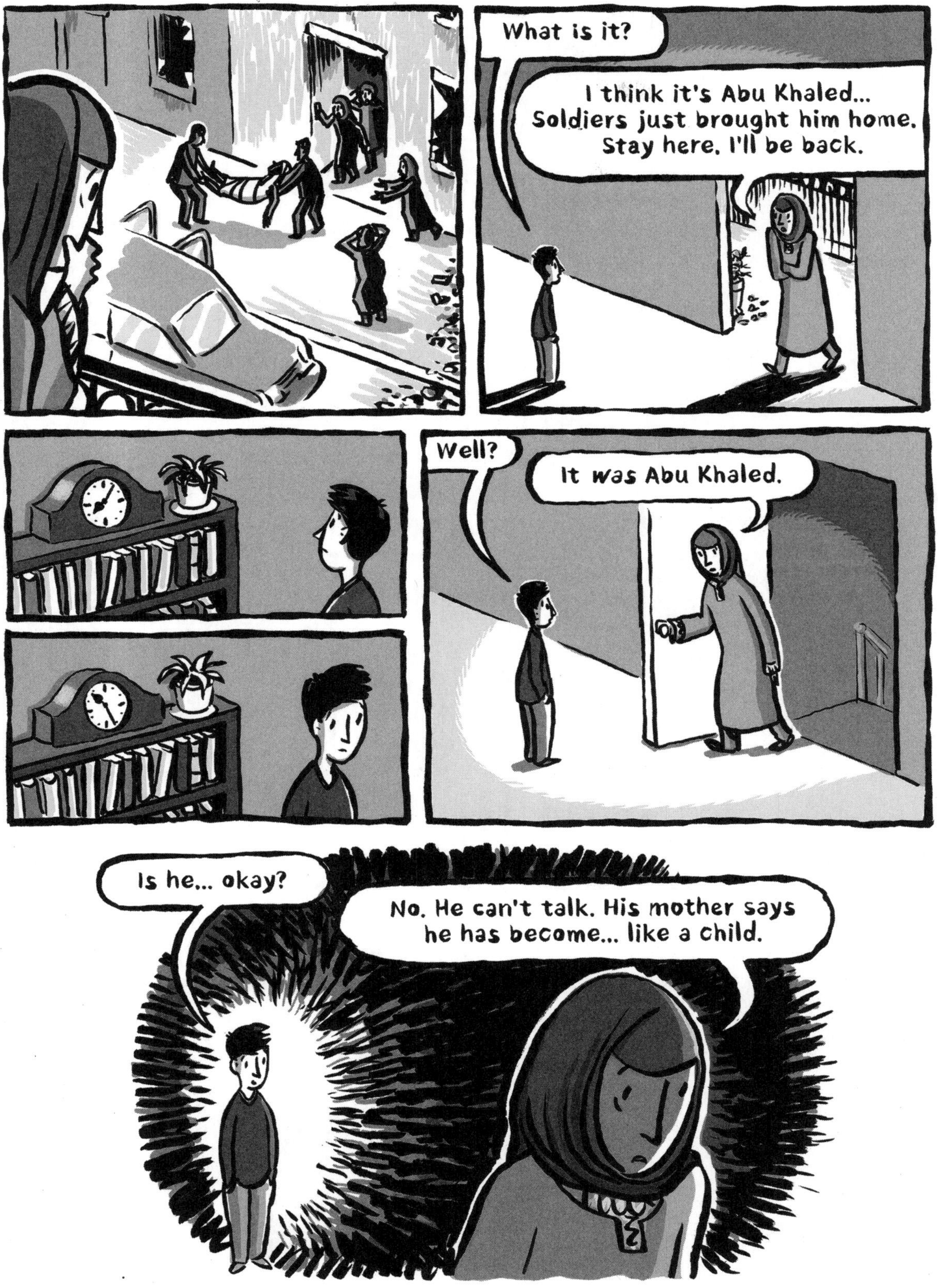
What is it?
I think it's Abu Khaled... Soldiers just brought him home. Stay here. I'll be back.
Well?
It was Abu Khaled.
Is he... okay?
No. He can't talk. His mother says he has become... like a child.

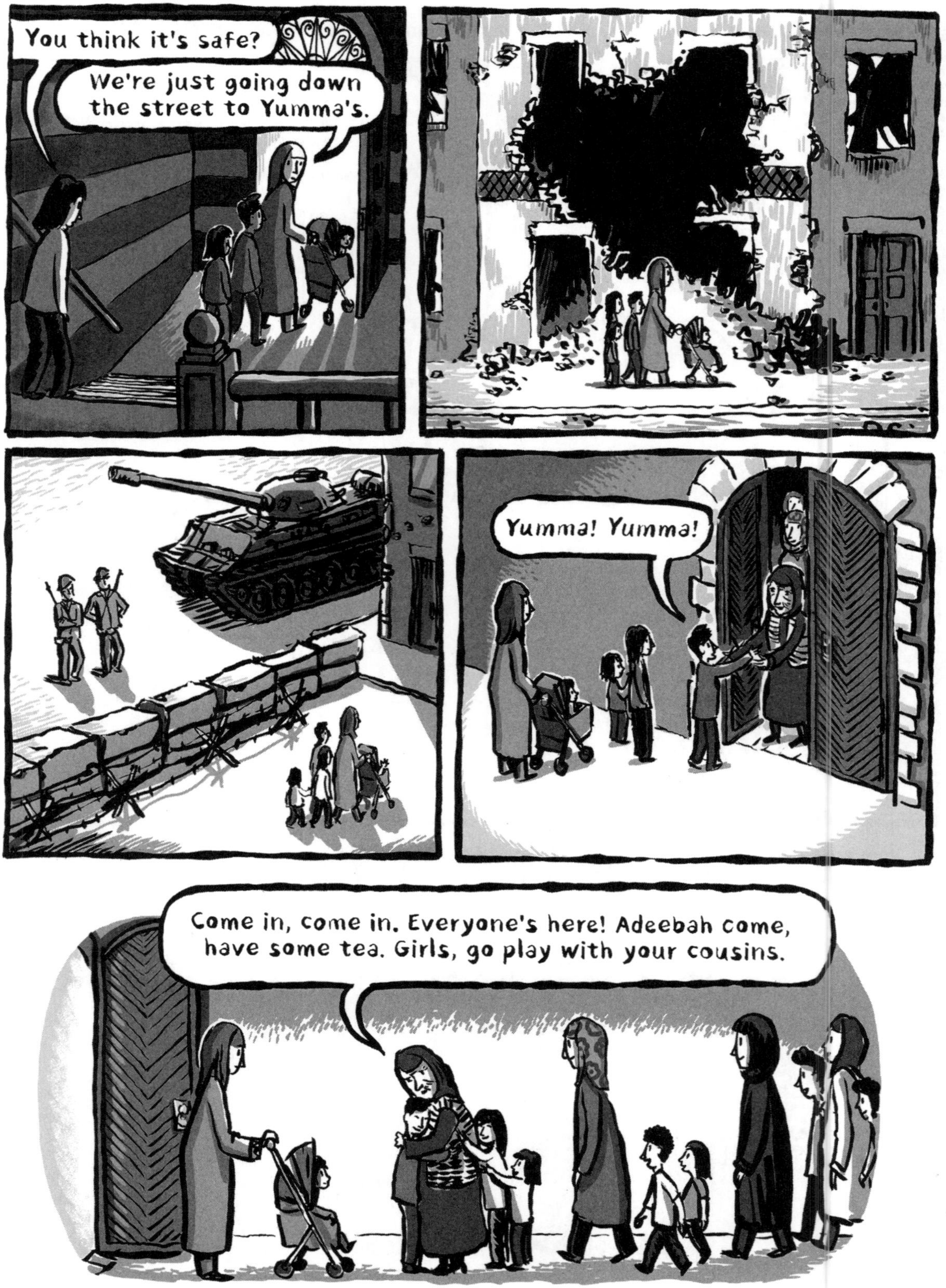
You think it's safe?
We're just going down the street to Yumma's.
Yumma! Yumma!
Come in, come in. Everyone's here! Adeebah come, have some tea. Girls, go play with your cousins.

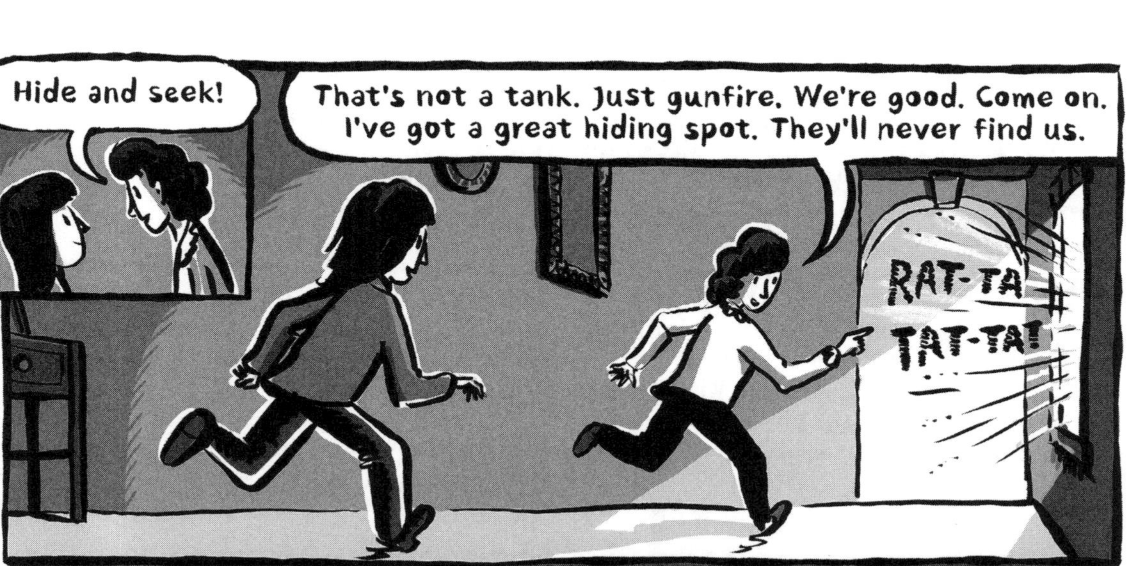
Hide and seek!
That's not a tank. Just gunfire. We're good. Come on. I've got a great hiding spot. They'll never find us.
RAT-TA TAT-TAT

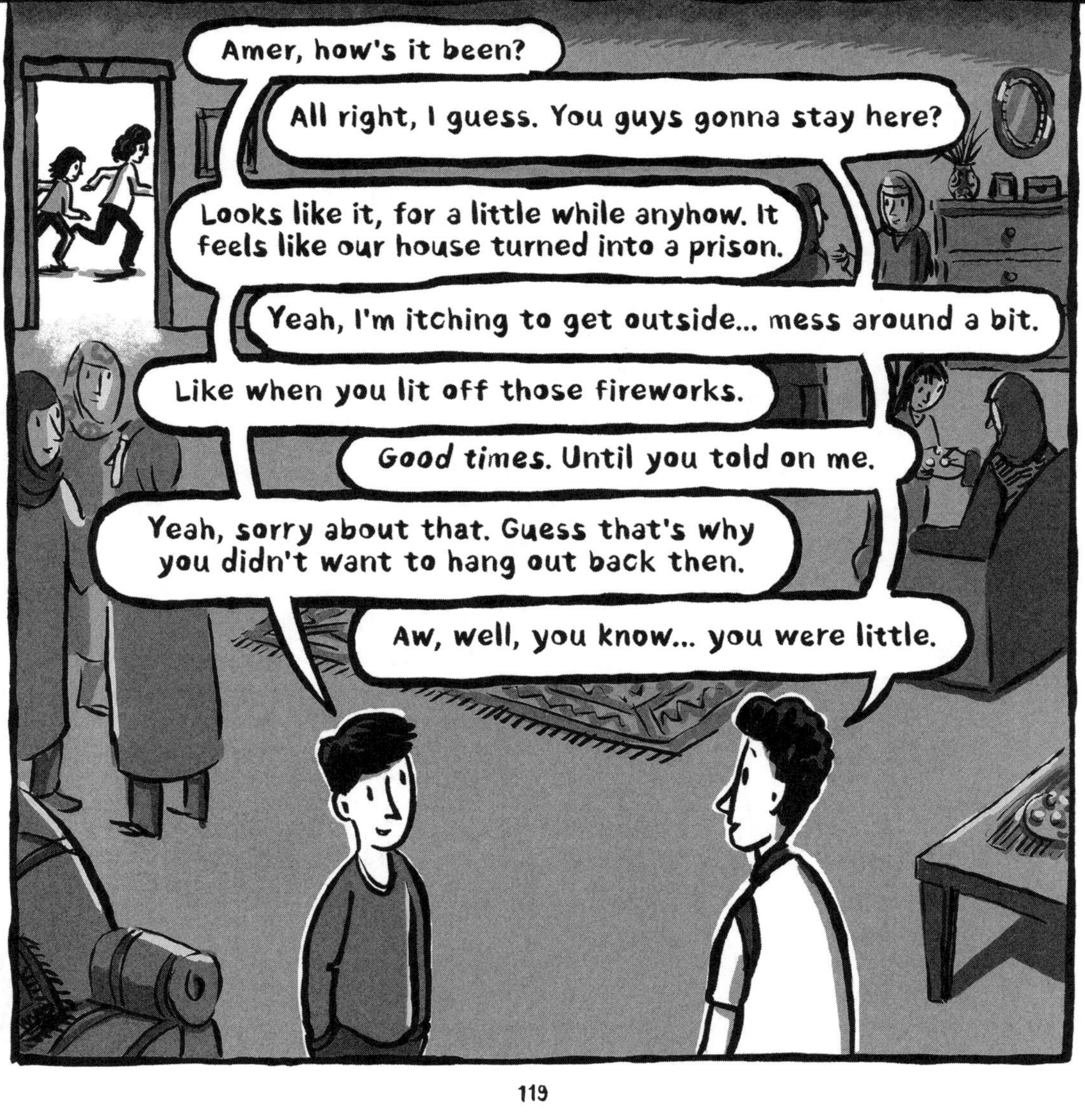
Amer, how's it been?
All right, I guess. You guys gonna stay here?
Looks like it, for a little while anyhow. It feels like our house turned into a prison.
Yeah, I'm itching to get outside... mess around a bit.
Like when you lit off those fireworks.
Good times. Until you told on me.
Yeah, sorry about that. Guess that's why you didn't want to hang out back then.
Aw, well, you know... you were little.

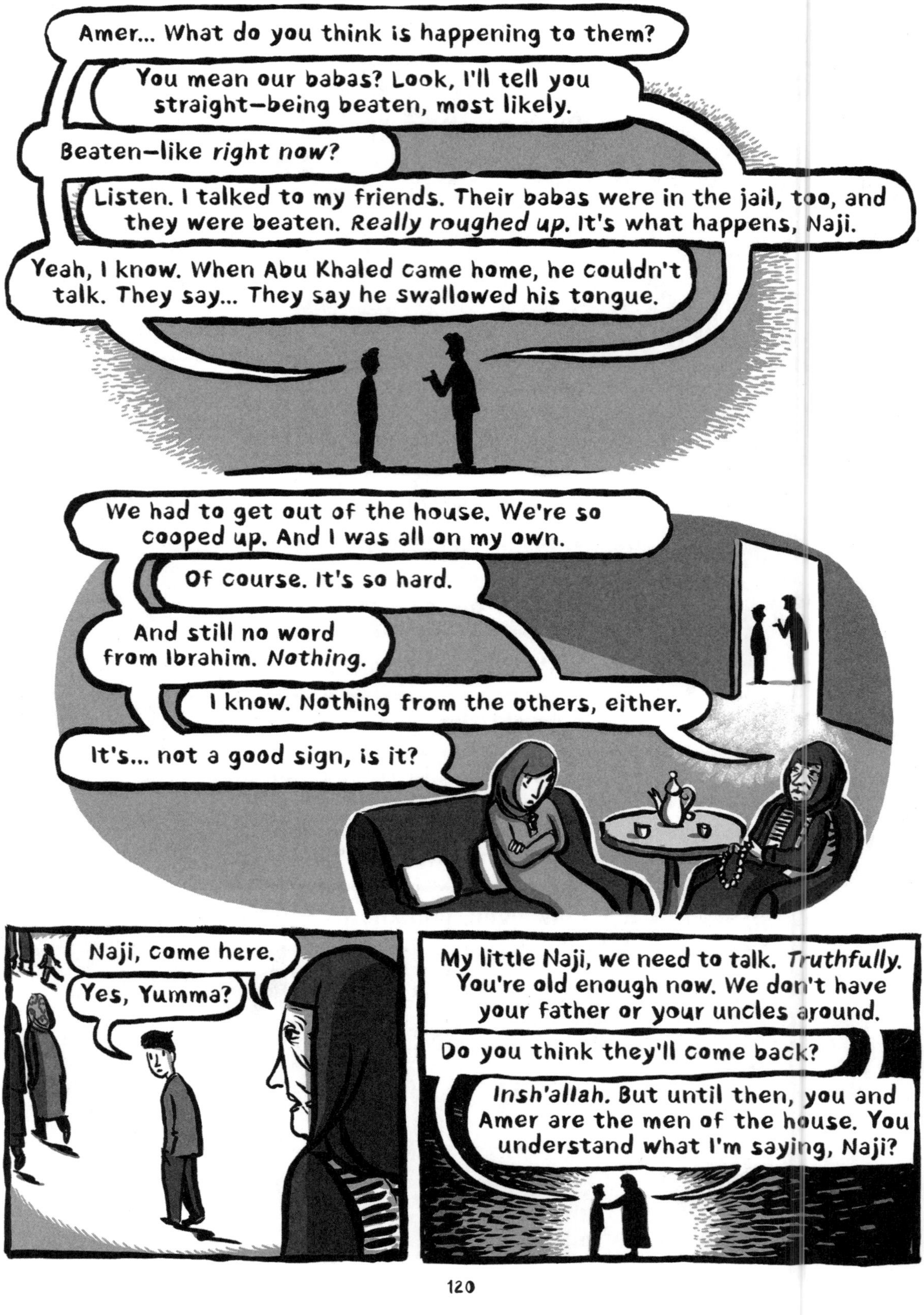
Amer... What do you think is happening to them?
You mean our babas? Look, I'll tell you straight—being beaten, most likely.
Beaten—like right now?
Listen. I talked to my friends. Their babas were in the jail, too, and they were beaten. Really roughed up. It's what happens, Naji.
Yeah, I know. When Abu Khaled came home, he couldn't talk. They say... They say he swallowed his tongue.
We had to get out of the house. We're so cooped up. And I was all on my own.
Of course. It's so hard.
And still no word from Ibrahim. Nothing.
I know. Nothing from the others, either.
It's... not a good sign, is it?
Naji, come here.
Yes, Yumma?
My little Naji, we need to talk. Truthfully. You're old enough now. We don't have your father or your uncles around.
Do you think they'll come back?
Insh'allah. But until then, you and Amer are the men of the house. You understand what I'm saying, Naji?

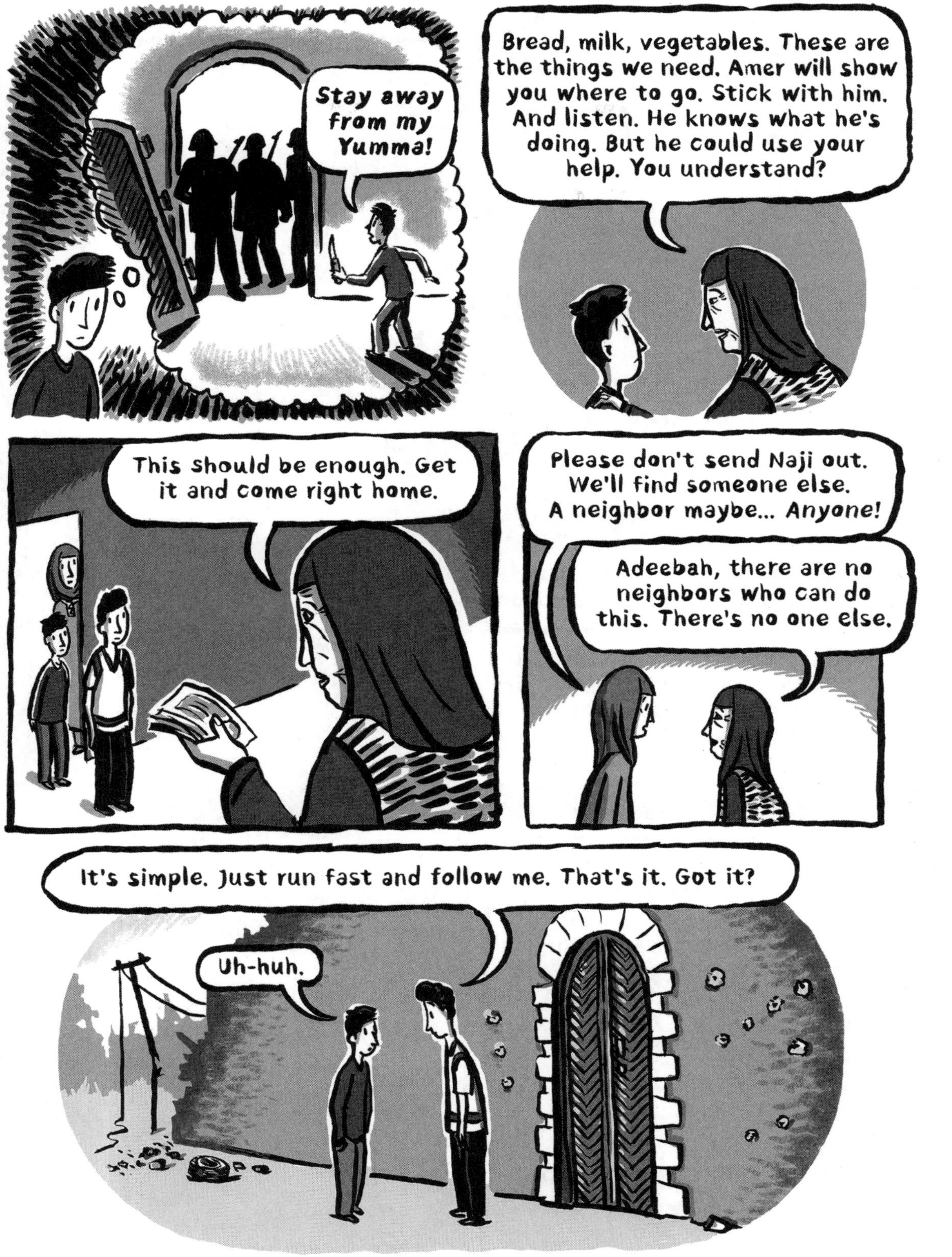

Stay away from my Yumma!
Bread, milk, vegetables. These are the things we need. Amer will show you where to go. Stick with him. And listen. He knows what he's doing. But he could use your help. You understand?
This should be enough. Get it and come right home.
Please don't send Naji out. We'll find someone else. A neighbor maybe... Anyone!
Adeebah, there are no neighbors who can do this. There's no one else.
It's simple. Just run fast and follow me. That's it. Got it?
Uh-huh.

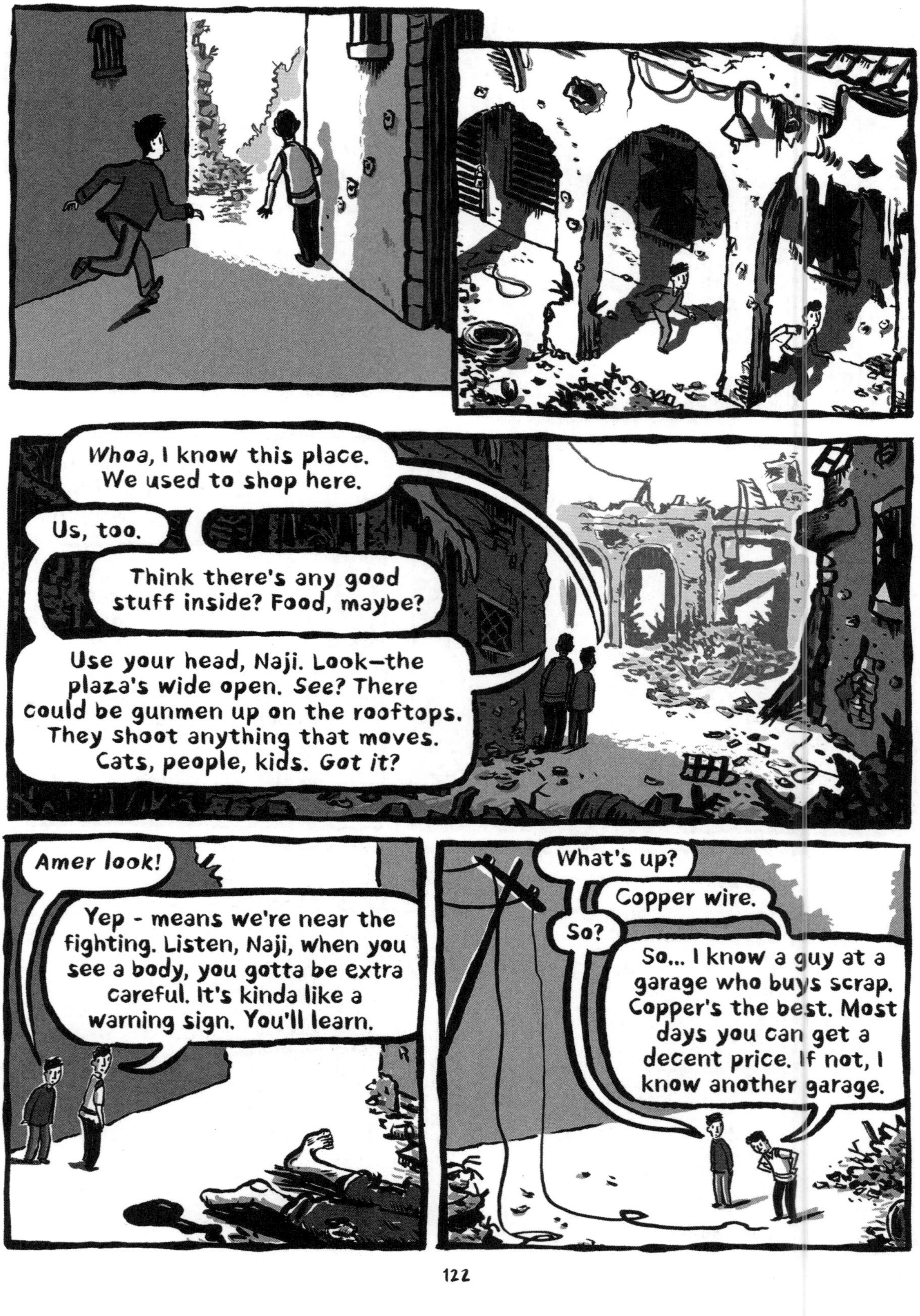

Whoa, I know this place. We used to shop here.
Us, too.
Think there's any good stuff inside? Food, maybe?
Use your head, Naji. Look—the plaza's wide open. See? There could be gunmen up on the rooftops. They shoot anything that moves. Cats, people, kids. Got it?
Amer look!
Yep - means we're near the fighting. Listen, Naji, when you see a body, you gotta be extra careful. It's kinda like a warning sign. You'll learn.
What's up?
Copper wire.
So?
So... I know a guy at a garage who buys scrap. Copper's the best. Most days you can get a decent price. If not, I know another garage.

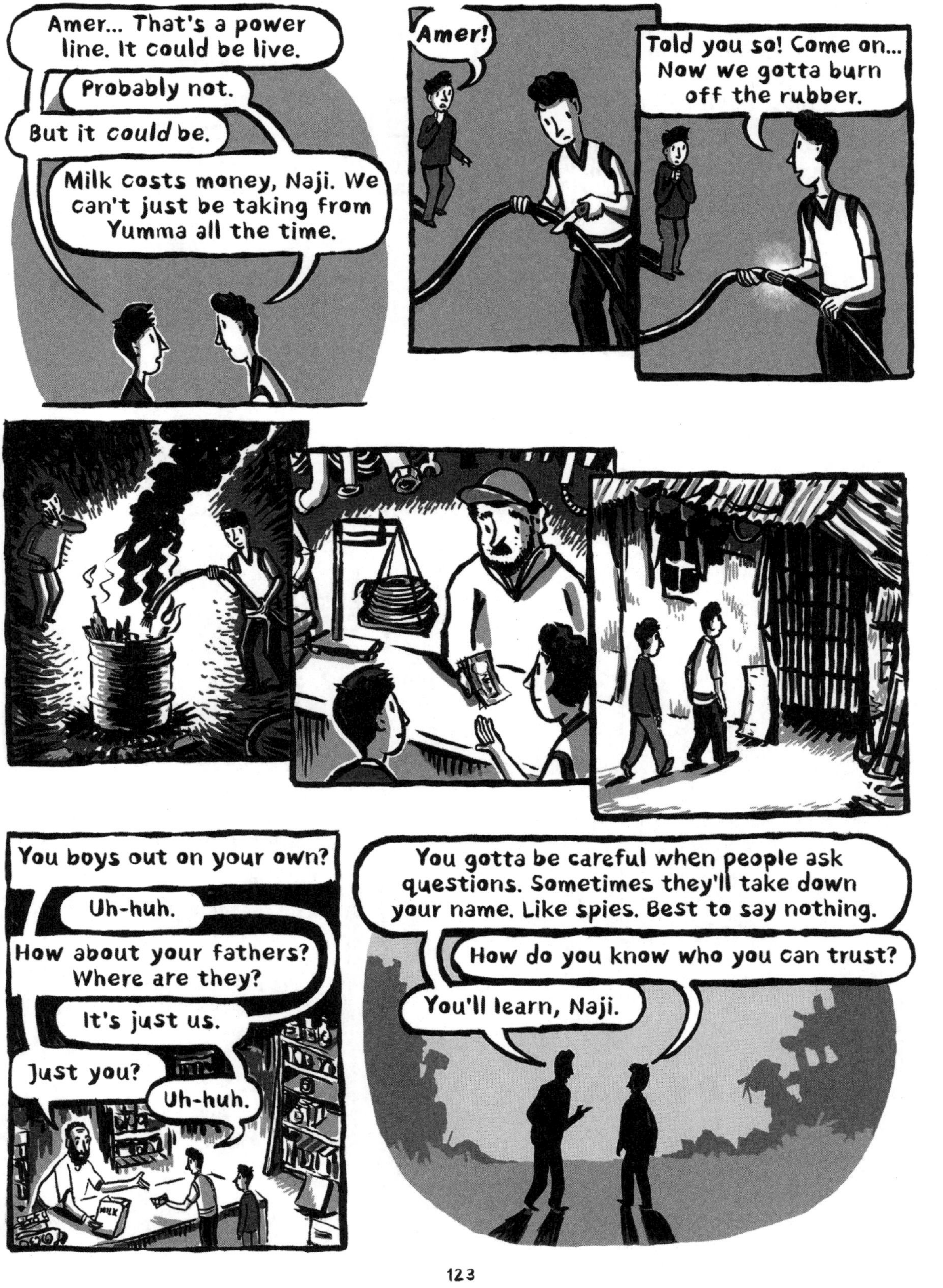

Amer... That's a power line. It could be live.
Probably not.
But it *could* be.
Milk costs money, Naji. We can't just be taking from Yumma all the time.
Amer!
Told you so! Come on... Now we gotta burn off the rubber.
You boys out on your own?
Uh-huh.
How about your fathers? Where are they?
It's just us.
Just you?
Uh-huh.
MILK
You gotta be careful when people ask questions. Sometimes they'll take down your name. Like spies. Best to say nothing.
How do you know who you can trust?
You'll learn, Naji.

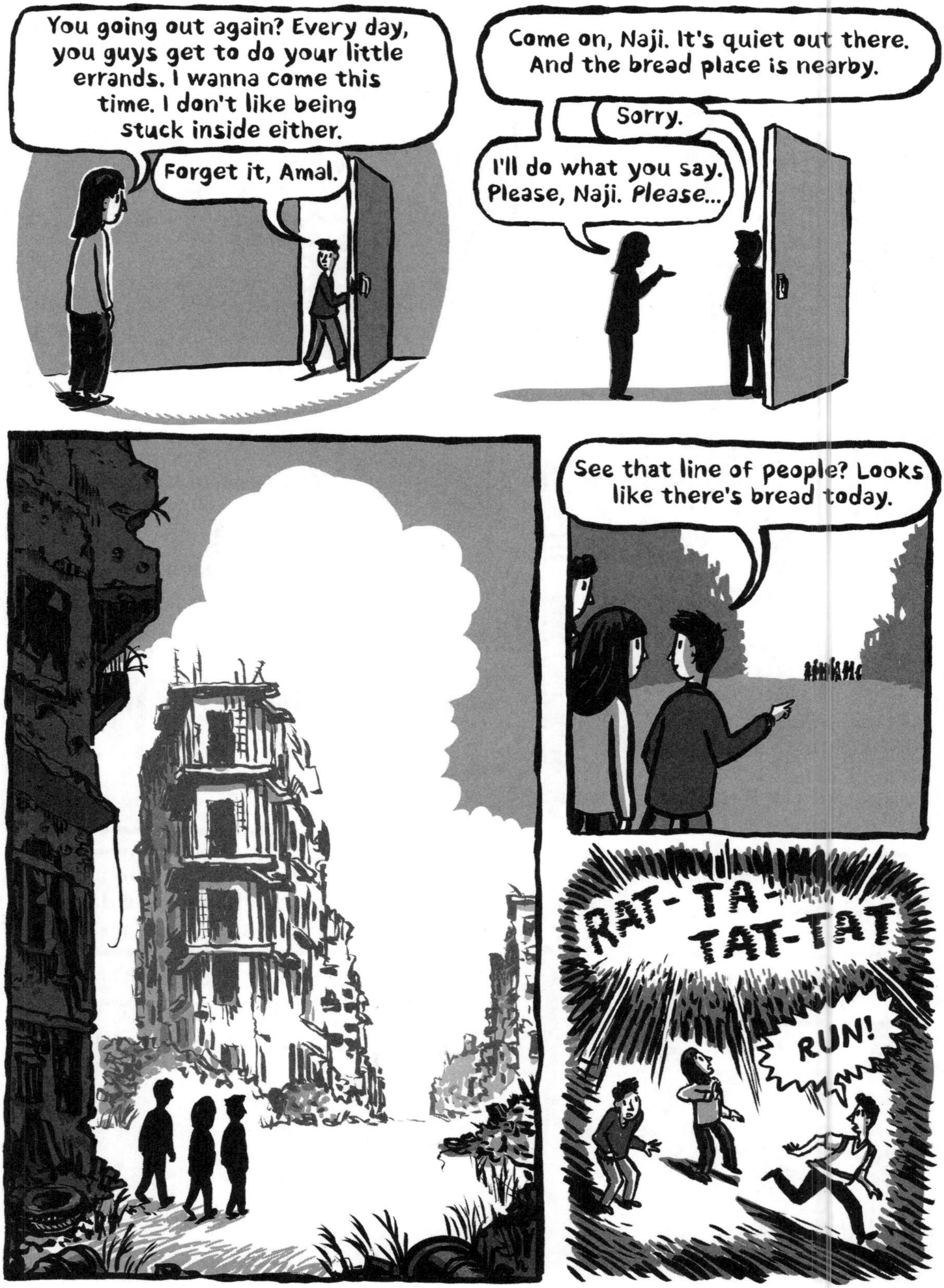
You going out again? Every day, you guys get to do your little errands. I wanna come this time. I don't like being stuck inside either.
Forget it, Amal.
Come on, Naji. It's quiet out there. And the bread place is nearby.
Sorry.
I'll do what you say. Please, Naji. *Please*...
See that line of people? Looks like there's bread today.
RAT-TA-TAT-TAT
RUN!

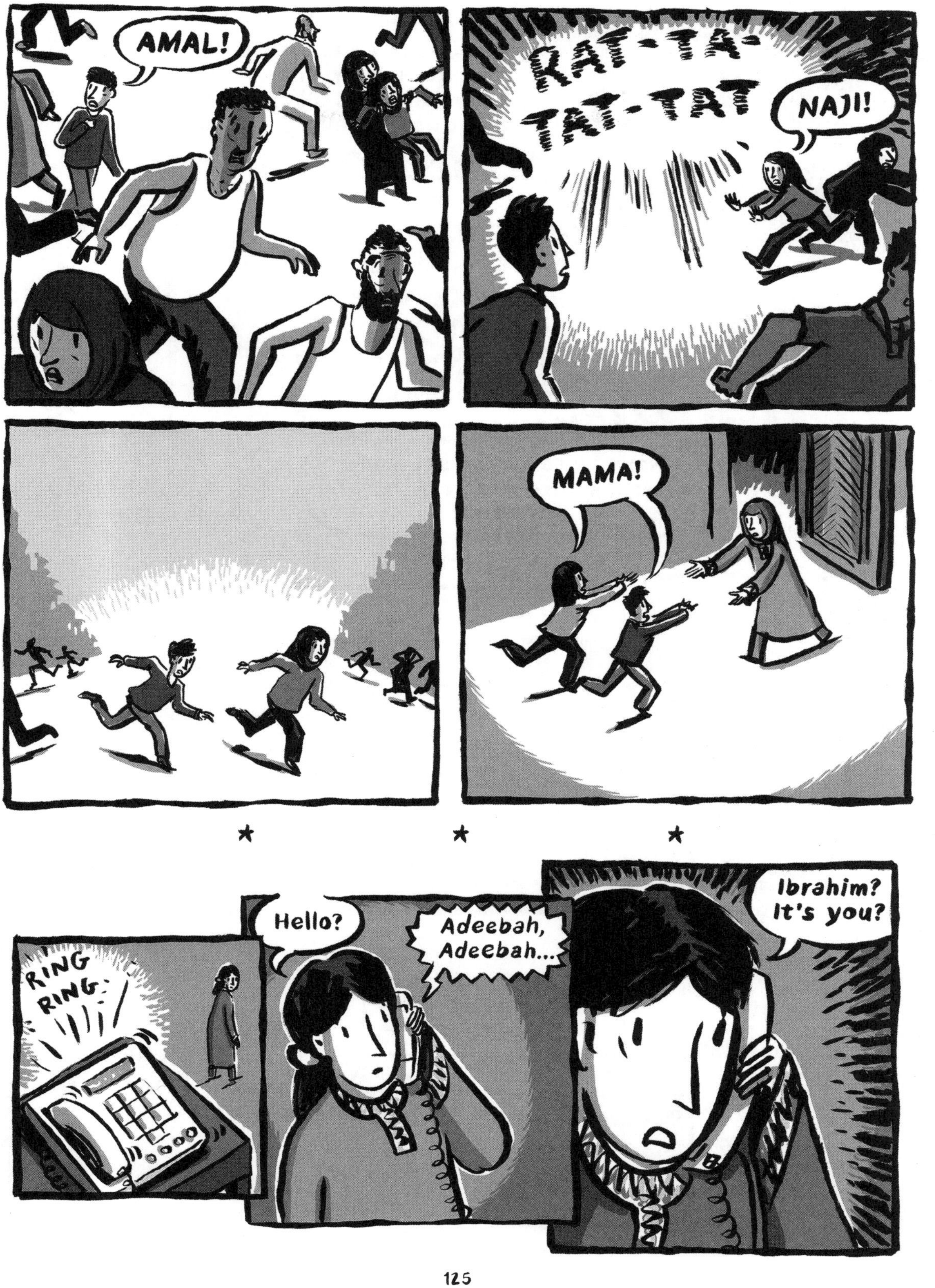
AMAL!
RAT-TA-TAT-TAT
NAJI!
MAMA!
* * *
RING RING
Hello?
Adeebah, Adeebah...
Ibrahim? It's you?

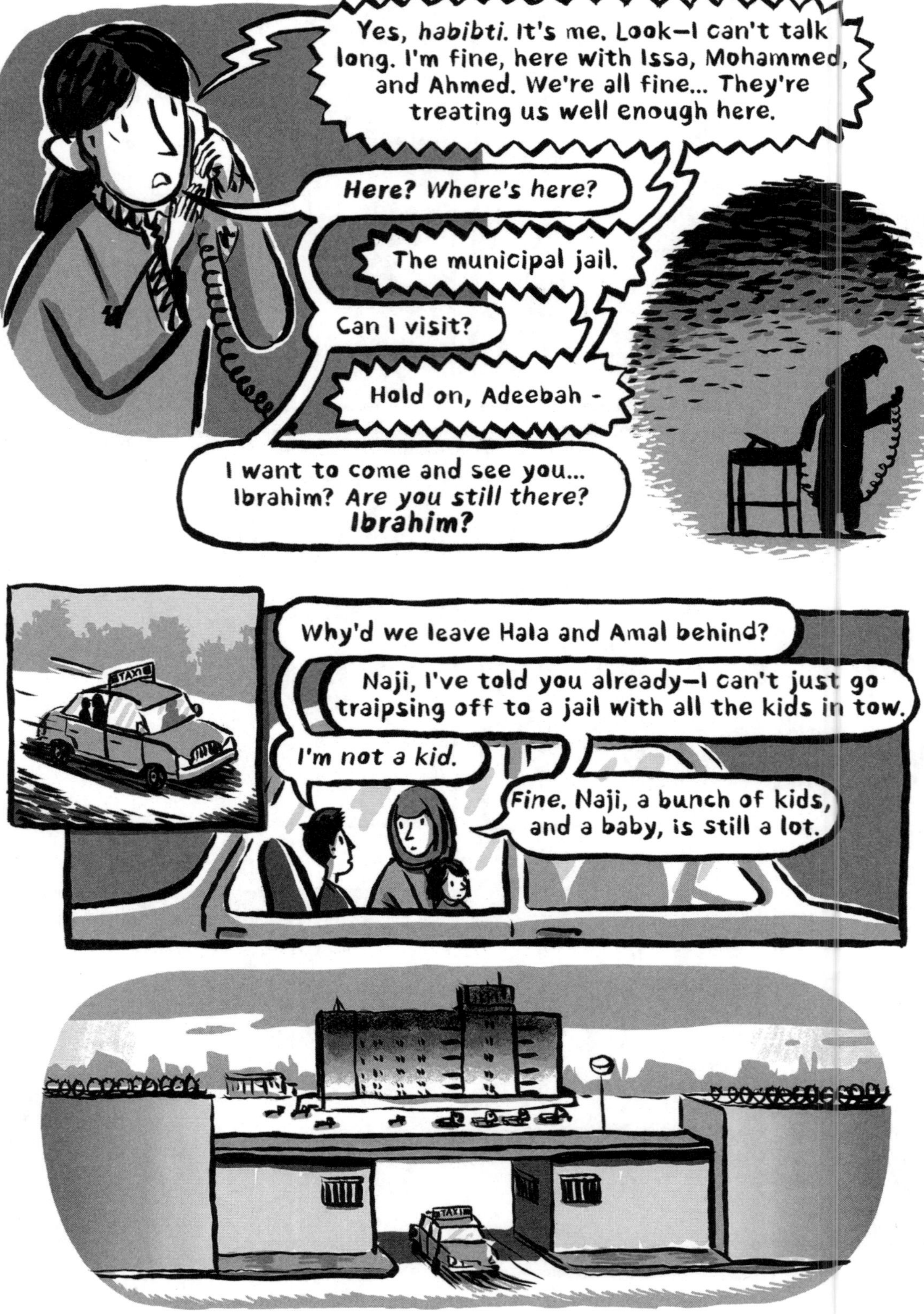
Yes, *habibti.* It's me. Look—I can't talk long. I'm fine, here with Issa, Mohammed, and Ahmed. We're all fine... They're treating us well enough here.
Here? Where's here?
The municipal jail.
Can I visit?
Hold on, Adeebah -
I want to come and see you... Ibrahim? *Are you still there?* **Ibrahim?**
Why'd we leave Hala and Amal behind?
Naji, I've told you already—I can't just go traipsing off to a jail with all the kids in tow.
I'm not a kid.
Fine. Naji, a bunch of kids, and a baby, is still a lot.

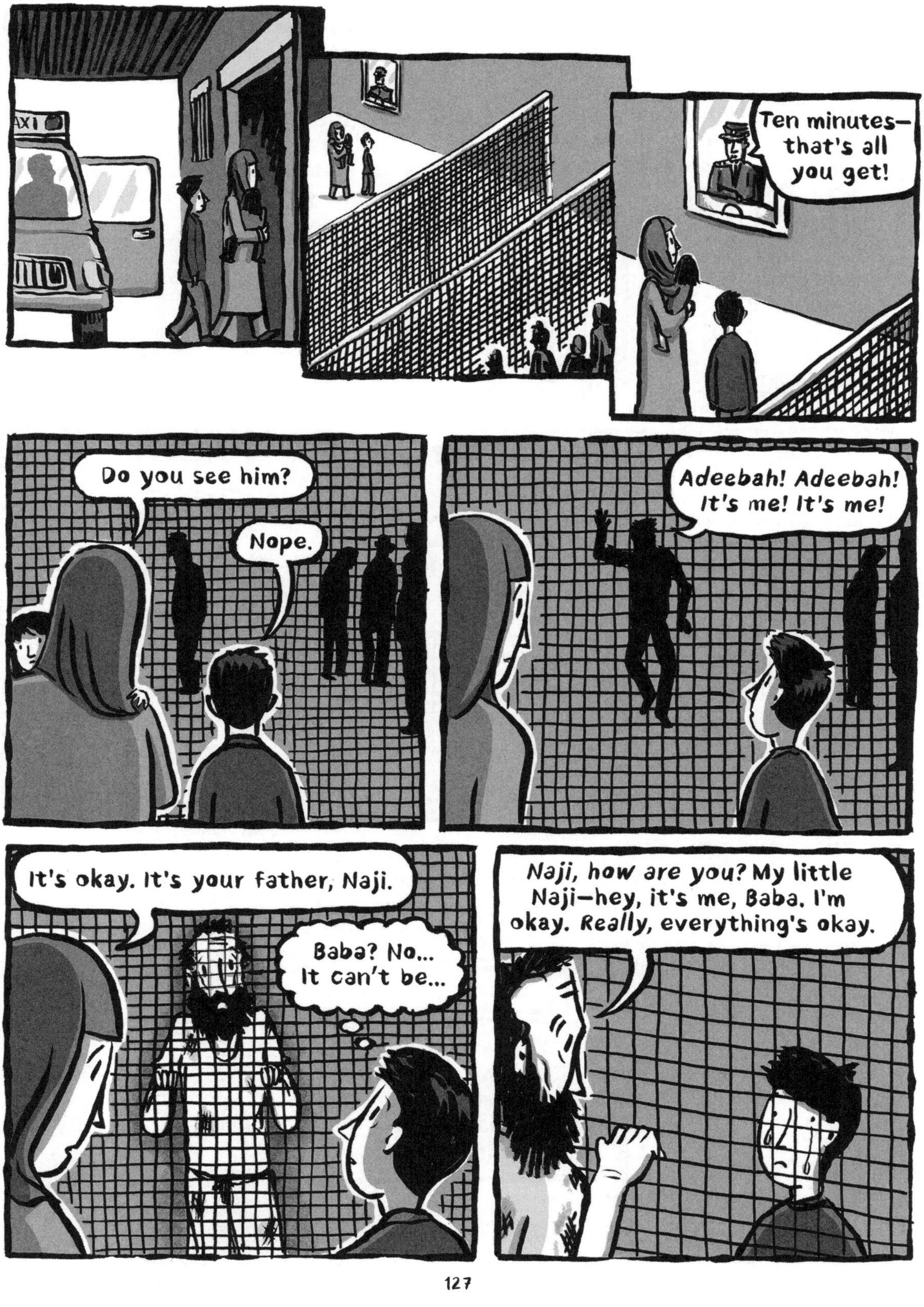

AXI
Ten minutes—that's all you get!
Do you see him?
Nope.
Adeebah! Adeebah! It's me! It's me!
It's okay. It's your father, Naji.
Baba? No... It can't be...
Naji, how are you? My little Naji—hey, it's me, Baba. I'm okay. Really, everything's okay.

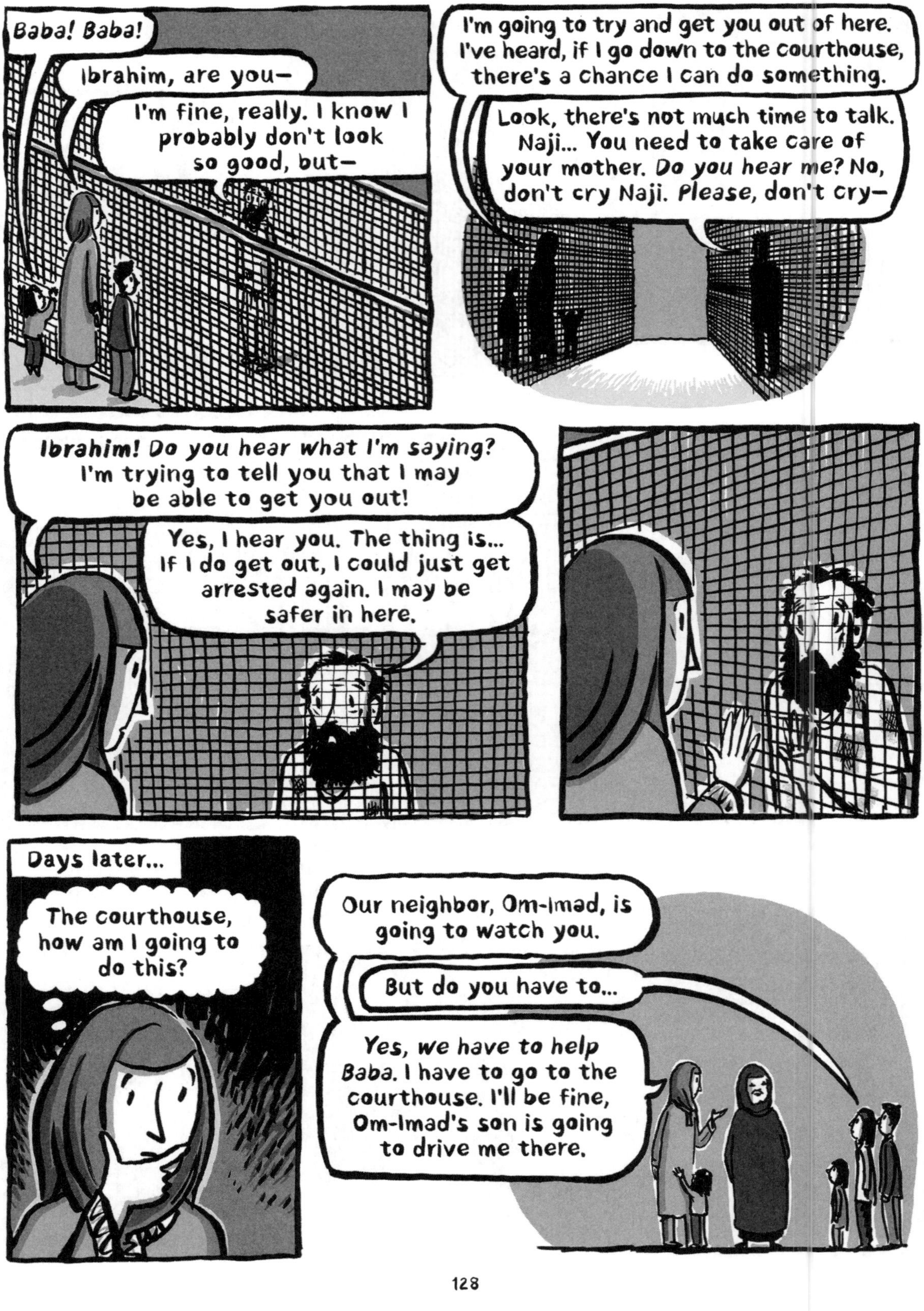
Baba! Baba!
Ibrahim, are you—
I'm fine, really. I know I probably don't look so good, but—
I'm going to try and get you out of here. I've heard, if I go down to the courthouse, there's a chance I can do something.
Look, there's not much time to talk. Naji... You need to take care of your mother. *Do you hear me?* No, don't cry Naji. *Please*, don't cry—
Ibrahim! Do you hear what I'm saying? I'm trying to tell you that I may be able to get you out!
Yes, I hear you. The thing is... If I do get out, I could just get arrested again. I may be safer in here.
Days later...
The courthouse, how am I going to do this?
Our neighbor, Om-Imad, is going to watch you.
But do you have to...
Yes, we have to help Baba. I have to go to the courthouse. I'll be fine, Om-Imad's son is going to drive me there.

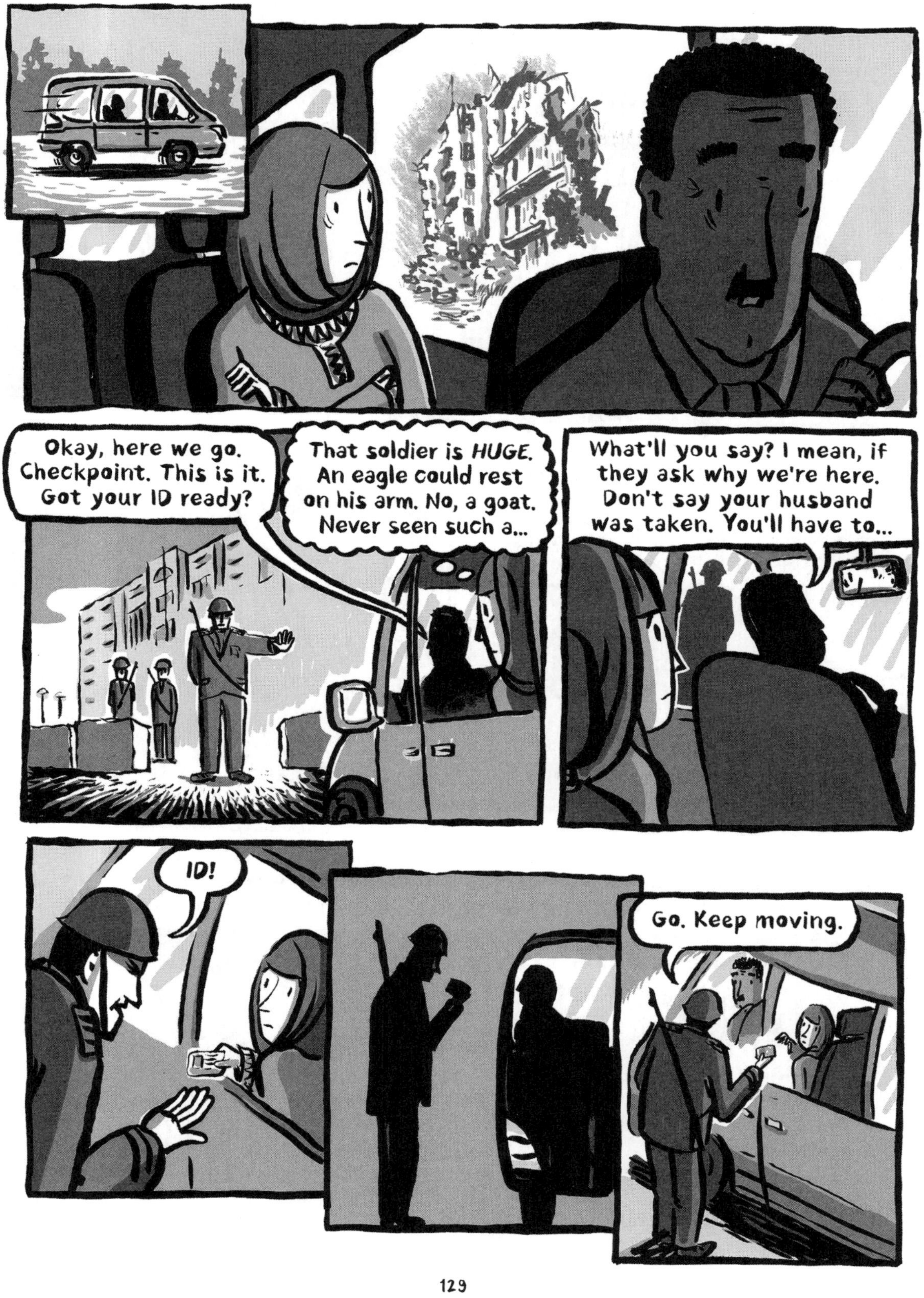
Okay, here we go. Checkpoint. This is it. Got your ID ready?
That soldier is *HUGE*. An eagle could rest on his arm. No, a goat. Never seen such a...
What'll you say? I mean, if they ask why we're here. Don't say your husband was taken. You'll have to...
ID!
Go. Keep moving.

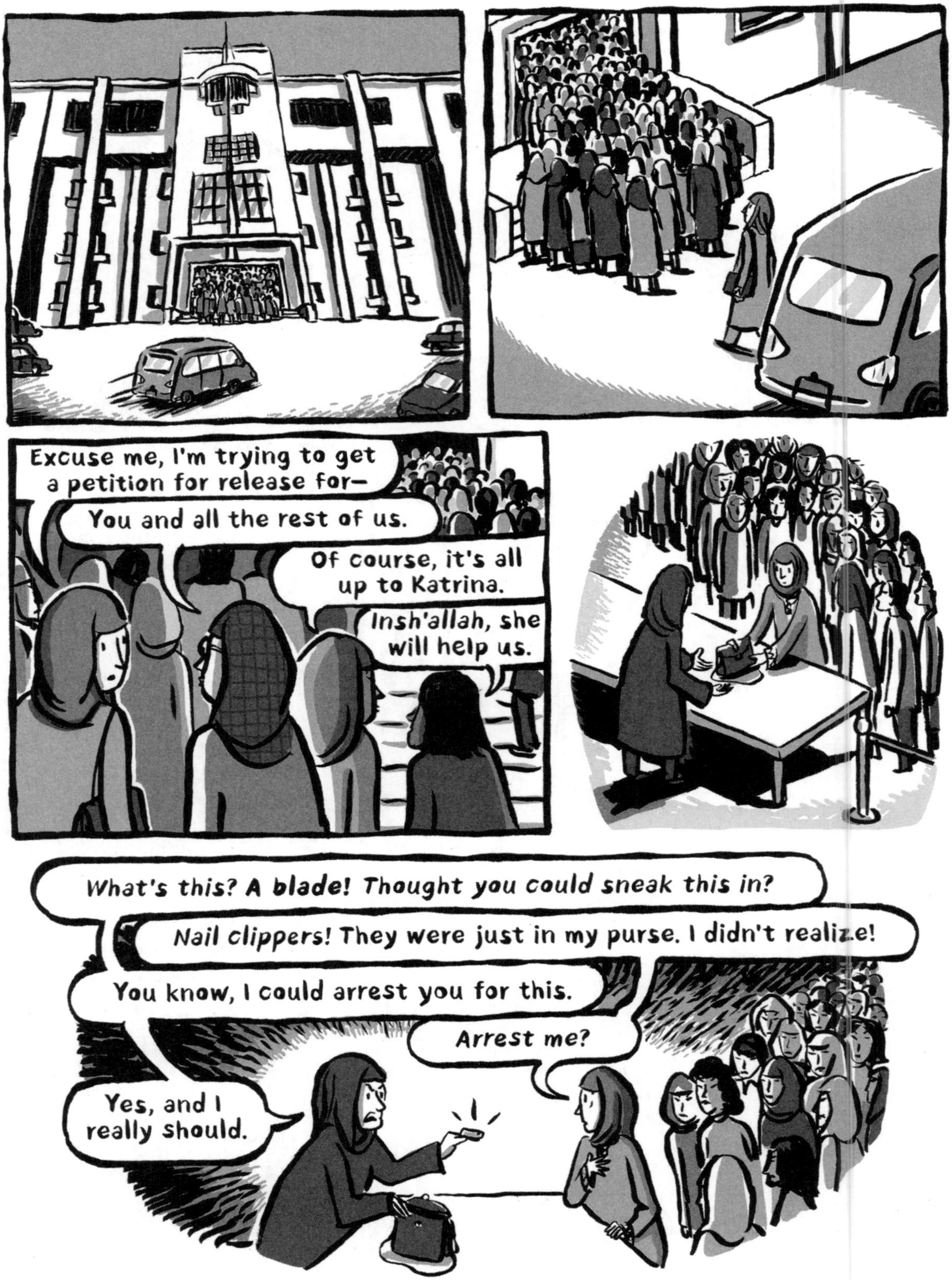
Excuse me, I'm trying to get a petition for release for—
You and all the rest of us.
Of course, it's all up to Katrina.
Insh'allah, she will help us.
What's this? A blade! Thought you could sneak this in?
Nail clippers! They were just in my purse. I didn't realize!
You know, I could arrest you for this.
Arrest me?
Yes, and I really should.

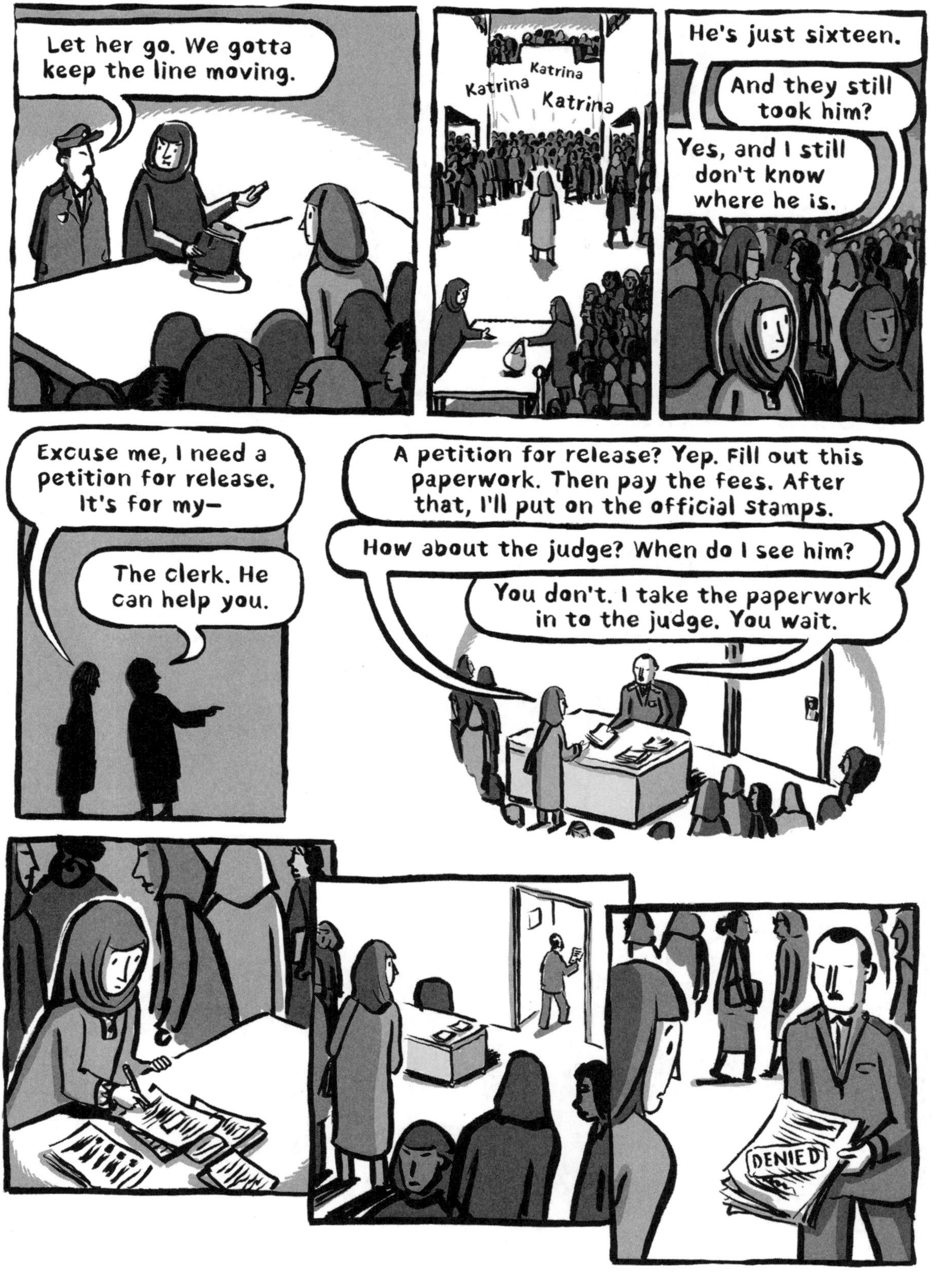
Let her go. We gotta keep the line moving.
Katrina
Katrina
Katrina
He's just sixteen.
And they still took him?
Yes, and I still don't know where he is.
Excuse me, I need a petition for release. It's for my—
The clerk. He can help you.
A petition for release? Yep. Fill out this paperwork. Then pay the fees. After that, I'll put on the official stamps.
How about the judge? When do I see him?
You don't. I take the paperwork in to the judge. You wait.
DENIED

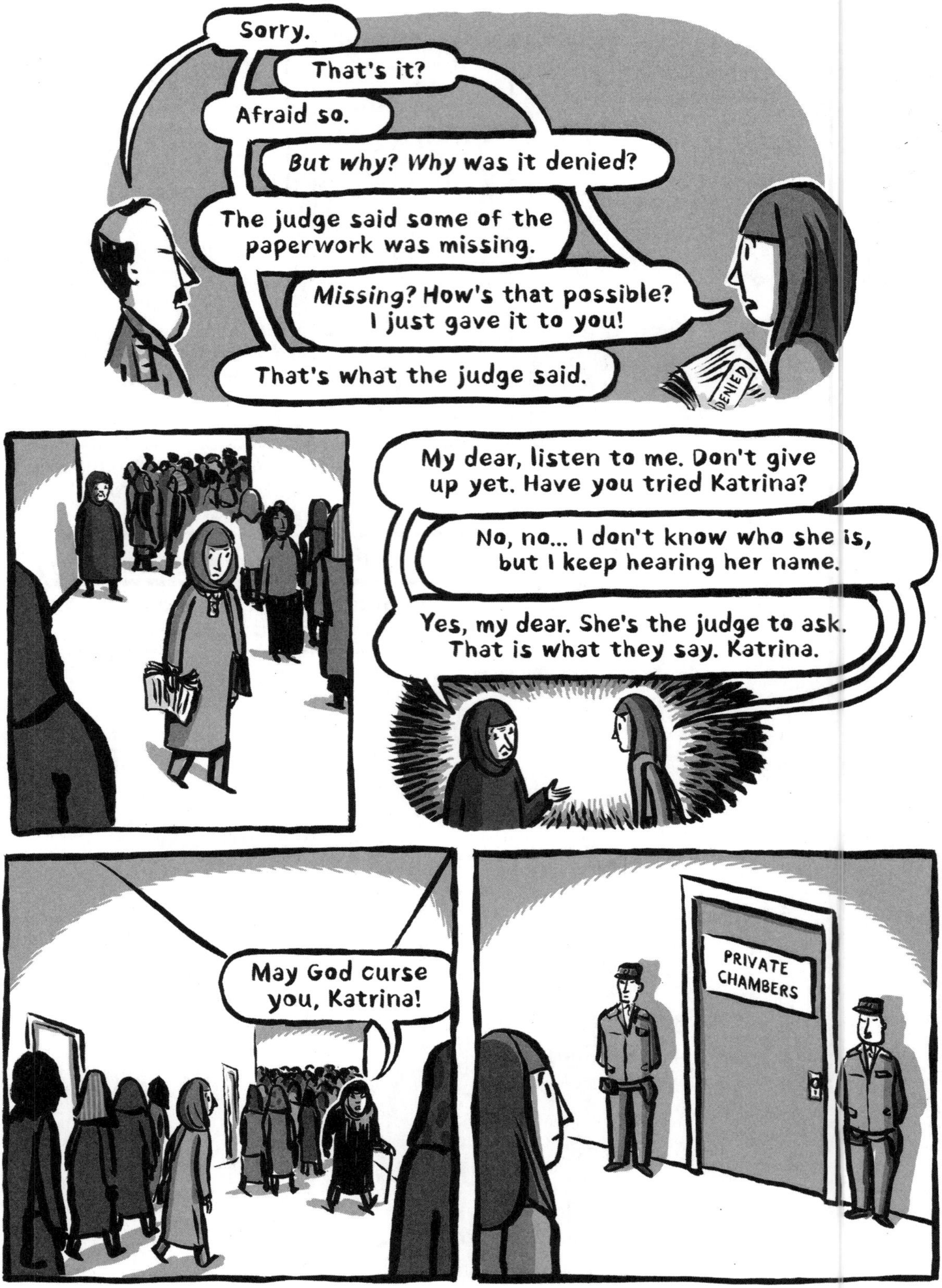
Sorry.
That's it?
Afraid so.
But why? Why was it denied?
The judge said some of the paperwork was missing.
Missing? How's that possible? I just gave it to you!
That's what the judge said.
DENIED
My dear, listen to me. Don't give up yet. Have you tried Katrina?
No, no... I don't know who she is, but I keep hearing her name.
Yes, my dear. She's the judge to ask. That is what they say. Katrina.
May God curse you, Katrina!
PRIVATE CHAMBERS

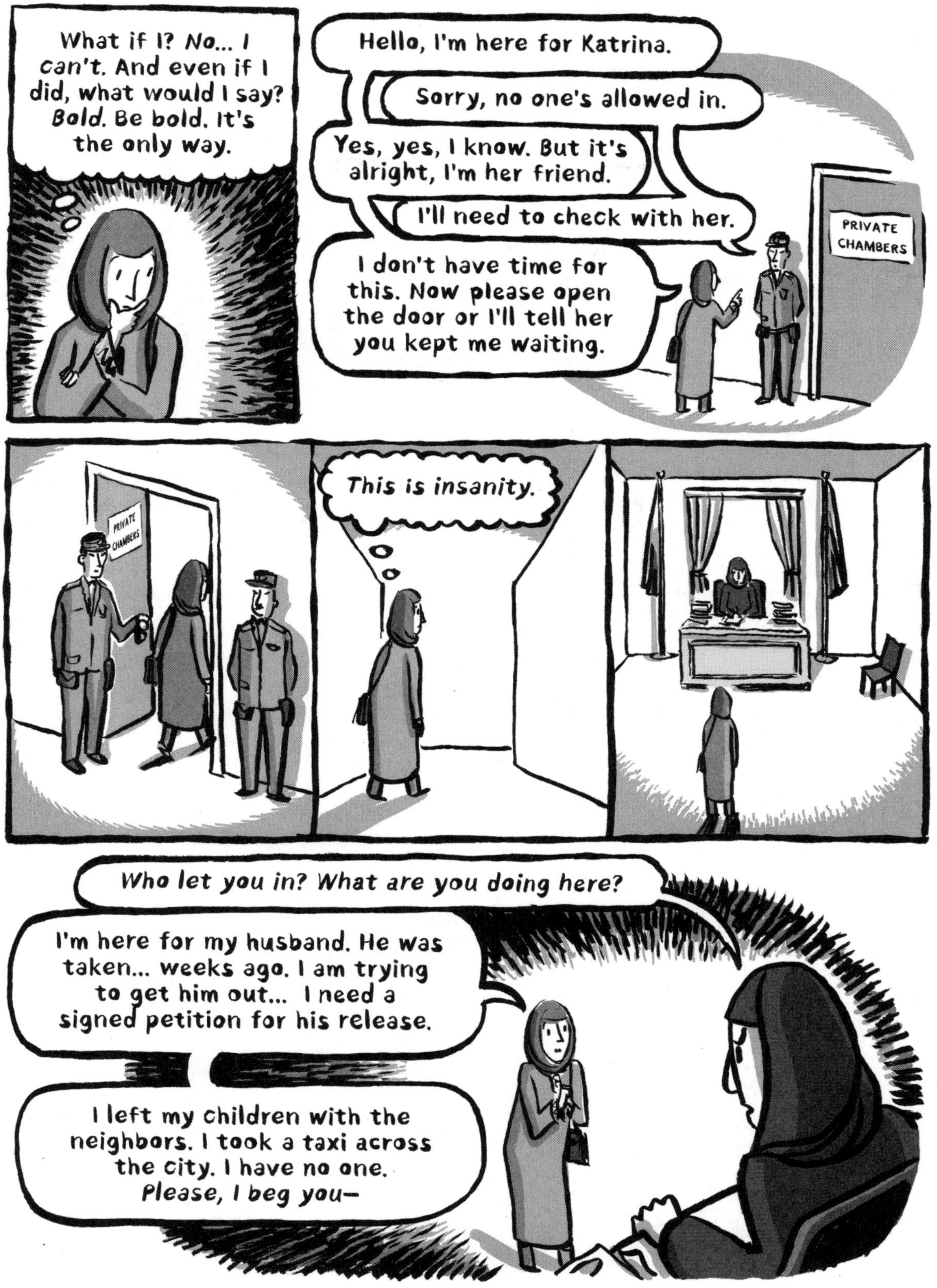
What if I? *No...* I can't. And even if I did, what would I say? *Bold.* Be bold. It's the only way.
Hello, I'm here for Katrina.
Sorry, no one's allowed in.
Yes, yes, I know. But it's alright, I'm her friend.
I'll need to check with her.
I don't have time for this. Now please open the door or I'll tell her you kept me waiting.
PRIVATE CHAMBERS
PRIVATE CHAMBERS
This is insanity.
Who let you in? What are you doing here?
I'm here for my husband. He was taken... weeks ago. I am trying to get him out... I need a signed petition for his release.
I left my children with the neighbors. I took a taxi across the city. I have no one. *Please, I beg you—*

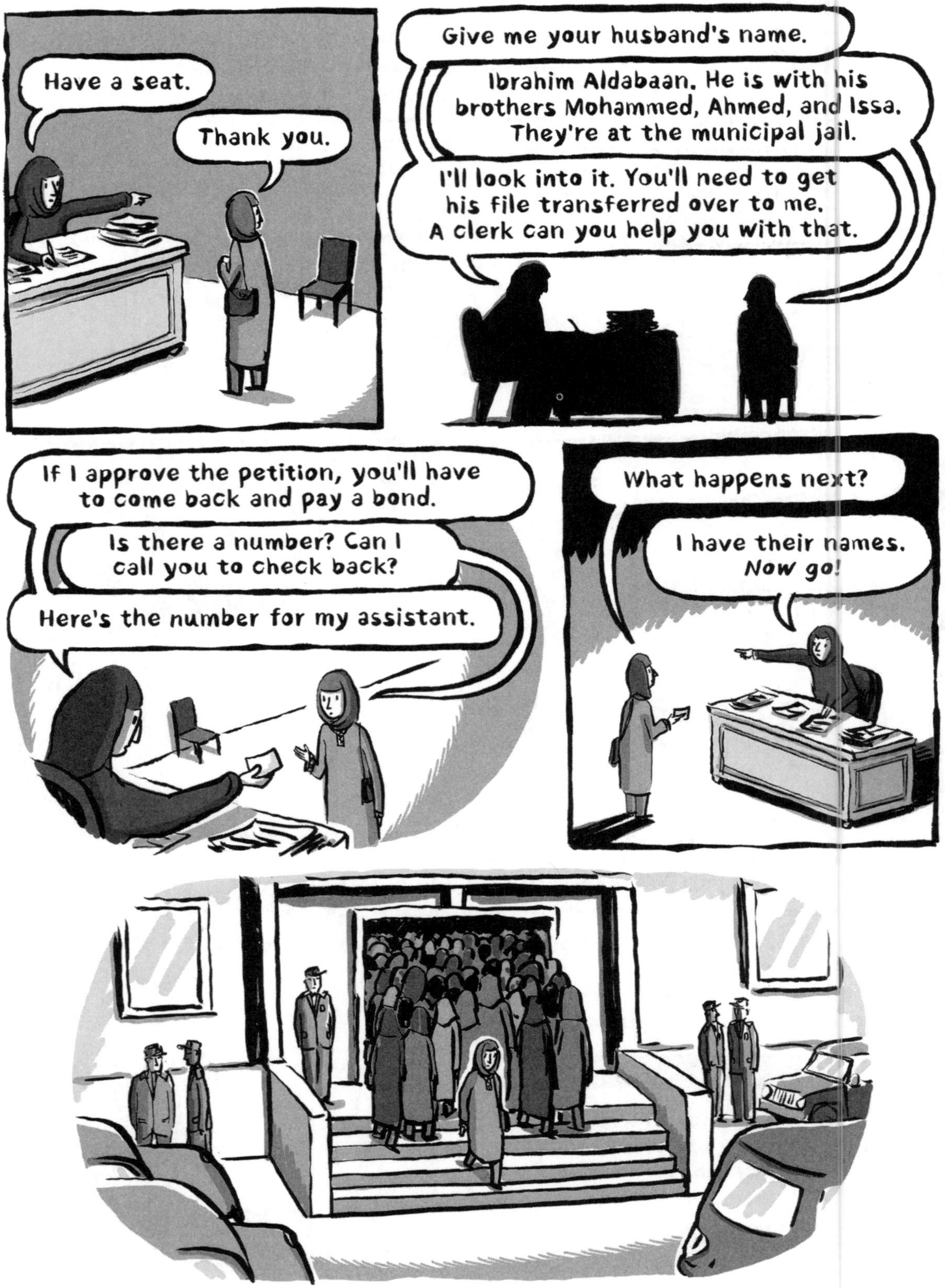
Have a seat.
Thank you.
Give me your husband's name.
Ibrahim Aldabaan. He is with his brothers Mohammed, Ahmed, and Issa. They're at the municipal jail.
I'll look into it. You'll need to get his file transferred over to me. A clerk can you help you with that.
If I approve the petition, you'll have to come back and pay a bond.
Is there a number? Can I call you to check back?
Here's the number for my assistant.
What happens next?
I have their names. *Now go!*

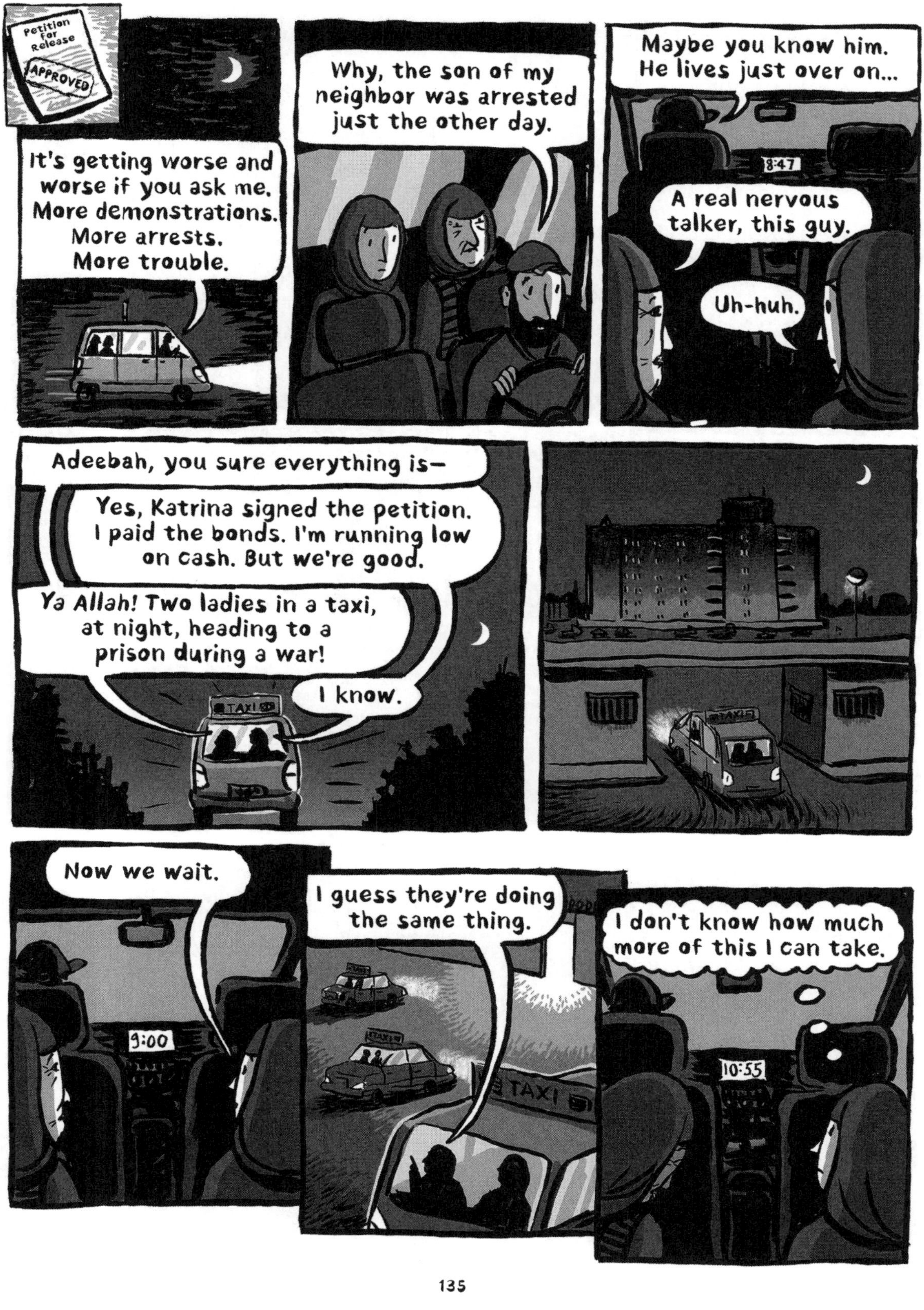
Petition for Release
APPROVED
It's getting worse and worse if you ask me. More demonstrations. More arrests. More trouble.
Why, the son of my neighbor was arrested just the other day.
Maybe you know him. He lives just over on...
8:47
A real nervous talker, this guy.
Uh-huh.
Adeebah, you sure everything is—
Yes, Katrina signed the petition. I paid the bonds. I'm running low on cash. But we're good.
Ya Allah! Two ladies in a taxi, at night, heading to a prison during a war!
I know.
TAXI
TAXI
Now we wait.
9:00
I guess they're doing the same thing.
TAXI
I don't know how much more of this I can take.
10:55

Look! I think that's Mohammed!

Are the others coming?

Don't know. It's chaos in there. Chaos. No one knows... anything, really. But I got the stamp. Once you get the stamp—

You sure you got it?

Sure. Trust me. I got it.

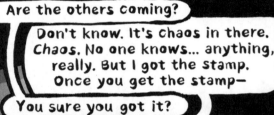

11:55

Ahmed!

What about Ibrahim?

He should be coming. Takes time though. They fingerprint you. And you gotta wait in this little room. Then they call you... And take you through this gate.

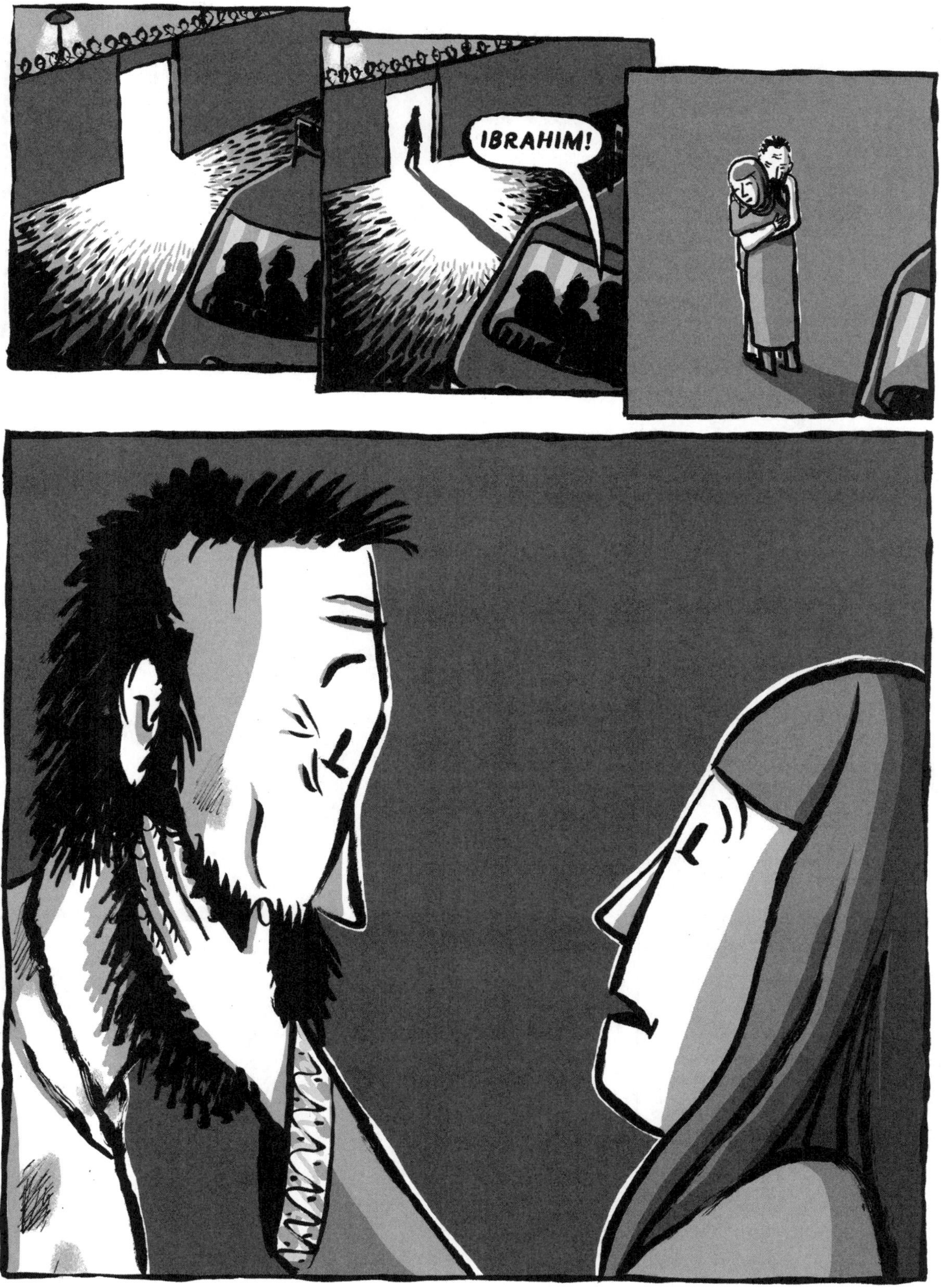
IBRAHIM!

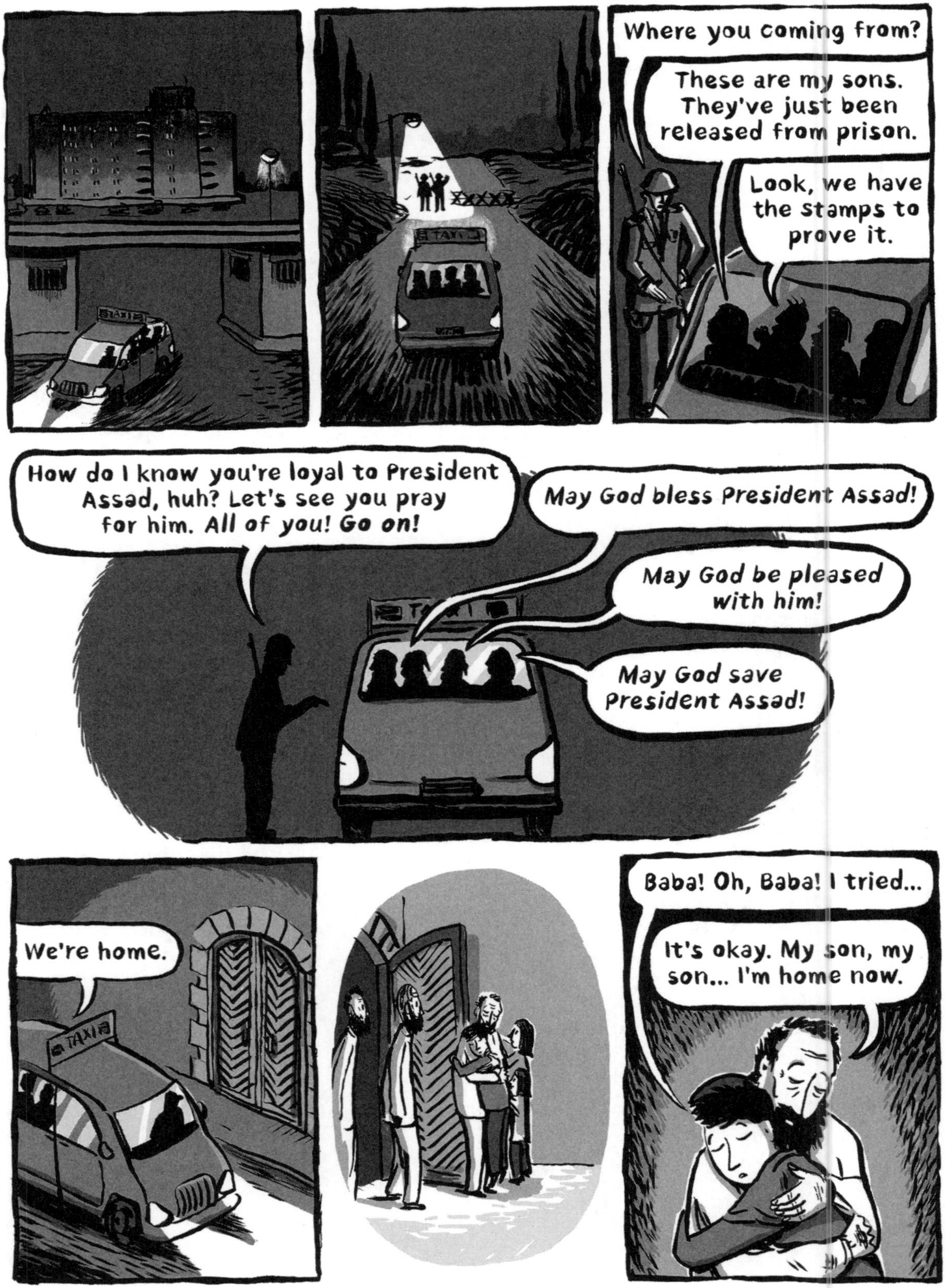
Where you coming from?
These are my sons. They've just been released from prison.
Look, we have the stamps to prove it.
How do I know you're loyal to President Assad, huh? Let's see you pray for him. All of you! Go on!
May God bless President Assad!
May God be pleased with him!
May God save President Assad!
We're home.
Baba! Oh, Baba! I tried...
It's okay. My son, my son... I'm home now.

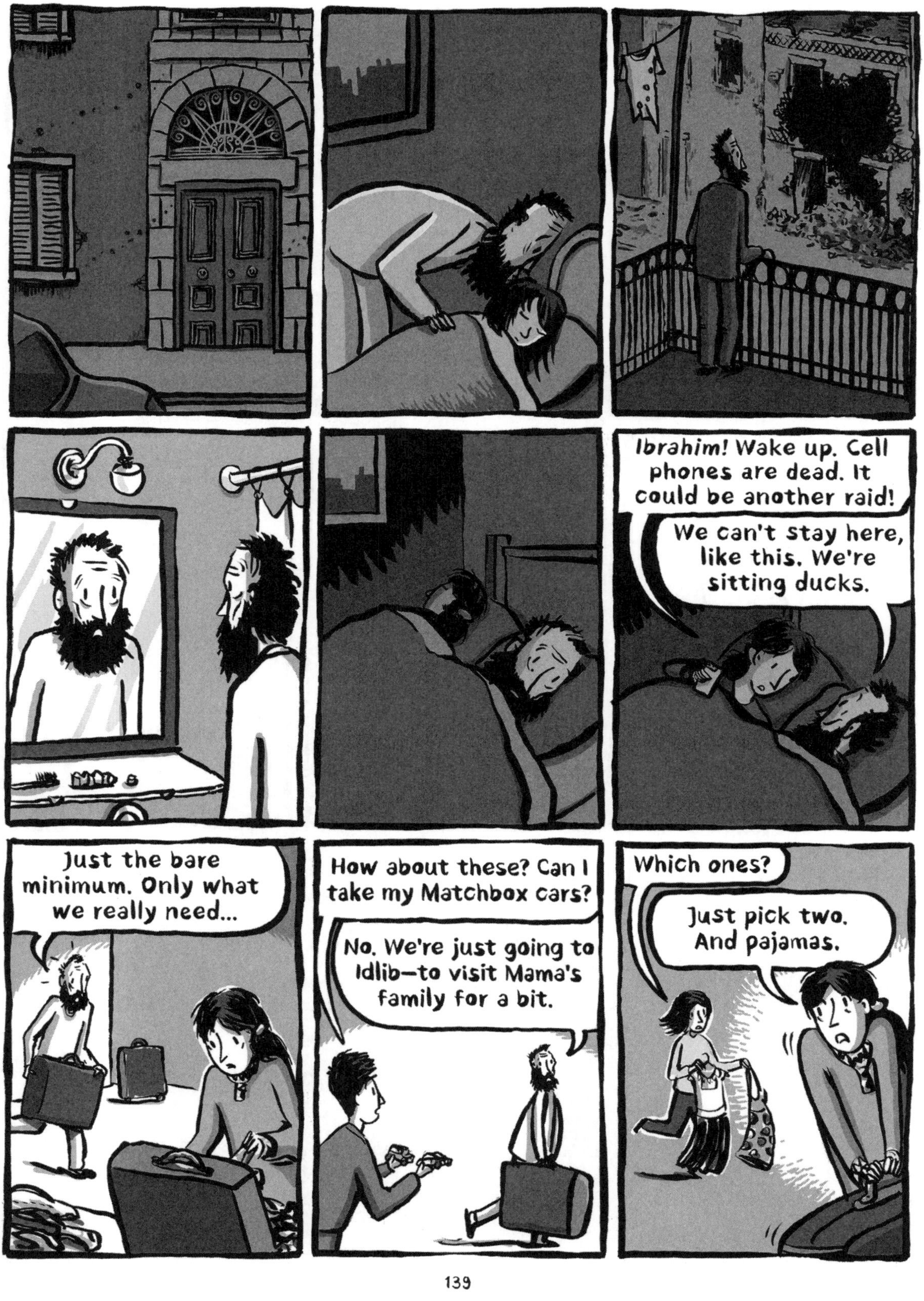
Ibrahim! Wake up. Cell phones are dead. It could be another raid!
We can't stay here, like this. We're sitting ducks.
Just the bare minimum. Only what we really need...
How about these? Can I take my Matchbox cars?
No. We're just going to Idlib—to visit Mama's family for a bit.
Which ones?
Just pick two. And pajamas.

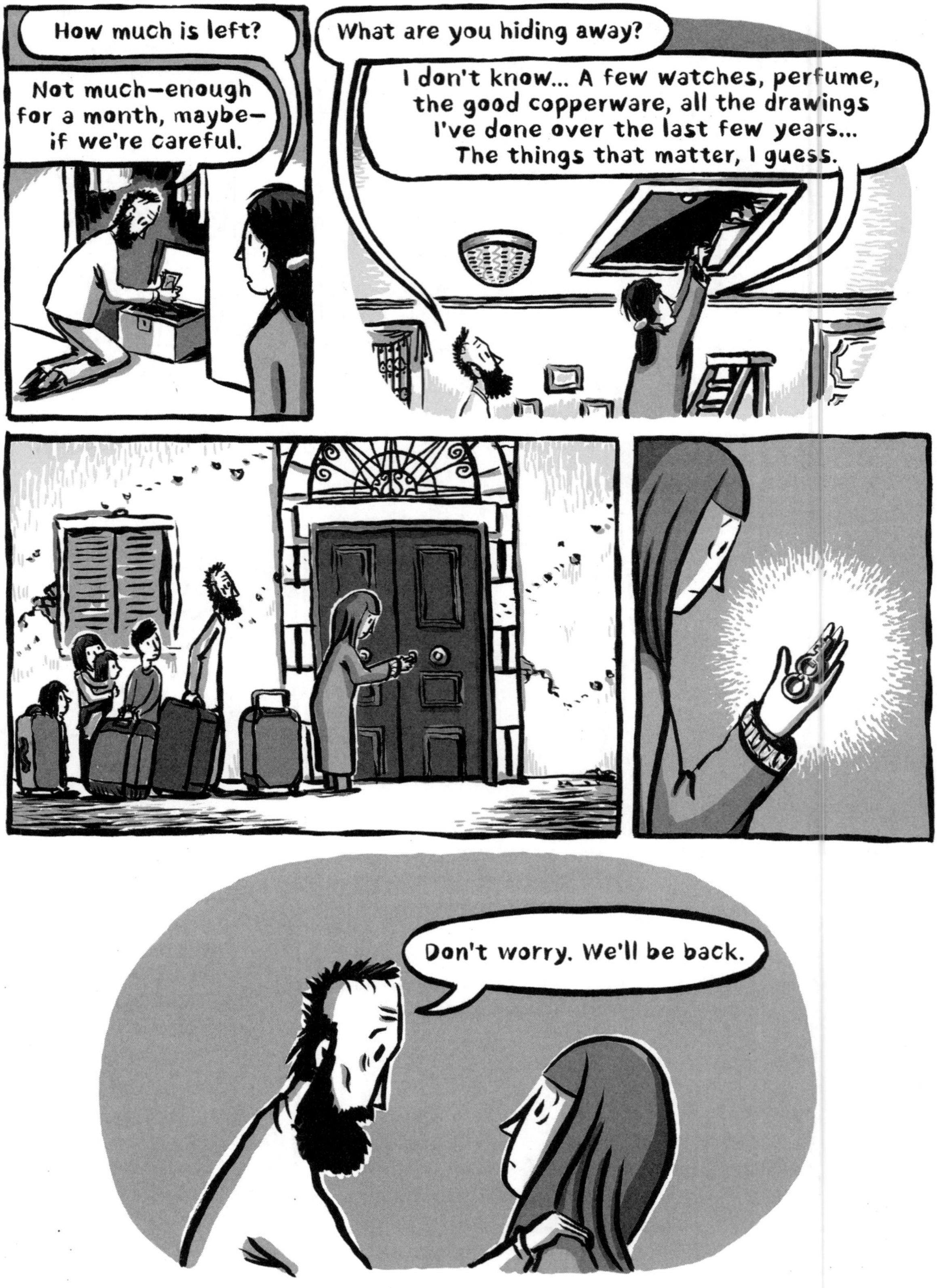
How much is left?
Not much—enough for a month, maybe—if we're careful.
What are you hiding away?
I don't know... A few watches, perfume, the good copperware, all the drawings I've done over the last few years... The things that matter, I guess.
Don't worry. We'll be back.

Chapter 5

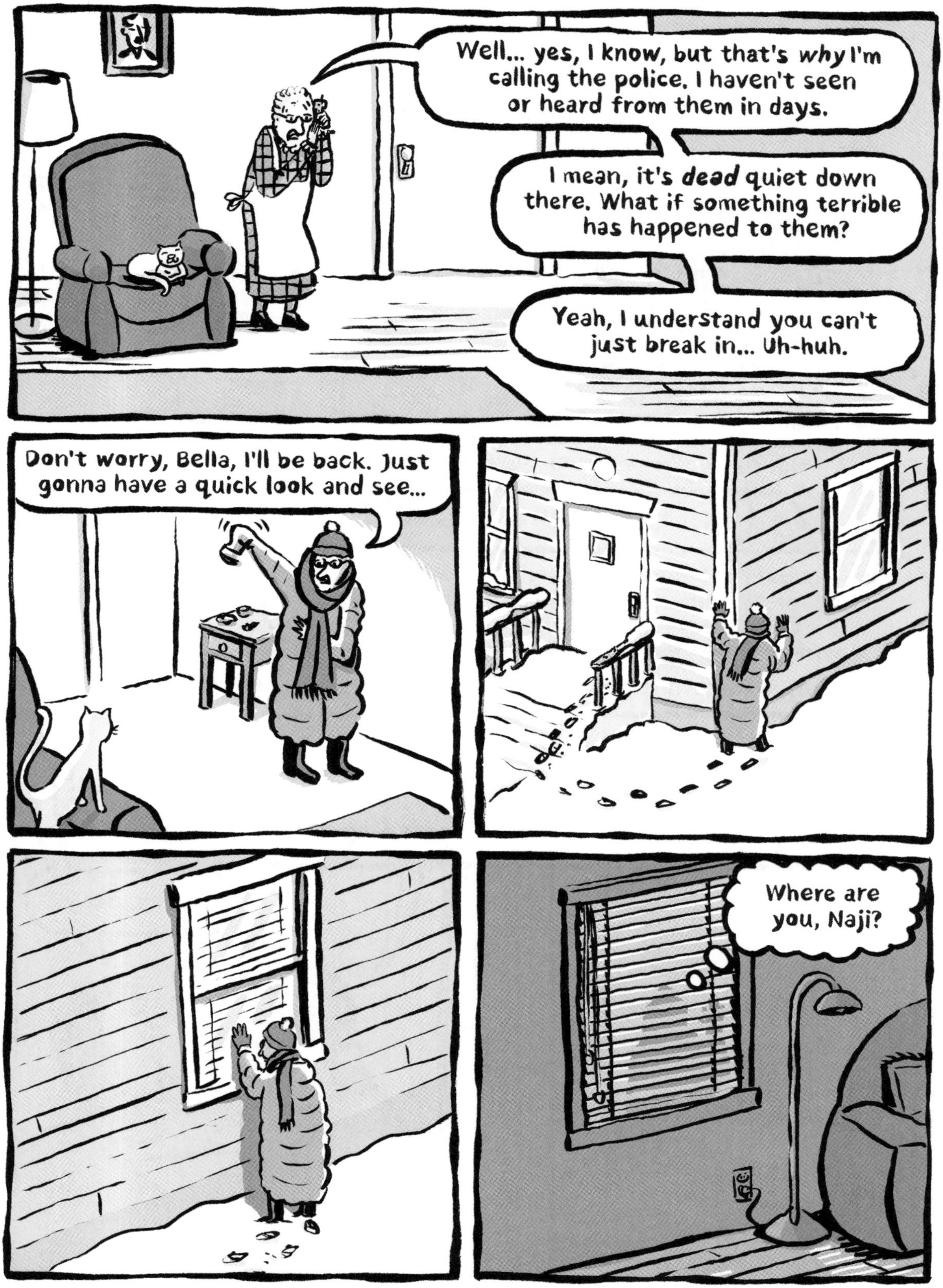
Well... yes, I know, but that's *why* I'm calling the police. I haven't seen or heard from them in days.
I mean, it's *dead* quiet down there. What if something terrible has happened to them?
Yeah, I understand you can't just break in... Uh-huh.
Don't worry, Bella, I'll be back. Just gonna have a quick look and see...
Where are you, Naji?

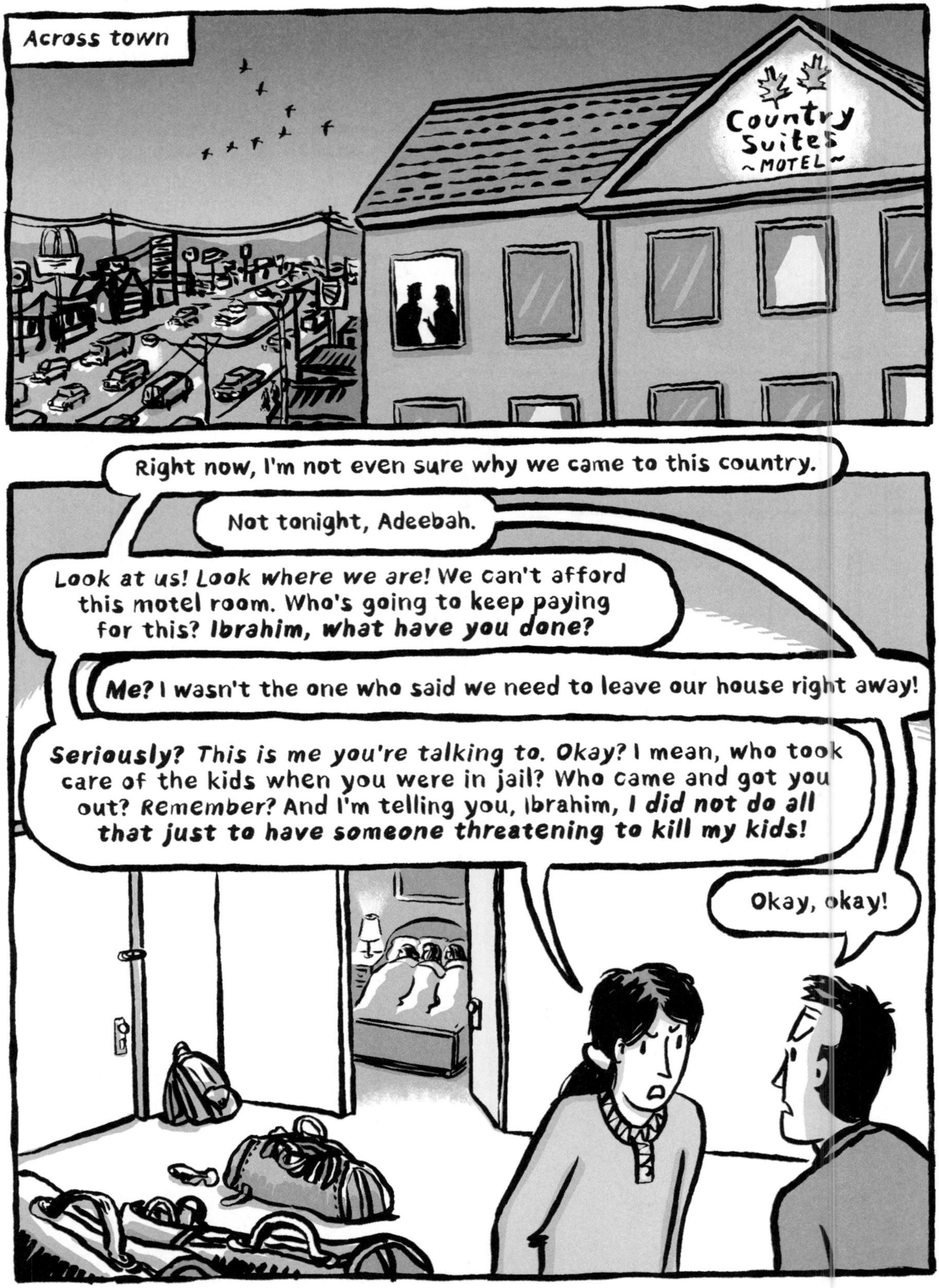
Across town
Country Suites ~MOTEL~
Right now, I'm not even sure why we came to this country.
Not tonight, Adeebah.
Look at us! Look where we are! We can't afford this motel room. Who's going to keep paying for this? *Ibrahim, what have you done?*
Me? I wasn't the one who said we need to leave our house right away!
Seriously? This is me you're talking to. *Okay?* I mean, who took care of the kids when you were in jail? Who came and got you out? Remember? And I'm telling you, Ibrahim, *I did not do all that just to have someone threatening to kill my kids!*
Okay, okay!

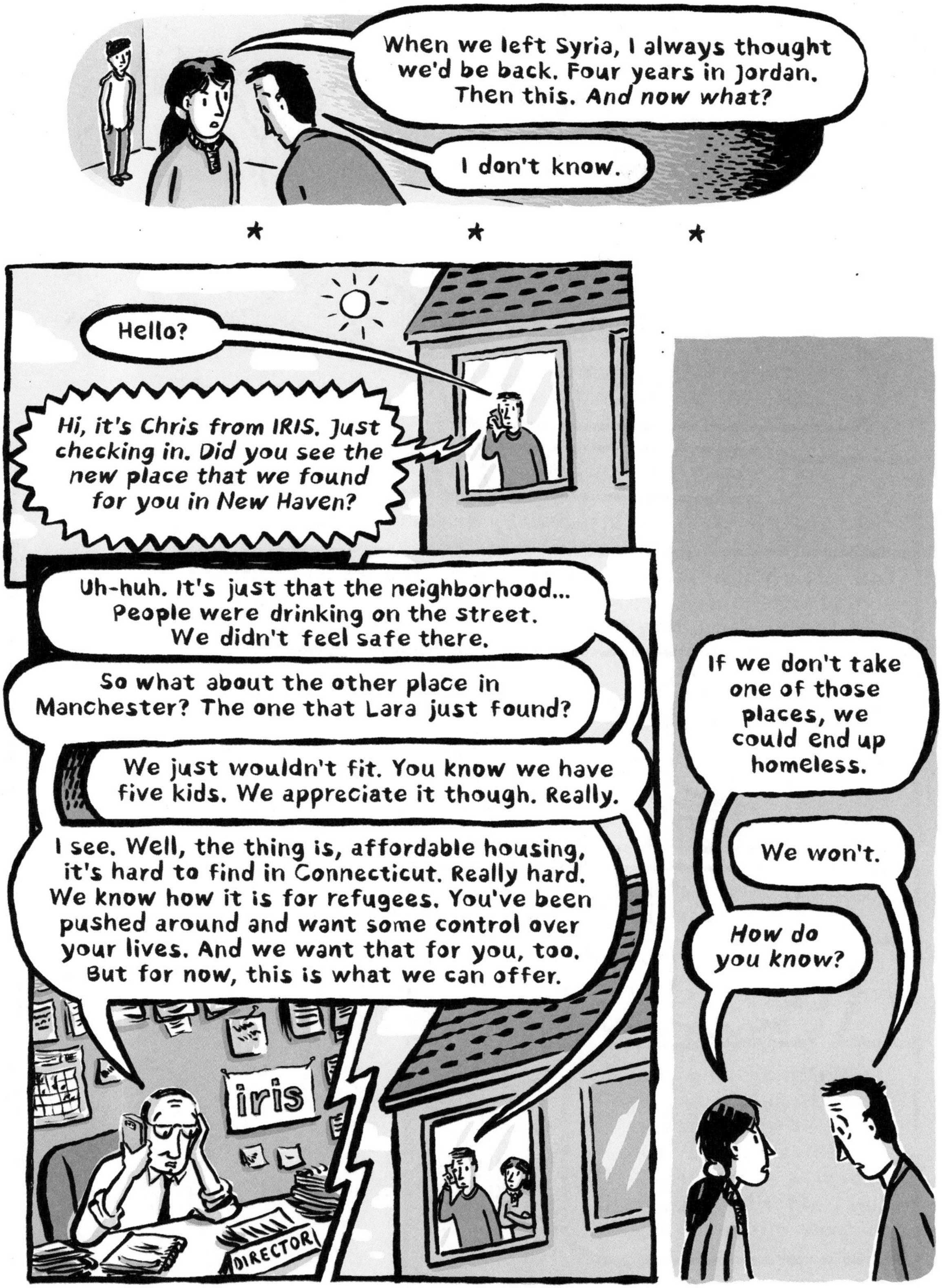
When we left Syria, I always thought we'd be back. Four years in Jordan. Then this. *And now what?*
I don't know.
* * *
Hello?
Hi, it's Chris from IRIS. Just checking in. Did you see the new place that we found for you in New Haven?
Uh-huh. It's just that the neighborhood... People were drinking on the street. We didn't feel safe there.
So what about the other place in Manchester? The one that Lara just found?
We just wouldn't fit. You know we have five kids. We appreciate it though. Really.
I see. Well, the thing is, affordable housing, it's hard to find in Connecticut. Really hard. We know how it is for refugees. You've been pushed around and want some control over your lives. And we want that for you, too. But for now, this is what we can offer.
iris
DIRECTOR
If we don't take one of those places, we could end up homeless.
We won't.
How do you know?

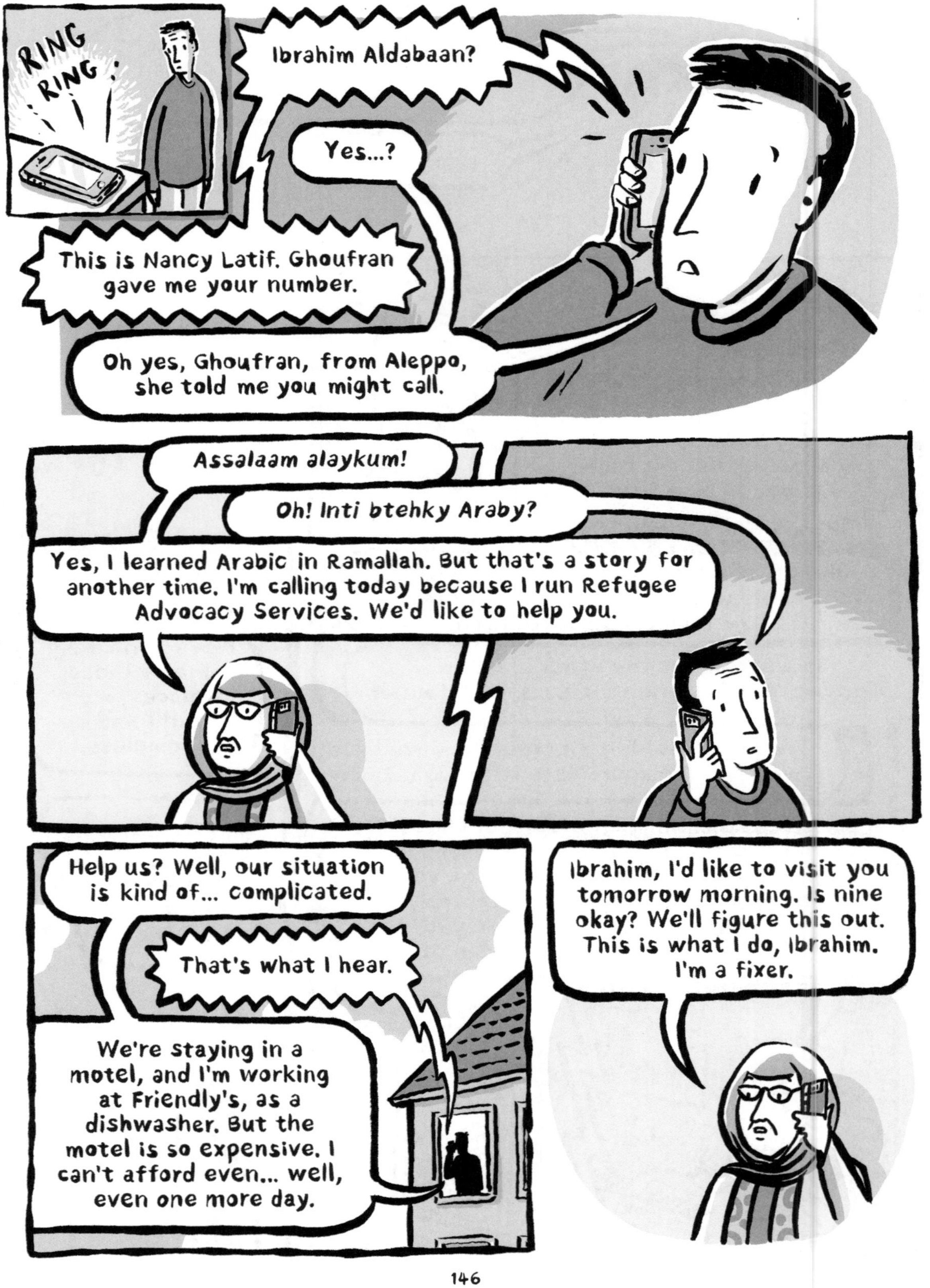

RING RING
Ibrahim Aldabaan?
Yes...?
This is Nancy Latif. Ghoufran gave me your number.
Oh yes, Ghoufran, from Aleppo, she told me you might call.
Assalaam alaykum!
Oh! Inti btehky Araby?
Yes, I learned Arabic in Ramallah. But that's a story for another time. I'm calling today because I run Refugee Advocacy Services. We'd like to help you.
Help us? Well, our situation is kind of... complicated.
That's what I hear.
We're staying in a motel, and I'm working at Friendly's, as a dishwasher. But the motel is so expensive. I can't afford even... well, even one more day.
Ibrahim, I'd like to visit you tomorrow morning. Is nine okay? We'll figure this out. This is what I do, Ibrahim. I'm a fixer.

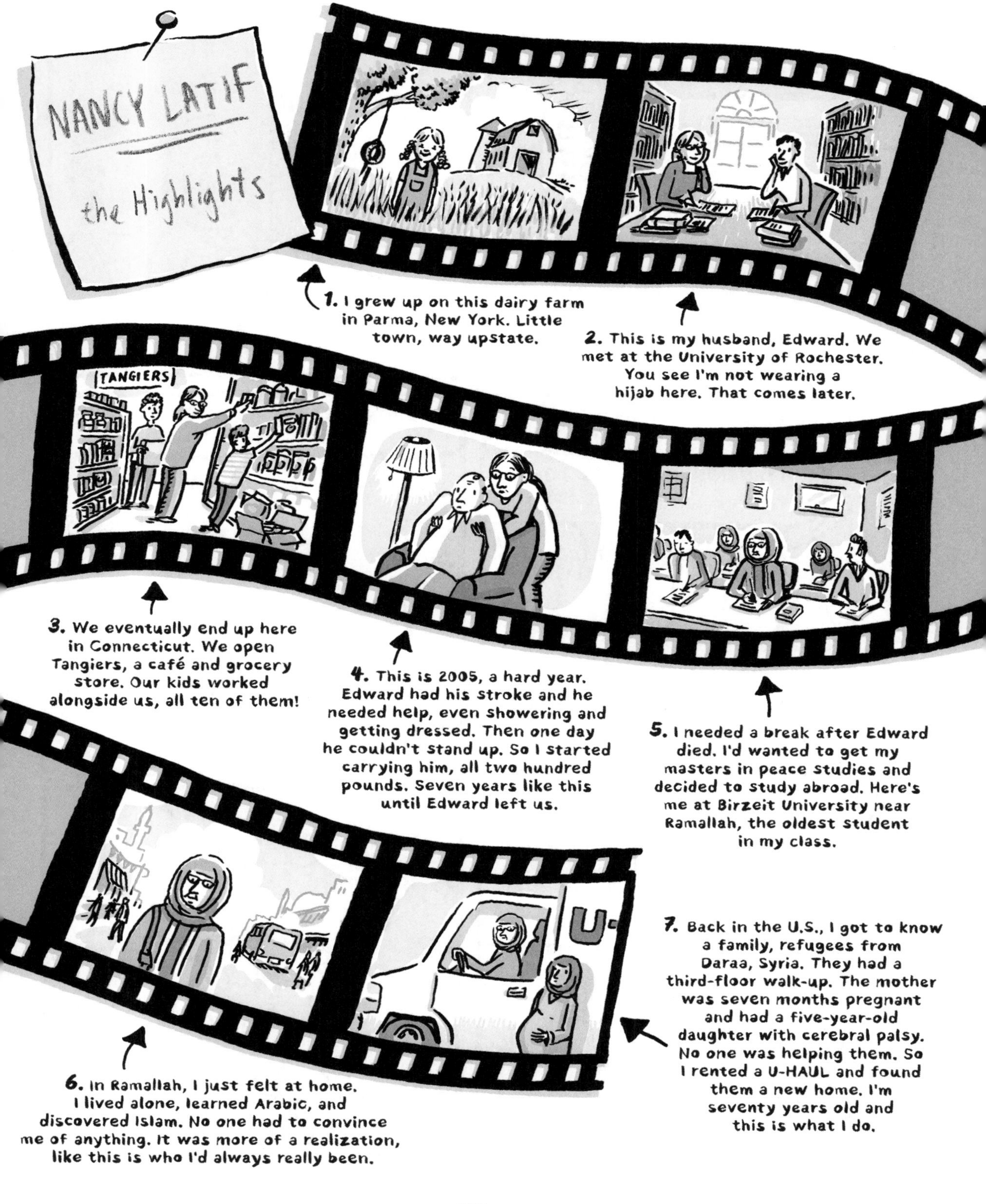

NANCY LATIF
the Highlights
1. I grew up on this dairy farm in Parma, New York. Little town, way upstate.
2. This is my husband, Edward. We met at the University of Rochester. You see I'm not wearing a hijab here. That comes later.
TANGIERS
3. We eventually end up here in Connecticut. We open Tangiers, a café and grocery store. Our kids worked alongside us, all ten of them!
4. This is 2005, a hard year. Edward had his stroke and he needed help, even showering and getting dressed. Then one day he couldn't stand up. So I started carrying him, all two hundred pounds. Seven years like this until Edward left us.
5. I needed a break after Edward died. I'd wanted to get my masters in peace studies and decided to study abroad. Here's me at Birzeit University near Ramallah, the oldest student in my class.
6. In Ramallah, I just felt at home. I lived alone, learned Arabic, and discovered Islam. No one had to convince me of anything. It was more of a realization, like this is who I'd always really been.
U-
7. Back in the U.S., I got to know a family, refugees from Daraa, Syria. They had a third-floor walk-up. The mother was seven months pregnant and had a five-year-old daughter with cerebral palsy. No one was helping them. So I rented a U-HAUL and found them a new home. I'm seventy years old and this is what I do.

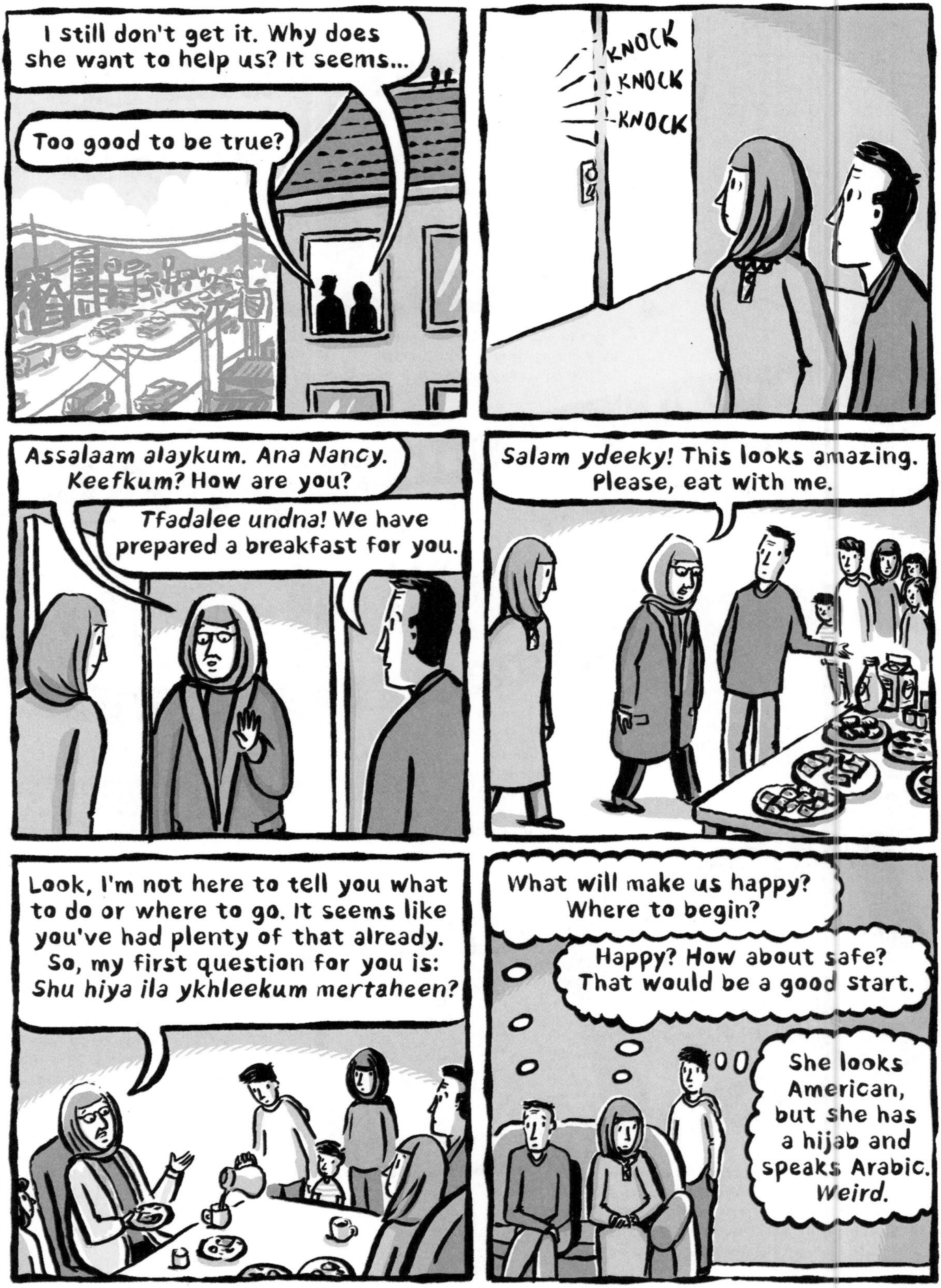
I still don't get it. Why does she want to help us? It seems...
Too good to be true?
KNOCK
KNOCK
KNOCK
Assalaam alaykum. Ana Nancy. Keefkum? How are you?
Tfadalee undna! We have prepared a breakfast for you.
Salam ydeeky! This looks amazing. Please, eat with me.
Look, I'm not here to tell you what to do or where to go. It seems like you've had plenty of that already. So, my first question for you is: Shu hiya ila ykhleekum mertaheen?
What will make us happy? Where to begin?
Happy? How about safe? That would be a good start.
She looks American, but she has a hijab and speaks Arabic. Weird.

Well, as long as you're asking. A safe neighborhood would be great, where the kids can play outside and Adeebah can walk in the street and not be afraid...

But one step at a time. What's your deal here at the motel?

How about West Hartford? It's safe and there are great schools.

Well, we're two days past due.

Sure... I'd need a job.

Yep, and a good one. Washing dishes isn't going to pay the bills.

Okay, I'll take care of that right now. Then we should start looking at places that would suit you. Adeebah, I have a few leads on apartments in West Hartford. Maybe the two of us can go together?

So, Adeebah, two things you need to know about me—two rules, I guess you could say.

Rules?

First, there's no smoking in my car. Because of my asthma. Second, if I help you, then you have to agree to help others. That work for you?

Yes, of course.

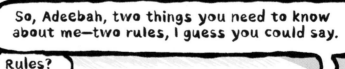

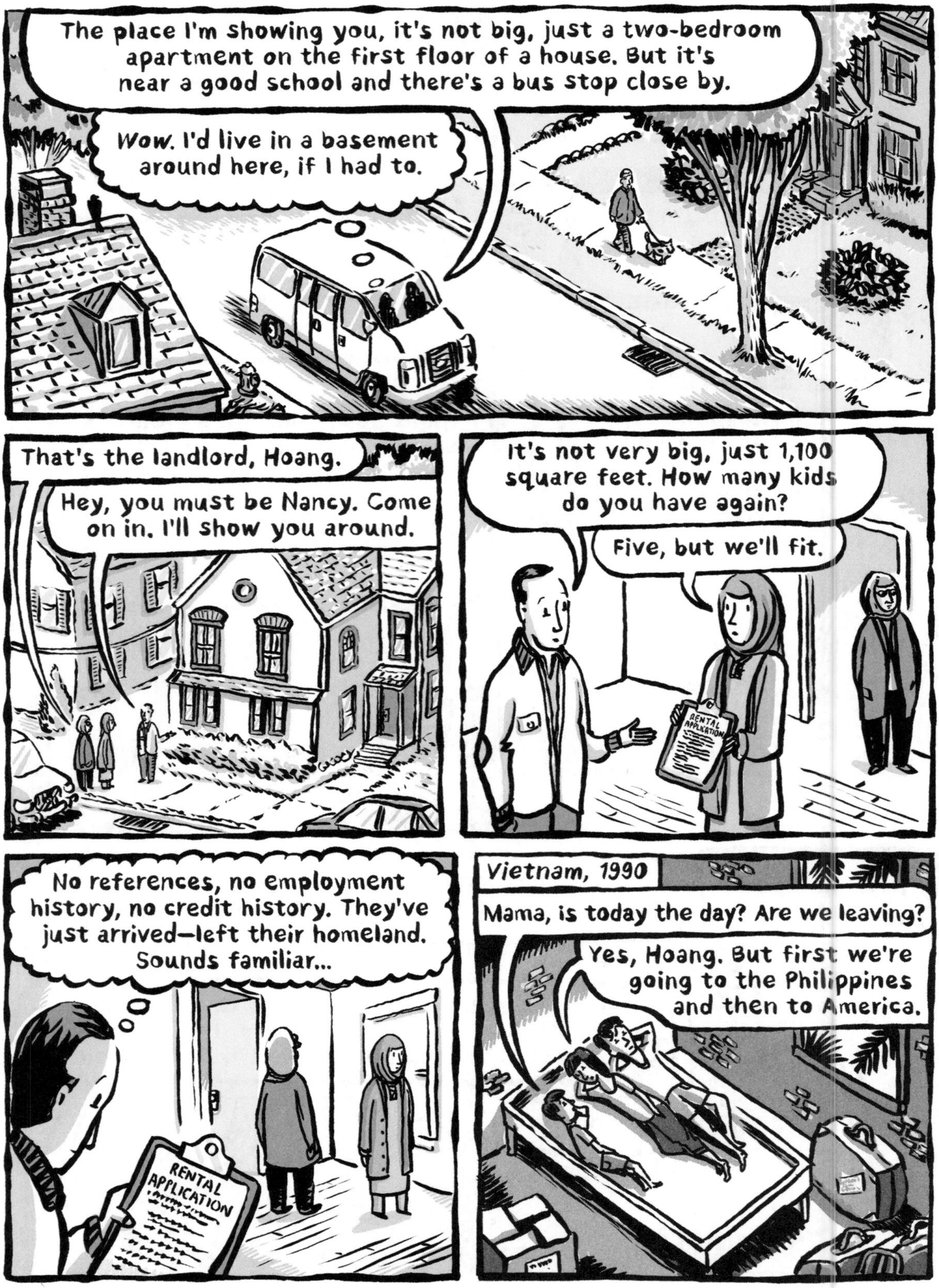
The place I'm showing you, it's not big, just a two-bedroom apartment on the first floor of a house. But it's near a good school and there's a bus stop close by.
Wow. I'd live in a basement around here, if I had to.
That's the landlord, Hoang.
Hey, you must be Nancy. Come on in. I'll show you around.
It's not very big, just 1,100 square feet. How many kids do you have again?
Five, but we'll fit.
RENTAL APPLICATION
No references, no employment history, no credit history. They've just arrived—left their homeland. Sounds familiar...
RENTAL APPLICATION
Vietnam, 1990
Mama, is today the day? Are we leaving?
Yes, Hoang. But first we're going to the Philippines and then to America.

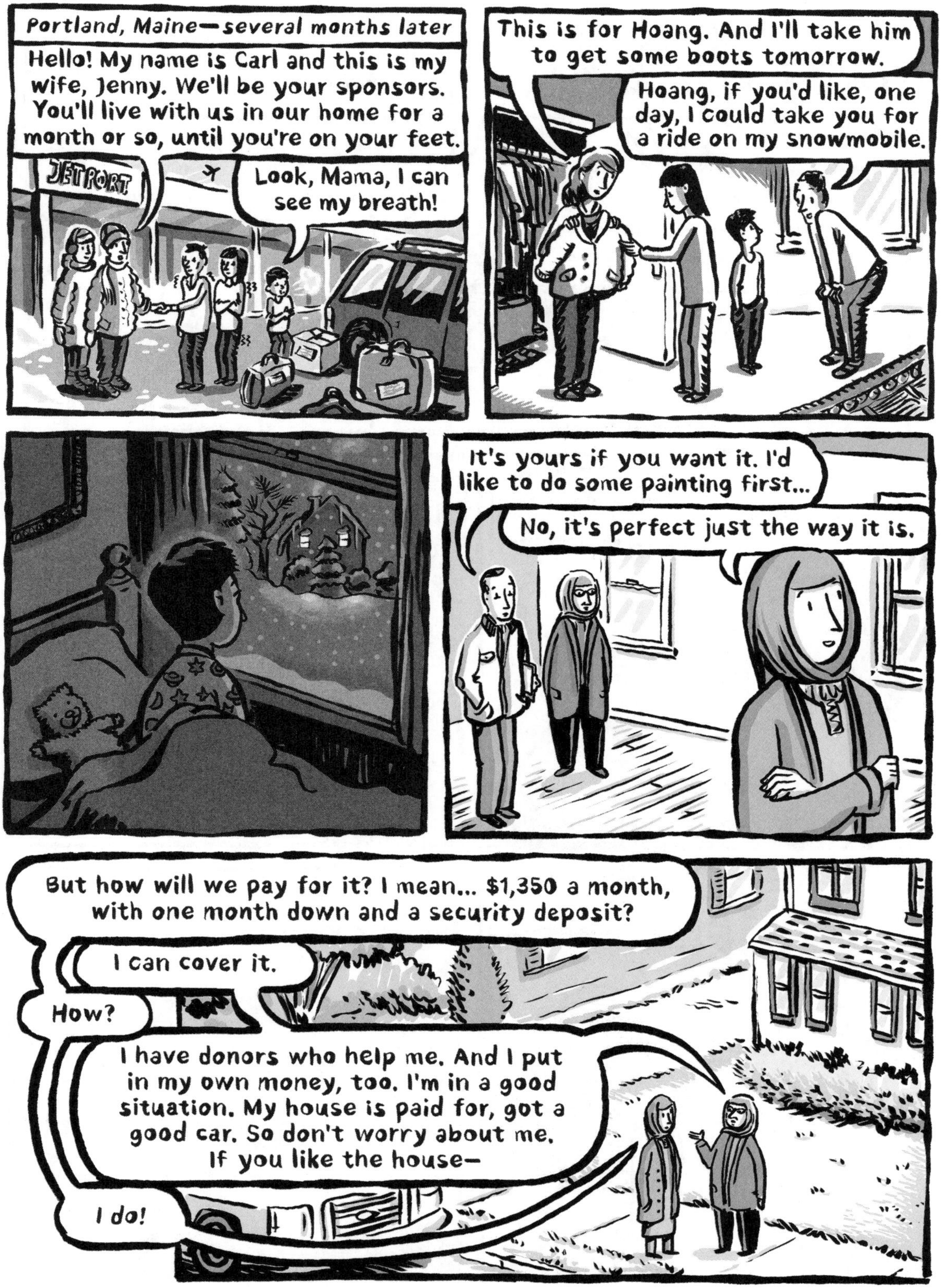
Portland, Maine—several months later
Hello! My name is Carl and this is my wife, Jenny. We'll be your sponsors. You'll live with us in our home for a month or so, until you're on your feet.
JETPORT
Look, Mama, I can see my breath!
This is for Hoang. And I'll take him to get some boots tomorrow.
Hoang, if you'd like, one day, I could take you for a ride on my snowmobile.
It's yours if you want it. I'd like to do some painting first...
No, it's perfect just the way it is.
But how will we pay for it? I mean... $1,350 a month, with one month down and a security deposit?
I can cover it.
How?
I have donors who help me. And I put in my own money, too. I'm in a good situation. My house is paid for, got a good car. So don't worry about me. If you like the house—
I do!

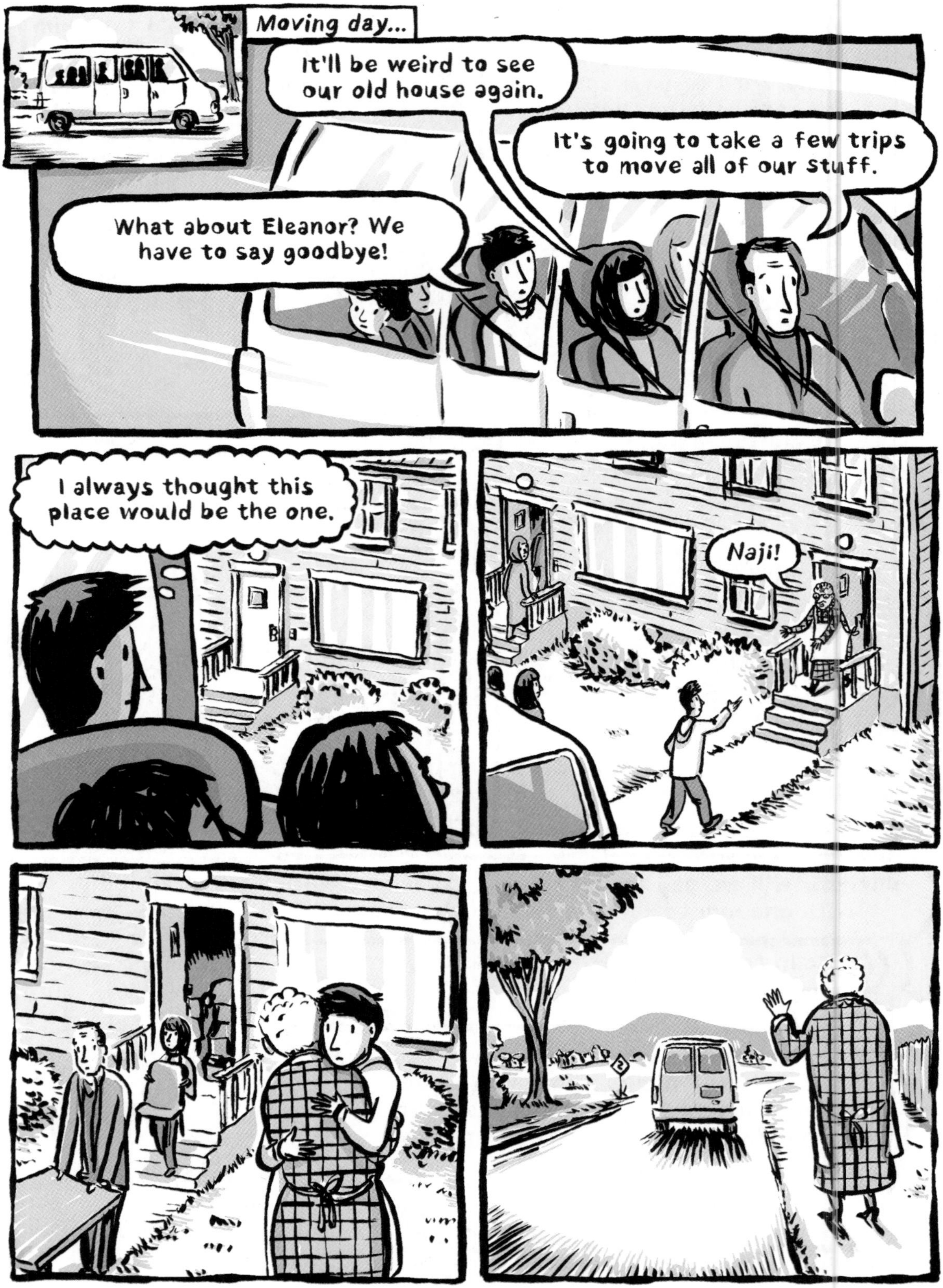

Moving day...
It'll be weird to see our old house again.
It's going to take a few trips to move all of our stuff.
What about Eleanor? We have to say goodbye!
I always thought this place would be the one.
Naji!

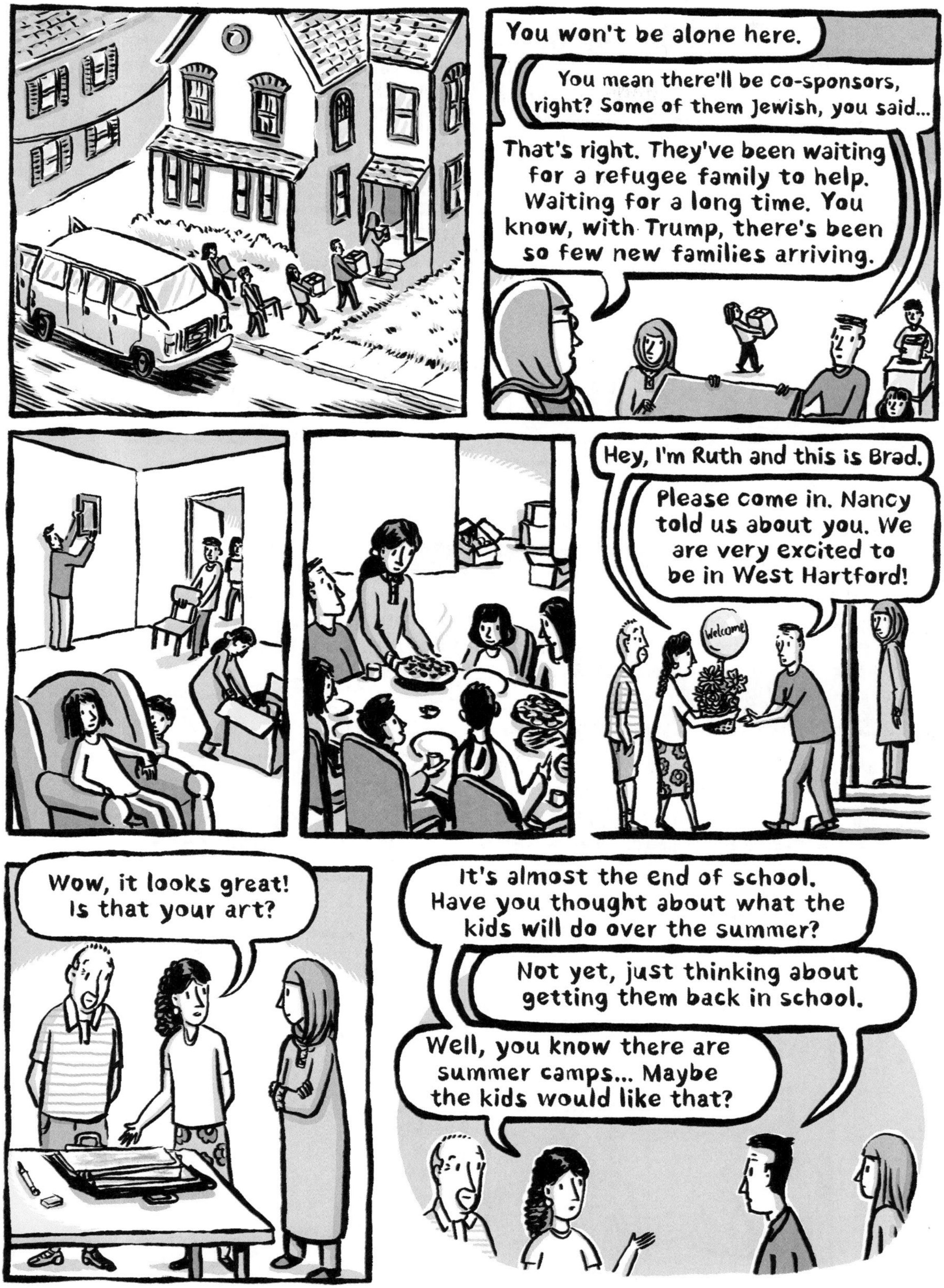
You won't be alone here.
You mean there'll be co-sponsors, right? Some of them Jewish, you said...
That's right. They've been waiting for a refugee family to help. Waiting for a long time. You know, with Trump, there's been so few new families arriving.
Hey, I'm Ruth and this is Brad.
Please come in. Nancy told us about you. We are very excited to be in West Hartford!
Welcome
Wow, it looks great! Is that your art?
It's almost the end of school. Have you thought about what the kids will do over the summer?
Not yet, just thinking about getting them back in school.
Well, you know there are summer camps... Maybe the kids would like that?

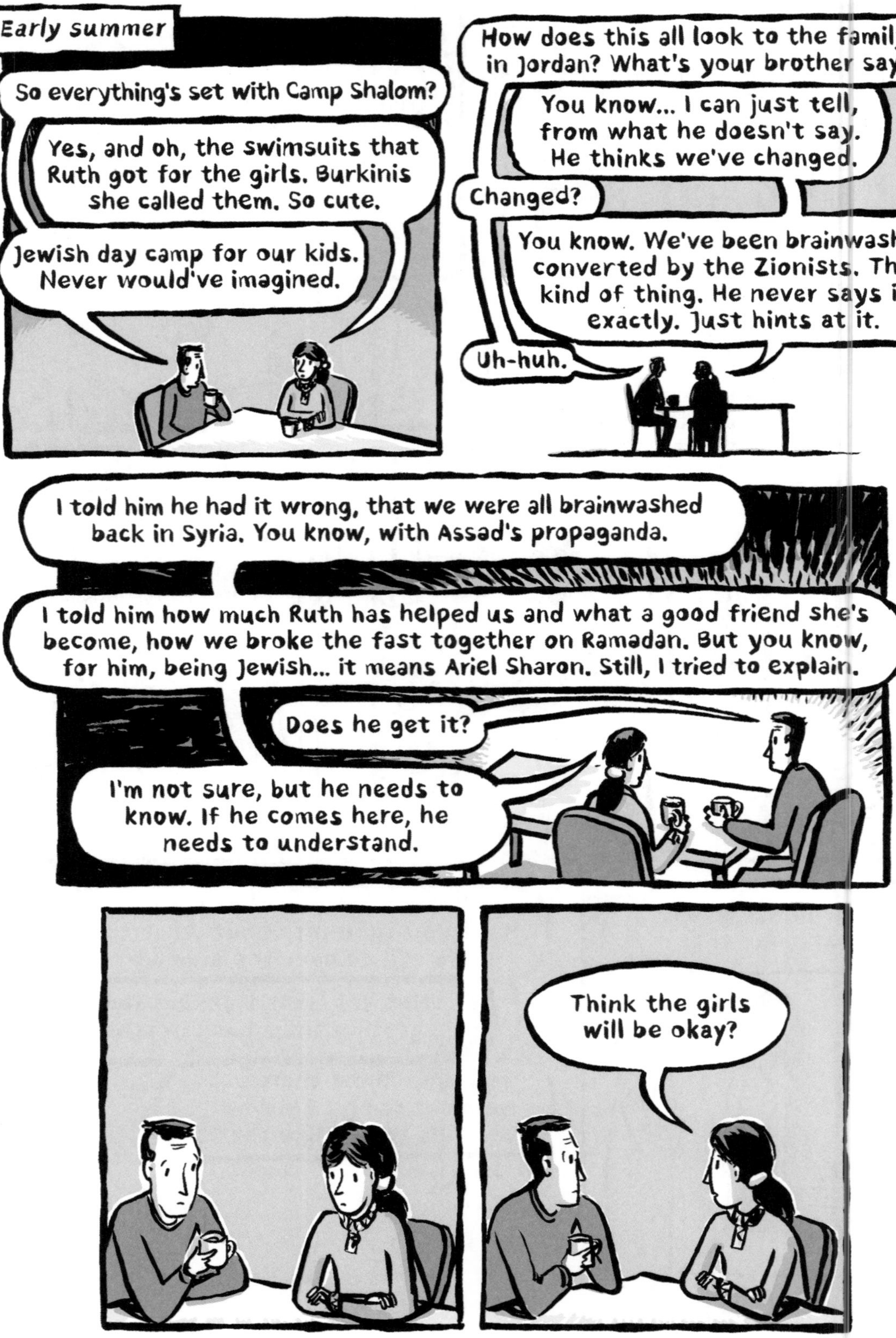
Early summer
So everything's set with Camp Shalom?
Yes, and oh, the swimsuits that Ruth got for the girls. Burkinis she called them. So cute.
Jewish day camp for our kids. Never would've imagined.
How does this all look to the family in Jordan? What's your brother say?
You know... I can just tell, from what he doesn't say. He thinks we've changed.
Changed?
You know. We've been brainwashed, converted by the Zionists. That kind of thing. He never says it, exactly. Just hints at it.
Uh-huh.
I told him he had it wrong, that we were all brainwashed back in Syria. You know, with Assad's propaganda.
I told him how much Ruth has helped us and what a good friend she's become, how we broke the fast together on Ramadan. But you know, for him, being Jewish... it means Ariel Sharon. Still, I tried to explain.
Does he get it?
I'm not sure, but he needs to know. If he comes here, he needs to understand.
Think the girls will be okay?

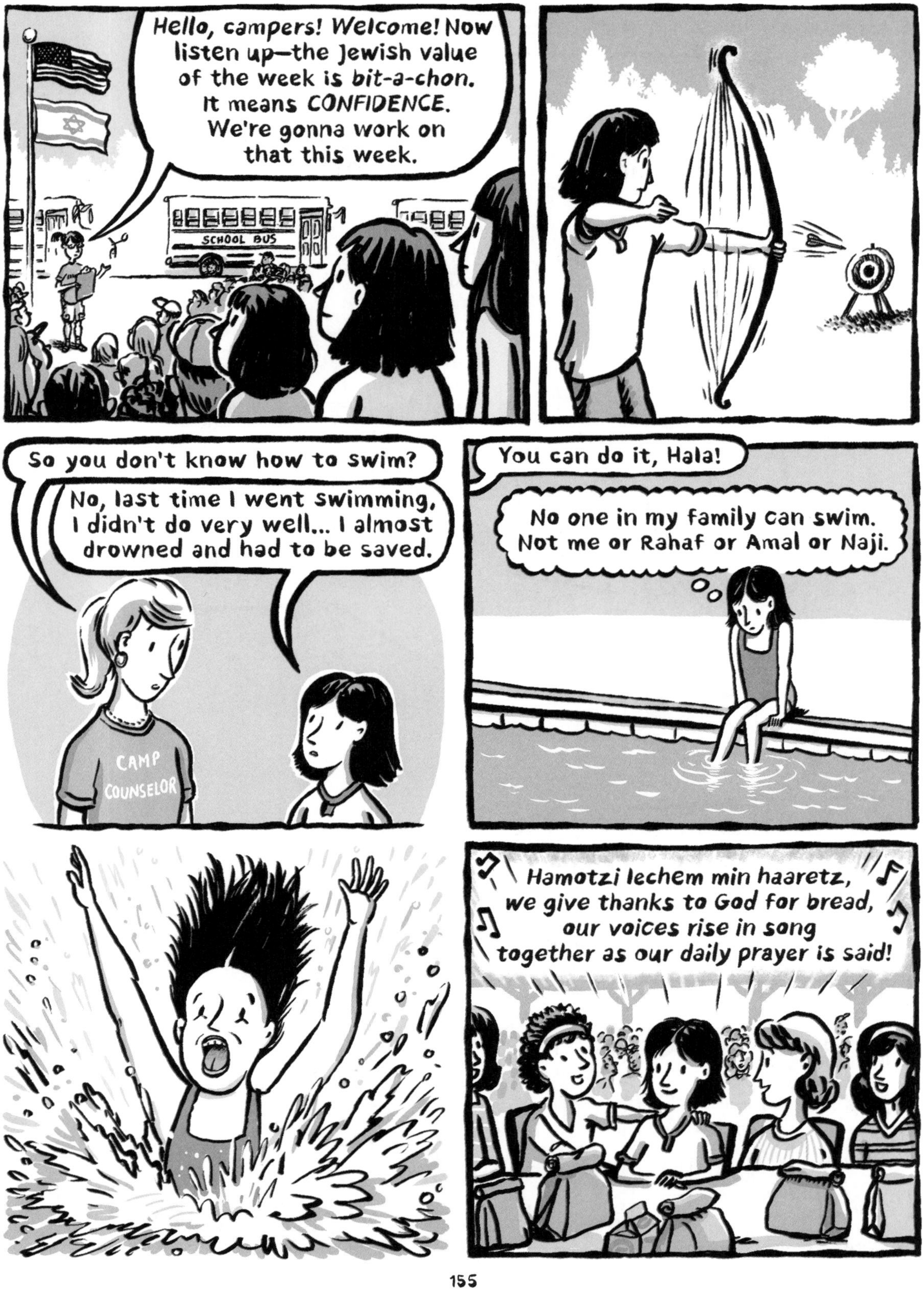
Hello, campers! Welcome! Now listen up—the Jewish value of the week is *bit-a-chon*. It means *CONFIDENCE*. We're gonna work on that this week.
SCHOOL BUS
So you don't know how to swim?
No, last time I went swimming, I didn't do very well... I almost drowned and had to be saved.
CAMP COUNSELOR
You can do it, Hala!
No one in my family can swim. Not me or Rahaf or Amal or Naji.
Hamotzi lechem min haaretz, we give thanks to God for bread, our voices rise in song together as our daily prayer is said!

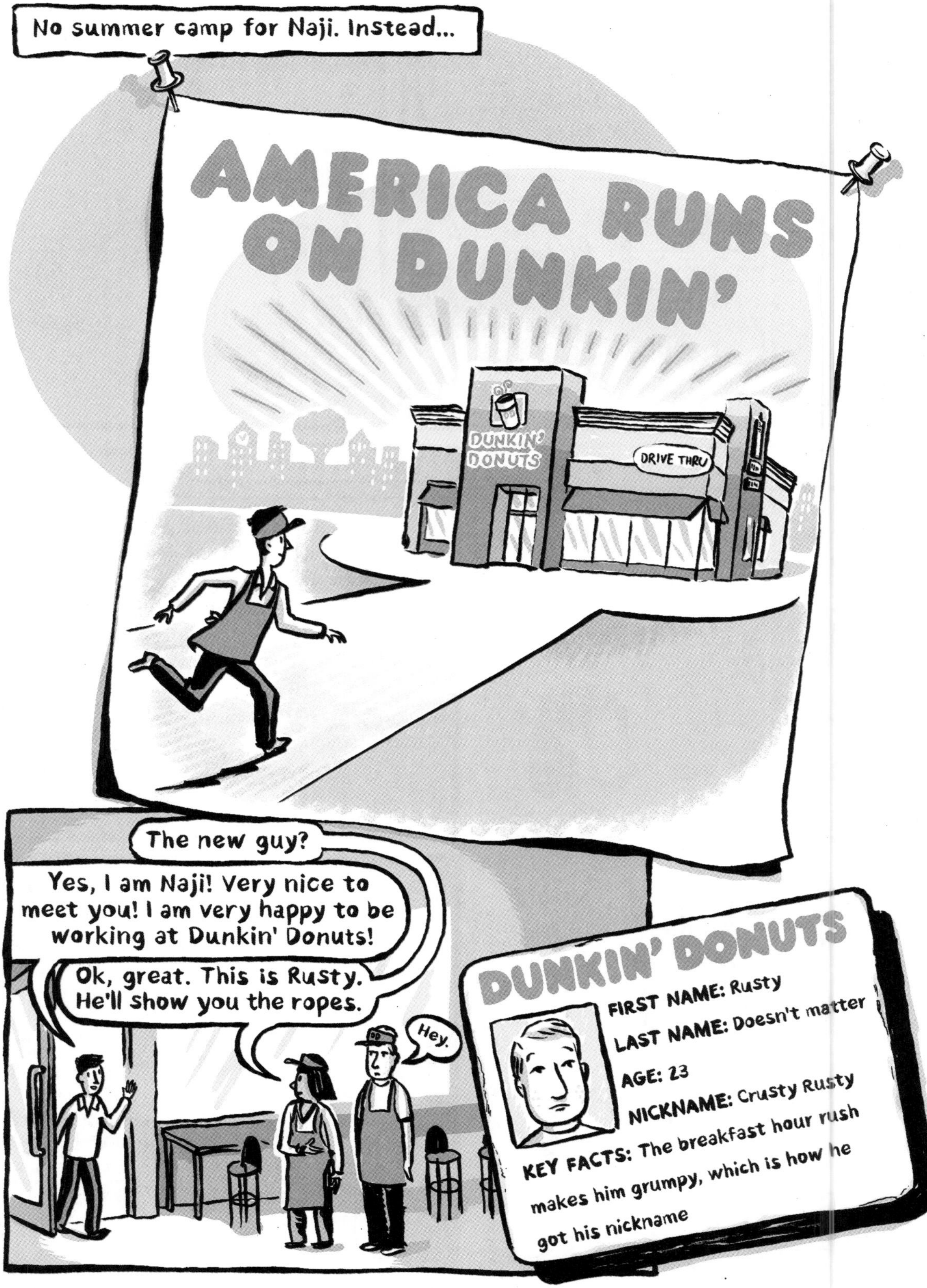

No summer camp for Naji. Instead...
AMERICA RUNS ON DUNKIN'
DUNKIN' DONUTS
DRIVE THRU
The new guy?
Yes, I am Naji! Very nice to meet you! I am very happy to be working at Dunkin' Donuts!
Ok, great. This is Rusty. He'll show you the ropes.
Hey.
DUNKIN' DONUTS
FIRST NAME: Rusty
LAST NAME: Doesn't matter
AGE: 23
NICKNAME: Crusty Rusty
KEY FACTS: The breakfast hour rush makes him grumpy, which is how he got his nickname

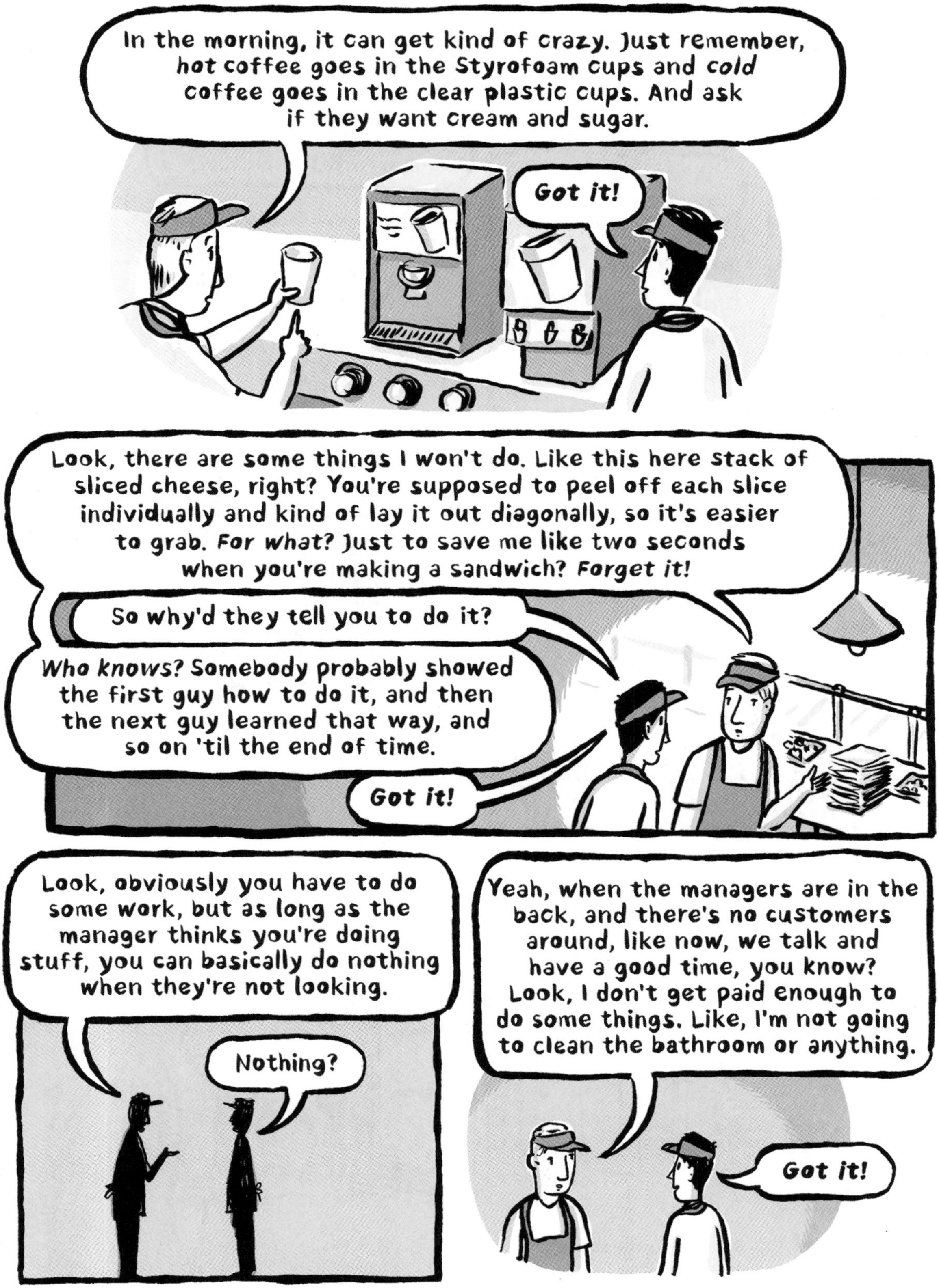
In the morning, it can get kind of crazy. Just remember, *hot* coffee goes in the Styrofoam cups and *cold* coffee goes in the clear plastic cups. And ask if they want cream and sugar.
Got it!
Look, there are some things I won't do. Like this here stack of sliced cheese, right? You're supposed to peel off each slice individually and kind of lay it out diagonally, so it's easier to grab. *For what?* Just to save me like two seconds when you're making a sandwich? *Forget it!*
So why'd they tell you to do it?
Who knows? Somebody probably showed the first guy how to do it, and then the next guy learned that way, and so on 'til the end of time.
Got it!
Look, obviously you have to do some work, but as long as the manager thinks you're doing stuff, you can basically do nothing when they're not looking.
Nothing?
Yeah, when the managers are in the back, and there's no customers around, like now, we talk and have a good time, you know? Look, I don't get paid enough to do some things. Like, I'm not going to clean the bathroom or anything.
Got it!

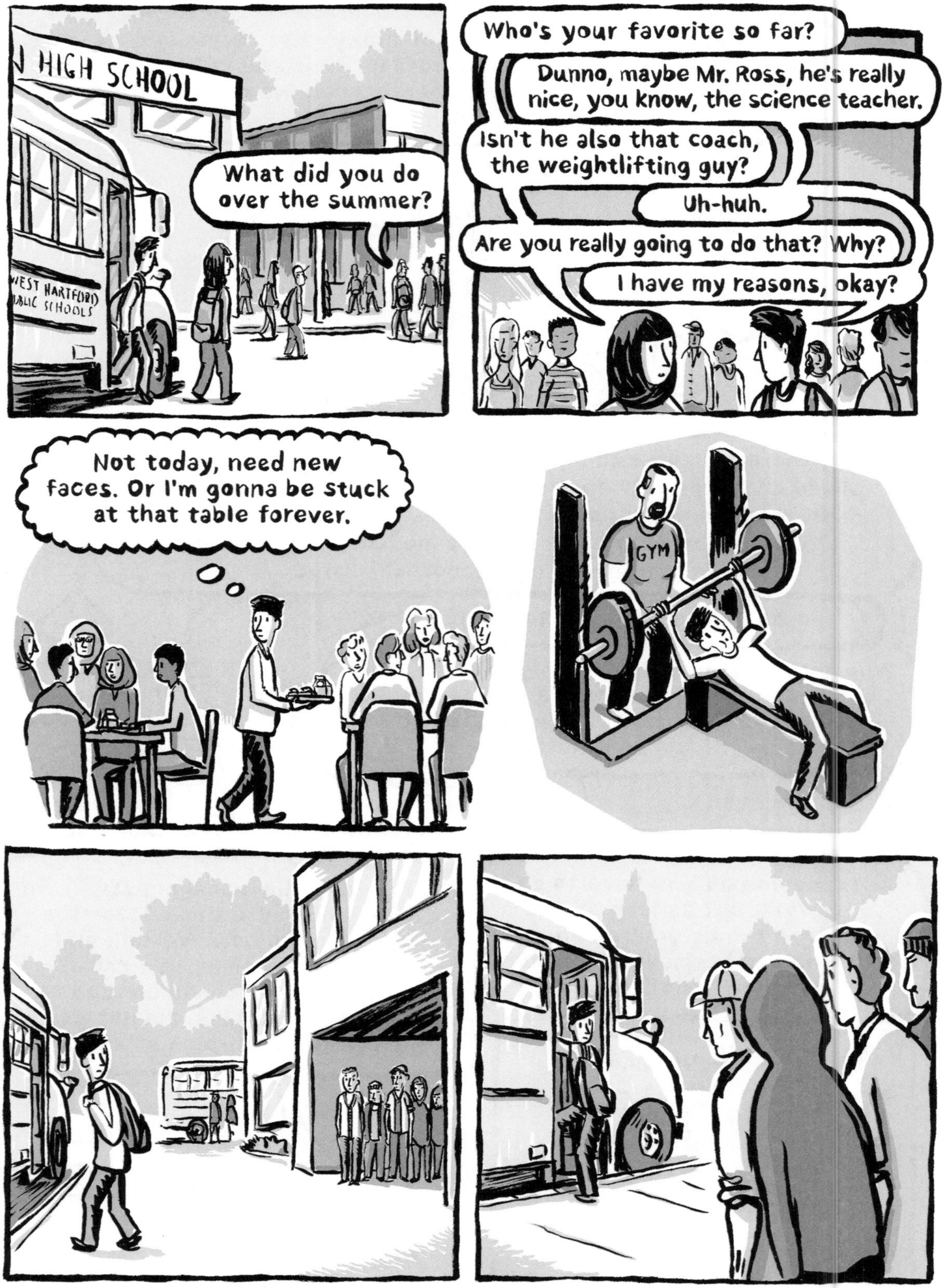

N HIGH SCHOOL
WEST HARTFORD PUBLIC SCHOOLS
What did you do over the summer?
Who's your favorite so far?
Dunno, maybe Mr. Ross, he's really nice, you know, the science teacher.
Isn't he also that coach, the weightlifting guy?
Uh-huh.
Are you really going to do that? Why?
I have my reasons, okay?
Not today, need new faces. Or I'm gonna be stuck at that table forever.
GYM

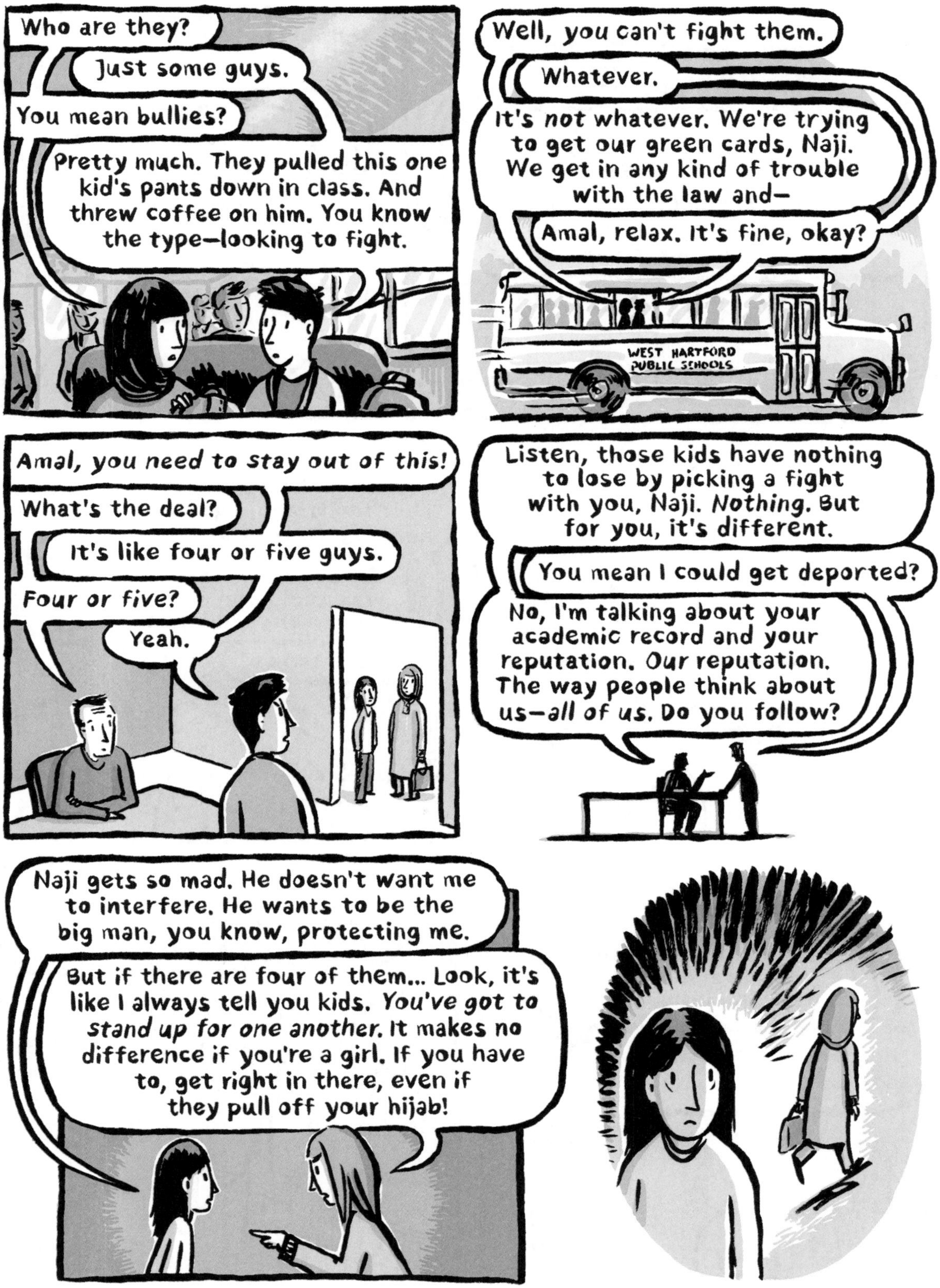
Who are they?
Just some guys.
You mean bullies?
Pretty much. They pulled this one kid's pants down in class. And threw coffee on him. You know the type—looking to fight.
Well, *you* can't fight them.
Whatever.
It's *not* whatever. We're trying to get our green cards, Naji. We get in any kind of trouble with the law and—
Amal, relax. It's fine, okay?
WEST HARTFORD PUBLIC SCHOOLS
Amal, you need to stay out of this!
What's the deal?
It's like four or five guys.
Four or five?
Yeah.
Listen, those kids have nothing to lose by picking a fight with you, Naji. *Nothing.* But for you, it's different.
You mean I could get deported?
No, I'm talking about your academic record and your reputation. *Our* reputation. The way people think about us—*all of us.* Do you follow?
Naji gets so mad. He doesn't want me to interfere. He wants to be the big man, you know, protecting me.
But if there are four of them... Look, it's like I always tell you kids. *You've got to stand up for one another.* It makes no difference if you're a girl. If you have to, get right in there, even if they pull off your hijab!

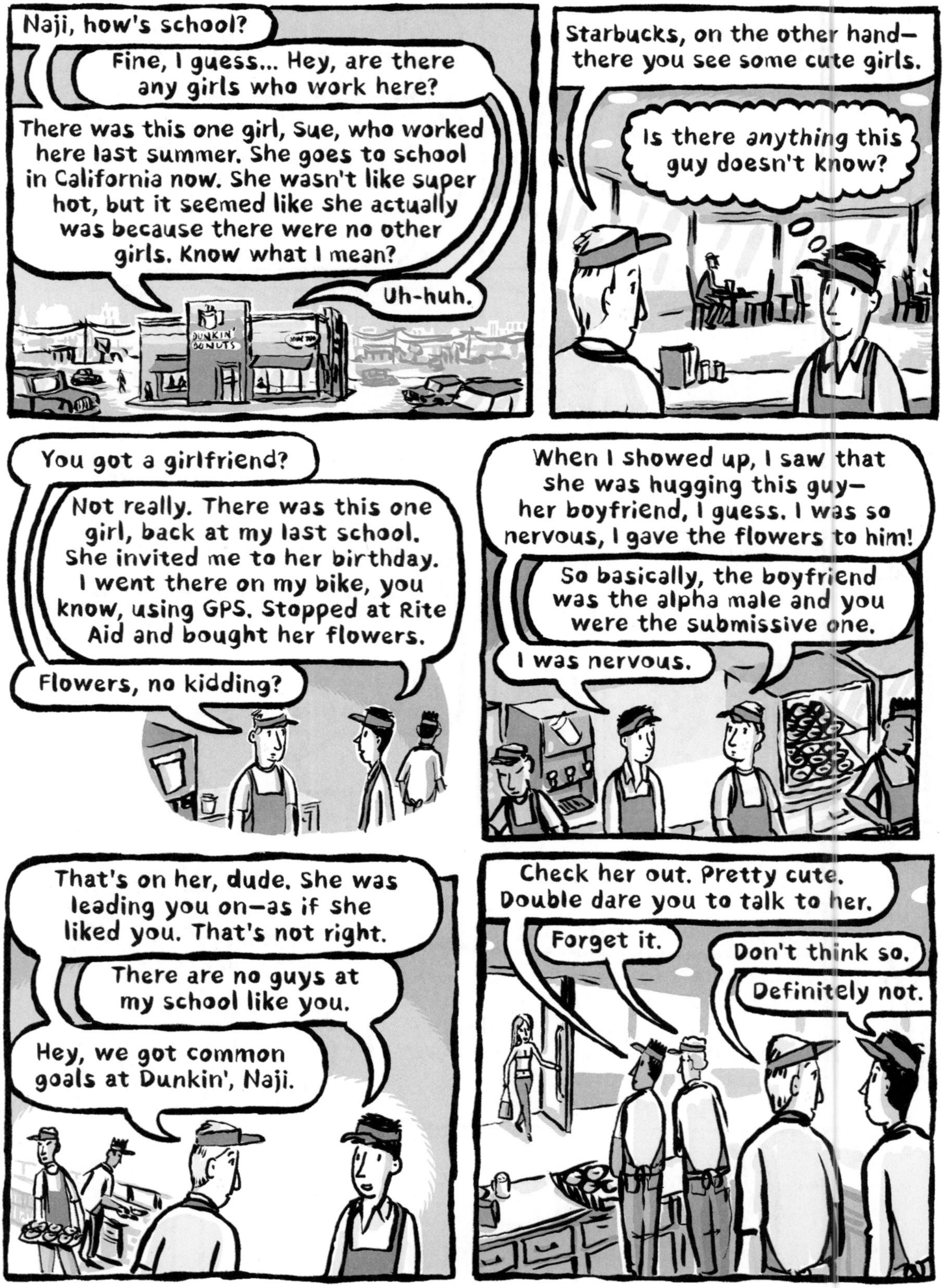

Naji, how's school?
Fine, I guess... Hey, are there any girls who work here?
There was this one girl, Sue, who worked here last summer. She goes to school in California now. She wasn't like super hot, but it seemed like she actually was because there were no other girls. Know what I mean?
Uh-huh.
DUNKIN' DONUTS
Starbucks, on the other hand—there you see some cute girls.
Is there *anything* this guy doesn't know?
You got a girlfriend?
Not really. There was this one girl, back at my last school. She invited me to her birthday. I went there on my bike, you know, using GPS. Stopped at Rite Aid and bought her flowers.
Flowers, no kidding?
When I showed up, I saw that she was hugging this guy—her boyfriend, I guess. I was so nervous, I gave the flowers to him!
So basically, the boyfriend was the alpha male and you were the submissive one.
I was nervous.
That's on her, dude. She was leading you on—as if she liked you. That's not right.
There are no guys at my school like you.
Hey, we got common goals at Dunkin', Naji.
Check her out. Pretty cute. Double dare you to talk to her.
Forget it.
Don't think so.
Definitely not.

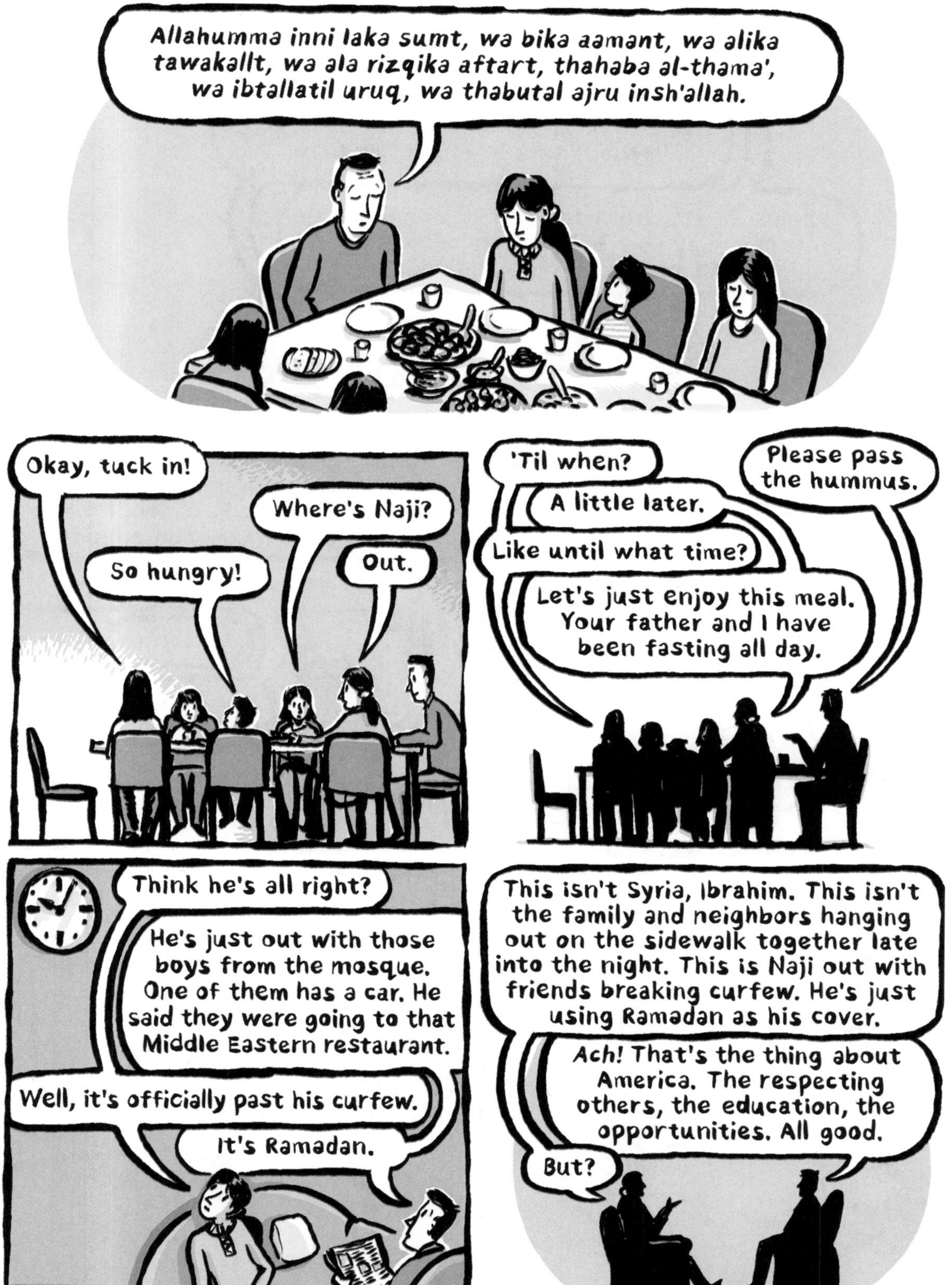
Allahumma inni laka sumt, wa bika aamant, wa alika tawakallt, wa ala rizqika aftart, thahaba al-thama', wa ibtallatil uruq, wa thabutal ajru insh'allah.
Okay, tuck in!
Where's Naji?
So hungry!
Out.
'Til when?
Please pass the hummus.
A little later.
Like until what time?
Let's just enjoy this meal. Your father and I have been fasting all day.
Think he's all right?
He's just out with those boys from the mosque. One of them has a car. He said they were going to that Middle Eastern restaurant.
Well, it's officially past his curfew.
It's Ramadan.
This isn't Syria, Ibrahim. This isn't the family and neighbors hanging out on the sidewalk together late into the night. This is Naji out with friends breaking curfew. He's just using Ramadan as his cover.
Ach! That's the thing about America. The respecting others, the education, the opportunities. All good.
But?

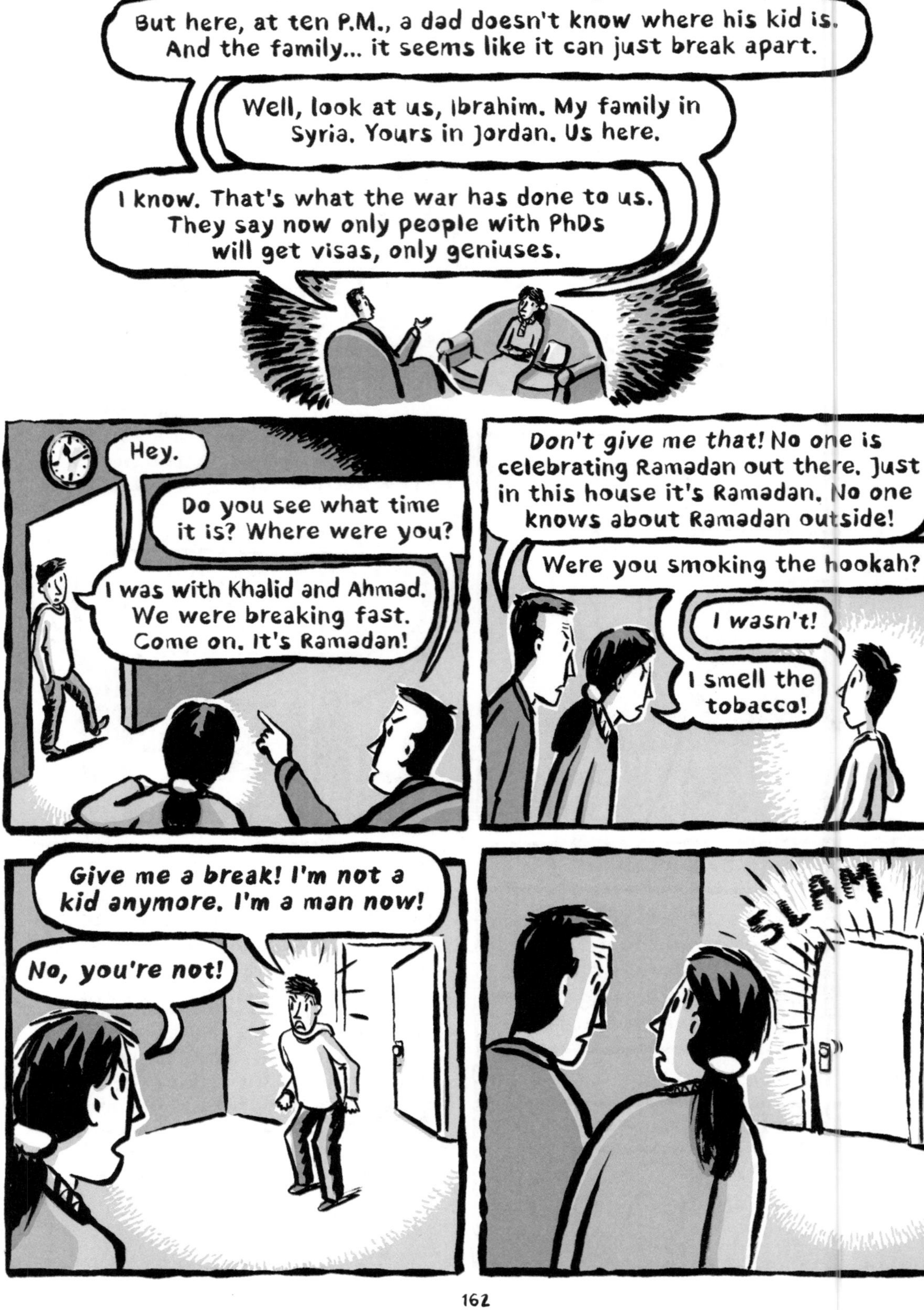
But here, at ten P.M., a dad doesn't know where his kid is. And the family... it seems like it can just break apart.
Well, look at us, Ibrahim. My family in Syria. Yours in Jordan. Us here.
I know. That's what the war has done to us. They say now only people with PhDs will get visas, only geniuses.
Hey.
Do you see what time it is? Where were you?
I was with Khalid and Ahmad. We were breaking fast. Come on. It's Ramadan!
Don't give me that! No one is celebrating Ramadan out there. Just in this house it's Ramadan. No one knows about Ramadan outside!
Were you smoking the hookah?
I wasn't!
I smell the tobacco!
Give me a break! I'm not a kid anymore. I'm a man now!
No, you're not!
SLAM

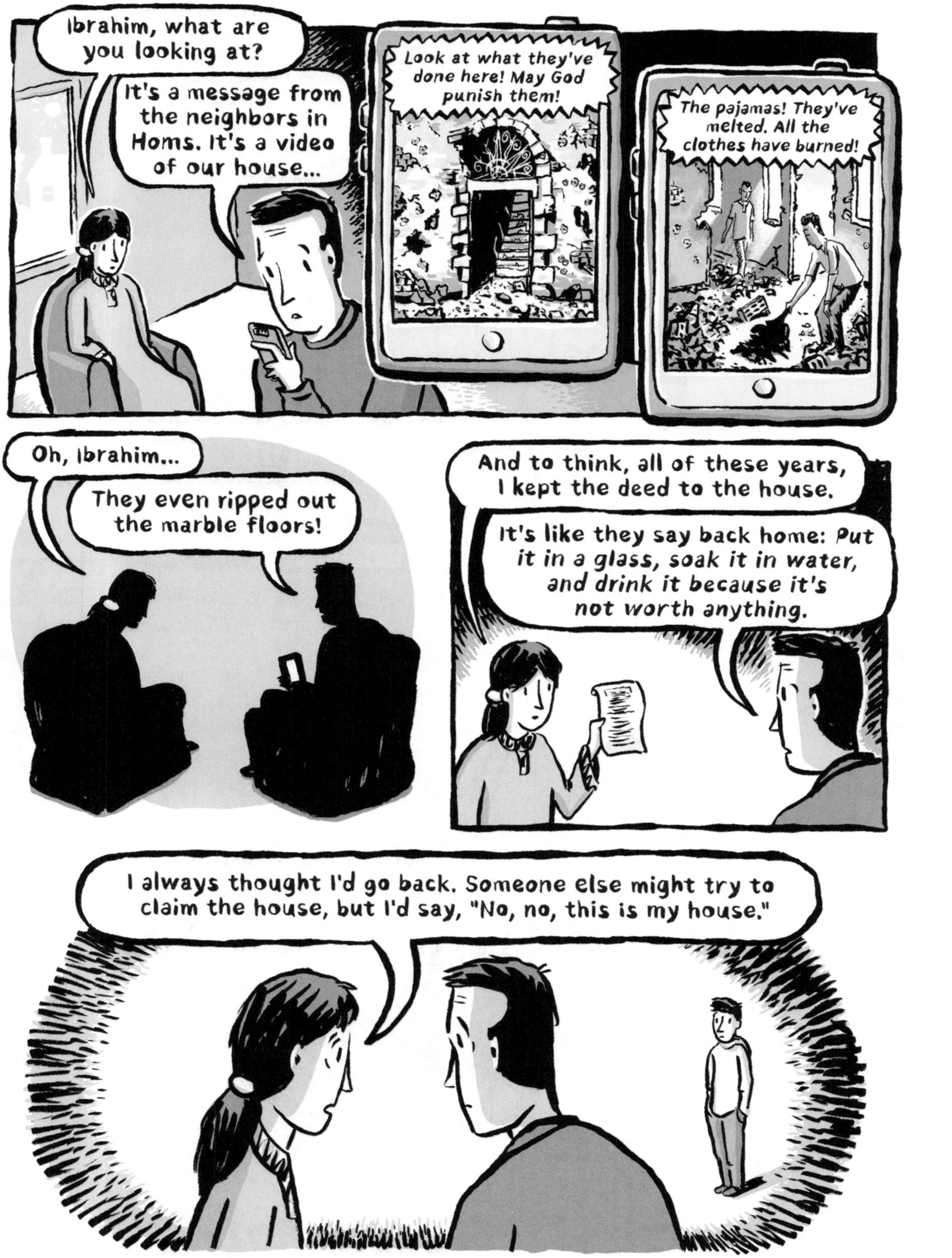
Ibrahim, what are you looking at?
It's a message from the neighbors in Homs. It's a video of our house...
Look at what they've done here! May God punish them!
The pajamas! They've melted. All the clothes have burned!
Oh, Ibrahim...
They even ripped out the marble floors!
And to think, all of these years, I kept the deed to the house.
It's like they say back home: *Put it in a glass, soak it in water, and drink it because it's not worth anything.*
I always thought I'd go back. Someone else might try to claim the house, but I'd say, "No, no, this is my house."

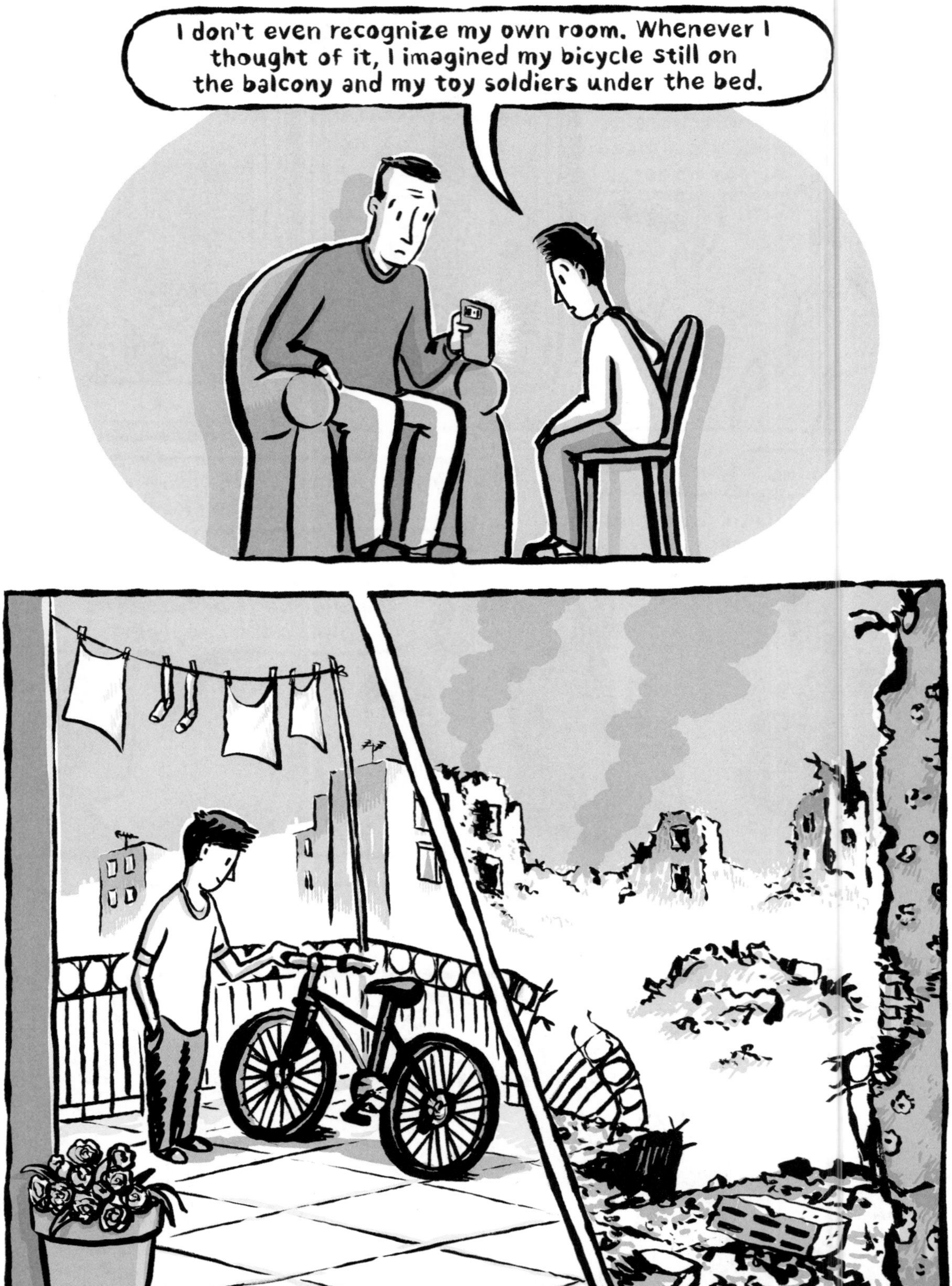
I don't even recognize my own room. Whenever I thought of it, I imagined my bicycle still on the balcony and my toy soldiers under the bed.

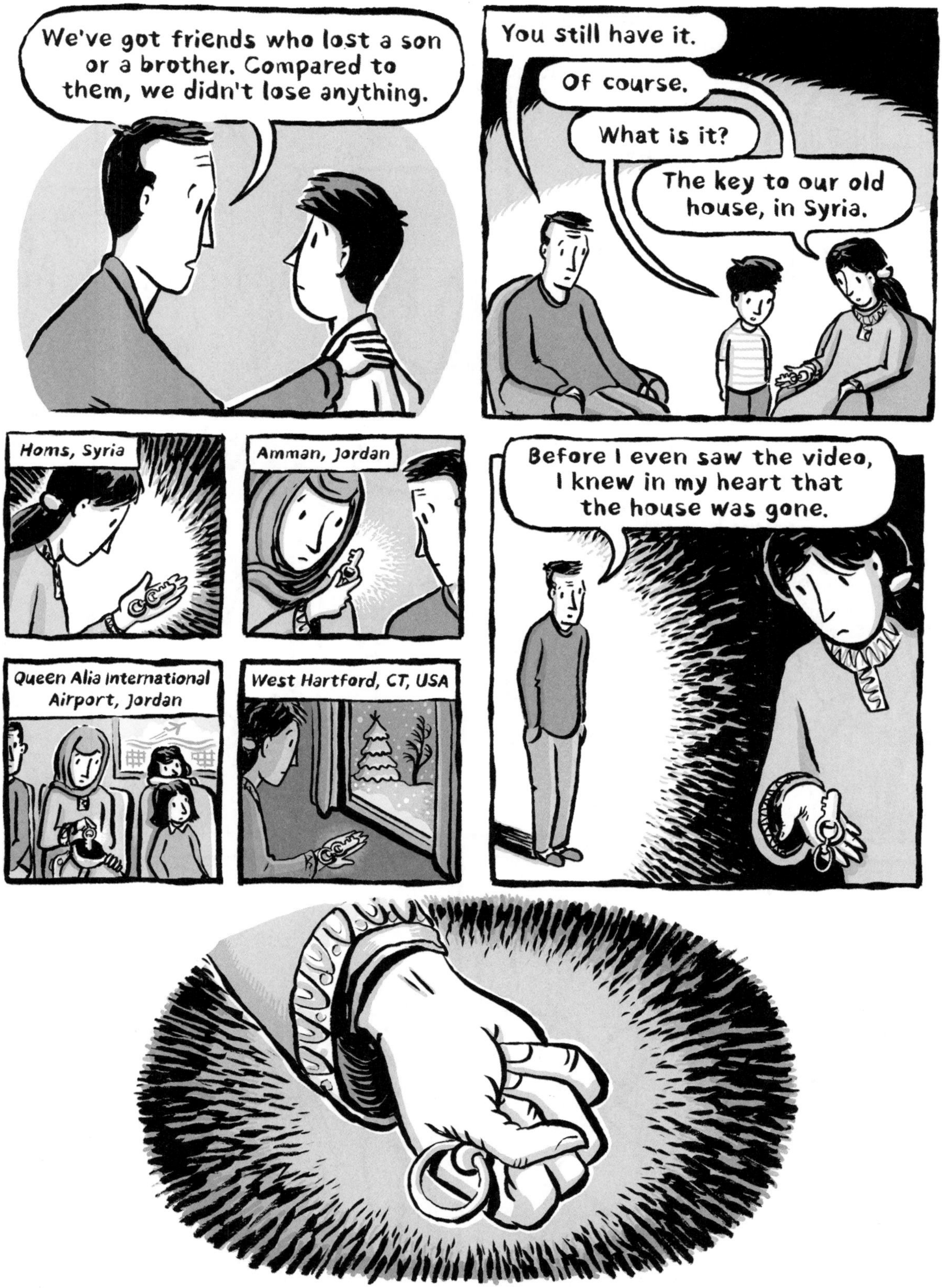
We've got friends who lost a son or a brother. Compared to them, we didn't lose anything.
You still have it.
Of course.
What is it?
The key to our old house, in Syria.
Homs, Syria
Amman, Jordan
Queen Alia International Airport, Jordan
West Hartford, CT, USA
Before I even saw the video, I knew in my heart that the house was gone.

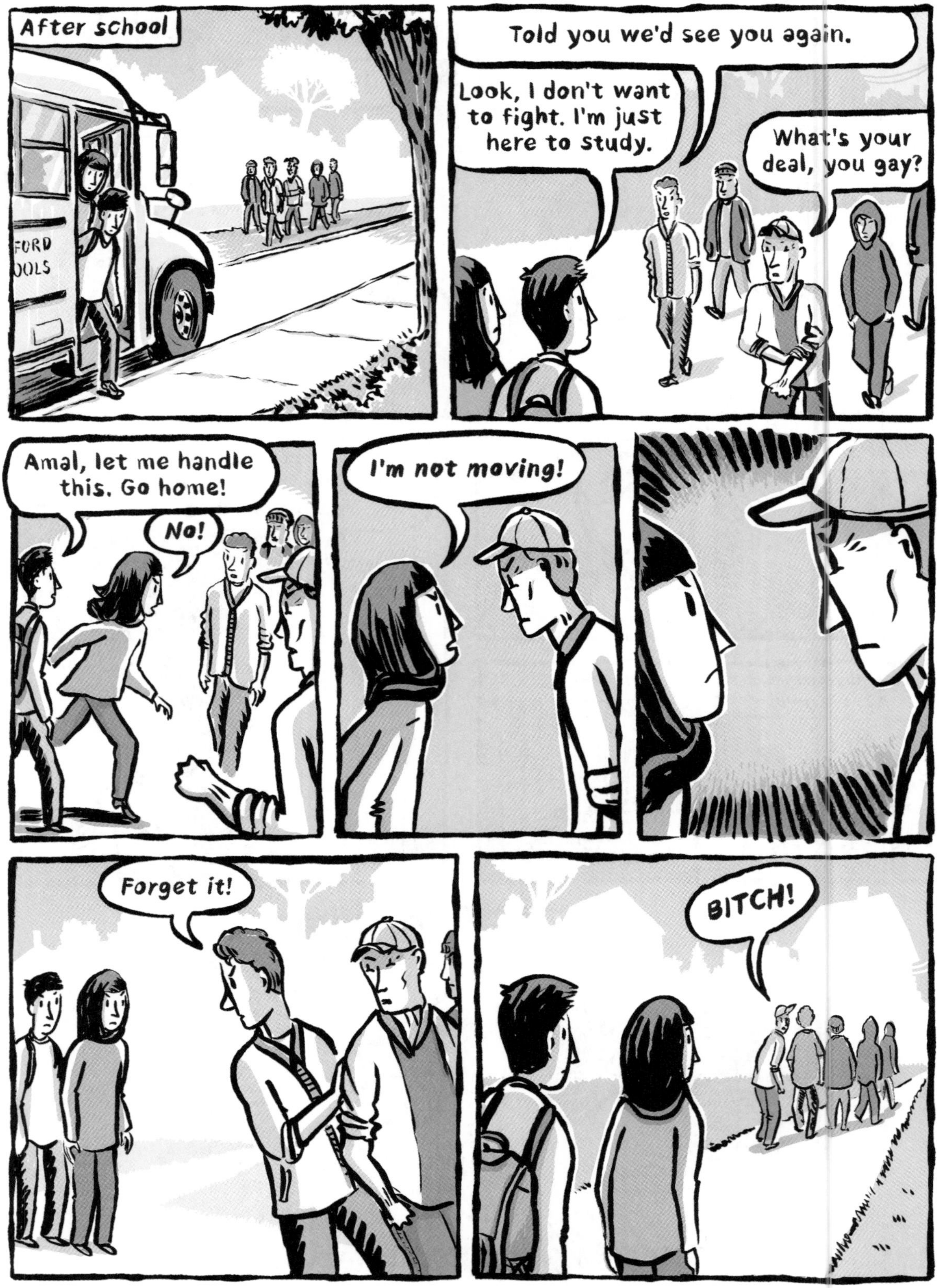
After school
FORD
OOLS
Told you we'd see you again.
Look, I don't want to fight. I'm just here to study.
What's your deal, you gay?
Amal, let me handle this. Go home!
No!
I'm not moving!
Forget it!
BITCH!

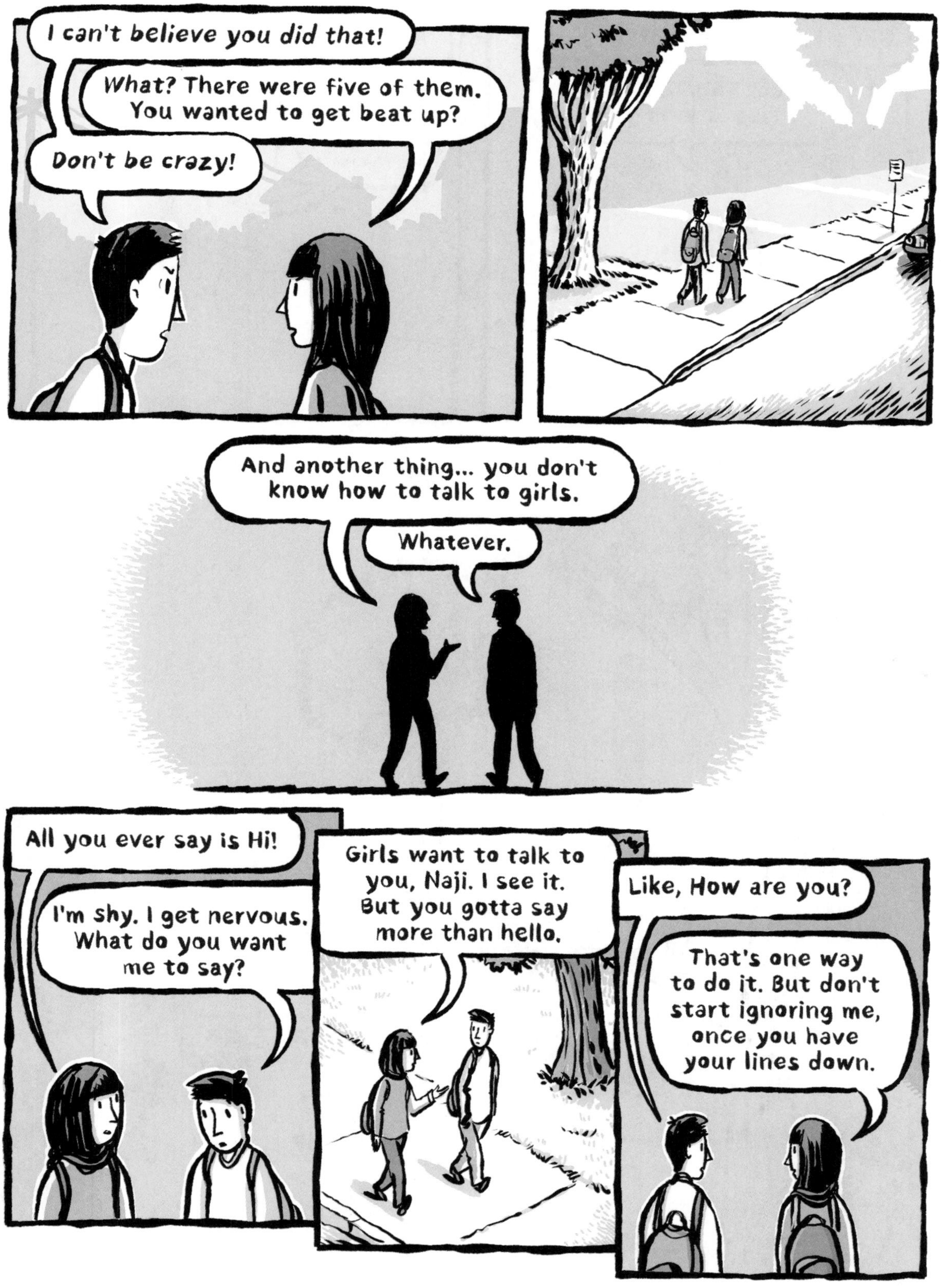
I can't believe you did that!
What? There were five of them. You wanted to get beat up?
Don't be crazy!
And another thing... you don't know how to talk to girls.
Whatever.
All you ever say is Hi!
I'm shy. I get nervous. What do you want me to say?
Girls want to talk to you, Naji. I see it. But you gotta say more than hello.
Like, How are you?
That's one way to do it. But don't start ignoring me, once you have your lines down.

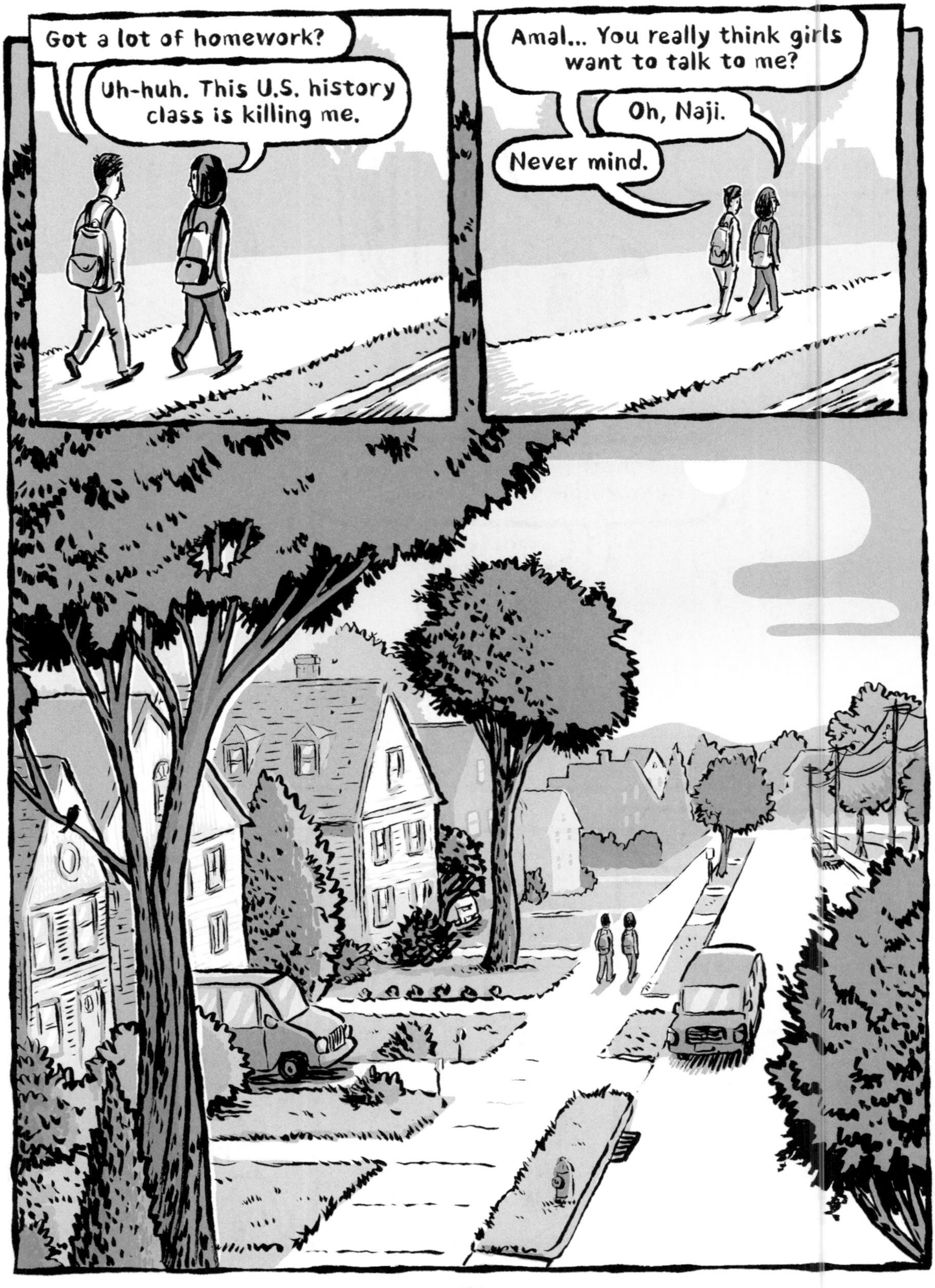
Got a lot of homework?
Uh-huh. This U.S. history class is killing me.
Amal... You really think girls want to talk to me?
Oh, Naji.
Never mind.

Epilogue

Michael Sloan and I spent more than three years with the Aldabaan family and much of what we witnessed was left on the cutting-room floor. What's more, even after I stopped reporting for this book, I continued to keep close tabs on the two families. What follows is an update for all those readers who want to know more about the fortunes of the Aldabaans.

Issa Aldabaan, who is Ibrahim's brother, still lives in New Haven with his family. He has been studying for his G.E.D., with the hope of going to college and finding a job in business administration. Issa's wife, Aminah, launched a successful catering business with the help of CitySeed, a nonprofit that seeks to provide all New Haven residents with access to fresh, local food. Aminah has become a well-known and beloved figure in the city and, for a time, her picture was featured on an enormous billboard in downtown, as an icon of New Haven's flourishing refugee population.

Issa and Aminah's children have thrived in school. Their daughter, Ammal, speaks flawless English and recently won a citywide award for her scholastic achievements. Their son, Faisal, also excels in school and on the soccer field. In fact, Faisal and my own son, Lucian, play on the same team, and on crisp fall evenings, Issa and I often stand together on the sidelines—like any other American dads—chatting casually and watching our kids play beneath a canopy of elm trees.

Issa sometimes hints at his regrets. Even though he is so proud of his childrens' success, he knows that his own prospects are far more limited. And this, of course, is a classically American theme: the first generation makes the sacrifice to come here and the next one realizes the dream.

Ibrahim and Adeebah are still living in West Hartford, Connecticut, and, while safe, the family is still struggling in many ways. Naji, who has repeatedly made the honor roll at school, was recently given the chance to go to a summer program at a local university to take college-level classes and live in the dorms. It was a tremendous opportunity and the program also offered him a full scholarship. Naji was thrilled, but ultimately turned it down. "I need to help my family earn money," he said, without a trace of self-pity. He spent the summer mowing lawns instead. For her part, Amal also sought to help the family financially by babysitting and is doing well in school, especially in math. "Working with numbers is easier for me," she told me, "because I can do it without using English."

Ibrahim has taken a job for Amazon as a delivery man, earning sixteen dollars an hour, working six days a week. He worries incessantly about providing for his five children. Adeebah has started a small catering business and continues to paint and draw. She has shown her work at Trinity College, the Hopkins School (in New Haven), and many local churches and synagogues. Like her sister-in-law, Adeebah has managed to achieve a modest degree of local fame and has been profiled in the *Hartford Courant* and on NPR. Even so, the family foresees years of struggle and financial precariousness.

Many people and groups have helped Ibrahim and Adeebah, including IRIS, their sponsors in Manchester and West Hartford, and Our Lady of Peace—a Catholic church in East Hartford. The parishioners at Our Lady of Peace offered to let the family live rent free in an abandoned house on church property, so long as the Archdiocese agreed. Adeebah and Ibrahim began preparing for the move and even unenrolled their children from Camp Shalom, their local summer camp. In the end, however, the Archdiocese of Hartford did not approve the idea, because of "insurance, legal, financial, and general operational risks to the parish and the Archdiocese of Hartford." The family was crestfallen and so were the parishioners who had advocated on their behalf. The entire episode demonstrated how difficult it is for refugees to build sustainable lives in America, even when they have the help of devoted supporters.

Ibrahim and Issa hold on to the hope that their mother, who is still living in Jordan, will someday be able to join them here in the United States.

Methodology

The stories chronicled in this book are true and represent over three years of reporting, starting in the fall of 2016. It all began when Bruce Headlam, an editor at the *New York Times*, called me and asked whether I was interested in doing an unusual project about Syrian refugees. His idea was to create a graphic narrative that would chronicle the arrival and experience of a single family, with a particular focus on the perspective of the children. He imagined a nonfiction comic strip that would be serialized on a weekly or biweekly basis. The project appealed to me, right away, for its sheer originality. I soon teamed up with Michael Sloan, who became the illustrator for the series.

When it came to finding a family to profile, we turned to Chris George, the director of Integrated Refugee and Immigrant Services (IRIS), a refugee resettlement agency based in New Haven. It was Chris who suggested that we follow the family members, from the very moment of their arrival in the United States. As much as I loved the idea, I was immediately concerned about consent; the family needed to participate freely and willingly, without feeling any sense of coercion or manipulation. Chris and I soon hatched a plan: I would show up and greet the family, on the day of their arrival, and then circle back, a week or so later—on my own—and ask them if they wanted to participate. If the family was uninterested or even hesitant, I would simply wait for another family.

So, on November 8, 2016—Election Day—I met the Aldabaan family, just hours after they landed in the United States. The family consisted of two brothers, Ibrahim and Issa, each of whom had come with their families. A week or so later, I visited Issa's new home in New Haven, along with Mohammed Hafez, a local artist and architect who served as my translator. With his help, I explained the project and even brought out a copy of *Persepolis*, by Marjane Satrapi, to show the family what the finished product might look like. To my relief, Issa immediately understood the proposition and was bullishly enthusiastic. I also visited his brother, Ibrahim, who was then living in Manchester, Connecticut. On that visit, I brought another translator, Dr. Mohammed Kadalah, a professor of Arabic. It was a successful visit and right away, Ibrahim and his wife, Adeebah, began sharing their stories.

In the coming months, I visited Issa and Ibrahim's families every few weeks or so. Although Ibrahim and Issa both spoke some English, I almost always went with a translator, to ensure that I understood them properly. With time, Mohammed Kadalah became the main translator for the two families. As chance would have it, he was from Issa and Ibrahim's hometown of Homs, and he was intimately familiar with the world they had left behind. And so, Dr. Kadalah became—not just my translator— but my indispensable intermediary and guide.

I soon began to have a series of long, free-ranging conversations with these two families, discussing everything that had happened to them: their prewar lives in Syria, how they survived the siege of Homs, their flight to Jordan, and their efforts to reach the United States. I recorded these conversations and often had them transcribed. Before long, I had hundreds of pages of transcripts. Simultaneously, I started following the families around and reporting on their new lives in the United States. I went to school with Naji and Amal, accompanied Ibrahim to his job-training program, attended Adeebah's art shows, and joined them at their orientation sessions hosted by IRIS. In effect, I embedded myself with the Aldabaans.

Because this book is not a memoir, but rather a work of journalism, the story also needed context and fact checking, beyond the families' own accounts and experiences. For that context, I spoke to many other people in their orbit—people like Lara and Sofia, who volunteered to co-sponsor the Aldabaans in Manchester. These were in-depth interviews. I spoke to Lara, for instance, numerous times over the course of a year and half. I did the same with Chris George at IRIS. When Ibrahim's family received a death threat, I contacted the FBI to understand how the bureau handled its investigation. When I accompanied Naji and Amal to school, I also spoke with their teachers at length. As in any work of journalism, I did everything possible to probe for the truth and resisted the temptation to take anyone's account at face value.

Once I had completed my research, I began working on creating a "script"—a scene-by-scene description that would lend itself to the comic format. In creating these scenes, I relied upon my transcripts from taped conversations or the handwritten notes I had taken. Sometimes, the script featured moments that I had witnessed myself, for example, at the orientation sessions run by IRIS. In such cases, I was able to re-create moments that I had observed and re-create dialogue directly from my notes and observations.

On other occasions, I depicted events that had occurred in the past, when I was not present, such as back in Jordan. Sometimes, I would consult my notes and discover that I did not have a precise record of dialogue—of who said what and when. For example, I wanted to include a scene in which Naji made his first friend, Tahsin, at school in Manchester. I was not present for their first encounter; Naji simply told me about it and I took notes. Here are my notes, with some clarifications in brackets:

Naji: We started talking together. I asked him: "Do you have any friends?" He [Tahsin] said, "I have been here a while, but no one has [really] talked to me yet." [A breakthrough moment for Naji. . .] I was like, that explains it. I thought it was me and I just didn't know how to make friends.

In situations like this, I would carve out space for a scene in the script, but I would leave the actual dialogue unwritten, almost like a fill-in-the-blanks story. Then days later, I would sit down with Naji and Tahsin and pepper them with detailed questions. What did you (Naji) say? How did you (Tahsin) respond? Where were you, in the cafeteria or the hallway? What exactly did you say, as best you can remember? Of course, memories are imperfect, but I tried to nail down the particulars as well as I could.

At times, the process was collaborative. I would sit down with all of the family members and ask them to recall what they were thinking or saying at a pivotal moment, like their first morning in America. The family members often really got into it. Of course, I retained editorial control over everything—the authority of "final cut," if you will—but this project simply demanded a level of collaboration that I had never even considered in any of my previous journalistic projects.

When I was done with my script, I would have a detailed document, which enumerated each panel, complete with a corresponding piece of dialogue and accompanying description of the scenery. My illustrator, Michael Sloan, would then take my script and create a detailed pencil sketch in which he rendered a rough draft of each scene or panel. Afterwards, we did a kind of "visual fact-checking" of what Michael had created. I would usually describe and (occasionally show) the sketches to the family members to ensure that the imagery was accurate. Other times, the family would send me photographs, for example, of the house where they resided in Jordan. My translator, Dr. Kadalah, also found photographs of key locations—like the jail or the courthouse in Homs—which Michael could then use to create settings that were more accurate.

There are several panels in the book that I would describe as "interpretive," in other words, where we took some artistic license. These panels include: the board game scene, where the family is exploring the house; the depiction of the volunteer drivers, who appear as playing cards; the calendar, with the family's schedule; the scene where the family is boarding the imaginary "Ball of Yarn Express" for Canada; and the scene where Naji is imagining everybody, back in Homs, fleeing and pressing their emergency locator beacons. Otherwise, we worked to make the imagery as realistic as possible.

There were a few occasions when we had to compress events—which unfolded over a lengthy span of time—into just a few panels. The most notable example involves the depiction of Naji starting high school in West Hartford. We show Naji arriving at school, joining a weight lifting club, and dealing with some bullies—all in a few brief montages. These events actually took place over the course of roughly a year, but we had to condense this time frame, visually, in order to tell the entire story before the book's end.

Finally, it is worth noting that while the names of the Aldabaan family members are all real, the names of some other characters have been changed in the interests of privacy.

Acknowledgments

The inspiration for this project first came from Bruce Headlam, our amazing editor at the *New York Times*. His vision and passion were crucial to its success. We are also enormously grateful to a cadre of other editors at the Times, including James Bennet, Rachel Dry, Jim Dao, Cassandra Harvin, Carmel McCoubrey, and Honor Jones, who helped conceive and sharpen the original comic strip. Quite simply, we couldn't have done it without their support.

Our translator and indispensable guide to all things Syrian was the brilliant Dr. Mohammed Kadalah. He worked tirelessly and with enormous heart to make sure that the stories in this book were told as accurately and thoughtfully as possible.

When it came time to develop the original series into a book, Tina Bennett, our literary agent, championed the cause and made it a reality. We are also thankful to Svetlana Katz, her deputy and our steadfast ally. Our publisher, Metropolitan Books, has done a marvelous job of shaping, publishing, and promoting the book, along with the invaluable expertise and support of First Second Books. Riva Hocherman, our editor, brought so much knowledge to bear on how the graphic narrative should unfold. She thinks in storyboard format intuitively and with great savvy. Riva, we learned so much from you. We would also like to thank a number of others in the greater Macmillan family, including Sara Bershtel, Jen Besser, Diana Frost, Brian Lax, Carolyn O'Keefe, Maggie Richards, and Don Weisberg. We're also grateful to Denzil Mohammed and Meghan Rosenberg at the Immigrant Learning Center for their pedagogical advice.

There were a number of other people who aided immeasurably in the reporting of this book. They offered their help generously, time and time again, to help make this a better, more accurate, and more nuanced story. Our thanks to Mohamad Hafez, Chris George, Ann O'Brien, Nancy Latif, Maher Mahmood, Leily Rezvani, Jean Silk, Judi Durham, Stefan Wawzyniecki, Vivian Batterson, Vivian Carlson, and Ruth Goldbaum.

Finally, and most important, our boundless gratitude to the Aldabaan family: Ibrahim, Adeebah, Naji, Ammal, Hala, Ahmed, Rahaf, Issa, Aminah, Faisal, Ammal, and Retaj. You welcomed us into your lives. Thank you for trusting us to tell your stories. It has been a privilege.

Jake would also like to thank . . . Tamar Halpern and Paul Zuydhoek, for supporting me and believing so passionately in this project. I am also grateful to Stephen Halpern and Elizabeth Stanton for their encouragement and steadfast love. My wife, Kasia Lipska, is my moral and spiritual compass; I tread northward with you. My children, Sebastian and Lucian, are the lights that glimmer even in the face of gathering darkness. To my brother, Greg: thank you for always making time. Michael, it has been a pleasure working with you and I'm so proud of what we've done. And, finally, thanks to the friends who were always there for me: Micah Nathan, Brian Groh, Emily Bazelon, Susan Clinard, and Kossouth Bradford.

Michael would also like to thank . . . David Goldin, my pal and mentor, for introducing me to the world of illustration. Steven Heller, former art director at the *New York Times Book Review*, for giving me my first break as an illustrator. All the art directors at the *New York Times* op-ed page with whom I've had the pleasure to work: there's a strong connection between my op-ed and letters illustrations and the artwork in this book. My fellow artists and musicians in the jazz band the Half-Tones: Joe Ciardiello, Barry Blitt, Chris Mariner, James Steinberg, Rob Saunders, Richard A Goldberg, and Hal Mayforth—our friendship and musical connection continues to inspire me. The Society of Illustrators and its executive director, Anelle Miller, have provided a supportive community and a home for the Half-Tones. My dear New Haven friends: I am so lucky to have you in my life. Richard Dannay, for your expert legal advice. Ed Ryan, for your wisdom and perspective. My friend Jake Halpern, for being such a wonderful collaborator.

Adeebah Aldabaan

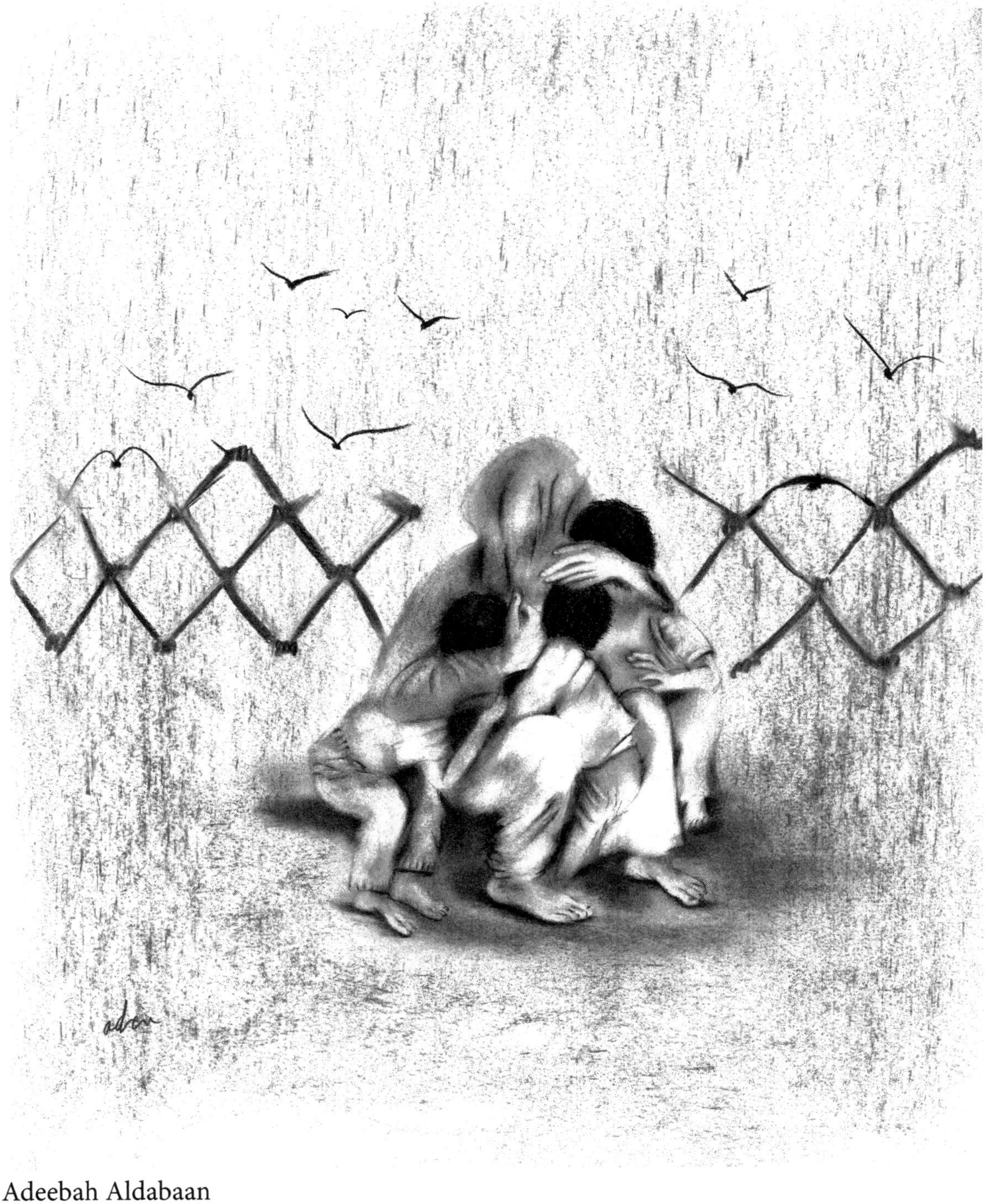

Adeebah Aldabaan

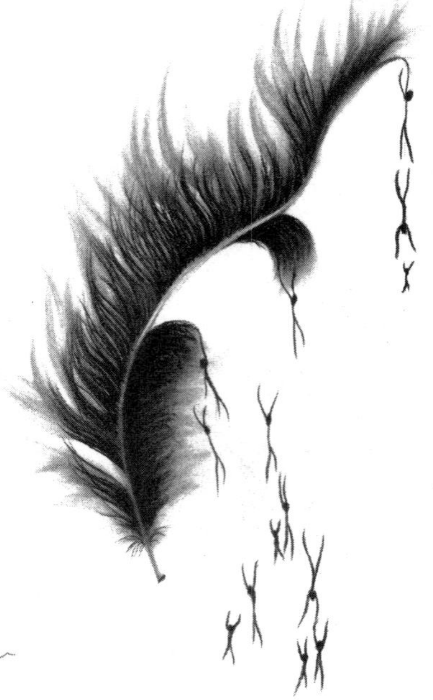

Adeebah Aldabaan

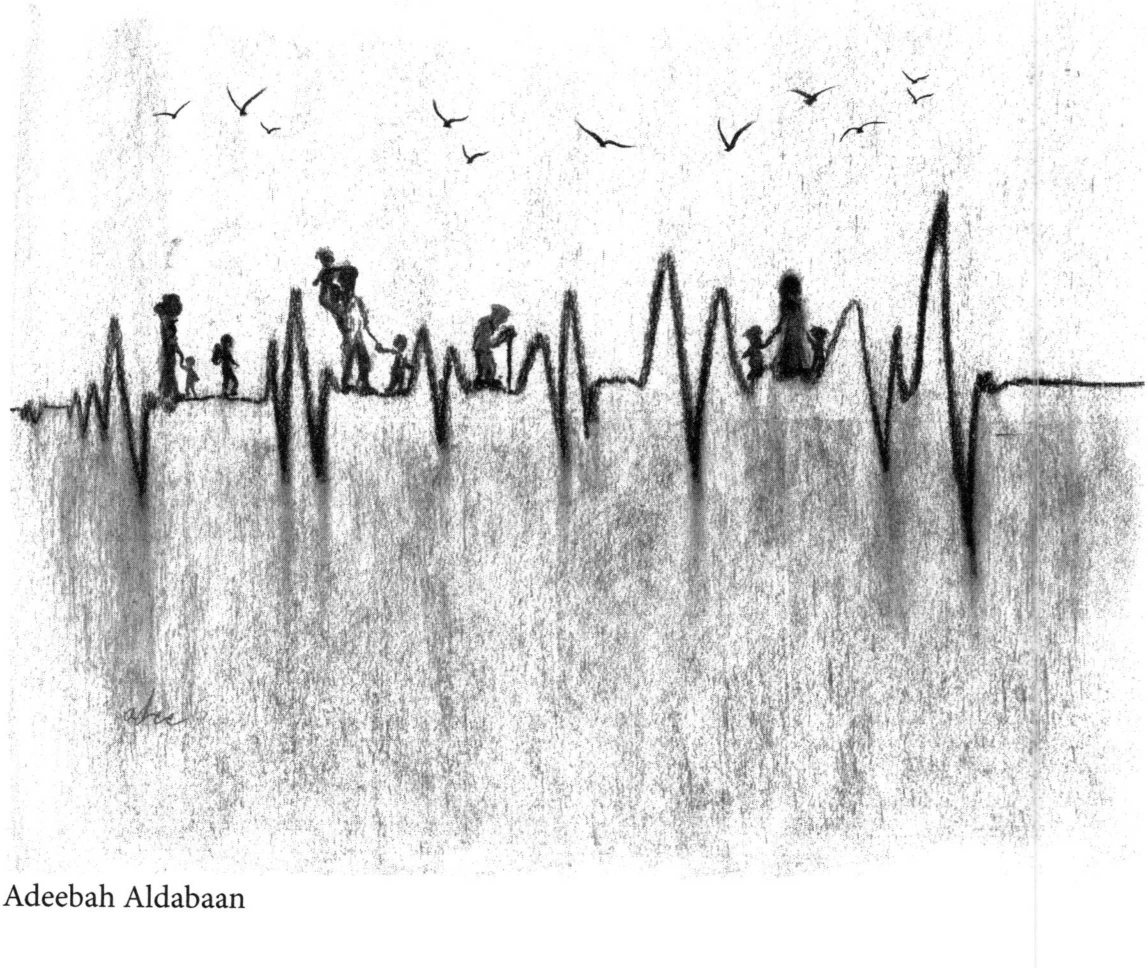

Adeebah Aldabaan

About the Authors

JAKE HALPERN is a Pulitzer Prize–winning journalist. He is the author of *Bad Paper* and coauthor of *Nightfall*. His journalism has appeared in the *New Yorker*, the *New York Times*, the *Wall Street Journal*, and the *Atlantic*. He teaches writing at Yale University in New Haven, where he lives.

MICHAEL SLOAN is a printmaker, illustrator, and Pulitzer Prize–winning editorial cartoonist. His artwork has appeared in the *New York Times*, the *Washington Post*, the *Wall Street Journal*, the *Boston Globe*, and many others publications. The Society of Illustrators has honored him with three silver medals for his illustrations. Sloan has lectured widely on his art and shown his work in solo exhibitions. He is also the creator of *The Zen of Nimbus* comic. He lives in New Haven.